D1594074

Islands of Truth

Daniel W. Clayton

Islands of Truth

The Imperial Fashioning of Vancouver Island

UBC Press · Vancouver · Toronto

F
1089
.V3
C58
2000

Printed in Canada on acid-free paper ∞
ISBN 0-7748-0741-5

Canadian Cataloguing in Publication Data

Clayton, Daniel Wright, 1964-
  Islands of Truth

  Includes bibliographical references and index.
  ISBN 0-7748-0741-5

  1. Vancouver Island (B.C.) – Discovery and exploration. 2. Vancouver Island (B.C.) – History. 3. Native peoples – British Columbia – Vancouver Island – History.* 4. Vancouver Island (B.C.) – Historiography. I. Title.

FC3844.5.C52 2000   971.1'2'02   C99-911285-6
F1089.V3C52 2000

This book has been published with the help of a grant from the Humanities and Social Sciences Federation of Canada, using funds provided by the Social Sciences and Humanities Research Council of Canada.

UBC Press acknowledges the financial support of the Government of Canada through the Book Publishing Industry Development Program (BPIDP) for our publishing activities.

Canadä

We also gratefully acknowledge the support of the Canada Council for the Arts for our publishing program, as well as the support of the British Columbia Arts Council.

Set in Minion by Artegraphica Design Co. Ltd.
Printed and bound in Canada by Friesens
Copy editor: Joanne Richardson
Proofreader: Dorota Rygiel
Indexer: Christine Jacobs
Cartographer: Eric Leinberger

UBC Press
University of British Columbia
2029 West Mall, Vancouver, BC V6T 1Z2
(604) 822-5959
Fax: (604) 822-6083
E-mail: info@ubcpress.ubc.ca
www.ubcpress.ubc.ca

*For June Clayton and to the
memory of Graham Clayton (1938-1999)*

We have now not merely explored the territory of pure understanding, and carefully surveyed every part of it, but have also measured its extent, and assigned to everything in it its rightful place. This domain is an island, enclosed by nature itself within unalterable limits. It is the land of truth – enchanting name! – surrounded by a wide and stormy ocean, the native home of illusion, where many a fog bank and many a swiftly melting iceberg give the deceptive appearance of farther shores, deluding the adventurous seafarer ever anew with empty hopes, and engaging him in enterprises which he can never abandon and yet is unable to carry to completion.

–IMMANUEL KANT, *THE CRITIQUE OF PURE REASON*

Contents

Illustrations

Acknowledgments

This book started its life as a doctoral dissertation in Geography at the University of British Columbia and would not have seen the light of day without the help and stimulation of many people and institutions. I would particularly like to thank Alison Blunt, Kate Boyer, Bruce Braun, Trevor Carle, Noel Castree, Brett Christophers, David Demeritt, Colin Maycock, Averill Groeneveld-Meijer, Jim Scott, Matthew Sparke, and Jock Wills, who made my graduate years at UBC so enjoyable and intellectually invigorating. I am also grateful to Alan Baker, Barbara Belyea, Mike Heffernan, David Ley, Chris Philo, Charlie Withers, and Graeme Wynn, who kindly read parts or all of the manuscript and made many valuable criticisms and suggestions. I owe special debts to Bob Galois and Richard Mackie, who have been my closest points of connection with early British Columbia for many years, and to April McIlhagga, who went out of her way to make my two years in Victoria comfortable as well as productive. Thanks are also due to the staff at the following libraries and archives for their assistance: British Columbia Archives, Victoria (especially Brent McBride); Public Record Office and British Library, London; Hudson's Bay Company Archives, Winnipeg; and Special Collections and Archives Division of UBC library (especially George Brandak and Francis Woodward).

I would like to express my deepest gratitude to my teachers and mentors, Derek Gregory and Cole Harris. I would not have undertaken this project, or become a geographer, without their encouragement and support, and I hope this book starts to repay them for their inspirational presence in my life.

It is a privilege to acknowledge the financial support of the I.W. Killam Foundation, the Social Sciences and Humanities Research Council of Canada, and the University of British Columbia. And it has been a pleasure to work with UBC Press on this book. I thank Jean Wilson for her interest in my work, and

Holly Keller-Brohman for the efficiency with which she guided the manuscript through the publication process. I am also grateful to Eric Leinberger for preparing the elegant maps that accompany Part 2.

The book is dedicated to my mother, and to the memory of my father, who died shortly before it was published. I hope that the following pages are some recompense for my years away from my parents and my brother Matthew, who have always been my rocks.

Introduction

Islands of Truth is about a series of Western encounters with the Native – Nuu-chah-nulth – peoples and territory of Vancouver Island in the late eighteenth and early nineteenth centuries, and some of the vantage points from which these encounters have been viewed over time. The book focuses on a particular period and Native region, but it is also a meditation on how representations of land and peoples, and studies of the past, serve and shape specific interests, and how the dawn of Native-Western contact in this part of the world might be studied 200 years on, in the light of a longer colonial history and ongoing struggles between Natives and non-Natives over land and cultural status.

Between the 1770s and 1840s the Nuu-chah-nulth groups of the west coast of Vancouver Island were engaged by three sets of forces that were of general importance in the history of Western overseas expansion: the West's scientific exploration of the world in the Age of Enlightenment, capitalist practices of exchange, and the geopolitics of nation-state rivalry. The British explorer James Cook visited Nootka Sound in 1778, George Vancouver mapped Vancouver Island for the British in 1792, and the Spanish reconnoitred the Northwest Coast between 1775 and the 1790s. Exploration was infused with the scientific and humanitarian spirit of the Enlightenment, but it was not sealed off from commercial or imperial expansion. Cook was instructed to search for the Northwest Passage – the fabled water route across North America, which Europeans thought would transform the structure of European trade with Asia. He cast doubt on its existence, but his observations about the resources of the coast encouraged a trade in sea otter furs between the Northwest Coast and China. Then, as the commercial potential of the Northwest Coast began to be harnessed, geopolitical disputes over rights of sovereignty arose between Western states. Politicians derived imperial claims from explorers' and traders' activities, and local, intensely corporeal, geographies of interaction were gradually subsumed into an abstract imperial space of maps and plans. The sea otter trade reached its height in the early 1790s during a dispute between Britain and Spain over rights of trade and settlement in the Pacific, and in the first half of the nineteenth century British and American politicians argued over the sovereignty of the Oregon Territory. These processes of imperial aggrandizement culminated in the Oregon Treaty of 1846, which divided the vast area west of the Rockies from Alaska to California between Britain and the United States of America. American pioneers occupied the region south of the 49th parallel (the international border), and in 1849 Britain established a colony on Vancouver Island. In fairly short order, then, Native peoples were observed through Western scientific lenses, and Native space at the eastern edge of the Pacific and western edge of North America was connected to the capitalist world economy, fashioned as imperial territory, and incorporated into empires.

Islands of Truth discusses this pre-colonial period of contact; the geographies it produced and worked through; and the stories about land, identity, and empire stemming from this period that have shaped the understanding of British Columbia's past and present. The book considers the ways in which Natives and Westerners were positioned in these projects of exploration, trade, and imperial aggrandizement. I chart how Native and Western interests and fortunes became intertwined through exploration and commerce and then diverged as Vancouver Island and the Northwest Coast were fashioned as imperial space.

This book is ostensibly an archival and geographical study of the past. The bulk of it focuses on the west coast of Vancouver Island in the late eighteenth century. I am interested in the geographical conditioning of processes of cultural interaction, modes of representation, and relations of power in different locales and at different scales. The three parts range between Nuu-chah-nulth villages and territories, where intricate contact relationships were forged, and Western corridors of political power, where imperial ideas about the Northwest Coast were moulded. Thus conceived, this book is about the connections between power, knowledge, and geography, and considers the intersection of local and global forces in a particular part of the world. I say little about the land-based fur trade and commercial initiatives of the Hudson's Bay Company west of the Rockies, which turned the mainland into a complex domain of Native-Western interaction, though I will touch on how local geographies of power in the company's vast Columbia Department became implicated in the imperial construction of the Oregon Territory.

One of the book's main themes is that regions like Vancouver Island are both products of the West and places with specific and irreducible identities. They have identities of and away from the West. They should not be studied in isolation from the translocal discourses and Western projects of encroachment that shaped them. Such discourses and projects brought different peoples into contact and conflict, and brought regions like Vancouver Island under the imperial aegis of the West. Yet Western projects of cultural engagement and territorial appropriation worked through local conditions, involved negotiation and resistance, and thus underwent translation. Processes of cultural contact, modes of representation, and strategies of imperial fashioning both created and destroyed identities and connections, settings and contexts.[1]

At the end of the eighteenth century, the west coast of Vancouver Island became a distant corner of the world economy, yet it was one where Natives and Westerners created spaces of interaction and power. Explorers, traders, politicians, and, later, colonists invoked the island's distance from hubs of civilization, yet Native-Western contact, imperial constructions of the region, and subsequent local constructions of the past gave Vancouver Island a distinctive identity. Stories about the links between exploration, trade, and empire in North America and the Pacific have never had single or simple meanings. Such links have been described from a range of perspectives, and with different – and often incommensurable – experiences, memories, and hopes in mind. Explorers juggled the familiar and the strange in complicated ways, traders had to improvise when they were in Native waters, imperial strategists worked with rarefied images of the non-Western world, and colonists occupied lands that were not replicas of the ones they had left.

In short, Western ideas and agendas were not imposed on Vancouver Island in a mechanical fashion. This region should not be regarded as a local product and example of global phenomena, and the Western forces that I discuss did not work like a machine. Scientific exploration, capitalism, and imperialism adapted to local terrain and gained a local texture. The contact process on the west coast of Vancouver Island involved a complex two-way physical and perceptual traffic between Westerners and Natives, and the imperial fashioning of the Northwest Coast involved an equally complex traffic between a body of Western ideas and a set of local facts and exigencies. Westerners developed knowledges that focused on Vancouver Island but were not altogether tied to it. The peoples and spaces represented in Western texts were simultaneously captured as part of a local scene and positioned elsewhere, in other registers, narratives, and imaginative processes; they became embedded and disembedded within Western systems of thought and experience.

Islands of Truth can also be read as a methodological commentary on how these projects and dynamics have and might be studied. I am interested in how other scholars have studied early British Columbia, and I attempt to recontextualize aspects of the recent critical literature on colonialism on Vancouver Island. I bring together a set of archival documents and a more eclectic body of theory. The colonial and postcolonial studies literature has helped me to conceptualize my archival materials.[2] Reading this literature while working in the archives was both an exhilarating and frustrating experience. On the one hand, the relevance of this literature to the interpretation of early British Columbia is perhaps only starting to come into focus. Much local scholarship on the past has been positivist in tone and provincial in outlook. On the other hand, much of the most provocative work on imperialism and colonialism deals with other parts of the world and does not have an instant or wholesale resonance in the setting I am studying. This theoretically adventurous literature sent me down some interpretive paths that other scholars of early British Columbia have ignored (or do not want to venture down), but we need to recognize that no body of ideas travels entirely intact. My narrative is punctuated by a number of conceptual and comparative digressions, where I variously seek to underscore the specificity of the dynamics I am dealing with, tease out the assumptions and agendas embedded in the Western projects of engagement I am tracking, and draw connections between this region and era and other times and places.

Local scholarship has shaped historical understanding and should be considered carefully. Early twentieth-century collectors, ethnologists, and historians of British Columbia played an important role in making this study possible. It was they who tracked down documents pertaining to the Northwest Coast and organized them in archives. Parts of this book are concerned with the formulation of "local" history and the geography of the archive: the questions that local scholars have asked, the concepts and tropes they have worked with, and what the past meant to them. Indeed, one of the most trenchant ideas in colonial and postcolonial studies is that writing on the past is directly implicated in the processes it describes. I am interested in how "local" scholars have handled the past, and the reader will see that my own narrative is mediated by a particular sense of the past and present.

I am concerned, more generally, with the truth status of texts: the meanings they create, the sites they work through, the realities and contexts they fashion, the understandings and stories they encourage and disguise, and the power relations they induce and bolster. I work out of the critical field of vision developed by Michel Foucault and Edward Said. Many studies of imperialism and colonialism now embrace Foucault's claim that the production of truth "induces regular effects of power," and many scholars work with Said's thesis that "the power to narrate" – the capacity to build and sustain some truths about land and people, and to denigrate and marginalize others – is a constitutive feature of Western dominance.[3]

There are thinkers who you think with to such an extent that they become part of you but are barely mentioned by name. For me, that thinker is Foucault. Yet his ideas do not have an automatic or wholesale purchase on Vancouver Island. I read Foucault long before I encountered Vancouver Island, and at many points the two do not touch. He dealt with European regimes of knowledge and power, and he focused on the institutional spaces they worked through, whereas I am exploring a circuitous Western outreach and a set of cross-cultural relationships. In turn, the theorists of colonialism who have done most with Foucault's ideas and the poststructuralist climate of thought and research he helped to create have worked on other periods and parts of the world, and often with a narrow range of historical materials (the official voices of empire and often just literary texts). The powerful arguments of theorists such as Edward Said, Homi Bhabha, and Gayatri Spivak – the so-called Holy Trinity of postcolonial theory – have a general purchase in North American settings, but their ideas spring, largely, from an engagement with the history of Western imperialism in Asia. They cannot simply be applied to Vancouver Island, and I do not want to make out that contact and colonialism were the same everywhere.[4] I am also mindful of Bhabha's point that the advent of poststructuralism in colonial and postcolonial studies may herald "another power ploy of the culturally privileged Western elite to produce a discourse of the Other that reinforces its own power-knowledge equation."[5]

Nicholas Thomas has criticized the valorization of global generalizations over local syntheses in much recent theoretical writing about imperialism and colonialism. We need to theorize these projects of exploitation and domination in global terms, he argues, because their effects are pervasive and thoroughgoing, but he thinks that many theorists "obscure the multiplicity of colonizing projects [and actors] and the plurality of potential subversions of them."[6] Thomas worries that grand theories about colonialism exaggerate and perpetrate the power of the West, focus too tightly on the agency of the colonizer, and gloss over the ways in which colonial power was contested and subverted.

I hold to the importance of generating theoretical – transposable and adversarial – statements about Native-Western encounters from detailed studies that work out of local cultural and political fields. I have a local commitment to theory. In this book, I am concerned foremost with Vancouver Island, the contact history of Nuu-chah-nulth groups, and some problematics in the British Columbian present. Yet local details do not make full sense unless they are studied in relation to the global agendas and contexts with which they were bound up, for it is difficult to extricate (post)colonial localities like Vancouver Island from the West. Colonial empires have been dissolved, but the legacies of colonialism are still felt in numerous ways.[7] In former settler colonies such as Australia and Canada, immigrant – European, colonial – societies have long since modulated into indigenous ones, made the land their own, and sidelined its first inhabitants. "Aboriginality," "indiginization," "postcoloniality," and other terms that signify late twentieth-century cultural, legal, and political struggles over authenticity, home, and identity are grounded in different ways in different places. In regions like Vancouver Island, they have discrepant and agonizing meanings that centre on land. Native and non-Native peoples still struggle to accommodate each other's attachment to land. This book looks at where some of these contemporary British Columbian tensions over land come from.

More conceptually, my analysis is informed by Foucault's genealogical formulation that there are "a whole order of levels of different types of events differing in amplitude, chronological breadth, and capacity to produce effects."[8] In the first place, the three parts of the book discuss different kinds of geography and history. I will start with an event, then explore a set of processes, and finally track the establishment of an imperial structure. Part 1 considers an event – Cook's well-documented sojourn at Nootka Sound in 1778 – and the light it sheds on subsequent ideas about the nature of historical meaning. The various sections in Part 1 tease out the relations between a vivid but fleeting moment in the contact history of the Northwest Coast, more general patterns of European and British Columbian thought, and some problematics in the British Columbian present. Part 2, on the other hand, focuses on the nature of Western-Native commercial interaction and tracks processes of territorial and sociopolitical change among Nuu-chah-nulth groups between the 1770s and early 1800s. I am concerned here with a more historically and geographically bounded realm of contact. Then, in Part 3, I try to show how the connections that Natives and traders made on the ground became circumvented by a set of imperial practices that operated at much longer range, over vast territories, and with considerable abstraction. Vancouver Island became part of a larger imperial domain, and politicians and diplomats produced effects of power that Native peoples could not influence. The imperial imagination ran with little direct information about the Northwest Coast, and for a long time this process of imperial reterritorialization, taking place in Western corridors of powers, had little direct bearing on the contact process. In the long run, however, politicians created an imperial space (the Oregon Territory) that formed the geopolitical framework of colonial appropriation. A distant set of metropolitan events, fuelled by partial facts about the Northwest Coast, had powerful implications for Native peoples.

Second, my argument about the intertwining and divergence of Native and Western fortunes is premised on the idea that the explorers, traders, and politicians who engaged the Native peoples and territory of the Northwest Coast each had a distinctive approach to the world. In Part 1, I represent Cook as an Enlightenment figure and evaluate his encounter with the people of Nootka Sound in terms of the aims and fault lines of this project. In Part 2, I explore how the ethic of profit adopted by traders shaped the contact process and what they wrote about Native peoples. These traders were capitalists, not Enlightenment figures. Then, in Part 3, I implicate explorers, traders, and politicians in processes of imperial aggrandizement and projects of state expansion that seized and devoured space from a distance and gradually turned Native land into Western territory from afar. "Local" scholars have tended to blur these distinctions, I think, and have thus lost something of the project-oriented nature of these

Western approaches to the Northwest Coast and the markedly different ways in which Native peoples were engaged in the first few decades of contact.

I have also tried to interpret Native agendas. Much of Part 2 focuses on Native projects of commercial engagement and the effects of the sea otter trade on Nuu-chah-nulth groups. It is obviously important to view Native peoples as thinking, breathing, historical actors (rather than as chastened and silenced "others," which is how they are often portrayed in books on the violence of colonial discourse), but I should say at the outset that the ethnographic record on the Nuu-chah-nulth is badly undertheorized and that I do not have the anthropological expertise to say as much about Nuu-chah-nulth society as I would have liked. But this does not meant that the ethnographic record should be ignored. It remains an important source of empirical information, and some of it can be cross-referenced with historical and archaeological records.

In short, the book explores the entanglements and divisions between Natives and newcomers. The first two parts show how explorers and traders sought to engage Native peoples – as people to be observed, befriended, and feared – and how Native peoples engaged them – largely as trade partners, allies, and actors in Native power games. On the other hand, Part 3 discusses modes of cultural effacement and how the colony of Vancouver Island was produced as an imperial space before it was colonized. These, I think, are the main themes of the book. As my account of this period and sense of British Columbia differs from that of other scholars, I should say more about how I engage local issues and scholarship, and mention some of the personal influences on my work.

Until the 1960s, British Columbia's history was narrated largely around themes of imperial affiliation and provincial and national becoming.[9] Native peoples barely featured in these accounts, except as the handmaids of a growing Western (and specifically British) interest in the Cordillera or as obstacles to colonial and national development. Anthropology was the first academic site from which this historiography was questioned, and Robin Fisher's 1977 book, *Contact and Conflict: Indian-European Relations in British Columbia, 1774-1890*, is perhaps the most accomplished overview of the Native past by a historian. Fisher dug deeply into the archival record and offered an impressive generalization about cultural change: that Native groups did not start to lose control over the direction of change until the onset of formal colonialism. Before colonists and the colonial state arrived, he argues, Natives and Westerners forged mutually beneficial, and largely peaceful, relationships; Native-Western interaction encouraged an "efflorescence" of Native material cultures, especially along the coast. With a few qualifications, Fisher still holds this view, and other studies of British Columbia's past still work within its general parameters.[10]

Fisher captured a basic dimension of change. To Native peoples, there were palpable differences between the presence of traders and the arrival of colonists. Traders could not afford to drive Native groups away, whereas colonists sought their own economy and harboured explicitly racist attitudes towards Native peoples. Between the 1770s and 1850s there emerged a cross-cultural economy of contact, or mediation. In the second half of the nineteenth century Native-White relations became rooted in a conflictual economy of colonizer and colonized – an order of exclusion.

It has become increasingly apparent that Fisher's thesis and model of inquiry has empirical and conceptual blind spots. Recent scholarship emphasizes the unintended consequences of Western encroachment. Epidemics of smallpox, malaria, and measles swept much of the Northwest Coast in the late eighteenth and early nineteenth centuries, devastating Native populations and disjointing Native societies in significant ways.[11] While Fisher does not suggest that Native cultures were ever static or immobile, his image of Native groups meeting traders on their own terms is considerably complicated by our understanding of this biological exchange. Another important switch in emphasis in the literature on early contact processes concerns Native-Western violence and inter-Native warfare. These themes were leitmotifs of late nineteenth- and early twentieth-century writing on the maritime fur trade and the North American Indian more generally. Native peoples were represented as volatile savages who attacked trade vessels and each other. One of the first and most prolific scholars of the trade, Frederic Howay, documented trader violence towards Native peoples and assumed that it was rooted in an ethic of profit. Fisher downplays conflict in the fur trade and between Native groups, and points instead to the structural violence of colonialism. He argues that Native attacks on traders, and vice versa, are less noteworthy than are the colonial strategies of power that ranged over Native communities. The colonial militia, British gunboats, the land laws and Indian reserve system, the rule of law, and the civilizing projects of missionaries and the colonial state transformed Native lives, cultures, and epistemologies.

As impressive as these generalizations are, Fisher made them in the 1970s and in a spirit of historical revisionism that can no longer quite accommodate current research and the context in which it has developed. Over the last twenty years, much more information has become available, work on early British Columbia has mounted, and research has become increasingly interdisciplinary. For this early period of contact, archaeologists, anthropologists, geographers, and historians have re-emphasized the violence of the fur trade, documented warfare, slave-trading, and territorial change among Native groups, and they have suggested that there were important regional variations in economic and cultural change within and between Native cultures. Generalizations about early contact are now harder to sustain.[12] These research developments stem from the growth of graduate schools in British Columbia's universities and the flowering of government-sponsored history and museum projects. They are also situated within a turbulent cultural and political context. Consciousness of the past has been affected by litigation over Native title of land. Researchers working for First

Nations or the federal and/or provincial governments have ransacked archives for evidence of Native settlement and territorial continuity. An academic sub-culture of consultancy has grown up around this court circus, and the courts have fractured scholarly formulations of historical continuity and discontinu-ity, of cause and effect. Historical records have been used to discount Native territorial claims, and judges have disparaged Native oral testimony.

Arguments about Native warfare, disease, and territorial change have obvious connotations in this context. The image of the "ecological Indian" in harmony with nature and at peace with her/his neighbours, which has figured in the per-ception and presentation of Native causes, is disrupted by evidence of violence. Evidence of extensive Native depopulation may refuel the colonial mythology of empty space. And evidence of territorial change disturbs the cartography of he-reditary tribal territories and Native occupation from "time immemorial." The kinds of questions scholars are now asking have been influenced by these court proceedings and, since 1993, by public debates about the purpose of the British Columbia Treaty Commission, which seeks a political solution to Native griev-ances and has recently produced the Nisga'a Treaty.

Scholars have responded to these developments by calling for a "disciplined analysis" of the past – a careful evaluation of evidence.[13] They do so, however, at a moment when scholarly objectivity is being associated with scholarly author-ity in resolutely judgmental ways. Litigators take shortcuts through the facts, and separate fact from fiction, by appealing to living and dead "authorities in the field"; and judges have run roughshod over the archival record, cutting and pasting together documents that best support their legal views, and forming impressions about the local past from the work of historians.[14] In British Co-lumbia, there is currently a "politics of pastness" (to borrow Arjun Appadurai's phrase) that beckons us to deal with the authoritativeness and circulation of evidence, ideas, and representations within and between the past and the present.[15] I visit these contemporary political issues most directly in Part 1, where I treat Cook's sojourn at Nootka Sound as both an event and a critical horizon for thinking about the handling of historical evidence and the making of his-tory. I argue that Cook's scientific and humanitarian mandate both embraced, and was confounded by, issues of vision, experience, and positionality. There were a number of *spaces of contact* embedded in this encounter.

Analysis of the production and dissemination of knowledge, the ordering of texts in archives, and strategies of representation present one way of re-routing connections between the past and present. The "real" events of the past cannot easily be separated from narratives of the past. Scholars such as Howay devoted many pages to the meaning of British Columbia's past. He was concerned with the nature of Britain's possession of the region. Such concerns have been deemed colonialist and archaic by a recent generation of scholars, but they are as impor-tant now as they were in Howay's day. Thinking about how the past is always being tailored in – and as – the present sensitizes us both to the selective shaping of historical understanding and to the organizing frameworks of our own texts.

These perspectives are truncated in ethnohistorical work on British Columbia because power tends to be seen solely at ground level, in the realm of face-to-face interaction, and regions such as Vancouver Island tend to be treated as self-evident and self-contained geographical and discursive entities. Scholars of "contact" are committed to approaching the past from "the bottom up," but they tend to avoid the global contexts in which Western projects were articulated. Facets of the eras of contact and conflict have been well documented by ethnohistorians, but their ideas about how the transition from "contact" to "conflict" occurred are quite narrow. In order to interpret this shift in Native fortunes more expansive formulations of power and representation are needed. A number of geographies of power worked on Vancouver Island over these two eras. Face-to-face interaction was basic and should not be trivialized. But other histories and geographies of power, stretching over longer distances, had a significant impact on the imperial fashioning of Vancouver Island: cartographic and geopolitical projects of inscription. The imperial archive of Western interest in the Northwest Coast has barely figured in the conceptualization of contact. This is probably because the annals of Western political decision making were the core of "top down" imperial histories that shuffled Native peoples out of the picture. It is time to reconsider this picture. Cartographic projects of representation, and models of sovereignty, induced and naturalized colonialism. I will suggest that an imperial history of power bridges the pre-colonial and colonial eras and prompts us to rethink the nature and moment of colonialism.

I do not think that Vancouver Island's double constitution as a locality of and away from the West can be seen very clearly if one skimps on historical research or if analysis is confined to Native shores. I cast a fairly wide archival net, and the processes of cultural accommodation and appropriation I have been introducing only came into focus when I drew in this net and began to see that Native-Western relations were fashioned in a variety of settings and circumstances. I also sense that my thinking about the past was influenced by the acrimonious court trial that was going on while I was working on this project – *Delgamuukw et al.* v. *The Queen*, involving the Gitksan and Wet'suwet'en peoples of north-central British Columbia – and the 1991 judgment on it. One of my colleagues was an expert witness for the Native plaintiffs, I had read the work of others who gave testimony on behalf of Native peoples and the Crown, and everyone I knew was affected by the trial. It was a depressing affair for Natives and for the many non-Natives who sympathize with Native causes. The colonialist quips about Native peoples that are enshrined in Chief Justice McEachern's "Reasons for Judgement" astonished many people. His judgment has since been overhauled in significant ways by a Canadian Supreme Court ruling, and the Treaty Commission now offers hope for many Native communities. But in the early 1990s I gained the vivid impression that I was writing into and about cultural divides. This impression was enhanced by my research, and I do not think that recent legal and political developments will transform the relations between the past and present overnight. I paint a less rosy picture of Vancouver Island's pre-colonial past than have scholars such as Fisher. I see narrower and more volatile avenues of cultural accommodation and the emergence of enduring cultural divisions.

Non-Native people have become increasingly aware of Native voices, protests, and cultural productions, but attempts to give British Columbia a more inclusive identity and to come to terms with the past have been chequered. There is White liberal guilt about the treatment of Native peoples, but there is also White racism. For Native peoples, court trials and First Nations-government negotiations will not cancel out the bitter memory of colonization and the colonialisms perpetrated by British Columbian and Canadian governments. Meanwhile, many long-established and newly arrived immigrant British Columbians worry that politicians are giving away their land and bankrupting the state. Land treaties and compensation packages will not dispel profoundly discrepant experiences of colonialism. Increasingly, it seems, cultural and political negotiations over land and resources are becoming numbers games that are shaped by principles of law, tied to government purse strings, and couched in a White rhetoric of "capitulation." Local newspaper headlines such as "Aboriginal Land Claims Total 111% of B.C. Land Mass" point to a modern, cartographic calculus of cultural strife that connects the past to legal and financial equations. This book is implicated in the appreciation of this calculus and of cultural differences in British Columbia. I argue that this calculus stems from the imperial construction of Native land between 1790 and 1846.

These lines of inquiry are also tempered by personal experiences. My tendency to see the work of empire where other scholars do not, and to situate Vancouver Island in theoretical realms that others have ignored, probably reflects my own experience of transplantation. I have not figured out how I am placed in empire, but growing up in England, attending an elite university where I received training in geographical and social theory but where (I now recognize) questions of empire were barely broached, then attending graduate school in British Columbia where I could not avoid colonial issues, and now working in Scotland (where my Englishness is noticed), I know I am of it. This book is perhaps an attempt to come to terms with aspects of this recognition.

I hope my title captures the various themes of the book. First, I adopt it in order to suggest that the engagement between Natives and Westerners was not a uniform process. Explorers, traders, Western politicians, and Native groups had different agendas, and Native peoples were implicated in these phases of exploration, trade, and geopolitics in different ways. These modes of engagement were shaped in a range of locales: they worked through different islands of meaning.

Second, I adopt this title in order to acknowledge that "Vancouver Island" means radically different things to Natives and to non-Natives. Analysis of the fashioning of the island – its cartographic shape, proper name, and imperial connotations – can give us insights into the creation of cultural divides that reach into the present. Third, I adopt this title in order to signpost the idea that the generation of knowledge and truths about peoples and places induces and supports relations of power. My subtitle refers to the island of truth – or constellation of knowledge, power, and geography – that has been least conceptualized in the scholarly literature on Native-Western relations but that has had a great bearing on the formation of imperial attitudes and colonial views.

My title is also styled upon my epigraph from Immanuel Kant's *Critique of Pure Reason*. As Captain Cook was opening up the Pacific to European inspection, Kant was opening up the place of "man" as an object of knowledge and a knowing subject. This passage from Kant points to the influence of scientific exploration and imperialism on European thought as well as to the notion that the Enlightenment was characterized by a doubly problematic relationship between thought and the world. As Enlightenment thinkers delved ever more deeply into the darkness and contradictions of reason, Europe continued to impose itself on the rest of the world in the name of reason and civilization. Europeans were fascinated by the power of reason to domesticate kingdoms of otherness and the capacity of "man" to live contemporaneously, without the crutch of the past. But there was also trepidation about territories of uncertainty, and there was recognition that Europe constituted itself as the enlightened centre and subject of History through myriad threatening – and often destructive – encounters with otherness. *Islands of Truth* traces something of Kant's world – these issues of certainty and doubt, superiority and anxiety, the Enlightenment and its shadows – to a particular corner of the world.

I will begin with a specific monument of truth and the stormy ocean surrounding it: a cairn at Nootka Sound commemorating Captain Cook's achievements, which was unveiled on a blustery day in 1924.

PART 1

Spaces of European Exploration

Possessing the Other, like possessing the past, is always full of delusions.

– GREG DENING, *PERFORMANCES*

Introduction

On 13 August 1924, HMCS *Malaspina* carried a party of dignitaries and about 150 spectators to Friendly Cove at the mouth of Nootka Sound to witness the unveiling of a cairn commemorating Cook's discovery of the sound in 1778 and subsequent European exploration in the region. A historian at the University of British Columbia, Walter Sage, reported on the event for the British Columbia Historical Association:

> Just as the *Malaspina* steamed into Friendly Cove two canoe-loads of Nootka Indians were seen pushing off from the village. As they came nearer there could be heard rising from their canoes a monotonous chant of three notes timed to the paddlestrokes. It was a song of welcome and goodwill to the white men ... Both canoes circled the *Malaspina*, the crews keeping up the vociferous welcome. Then Michael Brown, second chief of the neighboring Clayoquot tribe, a third cousin of Napoleon Maquinna, rose from his place in the men's canoe and commenced a long harangue in his own native tongue. His booming voice at once commanded silence and his flashing eyes compelled attention. While he spoke in a language unintelligible to the majority of his hearers, it seemed as if the mists of time had rolled away and that we were back again with Captain Cook on the deck of the *Resolution* looking down at the canoes of the Nootkans which surrounded the ship. Michael Brown may have been conscious of the illusion he was creating, for he swept his hand shoreward towards the village and appeared to be inviting us to land.

After the passengers had disembarked, Chief Brown welcomed them to "the country of the Nootkans." Over 150 Native people from different parts of the coast had turned out for the occasion. The memorial party then headed for the cairn, which was draped in the Union Jack and placed on a promontory close to the Native village of Yuquot (at Friendly Cove); it had been donated by the Historic Sites and Monuments Board of Canada and was the first one it had erected west of the Rockies.

A British Columbian judge and historian, F.W. Howay, opened the formal proceedings by encouraging everyone to sing the first stanza of Rudyard Kipling's *Recessional*. Sage noted that the refrain – *Lest we forget, lest we forget!* – "seemed perfectly in keeping with the spirit of the occasion." Howay then studied the cairn and invoked the Book of Joshua: "What mean ye by these stones?" "As every one knows," he stated, "the bare facts of history are mere dry bones. The tablet tells us that this sound was discovered by the great Captain James Cook." History had been built on this rock, and people had come to Friendly Cove "to show to the face of the day this pile of stones." The cairn, he continued, was a memorial to Cook and the triumph of two British imperial ideals: that sovereignty over waste lands went to the first civilized nation that took real possession and that the oceans of the world are free to all nations. Howay then made way for British Columbia's lieutenant-governor, W.C. Nichol, who delivered another speech, much of which was prepared for him by the provincial librarian, John Forsyth. Finally, the cairn was unveiled, the *Malaspina* gave a five-gun salute, and the spectators sang "God Save the King."

Back at Yuquot, Charles Moser, a Roman Catholic missionary on the west coast of Vancouver Island, acting as official interpreter, introduced Nichol to the Mowachaht chief of the area, Napoleon Maquinna. Sage noted that Maquinna was "arrayed in his robes of offices," shook hands with Nichol "with all due solemnity," and made a long speech in his native tongue. Nichol thanked the Natives for their hospitality, and then the grand chief factor of the Native Sons of British Columbia, Victor Harrison, addressed a group of Natives about their rights under Canadian law. The White visitors inspected the village – their cameras "snapping in every direction" – and bargained for Native artefacts. And lest the occasion be forgotten, a man from the Fox Corporation was on hand to film the proceedings.[1]

This remarkable event signposts a particular conjuncture between modernity and colonialism in British Columbia. Howay reintroduced what appeared to be a forgotten imperial landscape. Citizens of a young province and nation-state were at Nootka Sound to rediscover their past and give it meaning. There was a whiff of novelty in the air. Links between history, geography, and identity were being discussed as if for the first time. Howay, for one, had never been to Nootka Sound before.[2] Cook's discovery of Nootka Sound was being viewed as the foundation of history in British Columbia.

This unveiling ceremony points to the importance of images of discovery, constructions of the past, and tropes of possession in the formation of regional identities and power relations. I will return to it at the end of Part 1. It frames a broader analysis of how knowledge and truths about this encounter and Cook's three voyages have been shaped from a range of vantage points and points in history. The bulk of Part 1 focuses on Cook's sojourn at "Nootka Sound" in the spring of 1778.[3] But I want to set up this analysis by considering some more general interpretative issues relating to Cook and European exploration in the Age of Enlightenment. Cook's voyages raise some important and intriguing questions about the making of history and geography, I think, because he was the first European to reach many parts of the Pacific and because he now belongs to two – contorted – worlds: (1) a wide world of empire and decolonization, where European exploration and expansion was once conceived in triumphalist terms and history was written from the centre out, but where scholars in a range of disciplines are now sensitive to the material and symbolic violence that accompanied Europeans encounters with the non-European world and debate what it means to "write back" from the (post)colonial margins of empire; and (2) more discrete worlds of contact and colonialism, such as British Columbia, where figures like Cook have been viewed in markedly different ways by Native peoples, the colonists who took over their land, latter-day immigrants, and scholars who have produced regional histories that do not just refer back to Europe.

CHAPTER 1

Captain Cook,
the Enlightenment, and
Symbolic Violence

All had been ordered weeks before the start
From the best firms at such work; instruments
To take the measure of all queer events,
And drugs to move the bowels or the heart.

A watch, of course, to watch impatience fly,
Lamps for the dark and shades against the sun;
Foreboding, too, insisted on a gun,
And coloured beads to soothe a savage eye.

In theory they were sound on Expectation
Had there been situations to be in;
Unluckily they were their situation:

One should not give a poisoner medicine,
A conjurer fine apparatus, nor
A rifle to a melancholic bore.

− W.H. AUDEN, *THE QUEST*

ENLIGHTENMENT CREDENTIALS

James Cook's three voyages around the world (1768-80) heralded a shift in Europe's engagement with the Pacific, and Cook still holds a special place in the European imagination. He was not an "old South Sea" buccaneer wresting markets and resources from other countries, as Glyndwr Williams characterizes European mariners in the Pacific up to the 1750s.[1] He was sent on a scientific mission to map the Pacific and observe rather than exploit its peoples and resources.[2] He sailed with more sophisticated navigational aids than his predecessors, and he was a talented navigator who preserved the health of his crews.[3] Cook and his officers also kept detailed logs of their travels for the British Admiralty, and the artists and scientists who accompanied them represented the Pacific in intricate detail. The published journals of Cook's voyages, and the objects that his crews brought back to Europe, heightened curiosity about the non-European world, stimulated natural history, and contributed to the emergence of the human sciences. These scientific voyages influenced the shift in the order of European knowledge from the taxonomies and theological principles of the eighteenth century to the historicisms and secular principles of the nineteenth century.[4]

Cook rode a wave of public enthusiasm for overseas exploration and travel writing.[5] The official published accounts of his voyages, which were commissioned by the Admiralty and tailored from Cook's journals, sold out almost overnight.[6] They were translated into other languages and studied by European intellectuals.[7] Cheaper, abridged editions reached a broader reading public, and extracts from his voyages were published in newspapers, periodicals, and compendia. Some of Cook's crewmen tapped the huge European market for travel writing and achieved notoriety by publishing their own unofficial accounts, and many of the artefacts collected on Cook's voyages were displayed in European museums.[8] Cook gained an international reputation as a brilliant mariner and was heroized after he was killed by Hawaiian Islanders in 1779.[9] His voyages to the Pacific were among the most publicized events of the European Enlightenment.

In his dealings with the peoples of the Pacific, Cook was steered by an official code of conduct – a method and ethics of contact.[10] On his third voyage, which I will focus on below, he was instructed by the Admiralty to

> observe the Genius, Temper, Disposition, and Number of the Natives and Inhabitants, where you find any; and to endeavour, by all proper means to cultivate a friendship with them; making them Presents of such Trinkets as you may have on board, and they may like best; inviting them to Traffick; and shewing them every kind of Civility and Regard; but taking care nevertheless not to suffer yourself to be surprized by them, but to be always on your guard against any Accidents.[11]

These instructions stemmed from "hints" written for Cook in 1768 by the earl of Morton (James Douglas), the president of the Royal Society.[12] Cook was also cautioned to check the petulance and cupidity of his sailors when in contact with Native peoples and to avoid violent collisions. Firearms were to be used as sparingly as possible. This made logistical sense to both the Admiralty and the Royal Society. On these long voyages, Cook could not afford to lose men and supplies in skirmishes, and hostilities that drove his ships off shore would hinder scientific study. Trade was the preferred means of securing supplies and artefacts from Native peoples and was deemed an important way of breaking down language barriers. It also brought Native peoples within close range of Cook's artists and scientists.

Embedded in this injunction to "Traffick" was the notion that the peoples of the Pacific would have an irresistible desire for European goods and view them as the products of a superior culture. Dr. John Douglas (canon of Windsor and St. Paul's), who edited the official accounts of Cook's second and third voyages, captured such sentiments: "The uncommon objects [non-European peoples] have ... had opportunity of observing and admiring, will naturally tend to enlarge their stock of ideas, and to furnish new materials for the exercise of their reason. Comparing themselves with their visitors, they cannot but be struck with the deepest conviction of their own inferiority, and be impelled, by the strongest motives, to strive to emerge from it." Cook was to spread "the blessings of civilization" under the guise of trade.[13]

Cook's promoters hoped that the knowledge he generated would provide Europeans with new insights into their own civilization. Commentators suggested that explorers' discoveries helped Europeans to assess their own place in history and contemplate the "gradation" of societies "from barbarism to civility."[14] As knowledge about the non-European world grew between the sixteenth and eighteenth centuries, European thinkers no longer had to rely solely on European history as a measure of social change. In *Terra Australis Cognita* (1768) John Callender suggested that the Pacific would present "a faithful picture of the innocence and simplicity of the first ages ... men simple, and just as they came from the hand of nature."[15] Exploration fed European assumptions and theories about the world. Adam Smith, for instance, held that societies naturally progress over time through four distinct, consecutive modes of subsistence (hunting, pasturage, agriculture, and commerce), with different sets of ideas and institutions defining each – roughly labelled savage, barbarian, and civilized. His and other theories of historical development were bolstered by European discoveries in the New World and the Pacific.[16]

There were also humanitarian influences on Cook's voyages. "Shedding the blood of those people is a crime of the highest nature," Morton declared: "They are human creatures, the work of the same omnipotent Author, equally under his care with the most polished European; perhaps being less offensive."[17] This acknowledgment of the humanity of other peoples (albeit of divine creation) had complex intellectual roots in European ideas about "natural man" and the "noble savage," and in the anti-slavery movement.[18] Treating other peoples with "every kind of Civility and Regard" meant distancing oneself from "tribal" disputes and respecting other ways of life. This policy did not entail an unbridled relativism, however. There was a fine line between humanitarianism and moral righteousness. Callender, and many of his contemporaries, thought that "by adopting our ideas of a regular and well-ordered society ... [Native] minds would be opened, and formed, their savage manners softened."[19] Cook was to display Europe's cultural "acquisitions." His crews were meant to be models of social order and moral strength, and Cook was to lead by example.

This humanitarian agenda was closely connected to the rhetoric of science. The science of exploration was rooted in the Baconian belief that knowledge should be sought not for personal fame or gain but for the general advancement of "mankind." Barbara Stafford argues that respect for other peoples mirrored the tolerant, non-dogmatic implications of empirical science; the search for truth by induction was meant to be a multinational venture based on calm deliberation. Science was conceived as "a transcendent interest" above "narrowly commercial, military, or colonial exploitation." [20] The French geographer Charles de Brosses captured this spirit of benevolence in his *Histoire des Navigations aux Terres Australes* (1756): "Too much haste in enjoying the fruits of one's projects often leads only to their failure. In the beginning let us think of nothing but geography, of the pure desire to discover, of the acquiring of new lands and novel inhabitants for the universe."[21]

This scientific-humanitarian agenda has been discussed in detail. The economic and political motives for Cook's voyages remain obscure. Vincent Harlow claimed that after the Seven Years War (1756-63) there emerged a "second British Empire" of trade, rather than territorial dominion, with science in the service of commerce; Cook was Adam Smith's "global agent," as Bernard Smith has since put it, developing markets, spreading the idea of enlightened self-interest, and "bringing to prehistoric cultures the disguised checks and balances of a market economy."[22] These arguments involve a good deal of hindsight, however. It is unclear whether Cook's voyages were motivated by a grand imperial plan.[23] Political discussion about the Pacific as a new theatre of colonization was speculative. The British and French thought that the discovery of new riches in the fabled Terra Australis might alter the balance of power in Europe.[24] And Cook was instructed to make a careful inventory of the resources and commercial potential of the Pacific and to take possession of "convenient Situations."[25] The British did not want Cook's voyages to become a pretext for another war with France and had no immediate plans to colonize the Pacific; they had other worries.

Britain was enormously successful in the Seven Years War, but Ronald Hyam notes that British politicians signed the Peace of Paris "in remarkable ignorance of any but the most obvious British overseas interests."[26] Linda Colley thinks that this war challenged "long-standing British mythologies."[27] The conquest of Bengal and New France fractured belief in the symbiosis of the British nation and its empire – the idea that British power and character, at home and overseas, was based on Protestantism, commerce, and liberty. Britain's postwar empire, which included large non-Anglophone and non-Protestant subject populations, had to be managed and legitimized. Debates about the meaning of "Britishness" raged in England and Scotland, and questions of imperial alliance escalated in North America. Colley sees the British as "captivated by but also adrift and at odds in a vast empire abroad and a new political world at home which few of them properly understood."[28] Such anxieties forestalled thoughts of territorial expansion.

In his *Collection* of voyages to the South Pacific (1770), Alexander Dalrymple, the English East India Company's (and later the Admiralty's) hydrographer, re-iterated the old worry that distant colonies would strive for independence and argued that the Pacific should be regarded as a "new vent for manufactures" rather than a new arena of colonial conquest. Dalrymple was committed to com-mercial expansion, but in 1770 he was also concerned with the more immediate strategic import of "new discoveries."[29] "The subject of discoveries seems to be now reviving," he stated, and "demands immediate attention from every English-man, for it may be very justly said, the *being* of the British empire rests on our insular situation, and powerful navy. Were any of our competitors to gain the superiority at sea, the advantages of the *first* would be lost."[30]

Dalrymple's quasi-mercantilist logic has been explored by Daniel Baugh, who suggests that Cook's voyages were motivated, in part, by "a protective maritime imperialism."[31] They were part of a much longer history of Anglo-French ri-valry. The British government was anxious to maintain Britain's naval superior-ity. Cook and other British explorers were instructed to keep their eyes out for new naval bases, and the Admiralty hoped that Cook would produce seamen for Britain's dwindling merchant fleet. In fact, Cook's contemporaries did not try to hide these imperial undercurrents. For intellectual figureheads such as Sir Joseph Banks (the scientist on Cook's first voyage and, later, the president of the Royal Society), science and empire went hand-in-hand.[32]

Yet Cook made his name not as an imperialist, but as "the most moderate, humane and gentle circumnavigator who ever went upon discoveries," as Fanny Burney (Madame D'Arblay) famously remarked.[33] He followed his instructions, and commentators thought he fulfilled his scientific-humanitarian mandate. He did not wield British power so much as an enlightened world view – a new curiosity about the world and tolerance of other peoples.

BEAGLEHOLE'S COOK

This image of Cook as a humane scientific explorer was put on a scholarly footing this century by the New Zealand historian J.C. Beaglehole, who re-edited Cook's journals for the Hakluyt Society of London. Beaglehole represented Cook as a brilliant navigator, a judicious observer, and a flag-bearer of European civilization.[34] Beaglehole saw Cook as an Enlightenment figure: as a sailor of humble origins who broke out of the shackles of speculation and tradition and developed a self-conscious attitude towards observation, description, and interaction. Cook had "the sceptical mind: he did not like taking on trust," Beaglehole judged; he was "the great dispeller of illusion." He deployed his critical faculties using the science of his day and was "the genius of the matter of fact."[35] "He loved facts" and approached his journal writing with "a perfectly unassuming and primary wish to tell the truth."[36]

Similar views of Cook can be found in reviews from the late eighteenth century.[37] "In movement [Cook] realized his innermost nature," Bernard Smith has remarked more recently; and he continues: "Europe is like that; a geographical imperative impels it; it must be on the move or perish."[38] Beaglehole wrote at the tail end of this imperative – (1) after Cook had hooked up the world and (2) as a New Zealander. One implication of his work is that Cook's activities remain meaningful because he was a person like "us," struggling to make sense of the world diligently, objectively, and compassionately.

Beaglehole studied Cook during the era of decolonization, when there was an outpouring of anti-European sentiment, and science and humanism were being seen as the handmaidens of European power. His work on Cook's voyages can be read as a thinly disguised defence of the political disinterestedness of scientific knowledge. Yet his work counterbalances that of postwar liberal historians who reinvoked the nineteenth-century view that contact with Europeans was inherently and inevitably catastrophic for Native peoples – that Cook was a poisoner.[39] Far from inaugurating cultural disaster, Beaglehole argued, Cook's voyages set a standard of cross-cultural interaction that others ruined.[40] Beaglehole associated colonialism with formal European rule – not explicit features of Cook's agenda – and thought that the creation of knowledge itself did not found imperial desire or colonial power. By the standards of the nineteenth century, Cook's sweep of the Pacific was fleeting and his relations with Indigenous peoples were mostly congenial. As a New Zealander, Beaglehole must have known that all of this made Cook's status as an imperialist ambiguous.

IMAGINATIVE GEOGRAPHIES

These issues of knowledge and identity have recently been the subject of intense debate in the literature on the Enlightenment and colonialism. Recent scholarship pays close attention to the imaginative dimensions of Europe's engagement with the Pacific and to issues of representation. Europeans, like all peoples, imagined and represented the world in relation to themselves, but with the privilege of more power than most. Dorinda Outram demonstrates that Cook's voyages, and the voyage of his French counterpart, Louis-Antoine de Bougainville, focused European debates about civilization at a time when Europe's sense of itself was undergoing profound social and political change.[41] Thinkers such as Voltaire and Montesquieu had used knowledge about Asian and Amerindian peoples to highlight the specificity and peculiarity of European cultural practices.[42] Outram notes that Denis Diderot's *Supplément au Voyage de Bougainville* (1796) was of particular importance in moving "the debate on the 'noble savage' and on 'civilisation' away from its previous implicit exotic referent of the 'savages' of the New World on to the Pacific."[43] Diderot and many other commentators exoticized Native life in the Pacific, seeing in it, variously, archaic simplicity, classical perfection, goodness and purity, and savagery.[44]

Outram suggests that Europeans could configure Pacific Islanders as exotic, timeless, distant, and yet as strangely intimate, Others precisely because the discoveries of Cook and Bougainville did not entail colonization. The Pacific was not part of the bloody, exploitative traffic of the Atlantic colonial system. The Pacific figured in debates about the pros and cons of the slave trade as a paradisical space of contrast. As Henri Baudet diagnosed, "There was, on the one hand, the actual physical outside world which could be put to political, economic and strategic use; there was also the outside world onto which all identification and interpretation, all dissatisfaction and desire, all nostalgia and idealism seeking expression could be projected. And although one of these two worlds may have been circumscribed by fixed, material circumstances, the other remained infinitely variable, infinitely interpretable, adjusting itself with endless patience to all the twists and turns of our thought."[45] Bernard Smith's pathbreaking book *European Vision in the South Pacific* (1960) discusses these twists and turns. He noticed that Cook's ships "combined the values of a fortress and a travelling laboratory," and he identified two strains in Europe's construction of the Pacific: a neo-classical strain influenced by the philosophies of Europe's Royal Academies and characterized by the pursuit of purity in form and a unity of mood in graphic expression; and a scientific strain concerned with detailed observation and realism, which grew in stature between 1768 and the 1850s. Cook's artists and scientists championed the "empirical habits of vision" of the Royal Society.[46]

SPACES OF APPROPRIATION

Other critics have read much more into these constructions. They point to the symbolic and material violence embedded in this Enlightenment outreach. Greg Dening argues that in "acting out their scientific, humanistic selves" in the Pacific, the nations of Europe were competing over their place in history:

> It was a time of intensive theatre of the civilised to the native, but of even more intense theatre of the civilised to one another. The civilised jostled to see what the Pacific said to them of their relations of dominance. They vied in testing the extensions of their sovereignty and the effectiveness of their presence – through territorial possession, protected lines of communication, exemplary empire. They shouted to the natives, in that loud and slow way we use to communicate with those that do not share our language, the meaning of flags and cannons and property and trade, and lessons of civilised behaviour.[47]

European powers may not have planned to colonize the Pacific, but the region was constituted as a "theatre" of empire. Explorers' texts can be viewed as imperial allegories that combined a new self-conscious world view and much older European jealousies: old and new practices of cultural dominance.

Mary Louise Pratt traces these cultural imperialisms and reifications to the worlds of science and commerce. Between 1750 and 1850, she argues, the mercantilist equation of wealth, power, and empire modulated into an ambitious, bourgeois political economy of representation – a European "planetary consciousness" – which was driven by practices of classification.[48] The systematic mapping, naming, and classification of the lands, peoples, and resources of the world was geared to the search for markets and profits, and explorers conceived the world as "a chaos out of which the scientist produced an order." Pratt views the project of natural history as "a utopian image of a European bourgeois subject simultaneously innocent and imperial, asserting a harmless hegemonic vision that installs no apparatus of domination." This project, she continues, modelled "the extractive, transformative character of industrial capitalism, and the ordering mechanisms that were beginning to shape urban mass society in Europe under bourgeois hegemony. As an ideological construct, it makes a picture of the planet appropriated and deployed from a unified, European perspective."[49]

Pratt does not discuss Cook's voyages, and her reading is perhaps too sinister; but it is an important corrective to the view propounded by scholars such as Beaglehole – that these eighteenth-century voyages were innocent scientific forays.[50] Many explorers described non-European space as bounteous and ripe for colonization, and scientific exploration became "a magnet for the energies and resources of intricate alliances of intellectual and commercial elites all over Europe."[51] Exploration helped Europe to construct non-Europeans as different and distant – as Other – in order to constitute itself as a coherent geographical and cultural entity (the hearth and pinnacle of civilization), overriding imperial rivalries, papering over national differences, legitimizing imperial expansion, and stretching the capitalist world system to the ends of the earth through science.[52]

As Paul Carter notes, however, many critics often assume that "a narrative of eighteenth-century Pacific exploration is a narrative of European experiences."[53] They chart multifarious operations of power, and explorers' texts are mined for what they tell us about Europe. But now, as in the eighteenth century, appreciation of Native perceptions of Europeans is dimmed by the bright lights and specialist languages of European vision. All of Europe's energies are poured on to Native peoples, but the business of interaction in what Pratt herself terms "the contact zone" often remains dark, if not forgotten. The meaning of encounters for the lands and peoples encountered are willed back to Europe and into critical positions that turn around Europe and its others. It is Europe's presence on foreign shores that is the point of critical intrigue, not Natives' gist of European style. It is European practices of representations that are the focus of attention, not the meeting of cultures.[54]

SPACES OF CONTACT

These issues of Native perception reached a head with the publication of Gananath Obeyesekere's book *The Apotheosis of Captain Cook*. Obeyesekere, a Sri Lankan anthropologist, tries to debunk the long-held view that Hawaiians thought Cook was the embodiment of their god Lono.[55] He argues that Cook's apotheosis is a European myth and represents Cook and those who have eulogized his achievements as conjurers. He suspects that Cook had a narcissistic streak, presenting himself as an enlightened explorer at home but acting as a tyrant abroad. Cook, he implies, was a melancholic bore, at home with "savage ways" by his third voyage and treating Indigenous peoples with contempt.[56] There was a subtext of violence and deception beneath the scientific-humanitarian veneer of his voyages. Cook burned Native villages, shot thieves, and flogged his crew for misdemeanours.[57]

Deborah Bird Rose reads this book as a self-reflective meditation on the "insulated god-like position" that many scholars (she picks out anthropologists) assume when discussing other societies. "The apotheosis of Cook can be seen as a symptom of a more encompassing disorder," she argues: "that European conquest culture is not attuned to bridging intersubjective space, but only to dominating it."[58] She suggests that while Obeyesekere's interpretation of Cook's death may not be entirely cogent, his broader project of exposing European myth making is important, for "in making myths about his encounters with indigenous peoples, we tell ourselves stories about relationships between ourselves and others which conceal the violence inherent in our lives."[59] Obeyesekere tries to bridge the gap between Hawaiian and European perspectives on Cook's death by using European concepts of practical rationality. "The fact that my universe is a culturally constituted behavioural environment," he states, "does not mean that I am bound to it in a way that renders discrimination impossible. The idea of practical rationality provides me with a bit of space where I can talk of Polynesians who are like me in some sense ... to talk of the other in human terms."[60]

Marshall Sahlins, who is the most eloquent academic exponent of Cook's apotheosis and thus the main target of Obeyesekere's intellectual ire, has published a vitriolic (though very scholarly and in places highly amusing) book-length response to his critic. He accuses Obeyesekere of denigrating Hawaiian ways of knowing.[61] "The only difference between Obeyesekere's position and the garden variety of European imperialist ideology," Sahlins argues, "is that he reverses the values enshrined in the opposition between the West and the rest. "He would give the 'natives' all that 'rationality' Western people take to be the highest form of thought, while endowing Europeans, including the outsider-anthropologists, with the kind of mindless repetition of myth they have always despised ... The ultimate victims [of his study] ... are the Hawaiian people. Western empirical good sense replaces their own view of things, leaving them with a fictional history and a pidgin ethnography."[62]

This debate over Cook's death is part of a much broader debate in anthropology – and the humanities and social sciences more generally – about the politics of interpretation. To what extent can scholars observe or write about "other" cultures or the past without imposing their own categories and agendas on their subject matter?[63] Sahlins points out that concepts of reason and practical rationality are not culturally neutral or universally valid epistemological constellations. They are definitively European and have played an important role in colonial projects. They certainly inform Cook's representations, as I will show.

Carter thinks that Obeyesekere blurs "the primary spatial dynamic" of contact – "the profoundly different physical and conceptual spaces" that Europeans and Natives occupy and negotiate in contact situations – spaces that mediate the perception and construction of distance and difference, and the generation of meaning in the absence of a common language.[64] For Carter, the *site* of contact has historical significance. If one treats Hawaiian space as an inert stage on which the drama of Cook's death unfolded, as Obeyesekere does, then one perpetuates "the violence of the colonising eye and mind."[65]

Carter is interested in explorers' experiential dialogue with their surroundings – their *geo-graphy*, or "writing of lands." In his book *The Road to Botany Bay* (1987), he shows how Cook brought the Australian coast under his intentional gaze, and into his own intimate world of travel, using an elaborate, mischievous naming practice. He names Cook the founder of a "nomadic discourse" of "spatial history." Furthermore, Carter claims that the exploration of Australia was informed by open-ended, imaginative processes of movement and

observation rather than by the "passive and static" – taxonomic and imperial –
gaze of Cook's scientists.[66] Carter's book encourages non-dogmatic methods of
re-exploring history. He knows how precious acts of discovery are in the historical imagination of countries such as Australia, which do not have a long White
history, and how easily explorers' words and maps get translated into images of
territorial self-identification and power. Nevertheless, his reading of Cook is
exclusionary in that he ignores Cook's dealings with Native peoples.[67] While
Carter is adamant that it is Cook's engagement with the Australian coast that
matters, and not how we connect him to Europe, he still works backs to a European imaginary – an imaginary that Aboriginal peoples think stands for violence and appropriation. Carter uses none of Beaglehole's methods, but their
images of Cook are in some respects the same. Cook's journals remain the self-
contained locus of representation. For all of Carter's remarks about the spatial
dynamics of contact, his spatial history "begins and ends in language" and, thus,
cannot be invoked unreflexively as a means of decolonizing history.[68] His jour-
neying ethic of self-refashioning has a distinctly European heritage.[69]

The next two chapters explore Cook's transactions at Nootka Sound with these
issues and problematics in mind. Cook was then on his third voyage. He stayed
at Nootka Sound for a month repairing his ships, the *Resolution* and *Discovery*. I
read this encounter in three spatial registers: at the "local" site where face-to-
face interaction occurred (encouraged by Carter); in terms of Cook's experiential dialogue with the Pacific (sketched by Carter); and in the context of the
broader European-Enlightenment imaginary I have been discussing.

Space cannot be construed as an independent variable in the formation of
eighteenth-century European doctrines about the Other, in methods of contact,
or in the representational practices of explorers such as Cook. The imagination
and production of non-European space, I will suggest, was central to the design,
execution, and record of Cook's voyages. The three spatial registers I have mentioned were meshed in Cook's encounters with the peoples of the Pacific. In an
elliptical line in the preface to his edition of Cook's third voyage, Beaglehole
stated: "Where Cook went, why he said what he did, the accidents of the weather:
all this may be taken as matter of historical geography."[70] Beaglehole was interested in the geography *of* Cook's voyage – with Cook as the great dispeller of
geographical illusion. I argue that there were a number of geographies embedded *within* Cook's voyages. A number of viewpoints, stretching from specific
sites of interaction to the global trajectory of appropriation, were tucked un-
comfortably into this encounter.

CHAPTER 2

Successful Intercourse Was Had
with the Natives?

The two great mythical experiences on which the philosophy of the eighteenth century had wished to base its beginnings were the foreign spectator
in an unknown country, and the man born blind restored to light.

– MICHEL FOUCAULT,
THE BIRTH OF THE CLINIC: AN ARCHAEOLOGY OF MEDICAL PERCEPTION

THE RATTLE OF EMPIRICAL SCIENCE

Cook entered Nootka Sound on the morning of 29 March 1778, and by evening
his ships had anchored near the south end of Bligh Island. The official published
account of his third voyage states:

> We no sooner drew near the inlet than found the coast to be inhabited, and at the
> place where we were first becalmed, three canoes came off to the ship. In one of
> these were two men, in another six, and in the third ten. Having come pretty near
> us, a person in one of them stood up, and made a long harangue, inviting us to land,
> as we guessed, by his gestures. At the same time he kept strewing handfuls of feath-
> ers towards us; and some of his companions threw handfuls of a red dust or powder
> in the same manner. The person who played the orator, wore the skin of some ani-
> mal, and held, in each hand, something which rattled as he kept shaking it. After
> tiring himself with his repeated exhortations, of which we did not understand a
> word, he was quiet; and then others took it, by turns, to say something ... After the
> tumultuous noise had ceased, they lay at a little distance from the ship, and con-
> versed with each other in a very easy manner; nor did they seem to shew the least
> surprize or distrust.[1]

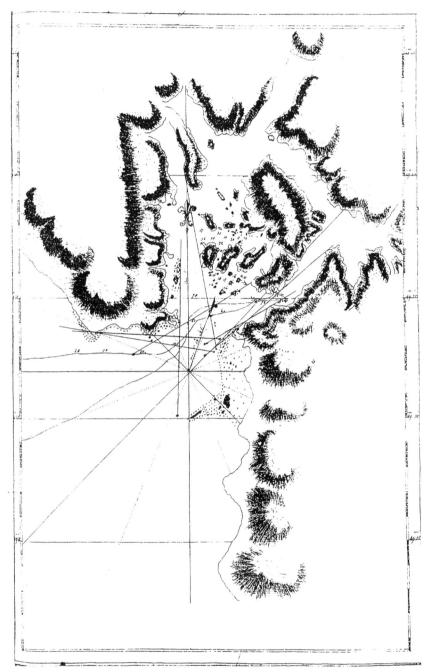

Figure 1   A chart showing the entry of Cook's vessels into Nootka Sound, March 1778
Source: Thomas Edgar, *A plan of King Georges Sound*, in "A log of the proceedings of his majesty's sloop *Discovery*," part 1, PRO ADM 55/21, fol. 150. Courtesy the Public Record Office, London.

As Cook's ships got closer to shore, the account continues, "the canoes began to come off in greater numbers," totalling thirty-two, and "though our visitors behaved very peaceably, and could not be suspected of any hostile intention, we could not prevail on any of them to come on board."[2]

For almost two centuries it was assumed that these were Cook's words, and this passage was read as a factual account of contact. (It is also the passage that Sage drew on in his report about the unveiling ceremony.) It established that Cook and his crew had *been there*. Exploration was a resolutely empirical science, and European thinkers put a premium on first-hand observation and systematic studies of people and nature. Scientific exploration revolved around what Barbara Maria Stafford calls "the valorization of the instant": explorers were expected to represent their active, physical engagement with new surroundings.[3] This passage in the official account undertook to mimic the immediacy of first contact. Nothing was expected of these inhabitants as they approached Cook's ships; Cook apparently had no preconceptions. These people presented themselves freely before Cook's gaze, apparently showed little surprise at the sight of the ships, and invited Cook to land. Communication at first depended on body language: motives and intentions were read from gestures.

Objectivity, and the supposition that an account was therefore reliable and true, was based on a particular textual stance towards the world. The task of the explorer, Stafford continues, was to find "an innocent mode of literary and visual expression" that could duplicate the experience of encountering the new.[4] Scientific explorers tried to match words to things without "the crutch of memory" or an "intervening human screen."[5] They were committed to observation. They did not want the eye to wallow in distant memories and vague connotations.

This search for objectivity implied disinterestedness and detachment: "the explorer – committed to the living of actuality, not to recollection; unwedded to the landscape; not endemic to his terrain – is an interloper in a raw world that functions without him," Stafford suggests.[6] The passage in the official account contains no value judgements concerning the Natives' behaviour; rather, it suggests that such behaviour indicates the natural attributes and cultural traits of this "new" group of people (their "dispositions," as it was put in Cook's instructions). The implication is that such actions were endemic to these people and that their reaction to Cook's ships was, therefore, quite natural.[7]

This account of first contact at Nootka Sound may be "objective" in the sense that Stafford unpacks the term, but how factual is it? When Beaglehole compared Cook's holographic journal (housed in the British Museum) with the official account, he discovered that Douglas had twisted Cook's descriptions, added information from the journals of some of Cook's officers, and added lines of his own to pander to popular stereotypes and to liven up Cook's sometimes wooden (factual, objective!) prose.[8] Scholars now work with Beaglehole's 1967 edition of Cook's journal in the belief that they are reading a more authentic Cook.

This is how Cook himself described first contact at Nootka Sound: "We no sooner drew near the inlet than we found the coast to be inhabited and the people came off to the Ships in Canoes without shewing the least mark of fear or distrust. We had at one time thirty two Canoes filled with people about us, and a groupe of ten or a dozen remained along side the Resolution most part of the night. They seemed to be a mild inoffensive people, shewed great readiness to part with anything they had and took whatever was offered them in exchange."[9] It is a shorter statement than Douglas's, but it is still matter-of-fact and seemingly "objective." But is it a disinterested, on-the-spot account? I.S. MacLaren has studied the four basic stages in the evolution of explorers' narratives – from the log book entry, to the journal, to the book manuscript, to "official" published accounts – and shows how, from stage to stage in this sequence, the physical scene of writing becomes more distant, the author relies more on memory, and questions of narrative structure become more central. Cook's journal, MacLaren points out, is a second-stage journal composed after the fact.[10]

MacLaren's point can be expanded. Explorers' first-hand observations were tempered by the recollection of other lands and peoples. The particular words and details that gave Cook's and Douglas's accounts of first contact at Nootka Sound their own vitality were drawn from a space of comparison developed during Cook's voyages. Each new encounter was made novel by virtue of the singular collection of statements employed to make it differ from others: here, at Nootka Sound, the Native inhabitants apparently showed little surprise at the arrival of strangers on their shores; there, in other parts of the Pacific, they appeared to be hostile; here, they approached the ships and threw feathers and dust; there, they brandished their spears. Cook's voyages had a textual momentum; his encounters with different peoples made sense as part of a whole. On his third voyage, especially, Cook tried to "*relate* as well as to *execute*" his voyage, as Douglas put it, by weaving his observations into a narrative.[11] Cook highlighted the differences between the peoples he met by pinpointing their "dispositions" – their character and attributes. Cook distinguished the "Nootkans" from other Native groups by emphasizing their trading abilities and notions of property. Douglas tried to illuminate Cook's space of comparison. He highlighted difference by dividing Cook's various encounters into chapters, by working with the journals of Cook's officers, and by drawing more acute contrasts than did Cook between Native peoples and Europeans.[12]

Cook's textual fabrication of difference was also influenced by the geographical momentum of his voyages. Carter argues that Cook tried to capture in writing "the zigzag map created by his passage" and that the place names he bestowed allude to his journey itself – to its dead-ends and successes, and to disagreements between Cook and the scientists on his ships.[13] Carter thinks that Cook did not simply try to capture the new and the strange in a factual, transparent, scientific manner; he also tried to record the imaginative act of exploring. For instance, as he approached Nootka Sound and glimpsed what appeared to be an inlet, he bestowed the name "Hope Bay," signalling his hope that a good harbour would eventually be found.[14] Cook was not mistaken, of course, but he kept the name, we might suggest, because it alluded to the way he had discovered Nootka Sound and his need at that juncture to find an anchorage where he could repair his ships.

We should not go overboard with such images. Cook was a British naval captain foremost, probably identified himself as a European second, and Carter's reading of him as a nomadic spatial historian is obviously retrospective. Yet Carter is right, I think, to say that Cook's cultural lenses became tinted by his experience of travel and that there was a physicality and materiality to the putatively disinterested science of observation and representation. In addition, representation became more intricate as each new encounter proceeded. Elsewhere – the trace of other encounters supplemental to accounts of new ones – became juxtaposed and interpenetrated with the experience of yesterday. Beaglehole shows that as events unfolded, Cook went back over his journal, reworking first impressions, adjusting statements, and polishing his observations. While his ships were stationary, his journal was still on the move. Towards the end of his journal of events at Nootka Sound, for example, he tried to reassess the Natives' readiness to trade and their use of iron. Had such facets of Native life been picked up from Europeans or were they indigenous? Cook knew that the Spanish had explored the north Pacific in the mid-1770s, though he did not know where they had anchored.[15] He could not resolve the issue and noted that these people "have been so many years in a manner surrounded by Europeans ... and who knows how far these Indian nations may extend their traffick with one a nother."[16] Douglas also tried to account for the possibility that these people had been contacted before by Europeans. "They were earnest in their inquiries, by signs, on our arrival, if we meant to settle amongst them; and if we came as friends ...; the inquiry would have been an unnatural one, on a supposition that any ships had been here before; had trafficked ... and had then departed; for, in that case, they might reasonably expect we would do the same."[17] In this passage from the official account, sixty-five pages on from the one describing first contact, Douglas informs us that Cook *did* understand the Natives' harangues – that they wanted to know why he had visited them. Yet Douglas still suggested that the Natives had only one endemic, or natural, way of viewing strangers and that they would have reacted to Cook and the Spanish in the same way. Cook himself, on the other hand, seemed to put parameters around the objectivity of his account of first contact, implying that the inhabitants' initial reaction to his ships was influenced by contact with other strangers and may not have stemmed solely from some natural disposition.

These processes of revision point to another possible interpretation of the accounts of first contact at Nootka Sound: that Cook, and then Douglas, wrote them as an introduction to, and prospect of, things to come; that they served a rhetorical purpose. I will return to this line of inquiry shortly. For now, I want to assess first contact from the margins of Cook's field of vision; that is, in terms of what we can now say he could not have known and did not discover.

FLOATING ISLANDS, BONES, AND BLOOD

A Spanish vessel anchored near Nootka Sound for two days in August 1774.[18] In 1789, an American trader was told by some Natives of the sound that this Spanish ship had terrified them.

> About 40 months before Captn Cook's arrival a Ship came into the sound and anchor'd within some rocks on the East side [of] the entrance where she Remain'd 4 Days and Departed. They said she was a larger ship than they had ever seen since; that she was copper'd and had a Copper Head, this I suppose to have been Gilt or painted yellow; that she had a great many guns and men; that the Officers wore Blue lac'd coats; and that most of the men wore Handkerchiefs about their heads. They [the ship's officers] made them presents of Large pearl shells some of which they still have in [their] possession ... When they [the Natives] first saw this ship they said they were exceedingly Terrified and but few of them even ventur'd alongside.[19]

Fear eventually gave way to curiosity, however, and there was some trade between the two groups. But this picture of Native fear was confirmed three years later by the Spanish botanist José Mariano Moziño.

> The sight of this [Spanish] ship at first filled the natives with terror, and even now they testify that they were seized with fright from the moment they saw on the horizon the great "machine" which little by little approached their coasts. They believed that Qua-utz [a deity] was coming to make a second visit, and were fearful that it was in order to punish the misdeeds of the people. As many as were able hid themselves in the mountains, other closed themselves up in their lodges, and the most daring took their canoes out to examine more closely the huge mass that had come out of the ocean. They approached it timorously, without sufficient courage to go on board, until after a while, attracted by the friendly signs by which the Spanish crew called, they boarded the ship and inspected with wonder all the new and extraordinary objects that were presented before them.[20]

And in the late nineteenth century, Augustus Brabant, a Roman Catholic missionary, was told by Hesquiaht people that their ancestors thought that the Spanish ship was a floating house. Some visited the ship and returned to their village saying they had seen "several of the deceased of the tribe" on board.[21]

Ingraham, Moziño, and Brabant started to piece together a Native picture of contact and a Native landscape with its own set of geographical, cultural, and spiritual contours.

These Native perceptions of the Spanish can be put together with other ethnographic fragments dealing with the arrival of Cook's ships. In the early twentieth century Chief George of Nootka Sound related a story about how, one day, the tops of three sticks were seen on the horizon. The sticks were soon identified as a watercraft, and people thought that Haitetlik, the lightening snake, was propelling it. Others considered it a salmon changed by magic. Two chiefs thought it was the work of Quautz. As the craft approached their village, "all the men and women grew very much afraid" and people were advised to hide. "A woman doctor named Hahatsaik, who had power over all kinds of salmon, appeared with a whalebone rattle in each hand; she put on her red cedar bark cap and apron and sang, saying that it must be a salmon turned into a boat." She called out: "'Hello you, you spring salmon, hello you dog salmon, hello you coho salmon.'" A canoe containing another doctor, Wiwai, then went out; then another canoe with Chief Nanaimis and ten strong men went to offer the thing two fine beaver skins. Nanaimis stayed in his canoe but got close enough to the thing to see "that Cook was not an enchanted salmon, but only a man." Maquinna, an important Nuu-chah-nulth chief, then went out, saying to Cook, "'I want you to come and stay with me next year.'"[22]

This text is complemented by others recorded in the 1970s and included in a provincial government publication that formed part of the Cook bicentenary celebrations. According to a story related by Winifred David, the Natives of the sound "didn't know what on earth" was approaching. Warriors were sent out in two canoes to see, and they thought it was "a fish come alive into people." The warriors took a good look at the men on deck. One of them, with a hooked nose, was thought to be a dog salmon. A hunchback sailor was in Native eyes a humpback salmon. The warriors reported home that this thing contained fish "come here as people." Chief Maquinna sent more canoes out to see what these people wanted. When the Natives were given some thick white pilot biscuits by Cook's crews, they thought these men were friendly and should be treated well.

In another account related by Gillette Chipps, Cook's ship was viewed as an island and the Natives danced around it. "They say Indian doctors go out there singing a song, find out, try to find out what it was. Rattling their rattles." They saw White faces on both sides of the island. "Maybe it was the same men on the other side when they go around the other side the same person but different places." Cook also visited their village, and his blacksmith, Tom, fell asleep in the big house as the Natives danced and entertained the captain. During this time the Natives also learned about pilot bread. "They didn't know what the heck to do with it." Some kept it as a good luck charm; others thought it was poisonous and would not eat it. In another account, Peter Webster related that Cook's ships got stuck at sea, unable to find their way into Nootka Sound, and that a whaling canoe went out to guide them to shore.[23]

In these Native texts the new and the strange, remembered from the past, have undergone historical translation. The four Native people who related these accounts all identified Cook by name. British and American traders came to Nootka Sound in increasing numbers in the late 1780s, and it is possible that oral histories of these first dealings with non-Natives in the late eighteenth century may have been improvised so as to incorporate such a famous figure as Cook. Floating islands, a White man and his blacksmith, now signify Cook and his ships. Strange objects that carry charms or poison have been identified as ship's biscuits. The anthropologists who went to Nootka Sound in the 1970s were probably looking for stories about Cook.[24] Some of the details in these Native accounts can be found in the European record of Cook's stay; others cannot.

Other Native texts that refer to Cook's visit do not carry as many of these historical traces, though that is not to say that they are necessarily any truer or more authentic than the accounts presented above. Around 1880, the missionary C.M. Tate recorded some details that had been passed down by Native elders of Nootka Sound. "We were all down at the ocean beach cutting up a large whale which had been found stranded the previous day when looking across the big water we saw something white that looked like a great seagull." Some thought it was a large bird from the sky that had come to earth to eat the people. "This made us all afraid," the account continues, "and we ran off to the woods to hide ourselves. We peeped out from behind the trees to see what it would do, when we saw it go right past the point and into the bay where our village was." The old people "got very much afraid," but the younger ones "were anxious to know what it was." The wise men of the tribe held a council and one old man said it was a moon from the sky using a sea serpent for its canoe. "As this great thing was now standing still, the old man suggested that two of the young men, who had no wives, should take a canoe, and go off ... to see what it was. If they were swallowed up, they would have no wives or children to grieve for them, and then we would know that it was dangerous." The two men who went out were afraid to go near the moon "for some time" but eventually decided to make "a bold dash" towards it. They found men with a great deal of hair on their faces and were frightened until one of "the strange men beckoned with his hand for them to go near." They plucked up the courage to paddle alongside the moon's canoe. "Very soon," the account states,

> a rope ladder was dropped down, and one of the moon men beckoned for them to come up. They tied their canoe to the rope ladder, and climbed up the side of the moon's canoe, when they were surprised with everything they saw. One of the men, with bright buttons on his coats, spoke to another man, who went down into the very heart of the moon's canoe, and soon came back with two dishes, one of which

was full of round flat bones, and the other full of blood [biscuit and molasses]. The man with the bright buttons pointed to the bones and the blood then pointed to his mouth; but the young man did not understand that they wanted them to eat, until one of the moon men took up a piece of the bone, dipped it in the blood, then put it in his mouth ... at the same time holding out the dishes for them to eat also; but they were afraid to touch the moon's food.

The two Natives soon realized that the moon men wanted the skins they were wearing, and an exchange took place. When the two men returned to shore, people were interested in the beads and strange clothing that they had received but "felt afraid" when they were told the people of moon's canoe lived on bones and blood. The next day some of the moon men came ashore and one of them had a "crooked stick [flint-lock gun] which he made speak with a very loud noise." "After a while," the story concludes, "the moon went away, and everybody felt glad."[25]

The last story I will draw on was told by Muchalat Peter to the ethnographer Philip Drucker in the 1930s. Two people from the community of Tcecis (see Figure 5) saw an island with people and fire on it that looked like "a spirit thing," a Tc'Exa. When this news reached the village, the chief assembled all the people for a meeting. A group of men and a shaman were sent to find out more. As the ship came into sight again, the shaman began to sing in order to see the spirit in the thing. "I don't think that's a Tc'Exa," she remarked; "I don't see the spirit of it." When they got alongside, they saw men eating fire who asked about "pish." The Natives didn't understand them. When they returned to the village, they looked back expecting the thing to have disappeared, but it had not. The old people of the village thought: "That's our great-great grandchildren coming from the other side of the ocean." Many more canoes returned to the thing and circled it. They did not understand what ladders were for, but they understood the gesture "come up." Chief U`kwisktcik was the first to go up, and others followed. They exchanged their cedar bark mats and returned to the village to get more blankets. When they returned, the Whites wanted to trade clothes but the Natives were not interested because they did not know how to wear them. They wanted iron spikes to make hooks. Back at the village, the chief wanted to know if any one had had a bad dream about the ship. When they said they had not, it was surmised that the ship was not a bad spirit. All the people then went to trade furs. A warrior saw a man with a gun. He "went up to the man, placed [the] muzzle of the gun against [his] own breast, because he had on armour ... that could stop [the gun from] 'blowing.' The white signed that [the] Ind[ian] would fall dead, took the latter's garment, folded it, placed it at the end of the ship, [and] shot [a] hole in [it]. Then they knew that was another Tc'Exa, for no arrows could pierce his armor." The people returned to the village and wondered what kind of Tc'Exa this was. A fleet of canoes then came from another village to wed a woman to a Tcexa man. As they began their feast, "2 boatloads of whites came ashore and stood looking in the doorway. The white captain gave a hat to the chief of the manuasatxa" (people from another village), but his host "became jealous and said the gift had been meant [for] them" and so it was surrendered.[26]

I have paraphrased these accounts but have tried to retain their narrative progression. They obviously provide a different set of understandings about Cook's arrival. As such they help us to probe Cook's way of seeing. Like Cook's journal, these accounts are culturally and geographically situated statements about contact. They also point to aspects of this encounter that are obscured in Cook's journal and the official account but that shine more brightly in the journals of Cook's officers: a more face-to-face, bodily process of interaction, where touch met sight, words failed to translate the meaning of gestures, and human activity on and around the ships could not be easily summarized.

These stories relate a mixture of wonder, astonishment, curiosity, and fear at the sight of strange objects and people. In the official account, gestures, speeches, and songs are registered matter-of-factly. In these Native accounts, such actions are invested with supernatural and spiritual meaning.[27] Chiefs, shamans, and wise people were called on to interpret the appearance of strange phenomena; they had their own discriminatory categories of knowledge, just as did Cook.[28]

Comments about first contact at Nootka Sound made by some of Cook's officers tally with these Native accounts. Lieutenant David Samwell observed that the Natives "expressed much astonishment at seeing the Ship."[29] And Lieutenant James King reported:

The first [Native] men that came would not approach the Ship very near & seemed to eye us with Astonishment, till the second boat came that had two men in it; the figure & actions of one of these were truly frightful; he workd himself into the highest frenzy, uttering something between a howl & a song, holding a rattle in each hand, which at intervals he laid down, taking handfulls of red Ocre & birds feather & strewing them in the Sea; this was follow'd by a Violent way of talking, seemingly with vast difficulty in uttering the Harshest & rudest words, at the same time pointing to the Shore, yet we did not attribute this incantation to ... any ill intentions towards us.[30]

Many of the "facts" of first contact included in the official account come from King's journal, then, though Douglas toned down King's prose.

Cook and his officers recorded some events that are recounted in the Native accounts, though in a different narrative order. In Chief George's story, Maquinna invites Cook to come and stay next year. Cook and some of his officers state that this invitation was extended as the ships were leaving the sound.[31] Cook did visit two Native villages, in two boats, with some marines (with "crooked sticks") and gave out presents. The first village he visited, Yuquot, is that mentioned in the accounts related by David and Tate. (It is depicted on Figure 1, on the western lip of the sound.) On the basis of Cook's journal, the second village was Tcecis, as Muchalat Peter's testimony confirms. The "Surly chief" that Cook reported meeting there may have been offended because the captain gave a present to a chief from another village and ignored him.[32] Midshipman Edward Riou noted that when Cook visited this second village, on 20 April, he "found more of our Old acquaintances than at the town to the So:ward," suggesting that these people had been trading regularly with Cook's ships.[33] Lieutenant John Williamson reported that some Native people asked him how his musket worked and that they laughed when he told them the ball would pierce their armour. Williamson folded a Native garment about six times, pinned it to a tree, and fired at it, putting a hole through it and embedding the ball in the tree.[34] The only difference between this account and that given by Drucker's informant is that the event occurred on shore. Finally, within two days of Cook's arrival, the Natives of the sound had boarded the ships and were trading furs and cedar blankets for metal goods. In short, these European and Native texts relate similar details about this encounter but from different cultural perspectives.[35]

The Native accounts also show that first contact was embedded in a complex human geography. They involve different Native groups, villages, families, and individuals.[36] Native histories are passed down along these lines. Events happened at the intersection of family routines and geopolitical rivalries, human dramas and emotions, material and spiritual life, and bonds of kinship and the exploits of individuals. Contact had composite meaning. The bodies of White strangers materialized with hooked noses and beards that were associated with natural and spiritual worlds. The two people in Tate's narrative looked on ship's biscuit and molasses as bones and blood: as signs, perhaps, of cannibalism.

SPACES OF PHYSICAL AND TEXTUAL (IN)DISCIPLINE

Why were these sentiments of fear and astonishment, picked up by some of Cook's officers, excluded from the official account – especially the observations of King, who helped Douglas edit Cook's journal? As I have already implied, Cook's and Douglas's accounts of first contact served a rhetorical purpose. During this era of scientific exploration, and especially in Cook's case, statements about first contact served as parables of Europe's scientific-civilizing mission. Such statements traded on the belief that "successful intercourse" would be had with the Natives.[37] Their lands were discovered, their cultures were recorded, people were treated fairly, and few got hurt because contact was executed and related in the pacific blink of a scientific eye.

Statements about first contact mesh past, present, and future. When Cook met a new group of people, he assessed the progress of his voyage and shaped its broader message at the site of his discovery. The images of friendship and the prospect of trade that Cook worked into his journal helped to confirm his status as a humane explorer trading the trappings of European civilization. His factual prose helped to confirm his status as an objective observer. Douglas tried to bolster this image of Cook in his account of first contact at Nootka Sound. When Cook arrived at Nootka Sound, he did not jump to conclusions. He also narrated the event using the collective pronoun "we," and Douglas followed suit. Cook highlighted that he contacted the inhabitants of Nootka Sound as a representative of his country and as an ambassador of European civilization. Charles Clerke, the captain of the *Discovery,* saw himself in a similar light and wrote at first contact at Nootka Sound: "We could not induce them to come on board, but they had no weapons, & behaved very peaceably & socially, which I hope & flatter myself we shall be able to improve upon."[38]

These ways of visualizing and representing Native peoples relied on a set of disciplinary practices: the control that Cook could wield over his own narrative, the discipline he could exercise over his crews, the confidence he could place in the military superiority of his ships, and the means he had at his disposal for keeping the lid on the unseen and the unthought. This ship's regime of physical and textual discipline can be traced back to the commercial ventures of the Portuguese in the Atlantic and Indian Oceans in the fifteenth century. And Greg Dening has shown that this regime grew in sophistication over the following three centuries.[39] John Law argues that such disciplinary practices were among a range of methods instituted by naval boards and governments for effecting "long-distance control" – ways of arranging matters "so that a small number of people in Lisbon [or London or Madrid] might influence events half-way round the world"; ways of making possible "an undistorted system of global communication and control."[40] Law focuses on the mobility, durability, self-sufficiency, and security of Portuguese vessels and the development of a "navigational context" for mariners that freed them from medieval conceptions of the universe (principally, the use of the planispheric astrolabe and quadrant to determine latitude while at sea from stellar and solar observation). On Cook's voyages, the art and science of representing "unknown" peoples was folded into this disciplinary regime. The Admiralty and Royal Society sought an "undistorted," empirical appreciation of the world.

Yet in order to maintain these forms of discipline, Cook had to delegate responsibility. He had to encourage his officers to keep detailed logs so that he might consult them to flesh out his own observations, base his dealings with Native peoples on a division of labour, and plan for the possibility of attack. In short, he had to allow his crews to see and do things out of the scope of his own vision. Cook could not be "the same person but different places," as Gillette Chipps related one of the Native accounts. The principles of consultation and exactitude that Cook forged to maintain his status as the chief author of his voyage disrupted the authority of his representations. Cook's officers paid close attention to their captain's actions, but their journals still drift off in different directions. These officers recorded many things that are not in Cook's journal, and some of their observations contradict those of their captain. Cook's officers also traded observations and borrowed passages from each other, breaking down the idea that something original or immediate about the new and the remote was being re-presented in a transparent – or undistorted – fashion.[41] And what about the "ordinary" sailors who made up the bulk of the ships' companies and were left mostly in the dark about official matters: instructions about what to observe and how to represent what they saw? "Is it not quite a different path that he travels and can this path ever cross that of the more experienced observer?" wrote one such sailor on Cook's third voyage; "is it not possible for one traveller to recall what another might forget?"[42]

Cook's crews found the time and space to do things behind his back. At Nootka Sound, truth and objectivity became decentred, and issues of representation were bound up with a broader set of epistemological questions about how to capture the *situatedness* of one's first-hand appreciation of non-European peoples and lands. The journals of Cook and his officers both reflect and problematize the institutional and discursive tactics of scientific-humanitarian exploration – the chains of command that were in place to keep order on the ship and to prevent conflicts between Natives and crewmen; and the search for a form of representation that was at once objective and spontaneous. These journals illuminate the fluidity of observation and diversity of interaction at Nootka Sound. And the Native accounts point to a multi-levelled geography of contact – an articulation of bodies, spaces, and texts – that has been largely lost in discussion of Cook's voyages.[43] These accounts point to the variety and physicality of this encounter, to actions and meanings that could not easily be represented or summarized.

CHAPTER 3

Captain Cook
and the Spaces of Contact
at Nootka Sound

We come here more unprepar'd & and have not that test within ourselves
whereby to judge of the workings of the human mind in its rude state.

– JAMES KING, NOOTKA SOUND, 1778

SPECTACLE AND SURVEILLANCE

On 30 March, Cook despatched Lieutenant King to look for a good anchorage.
King found one on the west side of the sound, but Cook himself had found a
"snug Cove" close to where his ships had anchored the night before and decided
to make it his base.[1] Meanwhile, the ships had been surrounded by Native canoes and Cook noted that "trade commenced betwixt us and them, which was
carried on with the strictest honisty on boath sides."[2]

Was convenience Cook's only consideration when he selected this anchorage?
King was instructed to find an anchorage "as far as Possible from the Village" on
the west point of the sound that they had passed the day before.[3] Cook had
good reasons for anchoring six miles away from this village – Yuquot (see Figure
1). Bernard Smith suggests that, on his third voyage, Cook became ill and disil-
lusioned with his Enlightenment mandate. His crews had spread venereal disease, and he pondered whether his encounters with the peoples of the Pacific –
and especially the introduction of European manufactures – had upset "traditional" power structures. He had also been accused, by British and American
radicals, of being an oppressor of "natural" societies. As such, Cook wanted to
prevent conflict and misunderstanding. Anchoring away from Native villages
was a tactic that he resorted to more and more often.[4]

30

Cook discussed his tactics of contact in his journal, but they were often depicted more vividly in the art of his voyages. On his third voyage, Cook used John Webber, his artist, to create images of peace, harmony, and detachment. Smith notes that Webber portrayed "a highly selective truth, from which all sense of violence had been removed ... All of Webber's developed compositions constructed on the voyage and for the official publication seem to be saying the same thing: the people of the Pacific are indeed pacific people."[5] Selective, of course, because Cook allowed Native-White tension and violence to breed on his third voyage.

This "Cook-Webber visual-art programme," as Smith calls it, is displayed no better than in Figure 2 – a panorama of Cook's ships at Nootka Sound. As Smith and Rudiger Joppien suggest, it is as if this sketch was shot with "a modern wide-angle lens."[6] Webber drew the ships larger than their proper scale, towering over the Native canoes.[7] The usual activities of the crew – wooding, watering, and trading – are in full view. On the shore, crew members are rolling water casks, and blacksmiths are forging fittings for a new mast. Contact proceeds in a routine atmosphere of peace, tranquillity, and understanding.

By all accounts, Cook's encounter with the Nuu-chah-nulth was peaceful, but peace did not necessarily entail understanding. Native gestures and intentions could be misread. Webber may have portrayed pacific people, but Cook remained alert to signs of misunderstanding and conflict. In the art of Cook's third voyage, the spectacle of Britain's presence in Native waters – the visual rhetoric of civilization and superiority – was never entirely divorced from surveillance: Cook's intricate supervision of Native-White relations. Webber tried to capture for the British public, in one panorama, Cook's transactions at Nootka Sound

Figure 2   Spectacle and surveillance: John Webber's panorama of Nootka Sound
Source: John Webber, *A sketch of Nootka Sound,* in J.C. Beaglehole, ed., *The journals of Captain Cook on his voyages of discovery,* vol. III, part 1, n.p. Courtesy National Archives of Canada, C11201.

(Figure 2). But while all seems calm, one senses that Native movements were being carefully monitored and that a set of strategic relations were being played out. Had this small space been ceded to Cook? Was his presence uncontested or was he studying the ground for signs of trouble? Did Cook expect his soliloquy of peace and tranquillity to be interrupted?

Within two days of Cook's arrival, Native people had boarded the ships. They "laid aside all manner of restraint, if they ever had any," Cook noted, "and mixed with our people with the greatest freedom."[8] But Cook soon found them to be "as light fingered as any people we had before met with." The thieves were soon caught, and their prizes were relinquished, "sometimes not without force," but having large groups of Natives on board ship – King counted ninety-four canoes (about 500 people) around the ships – could have endangered the security of Cook's crew.[9] Cook tolerated their presence, however, and implied that there was little threat of violence. But tension was never far from the surface. Samwell was agitated by the Natives' "wild & uncouth" songs and "seemingly ... warlike manner" and wondered whether they had come "to offer us a Challenge if we were Enemies."[10]

Then, on 4 April, a large number of Native canoes full of armed men assembled in the Cove. A Native attack on Cook's ships seemed possible. Native canoes were hauled on to the beach where some of Cook's crew were busy with chores. Unsure about Native intentions, Cook armed his ships and ordered the men on shore to retreat to the observation tents (depicted in Webber's panorama). "The Indians," he wrote, "seeing that they had given us some alarm, gave us to understand by signs, it was not us they were arming against" but a Native war party that was coming into the sound. Cook described the rest of this event in a measured, dispassionate tone, implying that he had been in control of the situation. "At length, the difference, whatever it was, was compromised," though he suspected that it involved Native competition over access to his ships.[11]

There was a great range of opinion about this incident. James Burney, first lieutenant on the *Discovery*, who recorded the event in the most detail (down to the size and shape of the arrowheads being brandished), seemed confident that the ships had not been in danger and stated that the officers dined while the ruckus was brewing outside.[12] But Cook evidently did not sit back and observe these Native proceedings. He despatched some armed marines to assess the situation.[13] Midshipman George Gilbert reported that while Cook did not want to intrude on what seemed to be a Native affair (this being part of his humanitarian mandate), he came very close to firing on some canoes.[14] Samwell thought that the Natives would attack the ships. Cook "expostulated" with the Native people who approached the *Resolution*, and an old sail was draped before the cabin windows to prevent them from being shattered by a hail of stones.[15] When more canoes entered the sound, Samwell and other officers conjectured that a joint attack was planned.[16] Captain Clerke of the *Discovery* understood by signs from the "local" Natives that the other canoes had come "to play the Devil with us all."[17] Riou thought that the "local" Natives might attack because they had not been paid for the wood that Cook's crew members had gathered.[18] Samwell judged that the quarrel had arisen because a canoe belonging to Native people from beyond the sound had been plundered a couple of days earlier by these locals.[19] William Bayly, the astronomer stationed on shore, seemed less worried about the effectiveness of an attack from the local Natives, noting that they had traded most of their dangerous weapons to Cook's officers over the first few days of contact.[20] But Nathaniel Portlock, master's mate on the *Discovery*, was not so sure. He judged that these Native weapons would "stand the test with an equal number of any men under heaven" and that their arrows could "give mortal wound" at twenty yards.[21] It was in the afternoon of 4 April, after the war party from beyond the sound had departed, that Williamson demonstrated the power of his firearm to the Natives, perhaps as a warning. What is more, the "strangers" from beyond the sound reappeared the next day, and the conflict continued.[22] Cook did not mention this in his journal entry for 5 April, but some of his officers recorded their anxieties.[23]

Such sentiments displace Webber's panoramic eye. Cook could not keep the lid on his officers' anxieties and private reflections. But nor, perhaps, did he seek consensus concerning the nature of an event before writing about it. He realized that his journal would form the basis of the official account.[24] He also trusted that his officers would hand over their journals before they disembarked in Britain and that the details of his voyage would not be leaked to the public until after the official account had appeared. Still, Cook expressed only one set of views – a set that reflects his duty to carry out and chronicle his scientific-humanitarian mandate.

Two narratives seem to run through Cook's journal entries at Nootka Sound. His reports on contact with Native people are interspersed with details about the progress of his repairs to the *Resolution* and *Discovery*. Cook mulled over his impending trip north in search of the Northwest Passage. His account of this event on 4 April was perhaps tempered by his sense of the purpose of his stay at Nootka Sound – to fix his ships and rest his crew. Webber's panorama served this purpose. Webber sketched this Native conflict but he did not embellish his drawing on his return to Britain, perhaps because he thought it would convey the wrong message about Cook's sojourn in the sound.[25]

Cook may have passed over such incidents lightly, but his officers knew that they were significant and worthy of examination. There was a lucrative market for accounts of Native-White tensions and actual conflicts. They were parables about social and moral distance, the nature of understanding, and the powers of communication. When Cook's officers wrote about this Native conflict, they did not defer to Cook's account, though some of them must have discussed daily events with their captain. But could Cook's officers trust their own judgment?

On 4 April Cook and his officers became aware that the Native groups of the sound were proprietorial and competed with one another. Cook noted that these Natives were not "united in the same cause" and that "the Weakest were frequently obliged to give way to the strong."[26] And he was not the only one who sensed that his ships were implicated in this Native quarrel.[27] As other parties of "strangers" came to the ships to trade over the following two weeks, it became clear that Cook's "first friends" were acting as middlemen. It became necessary to distinguish between different groups in order to prevent misunderstanding.

When Cook visited Yuquot on 22 April, he realized that these Native notions of property and control extended far beyond access to trade with his ships. He had to pay for grass that his crew cut and observed: "I have no w[h]ere met with Indians who had such high notions of everything in the Country produced being their exclusive property as these."[28] In fact, Cook did reassess the events of early April later in his journal, admitting, perhaps under the weight of his officers' observations, that they were threatening. He accepted that his presence may have inflamed Native rivalries but insisted that "we were the means of preventing them from coming to blows" and "oftener I believe than this once, for our friends sometimes carried it [themselves] with rather a high hand over strangers who occasionally came to visit us."[29] Cook surmised that his "first friends" frightened off the "strangers" by claiming that they were allied with his ships.[30]

Cook's officers were less interested in whether their presence sparked the Native conflict than in what this conflict said about Native dispositions. Samwell was interested in the "Engagement of [Native] Tongues" that occurred when "strangers" approached the ships. He described how one man "made a long Speech, sputtering his words out with the utmost violent Rage and agitation of mind, to which the motions of his Body corresponded which were violent to an extream ... his actions were those of a man out of his Senses." Such displays, he later reflected, showed that these Natives had a "brave" and "resolute" disposition.[31] Portlock remarked that Cook's crew thought that the Natives' harangues and war songs were "the most warlike and awfull thing they ever heard."[32] Burney, on the other hand, suggested that while these people were "rather quarrelsome" and "very apt to take offence at the slightest indignity," "to do them justice, when they are angry, any little degree of submission immediately pacifies them."[33] Native verbal altercations may have been passionate, but Riou emphasized how orderly they were. One protagonist would not interrupt another's speech, and harangues seldom resulted in fighting.[34] Midshipman James Trevenan put this down to their "fearless independent spirit which apprehended no danger from any other than the person with whom they had particularly quarelled."[35] Bayly wrote: "The Natives seem rather a dull heavy people but very quick of resentment for the

slightest injury – but quite free from malice & design & exceedingly good natured."[36] And King judged that, while the Native balance of power in the sound
was difficult to assess, the "superior tribes" seemed to be the ones with the best
manners.[37]

Clerke commented that Cook's "first" friends, "in whose boundaries or confines of Country we happen'd to lay, look'd upon us [as] so far as their property
as to be entitled to a right to monopolizing all kinds of Exchanges with us to
themselves"; when strangers tried to break this monopoly, "our landlords had
recourse to Arms," entering into "warm disputes sometimes to our surprize ...
but they never did go farther than mutual abuse and harsh words, and the general result was, that the visiting Party was allowed to trade with us, upon condition that some of these People attended them, that they might take care the
market was not hurt by an under sale of Goods."[38] Burney sensed that there was
a logistical aesthetic to the way the Natives managed competition and access to
the ships. He wrote of events on 8 April:

> The canoes from the outer part of the Sound visited us at daylight, leaving a Canoe
> without the mouth of the Cove to watch. At 7 the guard Canoe made signals, on
> which all the rest left the ships and paddled as fast as they could around the South
> Point of the Cove to prevent being cut off. At the same time, the party from the
> northward which was now the strongest, made their appearance. They stopped abrest
> of the middle of the Cove and single Canoes passed and repassed, in consequence
> of which, the flying canoes returned and after a short parley, erected their pikes and
> began a Song, beating time with the staffs against the sides of their canoes. Having
> finished, they laid down their pikes, and the other party, who had during the per-
> formance sat still, now reared theirs and gave a song in return; which being ended,
> the southern canoes saluted them with a parting halloo and went off, leaving the
> market to the quiet possession of the northern party for that day.[39]

Burney described Native routines and rituals of interaction, and he emphasized
that the waters of Nootka Sound were owned, managed, and patrolled just as
was the land. He implied that Cook sailed into a well-established Native "market." Burney represented himself as a detached observer – an interloper, perhaps, in a commercial world that existed without him. He studied signals and
movements, and he recorded entry and departure times. Neither Cook nor his
officers assumed "the neutrality of the ground." Clerke wrote of landlords, markets, and monopolies and was conscious that the ships were situated within patrolled "boundaries." Images of competition – or of a Native geopolitics of trade
and interaction – pervade these officers' discussion of Native dispositions.

When discussing the representational practices of Cook's officers (and Cook
himself), sharp distinctions should not be drawn between logs of daily events
and the more generalizing "manners-and-customs" descriptions of land and

people that usually followed them, as if the former point to a realm of spontaneous or engaged observation and the latter denotes detached, summary reflection or classification. There were not two distinct modes of knowing
enshrined in these different forms of description but, rather, a set of provisional,
situated knowledges.[40] Accounts of Native dispositions (attempts to discern a
Native subject) were compilations of observations made during the course of an
encounter.[41]

Some of Cook's officers described the nature of interaction at Nootka Sound
much more thoroughly than did their captain and wrote markedly different
things about Native life. These officers had different personalities, backgrounds,
and literary talents. What they recorded depended in good measure on what
they could see from where they were stationed on the ship or on the shore. The
kinds of dealings they had with Native people also depended on their rank.[42] It
was these issues of personality, location, and rank – of positionality in all its
senses – that were at play in these officers' range of opinion over different events
and in their more blanket statements about Native dispositions.

An Unerring or Unsteady Gaze?

But what was also at play, I think, was the basic dilemma of mid eighteenth-
century British empiricism: of "how to move from the particular to the general
without the latter merely collapsing back into the former."[43] This is Terry
Eagleton's formulation, and he argues that this conundrum was profoundly ideological. During the eighteenth century, "civilized conduct" – and, by implication, the model of the disinterested observer and the explorer-civilizer – became
associated with "common styles of sensibility." Eagleton suggests that this model
of civility rested on an uneasy "ideological *rapprochement*" between old and new
elites. A new aristocratic-bourgeois elite began to consider itself less as the "state
class" than as the leader of a "public sphere" rooted in a *civil* society, which, inter
alia, cherished individual sensibility. Social power became rooted less in the "potentially divisive realities of social rank and economic interest" than in "the sensuous immediacies of empirical life" connecting the individual to society.[44] This
empiricism was a problematical philosophy for civil *society*, however, because it
shunned abstraction and rational totalities. Eagleton asks: how was the ruling
elite "to root itself in the sensuously immediate, yet elaborate this into something more compelling than a heap of fragments?"[45]

This problematic, I suggest, runs through the empirical "science of the concrete" that many commentators associate with Cook's voyages. British thinkers
developed a variety of responses to this conundrum. Moralists such as the earl
of Shaftesbury thought that there was no need to abandon the senses because
order, harmony, and virtue could be found in one's very instincts. Eagleton remarks that, for Shaftesbury, social harmony and moral order resided in neither

utility nor duty but in the "delightful fulfilment of our nature."[46] This, in outline, is also Stafford's view of scientific exploration. Science and morality, of course, were effectively aestheticized.

This aesthetic celebration of the senses was fractured along class lines. Aristocrats such as Shaftesbury associated *social* harmony with *national* order based on privilege and patronage. Yet, as John Barrell notes, this "applause for Happy Britannia was not joined by everyone"; poets such as Thomas Gray were interested in "the virtues of more impoverished, primitive communities, where the poet instead of celebrating what the polite chose to hear [and see] as the harmony of nation ... could be the spokesman of a community less differentiated by rank or occupation."[47] Such poets, Barrell argues, resented the hierarchical trappings of British civil society, looked for spaces of private reflection, and saw in primitive man "an ideal which announces that a society is healthy only when its simple structure is visible to all its members."[48]

Theories about "natural man" were influenced by these eighteenth-century notions of public and private sensibility. To extrapolate from Eagleton and Barrell: was human fellowship, compassion, and virtue – order, harmony, and beauty in society – imprinted on the body itself, "in its most spontaneous, pre-reflexive instincts," or was it reflected in the "simple structures" of rural/primitive life? Had not explorers such as Cook shown that these instincts remained untainted in non-European societies – that Indigenous peoples lived a life of natural goodness, uncorrupted by the artifices of European culture? And had not Europeans, including Cook, corrupted such virtues? At Nootka Sound, the adjectives used to inscribe Native dispositions were bound up with the body (its appearance, motions, gestures, and noises) and the seemingly elementary structures of Native society (reflected in the orderliness of Native harangues and the harmonies of Native songs).

This problematic was also methodological, of course. Cook and his officers realized that they could not see or learn much from short stays in distant spots. Cook declared to James Boswell that he and his crews picked up so little of Native languages that they were at the mercy of their senses.[49] And it was difficult to discover the principles of Native government and religion.[50] At Nootka Sound, Cook and his officers produced tentative evaluations of Native social life. Bayly commented: "we saw very little of their manners & customs the ships being in a small cove distant from their residence so that they only came to us to trade out of curiosity."[51]

Did such remarks point to darker doubts? Did Cook and his officers skip along the surface of Native societies, reading the body in lieu of being able to judge the mind or chart Native life at Nootka Sound on some taxonomic grid? If Shaftesbury and other British moralists were trying to sketch a new "corporate" philosophy, as Eagleton suggests, then can Cook's voyages be seen as an attempt to inscribe the non-European world with and for that philosophy, or did Cook and his officers engage with the harmonies and harangues of Native life in a more private way?

Let us recall Mary Louise Pratt's account of this "corporate" philosophy – those taxonomic, bourgeois "imperial eyes" that "passively look out and possess."[52] Pratt asks crucial questions about how explorers *produced* the world for their European readers, but the texts I am reading do not point to a definitively European, coherent, or hegemonic bourgeois subject at work in the Pacific. However collaborative scientific exploration might have been in theory, the British still saw the French as a hostile Other, and the two nations had different imperial styles and traditions of thought.[53] I am also working in a different methodological vein than Pratt, towards the complexity of Cook's encounter at Nootka Sound rather than in terms of the coherence of European configurations of the world. In any case, the "ideology of the aesthetic," as Eagleton describes it, became rooted in the "sensuous immediacies of empirical life" during this period, in part because many doubted that order, morality, and identity could be modelled on the market at all. It was difficult to find any moral design in the ideology of accumulation apart from that of self-interest.[54] I am suggesting that the propagation of British imperialism, industrial revolution, or bourgeois hegemony was not uppermost in the minds of Cook's officers when they tried to capture Native dispositions at Nootka Sound. They came from a variety of backgrounds – aristocratic, bourgeois, and clerical. They lived in the fabricated environment of a British naval ship, with its own routines, hierarchies, disciplines, and forms of pleasure and deprivation.[55] Identities could melt in the sensitive heat of the distant and the new. Observations about the "springs" of Native sensibility were prompted mainly by interaction around the ships and might be read as unsteady disquisitions into the social "nature" of order and harmony.

Clerke's rhetoric of landlords, markets, and monopolies is revealing. If anything, it was the very *unnaturalness* of the Natives' proprietorial instincts – the implication that these people had left the "boundaries" of nature and were "out of their senses" – that prompted the use of such language. Others were more circumspect. Embedded in these accounts of Native dispositions were composite meanings, identities, and distinctions between sense and reason, rudeness and civility, nature and artifice. Cook's officers were attempting to bring the Native peoples of Nootka Sound within an aesthetic, as much as a taxonomic, field of vision. Nootka Sound, and the Pacific more generally, was maybe less orderable and more aesthetically excessive than critics such as Pratt suggest.[56]

Given the range of opinions and adjectives used to describe the dispositions of the people of Nootka Sound, we might ask whether Cook's officers merely ended up with a "heap of fragments" – whether their observations about Native life could be synthesized and used to fashion a corporate ideology of "moral sense" in Britain or Europe? King suggested that they could not:

We come here more unprepar'd & and have not that test within ourselves whereby to judge of the workings of the human mind in its rude state; or rather few of us are capable of seperating the invariable and constant springs by which we are all mov'd, and what depends on education & fashion. As we cannot be said to converse with the people, we can only judge from outward actions, & not knowing all the Causes that give rise to them, we must be constantly led into error; this also inclines us to form conclusions in the narrow confind [sic] sphere of our observations, & what has immediately happnd [sic] to our selves; whence one person will represent these People as Sullen, Obstinate, & Mistrustful, and another will say they are docile, good natured & unsuspicious; the former will prove his assertion from their Phlegmatick temper, from their unwillingness to comply with what has the smallest appearance of compulsion, & from their manner of bartering, examining with the greatest suspiciousness your articles of trade, & not relying on their own judgement but making them pass the same examination amongst not only all in the same boat, but in perhaps all the Canoes alongside, at the same time hold[in]g their own goods fast, which they will not trust out of sight, nevertheless they are on the whole honest in their dealings; he will also instance the perpetual Squabbles amongst themselves ... He who supports the Contrary character will say that they have a nice sense of affronts, & which their passionate & quick tempers immediately resent, that this makes them sensible to a courteous behaviour, & which is returned on their parts with perfect good Nature: that they are easy to be gained by a mild & flattering Carriage, & that a diff[eren]t procedure might be resent'd, and that all this is very contrary to a sullen obstinate character; that the quarrells amongst themselves are mostly of different parties & that they are the free'est from all invidiousness & deception in their Actions of any people in the world; shewing their resentments instantaniously, & totally regardless of the probable consequences of so ill tim'd an appearance of their displeasure; & these are strong marks against the charge of a sullen & mistrustful Carriage.

All that King concluded from this was that "the facts on which the above reasonings are founded are true."[57] The senses, by themselves, were not strong enough to separate truth from error. Partial truths stemmed from "the narrow confind sphere" of observation. Who could distinguish the "invariable & constant springs" of life from fashion, or nature from artifice? King's account of Native dispositions is riddled with the paradoxes of eighteenth-century empiricism. What assertions can I make? What proofs might I give? What adjectives do I choose? What sense do *I* have of what I see?

These paradoxes were epistemological as well as methodological. King refused to blend different observations and present some collective account of the Native character. When Cook's officers interpreted Native life at Nootka Sound, they relied on their own senses and referred to themselves. King respected the notion that they were private individuals with different perspectives as well as ranked officers on a British naval ship. Eagleton argues that if one clung too closely to this view of subjectivity, it would become increasingly difficult to find "objectivity":

> The wider the subject extends its imperial sway over reality, the more it relativizes that terrain to its own needs and desires, dissolving the world's substance into the stuff of its own senses. Yet the more it thereby erodes any objective criteria by which to measure the significance or even reality of its own experience. The subject needs to know that it is supremely valuable; but it cannot know this if its own solipsism has cancelled out any scale by which such value might be assessed. What is this subject privileged *over*, if the world has been steadily dwindled to no more than an obedient mirror image of itself?[58]

This, in the abstract, points to why Cook's officers found themselves so "unprepar'd" at Nootka Sound. The journalist's aim may have been to describe and evaluate other societies objectively, but King knew that objectivity came at a certain price. The only way to do justice to the new was by working with what one had experienced oneself – with what had "immediately happpnd." The spatially confined nature of observation aggravated this form of subjecthood. King did not extend his "imperial sway over reality" smoothly and inexorably, but cautiously and anxiously. Eagleton spells out what happened when caution was thrown overboard: "In appropriating the whole of external nature, the bourgeois subject discovers to its own consternation that it has appropriated its own objectivity along with it."[59] For Eagleton, the bourgeois subject grew up as a "tragically self-defeating creature"; James King, he might suggest, was not a Kantian "epistemological entrepreneur" but a "sluggish subject" of eighteenth-century empiricism.[60] None of Cook's officers wrote about these questions of subjectivity as openly as King, but such issues inform the writing of Burney and Clerke, especially. What King drew out was the heterogeneity of vision and experience at Nootka Sound, and a set of epistemological anxieties underwriting representation.

THE LIMITS OF CURIOSITY AND THE BOUNDARIES OF HONESTY

Cook and his officers may not have held the same opinions about Native dispositions, but they seemingly shared a pervasive, if indeterminate, sense of curiosity. Harriet Guest suggests that the British "repeatedly articulated their interest in the South Pacific in terms of the undetermined and ambiguously transactive notion of curiosity."[61] Undetermined, because at this time the notion of curiosity was not rooted in any systematic discourse about material culture or any rigidly evolutionary theory about indigenous societies. Yet transactive, because the desire for "curiosities," and curiosity about the Other, was what sustained contact between explorers and Native peoples. But ambiguous, because, as Nicholas Thomas notes, drawing on the ideas of Edmund Burke, curiosity denoted both "a subjective attitude and ... an attribute of things noticed."[62]

Burke characterized curiosity as a passive, childlike, and impressionistic attitude towards the object world.[63] The term implied that one was unable or unwilling to pass aesthetic judgment on novel objects. "Curiosity" did not point to a disciplined, methodical scientific view of natural or human life, Burke suggested, but to a realm of uncertainty and ambivalence in observation and representation. Nevertheless, there was a large market for curiosities in Europe, and Cook's crews had a great passion for them.[64]

At Nootka Sound, Edgar noted that Native masks were "ingenious" yet "curiously" carved.[65] Riou noted that they had "a very frightful appearance" but were "far from being ill-done."[66] And Samwell stated that they "were not badly designed or carved."[67] "Curiously made," "not badly executed," "strangely produced," "curiously ornamented," and "interestingly shaped" are terms that abound in the journals of Cook and his officers. They had trouble putting a commercial and aesthetic value on many objects, and the inhabitants of Nootka Sound seemingly knew it. Samwell noted that the Natives performed "some legerdemain Tricks" to raise the value of curiosities in the eyes of Cook's desirous crewmen.[68]

These ambivalences are captured in artists' graphic representations of artefacts collected in the Pacific. Take Figure 3, which displays artefacts from Nootka Sound. There are many similar engravings in the official folio volumes of Cook's voyages. Thomas suggests that such images show "a combination of interest, qualified aestheticization, and indeterminacy" in layout. No particular form of vision or reaction seems to be encouraged. Figure 3 does not signify what function the objects played in the daily life of a Nootkan. One would have to examine Cook's written descriptions to learn whether they had a practical or ceremonial function, or if they were meant to illustrate a particular form or state of society – be it "savage," "warlike," "ingenious," or what have you. Nor were such images necessarily representative of material life, since Indigenous peoples usually traded only a selection of their "manufactures."[69]

Thomas thinks that such images are marked by an "evacuation of signification."[70] But one might equally admit, as he indeed does, that this graphic, clinical form of representation illuminates the authority and disinterestedness of science. Native artefacts were decontextualized: arranged by scientists and artists, and inserted into European circuits of capital and culture. Disinterestedness was tied to appropriation. Thomas concludes that during the late eighteenth century, scientific exploration was characterized by a tension between "an unstructured apprehension of diverse things" and "a scientific and imperialist project" of classification and hierarchization.[71] We have only to recall Stafford's synopsis of the scientific gaze and Eagleton's sketch of eighteenth-century

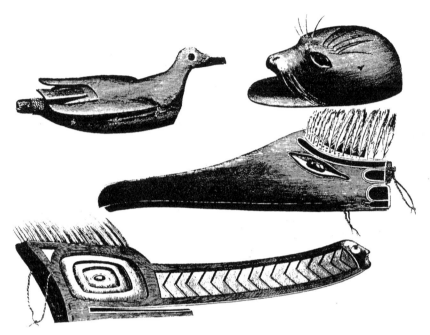

Figure 3   Drawing of artefacts collected at Nootka Sound
Source: J. Record, *Various articles, at Nootka Sound,* from a drawing by J. Webber, in James
Cook and James King, *A voyage to the Pacific Ocean ... in his majesty's ships the* Resolution *and
the* Discovery (London: G. Nichol and T. Cadell, 1784), II, plate 40, 306-307. Courtesy Special
Collections and University Archives Division, University of British Columbia Library.

aesthetics to appreciate how deeply felt this tension must have been. For the
dominant ideology of exploration was that alien people and things were part of
a raw, external world and that it was the explorer's job to represent the new and
the Other in situ. Had explorers, overwhelmed by the diversity of novel objects,
failed to rise to this challenge? What could the public learn about Native life, and
what could scholars say about the nature of Indigenous societies, from objects
that had been detached from their "natural" settings, shipped home, and displayed? Explorers still tried to judge and gradate other societies. They commented
on the status of women, which many Enlightenment thinkers viewed as a mark
of relative social advancement.[72] And they looked for signs of cannibalism, which
had a much longer genealogy in European thinking about the Other.[73] Thomas's
point is that material artefacts were not taken to represent the nature of non-
European societies until the nineteenth century.[74]

The most evaluative remarks that Cook and his officers made about Nootkan
society concern the veracity of the people – or what Clerke termed "the boundaries of honesty."[75] Cook, as we have seen, produced conflicting statements about
the honesty of the Nootkans, noting that trade was at first carried on with "the

Strictest honesty," and then declaring that the Natives of the sound were "as light fingered" as any people he had met.[76] Cook offered a more general evaluation of theft later in his journal: "In trafficking with us, some would betray a navish disposition and would make off with our goods without making any return, if there was an oppertunity, but in general most of them acted with different principles. Their passion for iron and brass and indeed any kind of metal was so strong that few could resist the temptation to steal whenever an oppertunity offered."[77] Many other things were traded and stolen besides iron and brass. Cook noted that "these people got a greater middly and variety of things from us than any other people we had visited."[78] Opportunities to steal arose when the inhabitants were on the ships. But Cook's statements about theft come with qualifications. He concluded the above passage by stating that the Natives "touched nothing but what was valuable in their eyes." And in his journal entry for 12 April he states: "I got them down into the Cabbin for the first time and observed that there was not a single thing that fixed their attention for a single Moment"; they "looked upon everything with the greatest indifferency," though "there were some who shewed a little curiosity."[79]

Was Cook suggesting that theft was understandable (though unacceptable) because Indigenous peoples had an irresistible attraction to European goods (that few "could resist the temptation" to steal)? He admitted that these people were selective and did not stand aghast at the "middly and variety" of goods on board his ships. He could not summarize Native attitudes towards theft, and some of his officers reiterated his inconclusive remarks. Bayly noted that the inhabitants were "well versed in thieving."[80] But Riou commented: "We sailed out of this place with less mischief and less things stolen from us by the Natives than ever we have done before at any place."[81]

Cook was highly sensitive about acts of theft on all of his voyages and reported them in his journal.[82] When Native people stole articles of trade or pieces of equipment, Cook went to the local chief or village with some armed marines to ask for them back and sometimes held chiefs hostage until the stolen items were returned. When his crewmen stole from Native people, they were lashed on the quarterdeck.[83] Cook tolerated many forms of behaviour on his voyages but not theft. Beaglehole and other scholars argue that Cook thought that anarchy would break out on his ships, and between Native people and his crewmen, if such acts were not punished. He considered the putative honesty – discipline – of his crews to be one the chief symbols of their civility. More pragmatically, he noted incidents of Native theft in order to inform other navigators of what to expect when they encountered a particular Native group. King noted: "We had the good fortune for near a months residence of having no serious quarrels ... but I can hardly conceive that a like good fortune will attend any future ships that may visit them & have at the same time so free an intercourse. In the first place their thefts, but more particularly their high Spirits ... will draw upon them a severe Chastisement."[84] Here King speaks for his captain and his mandate, suggesting that other navigators, bent on the pursuit of profit rather than science, might get themselves into trouble at Nootka Sound. And indeed they did, as I show in Part 2.

Cook's remarks about theft hinge on the spatial demarcation of vice from virtue. Cook implied that his ships were bastions of discipline and order, where trade with the Natives would be conducted fairly and peacefully. When the inhabitants boarded the *Resolution*, they stepped out of a world that Cook saw only in outline (but where the theft of European goods may not have been viewed as a vice) and entered a space that Cook controlled (and where theft could only be viewed as a crime). At Nootka Sound, as elsewhere, the appreciation and protection of property was a primary spatial dynamic of contact, and an important symbolic realm within which Cook's writing gathered global meaning. Cook instituted boundaries between his ships and Native canoes, and he policed the trading activities of his crew. But he realized that these boundaries would likely become permeable. Riou claimed that at Nootka Sound there was a "want of certain restrictions" respecting trade.[85] Many sailors traded their personal wares, and maybe some of the ships' fittings, without the permission or supervision of Cook or his officers. As a midshipman, tied to the quarterdeck and responsible for relaying orders and disciplining the lower ranks, Riou could size up trade and interaction from different positions. And Trevenan, another midshipman, commented on what happened when crew members crossed these boundaries.

> An old North Briton of a most irascible spirit had been fixed upon as a boatkeeper ... [but was] so often outwitted and of course reprehended for neglect of duty, that he was become as savage as the most savage tribe around him, with whom he had perpetual quarrels; and at last in an attempted theft, resolving to take full vengeance on the offender, he made a blow at him with the boat's stretcher ... but missing him it fell with such force on the side of the canoe as to break it down to the water's edge.[86]

The offended Native threatened the Old Briton, and Molesworth Phillips, one of the marines, was called to restore calm. This boatkeeper worked at the side of the ship, in an interstitial space between the security and "civility" of the ship and the potentially threatening world surrounding it.

Later in his journal Cook suggested that this surrounding Native world was in many respects as ordered as that of his ships. When he visited the village of Yuquot, he was received "very curtiously" and noted that the Nootkans held strict views about property. This did not move him to re-evaluate the nature of theft on board his ships, however; it simply made it seem more striking and puzzling. Did these people have two standards of intercourse? King lamented that when the Natives were on the ships, they "did not act faithfully up to the rule laid down by themselves" on their own turf.[87]

Greg Dening notes that "on a voyage his [Cook's] property was his limited capital ... He was transient; he came and went on the winds. His wealth lay in what he possessed, not in his distribution against tomorrow's needs and moral bonds. So a theft took proportions beyond the value of the thing stolen. It was a breach of a system of property and all the relationships that entailed. Prevention and punishment of theft became symbolic acts."[88] Parables of civilization were played out in the minute particulars of interaction. Explorers themselves were no doubt aware of the domestic import of their comments on theft. Margaret Hunt notes that in late eighteenth-century Britain, the business community tried to distance itself rhetorically from thieves and swindlers. Debt and fraud, particularly, were viewed as inherent traits of a riotous, polluting other.[89] Cook's remarks about the veracity of Native peoples may have been read as commentaries on economic and social cleavages within Britain.

MASCULINE BOUNDS OF INTERACTION AND OBSERVATION

Nor could Cook prevent the prostitution of Nootkan women to his crew.[90] Cook himself rarely discussed the sexual activity of his crewmen. It was considered a "rude" issue in "polite" circles, and late eighteenth-century commentators viewed Cook's own sexual abstinence as one of his greatest virtues. Bridget Orr suggests that Cook

embodied a markedly paternalistic form of masculinity that seemed to inform both his public virtues and his private character; thus his stern but careful treatment of his crew and much-lauded sense of responsibility towards the natives was matched by celibacy on board and the generation of a large family at home. The cultural power of this image was not inconsiderable. It provided a model of masculinity that rendered male chastity plausible by combining it with manly action ... It also dignified the role of the explorer, who served as civilization's advanced guard before conquest and settlement, suggesting that his benevolent disinterestedness represented the purity of the colonial mission.[91]

Some of Cook's officers and crewmen had a different sense of manly action, however, and described their sexual activities in lurid detail. And fitting the mode of representation I have been tracking, they held diverse opinions about Native women, reflecting their own desires and different senses of morality. Burney apparently avoided the women of Nootka Sound but judged they were "jolly likely wenches."[92] Williamson, who seemingly looked for sexual liaisons wherever he went in the Pacific, noted that the women of Nootka Sound had "no objection to bartering their favours & are by no means exorbitant in their demands."[93] Bayly, on the other hand, did not find these women "desirable objects" and reported that the crew "seemed quite easy about them," though he admitted that some officers, "whose stomachs were less dellicate," did buy women. At one point in his journal, Bayly observed that the Native men were "affronted" when anything was offered for women, but he later reflected that some Native men would sell their daughters if it was for something they could not otherwise get.[94] And Samwell, who was one of Cook's most licentious officers, declared that once the "favours" of Native women had been secured, the officers took erotic pleasure in conducting "a Ceremony of Purification" – scrubbing the dirt and red ochre off their bodies, or "cleansing" the women of their "different Ideas ... of Beauty and cleanliness," as he put it.[95] Finally, Riou struck a tone of moral indignation, arguing that the men of the sound "keep their Women under great Subjection, as much so as at the Society Isles."[96]

Riou's comments about the subjection of women were atypical. Cook and his officers generally did not discuss gender relations at Nootka Sound. Women are not distinguished in their discussions of trade and Native competition. When women do appear in these journals, it is as sexual objects to be bartered for along with other Native goods. When Burney or King reported that "the" Natives performed this ritual or that harangue, they were referring to Native men, even though women also acted as performers on such occasions, as some of the Native accounts of this encounter state.

How might we interpret this miscellaneous discursive relationship between sexual desire and the invisibility of Native women in discussions of trade? There is a growing literature on how explorers, literary figures, artists, and scholars gendered European and non-European nature and space. Derek Gregory argues that, during the nineteenth century, "Western 'nature' is made ever more elaborately feminine ... whereas Western 'space' is made over in the image of a masculine, phallocratic power ... space is *itself* represented as the physical embodiment of (masculine) rationality whose structures are to be superimposed over 'nonspace.'"[97] Non-Western "nature," on the other hand, was seen as feminine, fecund, often virginal, and ripe for colonial penetration. And non-Western "space" was struck in the image of male explorers and colonists; explorers' charts and colonists' maps and inventories brought non-Western "nature" into "spatial" existence.

Alan Bewell suggests that over Cook's three voyages, "an even more powerful feminization of [the] landscape [of the Pacific] took place."[98] Whereas Asia was seen to be "dominated by a surfeit of pleasure," the Pacific "came to be embodied in the image of pleasure to come."[99] As I noted earlier Cook's artists and scientists exoticized and romanticized the Pacific (especially the Polynesian Islands). Bernard Smith claims that on Cook's third voyage, Webber developed an image of the Pacific "as young, feminine, desirable, vulnerable, an ocean of desire."[100]

At Nootka Sound, however, matters were different. As this encounter proceeded, Cook and his officers began to realize that the Nootkans were a calculating, competitive trading people. And, as the opinions about the Native women of the sound documented above imply, Nootka Sound was not seen as young, feminine, or vulnerable. It was situated at the edge of this ocean of desire.[101] What pervades discussion of Nootkan trading abilities is the notion that an ordered Native space had been superimposed on nature – a network of territories, a theatre of commercial transactions, markets, and monopolies. Clerke and Burney described a geometry of power. They implied that the Nootkans lived against the grain of nature, in a *manufactured* space. The Nootkans lived *from* nature but seemed to have climbed out of a Hobbesian state *of* nature. Competition rarely led to violence.

To answer my question, then: Cook and his officers seemed to view trade and competitiveness as masculine traits, and this influenced the way they described interaction at Nootka Sound. They presumed that this society was run by men because interaction was routinized and ritualized, and seemed planned and controlled. There was a *spatiality* to trade that Cook and his officers (and, on Gregory's account, Europeans more generally) identified as fundamentally masculine. Bewell argues that "the differences between continents, nations, regions and cultures were given their most powerful iconic form in descriptions of the differences in the intellectual, physical, and reproductive capacity of the world's women."[102] Yet women were seen as embodiments of nature, and non-European women "were used to represent geographical regions ... as naturalized or indigenous embodiments of place" – of untouched nature. Nootka Sound was not "nature" or "woman" in these senses; it spoke to that marriage of "male power and a transformed nature." For Cook and his officers, "the Nootkan" was generically male.

This formulation is tentative. These presumptions about masculinity were no doubt more complex than I suggest and may not have been tied so tightly to European conceptions of nature and space.[103] But once again, I think, the particularity of Nootka Sound compounded the fragmentation of representation.

FRAGMENTS OF AN ENCOUNTER

I.S. MacLaren outlines the rhetorical devices that Douglas used to "polish" Cook's journal and turn him into a superior.[104] He dwells on Douglas's account of Cook's trip to Yuquot on 22 April. Cook wrote in his journal: "The inhabitants ... received us in the same friendly manner they had d[o]ne before, and the Moment we landed I sent some to cut grass not thinking that the Natives could or would have the least objection, but it proved otherwise."[105]

And this is what appeared in the official account: "The inhabitants received us with the same demonstrations of friendship which I had experienced before;

and the moment we landed, I ordered some of my people to begin their operation of cutting. I had not the least imagination, that the natives could make any objection to our furnishing ourselves with what seemed to be of no use to them, but necessary for us. However, I was mistaken."[106] In Douglas's version of the event, McLaren argues, Cook's readers see "a masterly captain, if not quite a monarch giving orders to *his* people."[107] Underlying the pronouncement that the grass was "of no use to them" was the assumption that this – and other – Native societies did not cultivate the land and therefore had no exclusive right to it: a Lockean point.[108] Cook's was more equivocal. He was perhaps thankful that the villagers asked him to pay. Otherwise, his actions might have sparked resentment and distrust. And regardless of whether the Natives harvested the grass, Cook simply noted that "there was not a single blade" of it "that had not a separated owner."[109] Douglas tampered with Cook's journal and tried to represent his stay at Nootka Sound as an encounter between unequals. Cook presented himself to these villagers and to his readers as a tolerant explorer.

We might now read Cook as a cautious observer who was prepared to rethink the nature of his encounters as they unfolded and as he moved around the Pacific. Representing him as an explorer who simply distorted Pacific realities or polluted Native cultures may recycle monolithic and imperious accounts of European-Native encounters. We might now cherish and embellish Cook's open-mindedness – his relativism, if you will. Yet we should not ignore the fact that Cook worked with a particular discourse. He believed in his scientific-humanitarian mandate and wielded a European rhetoric of civilization. The Native accounts I discussed in Chapter 2, and the logs and journals of Cook's officers, help us see these facets of Cook's work. He represented his stay at Nootka Sound as a model of cross-cultural harmony and order. "Successful intercourse was had with the natives." These other texts reveal realms of interaction and representation that were performed in and from a number of cultural and corporeal positions.

Stafford and Smith argue that mimesis was central to the way explorers such as Cook tried to capture otherness. But these and other scholars also suggest that mimesis was shot through with a set of anxieties about the relationship between the viewing subject and the object world. These anxieties peep through the writing of some of Cook's officers at Nootka Sound. The relationship between representation and reality in some of these journals appears unstable and truncated. Yet I would not go as far as Paul Carter and suggest that "a geographical feature is made no bigger than a page of writing" – that representation and reality, events and the discourses they figure in, are irretrievably yoked together.[110] Such implications emerge from Carter's writing because he focuses entirely on one set of texts – explorers' "official" narratives. The historical record of early contact in British Columbia is composed mostly of White texts. But in the case of Cook's stay at Nootka Sound it is possible to consider different perspectives.

The Native and White texts I have discussed construct truth and reality in different shades. They both push Cook from centre stage and help us to pinpoint his subject position.

The perspectives I have been unravelling also suggest that representation was a spatial problematic. It revolved around the location of Cook's ships in Native waters and the position of his officers on those ships. It was mediated by the physical and rhetorical demarcation of distance and difference between Europeans and Natives. And in a much grander and profoundly compromised sense, the representations I have discussed revolved around the traffic of European ideas, agendas, and epistemologies in non-European space.

It is important to chart such fissures and instabilities, as I will now finally make plain, because Cook's and Douglas's words have been treated as reliable, objective, historical documents and have been used for particular ends. I will return, then, to the unveiling of that cairn at Nootka Sound.

CHAPTER 4

Cook Books

We should have copies in our archives for Captain Cook, by all regarded as the discoverer of our province; at any rate he was the first person to give any knowledge of our land to the world.

– F.W. HOWAY, "HISTORICAL RESEARCH IN BRITISH COLUMBIA" (1926)

The unveiling ceremony at Nootka Sound in 1924 marked the first time that Cook's sojourn at Nootka Sound was treated as the foundation of history in British Columbia. Cook does not figure prominently either in H.H. Bancroft's histories of the Northwest Coast (1880s) or in Alexander Begg's *History of British Columbia* (1894), which he termed "a continuous history of this portion of the British Empire."[1] Historians gave the history of the region various starting dates.[2] Allan Smith argues that these first historians of British Columbia, who were not born in the province, worked with the conceptual tools of Victorian Britain, judging "local" activity in terms of "the extent to which it released the wealth of the world, created moral communities and illustrated the truth that the individual was the master of his fate." "British Columbian experience did more than meet the test," Smith continues, though historians disagreed on how and when wealth, achievement, and virtue had been harnessed.[3] British Columbia was seen as a land of plenty, where pioneers could serve themselves and the interests of the British Empire concurrently. The province signified something greater than itself.

F.W. Howay, who was born in British Columbia, held some of these views, but he was also one of a number of Canadian intellectuals working in the interwar years who began to look beyond the bonds of empire and think about the nature of regional identity. The cairn was offered by the Canadian government as a beacon of interpretation rather than as a marker of destiny or some completed development. Howay represented these currents of thought in his speech at Nootka Sound. He was not garnishing a British imperial philosophy of history with local produce but, rather, using this event to suggest that history and identity needed to be put on a White-Indigenous footing. The editor of the *Daily Colonist*, a local newspaper, noticed as much: "The unveiling is of more than average historic interest. A country is acquiring stability and giving direction to its ideals when it commemorates with fitting ceremony the events of the past which are interwoven with its growth and progress ... [Nootka Sound] is perhaps the most historic site of all in British Columbia ... [By unveiling a cairn there] we are keeping one hand on the traditions of the past."[4] Howay wrote to Ottawa in 1921 complaining that "so little interest have we shown in historic Nootka that it has been left to foreigners to mark it!"[5] The Washington State Historical Society had erected a monument there in 1903. And reflecting on the importance of the Historic Sites and Monuments Board in 1926, Howay stated that "real nationality must be founded on an interest in local history."[6] W.N. Sage also reflected on these issues of identity. In 1939, he suggested that "with the growth of a Canadian national feeling ... [came] the desire to see Canadian history in perspective from sea to sea ... [but] many Canadians were still 'colonials' in thought."[7]

Where were Native peoples in this discussion of national and regional identity and its colonial hangovers? Moreover, how was this talk of tradition possible when (according to the colonialist paradigm of progress sketched by Smith) it was Native peoples who were assigned the station of tradition, when tradition carried the connotations of fable and barbarism rather than reason and opportunity? And how could Nootka Sound be called a historic spot that was indigenous to White British Columbians when Captain Cook had encountered Native peoples who obviously thought that *they* owned the place?

This invocation of tradition and the search for historical-geographical identity smudged the idea that British Columbia had coeval foundations in a Native-White contact process and ruled instead that historical spaces such as Nootka Sound had thoroughbred roots in the civilized ideals of explorers such as Cook. Howay and Sage were struggling with issues of indigenization – or what Terry Goldie calls the "the impossible necessity of becoming indigenous" – and incorporated Native peoples into their speeches and writing in highly selective ways.[8] For White Canadians, Australians, and New Zealanders to imagine themselves belonging to more than just the British Empire, Goldie argues quite bluntly, they had "to look at the Indian. The Indian is Other and therefore alien. But the Indian is indigenous and therefore cannot be alien. So the Canadian must be alien. But how can the Canadian be alien within Canada?"[9] Goldie thinks that there were – and are – only two possible answers: either to incorporate signifiers of Native indigeneity within a White "semiotic field" (he uses the example of Mohawk Motors) or to reject the presence of the indigene by simply claiming that countries such as Canada began with the coming of Whites.[10] Goldie's formulation is too dichotomous, I think, but in the early twentieth century British Columbia's intellectual elite grappled with these issues of indigenization. E.O.S. Scholefield, for instance, wrote in the first volume of his and Howay's *British Columbia: From the Earliest Times to the Present* (1914): "The pagan tribes of Nootka occupy a place in the history of British Columbia analogous to that of Caesar's Britons in the annals of England."[11] Native peoples belonged to a distant – and perhaps irrelevant – past; Scholefield incorporated them into a White lexicon of British Columbian modernity as prehistoric ancestors.

Such sentiments can be found in Sage's report on the unveiling ceremony. We do not hear what Maquinna had to say. Nor do we learn what the Native groups assembled at Nootka Sound might have thought about the ceremony or about the conditions of their participation.[12] Sage's passage about the arrival of the *Malaspina* mimics Douglas's account of first contact at Nootka Sound. The Nootka re-enacted history itself. Sage was simply a scrivener. It was "as if the mists of time had rolled away." The enlightened heirs of Cook re-encountered a Native Other. The Native harangues were still unintelligible, and history repeated itself as spectacle. And so read a newspaper headline at the time: "Memorial Party's Vessel Thrice Circled by Flotilla of Indian War Canoes on Approach to Historic Spot – Learned Scholars and Ignorant Natives Stand Together at Foot of Monumental Cairn."[13] The Natives remade and fell out of history at the same time. Their actions had a literal meaning. We do not know how Chief Brown saw matters, but Sage reported that he was inviting the *Malaspina* to land just as Cook and his officers guessed that they were being invited ashore. By re-presenting the imagery of Douglas's account, Sage ensured that first contact retained its metaphoric status. Cook pointed to the future; Sage folded his advent on Native shores into the present.

Yet this unveiling ceremony was not staged in a political vacuum. It should be seen in the context of the Indian Rights Association (a pan-provincial Native organization that protested the land question at the start of this century); Native resistance to a Dominion law banning the potlatch; and, I will note in Chapter 11, agitation among non-Native intellectuals about the influence of Spanish and American toponymy on the coast (HMCS *Malaspina*, ironically, was named after Spain's illustrious scientific explorer Alejandro Malaspina, who visited the coast in 1791).[14] White scholars largely ignored these forms of Native dissent at public functions. In 1908, for example, Scholefield wrote to his friend G.M. Sproat (a former Indian reserve commissioner in British Columbia), asking him about what to include in a public lecture on the history of Vancouver Island. Sproat thought that the challenge was to know "what to leave in the ink pot," and he told Scholefield to avoid discussion of Natives "as an ordinary audience cares nothing about aborigines ... and some may charge you, as an official, with discussing disputed questions of rights."[15] Most White British Columbians probably did not care much about "aborigines," and Native resistance to colonialism did not threaten their grip on the land or sense of cultural superiority. But cultural superiority did not sit easily with moral confidence in the legitimacy of colonial dispossession. Sproat had thought long and hard about "the Indian problem"; when he was Indian reserve commissioner, he noted that it was "almost insoluble" or, at least, that it required "a larger brain or a more sensitive and charitable heart" than was possessed by most White British Columbians.[16] One of the ways in which White British Columbians identified themselves locally – and especially in relation to Native peoples – was by marginalizing and degrading competing cultural claims to land and actively maintaining Western, British, and colonial standards of distinction. British Columbia was no longer a British colony, but these scholars and public figures were indeed colonials in thought, preserving those boundaries and hierarchical distinctions between the White and Native that scholars such as Edward Said have shown defined the ideology of high imperialism around the turn of the twentieth century.[17]

For Sage, Douglas's account of first contact served this purpose. Cook, apparently, was welcomed by Natives who were eager to trade. Under the telos of local history, truth is most precious at its moment of origin – in that original discursive spark when Cook discovered Nootka Sound. Sage perhaps found this passage both revealing and comforting because it implied that Native dissent was an aberration of history. In the beginning – back in 1778 – everything was peaceful and uncontested. Cook was invited to land and, by implication, to take nominal possession of the coast for Great Britain. Sage's report amounts to what Foucault called "traditional history" – history conceived as a "patient and continuous development" and written as a "consoling play of recognitions."[18] As the *Malaspina* approached Friendly Cove, the mists of time rolled away and the spectators sensed that that they were Cook's acolytes. Sage's climatological metaphor can also be put in ocular terms. His report conforms to what Paul Carter means by "imperial history" – history that has "a satellite eye" and is "not random, open-minded, [and] equally attentive to all directions ... [but which] looks down a telescope."[19]

As with Cook's journal, Sage's report is selectively blind. I am not speculating here, for Sage kept a diary of this event that reveals that he papered over signs of Native dissent. Nor did he mention in his published report that the memorial party could not reach the cairn because of a high tide. Howay staged the event from the deck of a tug that bobbed around the promontory in bad weather, and the spectators quickly tired of the formalities. At Yuquot the Natives objected to the man from the Fox Corporation and wanted to "trample on his films and break his camera." Sage was told that things would have gone more smoothly if Maquinna had been paid twenty-five dollars for the privilege of filming his people. The villagers also demanded that the spectators pay a fifty-cent admission charge for the privilege of inspecting the village.[20] If the mists of time had rolled away, it was because these White visitors were back there with Cook having to pay for what they viewed and wanted. In all, the British Columbia Historical Association was presented with a spectacular version of this event.

Foucault treated the notion of "rediscovery" (in literary and especially scientific texts) as "a retrospective codification of a historical position."[21] In his address at Nootka Sound, Howay both raised and questioned these notions of rediscovery and retrospection. He was not as confident as Sage that there was some isomorphism between the past and the present. Had history been shaped? Much of what came between Cook and the present was still misty. Howay had gone to Nootka Sound to ground the connections between Cook and local historical identity.[22]

In his popular history, *British Columbia: The Making of a Province* (1928), Howay wrote that there is "a twilight period, before the dawn, in which fact and fiction are intertwined," when it was difficult to decide what came under the domain of history, thus making it difficult to forge a "consoling play of recognitions."[23] For Howay, Native peoples entered the domain of history for only a short period of time, in the "earliest pages" of exploration and trade. He thought they were largely irrelevant to the development of the province and argued that the study of Aboriginal life lay in the domain of anthropology. It was Cook who had illuminated the Northwest Coast and "made" history. Yet Cook still featured in Howay's twilight zone. The explorer's relevance to the developments of Howay's own lifetime still had to be mapped out. "The clouds of doubt and darkness that from the beginning of time had rested upon the western coast of North America found their last abode with the confines of the province of British Columbia," he wrote in 1923; but Cook's search for the Northwest Passage had only "lifted these clouds for an instant."[24] Cook's flash of brilliance had to be marked, and murky images of the past had to be weighed up and carefully arranged like stones in a cairn. Shortly after the unveiling ceremony, Howay wrote to C.F. Newcombe (an ethnologist and collector), complaining that little was known about the "early history" of the province and stating that he preferred history based on "a careful and critical reading and studying of the old books and writers to all the so-called information one may pick up as one travels."[25] "There is only one proper historical spirit," he wrote elsewhere, "and that is the spirit of doubt." The historian needs an open mind and "must not approach historical material and examine it with the coloured light of romance or bias, but with the bright clear light of the seeker after truth."[26] Yet standing before that cairn at Nootka Sound, Howay *was* trying to generate this "so-called" information. The party from Victoria was there to see as well as to commemorate history. At the unveiling ceremony, Howay suggested that one had to visit old landmarks as well as read dusty old library volumes to understand "the face of the day." This was the point of having a monuments board. Howay was to compose the epitaphs and resuscitate the "dry bones" of history. The site as well as the facts of history had significance.

Howay's response to the issue of indigenization, then, was to appeal to the authority of *witnessing*. "Everything in the European dream of possession rests on witnessing," Stephen Greenblatt argues; "a witnessing understood as a form of significant and representative seeing. To see is to secure the truth of what might otherwise be deemed incredible."[27] In some senses, Howay found it incredible that Cook's discovery had culminated in Britain's colonization of the Cordillera. Howay's essays on the "earliest pages" of British Columbian history are marked by a language of contingency and doubt. He noted that the maritime fur trade "owed its origin to an accident": the discovery made on Cook's voyage that sea otter furs collected on the Northwest Coast fetched high prices in China.[28] In turn, he characterized the maritime fur trade as "spasmodic" and argued that the land-based fur trade played only a small part in the economic development of the province.

For all of these contingencies, however, Howay still sought to give history direction. He concluded his essay, "The Fur Trade in Northwestern Development," with the thought that the fur trader had "pointed out to the home-builder [prospective colonist], who in the natural evolution must follow him, the paths which have led us to the proud position of today."[29] In 1924, he was trying to trace this narrative back to Cook, suggesting that Nootka Sound was the wellhead of local history. White British Columbians could dampen their worries about how these historical pieces fitted together, and satiate their thirst for identity, by revisiting Cook's discovery. Howay was trying to manufacture a past through an act of representative seeing – in his capacity as a scholar, collector, and custodian of British Columbian history.

Again, though, Howay was obscuring British Columbia's roots in cross-cultural interaction. Howay may have thought that the history of British Columbia was unelaborated, but, like Sage, he still thought of it as a shibboleth. He introduced his popular history of the province with the claim that "contact with civilization" had been "mortal for the native race."[30] When he spoke of fashioning local identity, he thought it unnecessary to include Native peoples because it was largely assumed that they were becoming extinct. In 1868, Sproat wrote that "colonization on a large scale ... practically means the displacing and extinction of the savage native population."[31] Bancroft wrote of the "divinely preordained extinction" of the Indian.[32]

Cook has had many posthumous reputations. In 1920s Britain, he was being "enrolled among the most celebrated and most admired of the benefactors of the human race."[33] In British Columbia, he was being enlisted as a historical figure conferring an uncontested history of British sovereignty. As I will show in Part 3, the British explorer George Vancouver also loomed large in these acts of historical consecration.

"THE ARCHIVIZATION OF KNOWLEDGE"

The correspondents I cite – particularly Howay, Scholefield, Sproat, and Newcombe – were prominent public figures and some of the principal architects of a colonialist historiography of British Columbia. They constructed a local archive and hoped it would foster a new sense of local identity. Newcombe kept a massive collection of natural specimens and ethnological artefacts (including many Native objects procured for the British Museum). Howay searched the world for books and manuscripts pertaining to British Columbia and built up an impressive personal library.[34] In 1893, R.E. Gosnell became British Columbia's first provincial librarian. When he started, the library contained only ten books (including *Ben Hur* and a *Life of Queen Victoria*) and some government journals. He appealed to the public to send him information about "early events."[35] It was difficult to discover the past overnight, though. In 1911, J.S. Helmcken (one of the first colonists on Vancouver Island) bemoaned that it was still "impossible for the present generation to understand the condition of the early settlers" because there was a dearth of information.[36] By 1923, however, Gosnell (then in retirement) boasted to Howay that the provincial library had the best collection of Northwest Americana in the world.[37] A separate archives department was established in 1908, which Gosnell started. Scholefield succeeded him as provincial librarian in 1898 and became provincial archivist in 1910, holding both posts until his death in 1919.[38]

Between the 1880s and 1920s, there was an enormous drive to collect information, discover and rescue historical origins, and shape British Columbia's past. As the librarian Terry Eastwood has commented: "The collective vision [of these archivists] became fixed on the remote glimmerings of a society now coming to feel itself established"; Gosnell and Scholefield attempted "national building on a provincial scale."[39]

This information drive was by no means peculiar to British Columbia. Thomas Richards argues that in the late nineteenth century the "archivization of knowledge" became a definitive feature of European empire-building. For the British and French, especially, the archive became the principal "place of transit" between imperial knowledge and power, "the collectively imagined junction of all that was known or knowable, a fantastic representation of an epistemological master pattern, a virtual focal point for the heterogeneous local knowledges of metropole and empire."[40]

Richards analyzes literary texts and other parts of the world, but I want to push his basic point: the "archivization of knowledge" in the late nineteenth century was central to the propagation of colonialist discourse in British Columbia. It was with the aid of a provincial archive, and the creation of private libraries such as Howay's, that scholars developed a local epistemological pattern and remained "'colonials' in thought," as Sage put it. Before this era of the archive, colonial discourse in British Columbia was fashioned around a discrete set of events, and knowledge and power was channelled through a number of agencies and institutions. Explorers, traders, governors, and colonial officials wrote in different ways, for different audiences, and with different aims in mind. There was a spectral relationship between knowledge and power. British colonialism on Vancouver Island in the second half of the nineteenth century was part of a highly dispersed apparatus of British knowledge and power. A general set of British imperial ideas and colonial policies towards governorship, settlement, and Native peoples – summarized in tracts such as Herman Merivale's *Lectures on Colonization and Colonies* (1861) – were interpreted and localized in different ways in different British colonies. In the late nineteenth century, on the other hand, there was a huge investment in local *narrative* history. Historians such as Howay sought to domesticate colonial discourses about British Columbia – to knot them up in local space. Colonialism was given a British Columbian cast through the careful arrangement of local knowledge and the dissemination of a local will-to-know that was pointed out in these information drives and boasts about historical collections.

Scholefield sent people to European and North American archives to copy a panoply of records relating to British Columbia. These heterogeneous knowledges were housed in the Legislative Building in Victoria for the consultation of scholars and government officials. The provincial archive was not opened to the public until the 1920s. The unveiling ceremony prompted Howay to search for the journals of Cook's officers, and in a essay on historical research on British Columbia written in 1926, he suggested that the task of "seeking everywhere" for "lost books" on the region remained central.[41] In 1958, Sage reflected that during the early twentieth century the historian had to be "a jack of all trades," using archives and libraries, conducting "historical fieldwork," and being a collector as well as a writer.[42]

We should be indebted to these early collector-historians. Without them, the past would indeed be much murkier. But we should not forget that this enthusiasm for the collection and synthesis of knowledge – which characterized the work of anthropologists as well as historians – conditioned the nature of the historical imagination. Scholars spoke of unveiling the past, peering through the mists of time, rediscovering origins and discovering lost chronologies: of moulding events into a local master narrative. These currents of thought were expressed most distinctly by Scholefield, who wrote to Howay in 1911:

> It is such a great thing, such a fascinating thing, this founding and building up of a [archives] department devoted to the gathering together and preservation of historical records. It is also a work that must tell in the future. Humble as our beginnings were, we laid, broad and deep, a foundation for a structure which will be the splendid, crowning glory of this great Dominion of ours. The study of our early history fascinates me. I look back and I see, as through a mist, an illimitable coastline, a vast wilderness, unexplored and unknown, indefinably grand. And then, little by little, the veil is lifted. Great explorers, bluff sailors and hardy fur traders in their matter of fact and direct way, smash the theories and explode the fallacies advanced by old map-makers and credulous historians.[43]

Scholefield tied the European discovery and colonial settlement of British Columbia to the development of the archive. Historical knowledge would be the "crowning glory" of the province and the nation. Scholefield identified himself with these "matter of fact" explorers and traders. They shared a taste for discovery. The accumulation of geographical knowledge and historical texts went hand-in-hand. Under the spell of the archive, Scholefield saw history as an exploratory process, and one supposes that his archival thirst was never satiated. The more texts he had at his disposal, the more "illimitable" and "vast" the historical canvas seemed. Imagined through the archive, the past became "unexplored and unknown, indefinably grand" – a historical wilderness to be harvested by historical knowledge.

In Scholefield's imagery, the development of the archive also doubles as historical progress. The explorer-archivist smashes the theories of "old-mapmakers and credulous historians." In short, the colonial archive has its own historicity and spatiality. It both creates, and attempts to fill, a terra incognita with historical meaning. Thus imagined, Native peoples were again being erased from the local historical imagination. The archive contributed greatly to the conception of British Columbian modernity. Scholefield posited what Homi Bhabha calls the "non-place" from which any "historiographical operation starts." "For the emergence of modernity – as an ideology of *beginning, modernity as the new*," Bhabha argues, "the template of this 'non-place' becomes colonial space ... The colonial space is the *terra incognita* or the *terra nulla*, the empty or wasted land whose history has to be begun, whose archives must be filled out; whose future progress must be secured in modernity."[44] This was not European modernity; Scholefield was in colonial space. But it was a colonial space fashioned and revised for the needs of a White society trying to see its indigeneity, paper over historical contingency, and veil colonialism in a particular sense of modernity.

THE COOK BICENTENARY AND THE COURTS

In 1978, the British Columbia provincial government planned tourist trips to Nootka Sound as part of its Cook bicentenary celebrations. But this time it heard from the West Coast District Council of Chiefs, which refused to participate in the official proceedings unless it was granted a multi-million-dollar economic development package to ease unemployment in Native communities and to build a longhouse at Yuquot. When Grace McCarthy (the province's tourism minister) dismissed these proposals as "silly," the council boycotted the celebrations and vowed to keep visitors away from Yuquot.[45] The press dubbed the village "Not-So-Friendly-Cove."[46]

A White ritual was forestalled, but colonialist ideas and stereotypes had not been dismantled. The editor of the *Victoria Times* saw no reason why Native peoples would want to celebrate, for "it was only after the white man came and settled that things went bad for them."[47] (Natives had not disappeared, but they had been mortally wounded, as Howay claimed.) The *Daily Colonist* stated that the Mowachaht had been the real losers of history: "They have changed. Friendly Cove hasn't."[48] (Friendly Cove remained a wellhead of local history.) Some historians could not understand what the "fuss" over Yuquot was about, as Cook had actually anchored a few miles away.[49] (Like many historians, they were giving stage directions that were far too technical for most people.) And an English couple from Middlesborough (near Cook's birthplace), who had won a ten-day holiday to British Columbia in a competition sponsored by the Bicentenary Committee and had hoped to visit Cook's landfall, conceded that no one could blame Native peoples for upsetting the show. They mused instead about the fact that they could not get a pork pie in Victoria.[50] (Why all the fuss over such a distant ex-colony?) George Watts, the chair of the Council of Chiefs, stated that "Land claims are at the root of the whole matter."[51] He was reiterating a Native grievance as old as colonial settlement itself: the appropriation of Native lands and resources without compensation or treaties.

In 1978, an academic conference was also held in Vancouver to mark the bicentenary. In their introduction to the published proceedings of the conference, which attracted Cook scholars from around the world, Robin Fisher and Hugh Johnston (two historians at Simon Fraser University in Burnaby) noted that the memory and legacy of Cook had been manipulated by both Natives and Whites "to suit current social and political concerns."[52] This remark was perhaps prompted by the "fuss" over Yuquot, but the issues lying behind it barely reached the conference floor. There was much debate about the influence of Beaglehole on Cook scholarship, and most of the papers dealt with the motives for, and legacies of, Cook's travels from a European perspective. Fisher was the only scholar who tackled the substance of Cook's encounters with Indigenous peoples. In his essay "Cook and the Nootka," which is perhaps the classic revisionist statement of the beginnings of Native-White contact in British Columbia, he argued that the two groups forged a reciprocal relationship.

> Some appear to want to see Cook's arrival at Nootka in terms of "good" and "evil." There were no such extremes at Nootka Sound in the spring of 1778. There was a balance in the relationship that developed between Cook's crews and the Indians. It is true that opposites can be balanced, but at the point of contact at Nootka Sound each group was subject to the culture of the other, each found things that were familiar, and each had to comply with the demands made by the other. Neither group asserted a dominance, neither perceived the other as superior and, therefore, neither responded with submission.[53]

Fisher criticized the "fatal impact" thesis then permeating much scholarship on European exploration, but the above passage also summarizes his view of early contact relations in British Columbia as sketched in *Contact and Conflict* (see Introduction). He claimed that explorers and traders "reacted to what they saw" of Native life, while settlers "tended to react to what they expected to see" (roughly, that Native peoples were primitives who could be easily pushed aside). In Fisher's opinion, the former generated more objective observations and held more open-minded opinions about Native peoples than the latter.[54]

While Fisher attacked the monoliths of colonial historiography, Cook still holds a special place in his thesis. He represents Cook as the arch reciprocator, the most experienced and sophisticated exponent of his first economy of contact. Fisher echoed Beaglehole's view that Cook was a dispassionate, open-minded, and humane explorer, thus ostracizing the explorer from local colonial historiography and placing him in an ideologically cleaner past. Fisher worked with the journals of Cook's officers but used them largely to bolster this image of Cook.

During this century, the European intellectual history of Cook's voyages – especially his place in the Enlightenment – has had a wayward life. In British Columbia, the details of Cook's encounter with the Nootka, and the European world Cook came out of, have been localized in particular ways. Sage transmuted Douglas's account for the purposes of his present, implying that Native dissent was an aberration of history and attempting to shore up the vicissitudes of a local master narrative of British Columbian history. Howay was the principal and most intricate architect of this local colonialist historiography. More recently, Fisher has tried to put this historiography in a bifocal light, trading on Cook's scientific-humanitarian agenda in order to suggest that early contact relations did not forecast the exploitation and marginalization of Native peoples. In all of these cases, discussion of Cook's sojourn at Nootka Sound has been bound up with local constructions of the British Columbian past.

As my discussion of Cook at Nootka Sound shows, we can challenge the objectivity and putative majesty of Douglas's account of first contact by studying the journals of Cook's officers and Native accounts of this event. Most of these accounts were not at Sage's disposal, but he was quick to recycle Douglas's imagery of first contact because it conveyed a reassuring message at a time when questions of identity and land in British Columbia were volatile. Fisher, on the other hand, did not explore the view that the images of tranquillity and trade that pervade Cook's journal are, in part, fabricated truths connected to the explorer's self-estimation as a peaceful representative of the British Crown and a messenger of European civilization.

Scholarship is always inflected by one's own present, and it is impossible for one scholar to appreciate fully the situatedness and genius of another scholar's writing. But however iconoclastic, scholarship is always tied to a broader horizon of discourse, and, until recently, questions of representation were never treated seriously in historical writing on British Columbia. Much scholarship was empirical in tone and parochial in outlook. This was perhaps because many aspects of the past still awaited consideration, especially the role that Native peoples played in the making of the province. One of the main aims of Fisher's work, as I read it, is to undermine the teleological narrative of sophisticated European cultures bowling over primitive societies.

But in spite of Fisher's efforts, colonial ideas about Native peoples and the land live on. They have been played out in the courts and are being marketed in corporate and public culture. For instance, did the Hudson's Bay Company judge its clientele's idea of local history correctly when it ran a newspaper advertisement in August 1993 selling the idea "our history is your history" with the slogan "First came the English, Then came the Bay"? "Oh!," pondered Stephen Hume, a *Vancouver Sun* columnist, "I wonder what ... First Nations [people] have to say about that view of things."[55]

In the courts Native groups have encountered judges who think that the observations of White explorers are more factual, objective, and reliable than Native oral traditions. In *Delgamuukw et al. v. The Queen*, the most controversial judgment in British Columbia on Native land claims, Chief Justice Allan McEachern stated that he worked with "a different view of what is fact and what is belief" than did the Native plaintiffs, who, he thought, had "a romantic view of their history." Patched Native histories that exist "only in the memory of the plaintiffs," he argued, are subsidiary to the knowledge created by the "continuum ... [of] great explorations" that brought Native peoples "into history" and govern the legal view that "authentic" Aboriginal practice is defined by what Europeans recorded when they discovered particular Native groups. He stated that he accepted "just about everything" historians put before him but not the work of anthropologists; participant observation, he noted in his judgement, was "fatal to the credibility and reliability of their [anthropologists'] conclusions." Most notoriously, McEachern donned the cap of the colonial Leviathan and described pre-contact Aboriginal life as "nasty, brutish, and short."[56]

There are strict legal rules about what counts as admissible evidence in court, of course, but in applying such rules to Native land issues judges like McEachern have also adhered to the ideology of scientific exploration and a much more diffuse yet entrenched body of colonialist ideas and assumptions. Judges, and some historians, have assumed that the texts of explorers are reliable because they conform to a European model of truth – that these texts are truthful because they are first-hand reports that were written on the spot. I have argued that while Cook and his officers may have endeavoured to follow this model, they did not, and perhaps could not, conform to it entirely. When we think about issues of representation in relation to these current political issues, we can see that models of truth are always bound up with cultural relations of power. Native oral traditions are also constructions of reality, of course, and have been revised over time in response to different needs. But to dismiss them as unreliable narratives on the basis of a definitively European notion of truth is to deny the saliency and historicity of cultural difference.

In late twentieth-century British Columbia, Native voices have been heard, but there is no agreement about how they should be treated. There are colonialist discourses embedded in these court judgments and newspaper advertisements – discourses that still need to be challenged. I have set up and challenged these discourses from the White side of the fence, so to speak, suggesting that work on historical icons such as Cook needs to be methodologically reflexive. Analysis of European-Native contact should include some discussion of how facts and evidence are derived from historical texts, how truths are constructed, and how representations are disseminated. We are fortunate that with Cook there are sufficient data to do this. We have a much more limited range of records for studying other phases and forms of contact in early British Columbia.

CHAPTER 5

Histories, Genealogies, and Spaces of the Other

I have worked from the unveiling ceremony at Nootka Sound, through some of the intellectual histories associated with Cook's voyages, into Cook's encounter with Nuu-chah-nulth peoples in 1778, and on to the annals of British Columbian history in order to illustrate that colonialism is as much an ongoing, arbitrary, and variously conceived process of inscription as it is a process of physical occupation, resettlement, and domination. However assiduous our scholarship on Cook might be, we cannot avoid the issue that Cook the man, the actor, and the messenger is, in good measure, a construction. He has been constructed in various ways from the 1770s to the present. There is no original or definitive Cook. From Douglas and Beaglehole, to Howay and Sage, to Fisher, and, most recently, to Obeyesekere and Sahlins, the explorer has been used to ignite issues of historical development, colonial and postcolonial identity, and the appreciation of cultural difference.

I have used Cook to put contemporary British Columbia in a specific light. None of the texts I have considered defines Cook's stay at Nootka Sound: they each contain partial truths hatched at the intersection of European and Native perceptions of the other in 1778 and onwards. But taken together, these texts raise questions about how and why certain representations are taken to be factual and true, while others get buried, ignored, or dismissed. To tackle these questions of representation, we need a vigilant sensitivity to the ways in which people and ideas move and act in different settings as well as a sensitivity to questions of position, location, and territoriality. British Columbia has been imagined and constructed geographically as well as historically. The agendas and cultural filters that Cook and his officers brought to bear on Nootka Sound came out of a specific corporeal and intellectual context. They worked within the disciplinary parameters of a British naval ship and in Native spaces where

European discourses of science and civilization were fleshed out, corroborated, and confounded by vision and experience. More materially, the history of British Columbia has involved an immense struggle over land and territory. What is dimmed in much historical work on British Columbia, but is acutely apparent in the history of the province and in these recent court judgments, is that it is impossible to study British Columbia's past or present without running into a shifting set of connections between power and space. If early British Columbia should be approached geographically, it is not because geographers wield better analytical tools than scholars from other disciplines; rather, it is because colonial and postcolonial forces are fundamentally territorial.

Cook's encounter with the Nuu-chah-nulth does not point in any single historical direction. It has a value all its own, as a discrete event. Cook's mandate muddled his observations, and the observations of his officers muddied the waters of representation even further. This "earliest page" of contact has multiple meanings, and the discussion of foundations seems precocious. Yet this encounter became part of a global history and local genealogy of cultural dominance. For Europeans, it was Cook's illustration of civilization on Native shores and his powers of observation that mattered. What mattered to Howay was that Cook was "the first person to give any knowledge of *our* land to the world." However, if it is *our* land that matters, rather than how the world came to know British Columbia, *whose* land it is remains contested and partly unknowable outside of the European contexts I have explored. Howay worked with a split imaginary of European exploration and regional becoming. His spirit of doubt lay on the ground and in a local archive. He was trying to gather together threads of regional identity at places like Nootka Sound. But he knew that "the seeker after truth ... [who] allow[s] the accumulating testimony to evolve the explanation" – as he saw historical inquiry – needed to look elsewhere, in metropolitan archives, for his testimony.[1] Judges and historians still work from European ways of knowing. They work with a European model of knowledge that tries to marginalize doubt and slough off the complicity of truth and power. They have tried to master Kant's wide and stormy ocean. My discussion of Cook also comes out of a European horizon of thought, of course. I have tried to get inside Cook's sojourn at Nootka Sound with a number of stories and a philosophy that draws connections between the production of truth and the exercise of power.

These issues of identity, doubt, testimony, and argument will continue to articulate the past and present. To change current relations of power would involve altering spatial bases of power that were put in place during the colonial period, but current power relations are also tied up with categories of knowledge about Native peoples, and strategies of representation, that are inflected by this global and local history of colonialism. In different ways, Howay and Fisher have battled with a postcolonial horizon of history. What made the history of the province British or British Columbian, or Native and European?

These historians have fashioned historical spaces within which particular narratives of self and other can be told. I have been trying to undo and redraw some methodological boundaries, suggesting that the archive on Cook and British Columbia is not a mute or transparent record of things past: it is a shifting arrangement of things past and present.

I have been using the terms "history" and "genealogy" along the lines suggested by Arjun Appadurai: that "history leads you outward, to link patterns of changes to increasingly larger universes of interaction; genealogy leads you inward, toward cultural dispositions and styles that might be stubbornly embedded both in local institutions and the history of the local habitus."[2] It matters how we connect figures like Cook to Europe. His voyages fuelled a broader Eurocentric vision of the world and the discourses of civilization and progress that characterized modern colonial projects. Much scholarship on Cook is still concerned with European vision. But it also matters how we connect Cook to places like British Columbia. Stories about his voyages do not just revert back to Europe; non-Native British Columbians and Australians have seen Cook as their own. His invocation as a local historical icon, rather than as a global player of Enlightenment ideals, has played an important part in the fashioning of colonial identities – of colonial particularity. Yet even at their most innovative, as with Carter's formulation of spatial history, attempts to ground Cook's posthumous particularity struggle to leave behind European – and often specifically British – models of experience and truth, and discourses of civilization and imperial incorporation. I have tried to acknowledge this bind and to develop a two-way geography of European and British Columbian constructions of the past and future. Places such as Nootka Sound were both theatres of European symbolic action and sites that adumbrated local historical discourses. They were the variously situated spaces through which histories and genealogies were made.

Native peoples have their own histories and genealogies, of course, and I have said little about the make-up of their texts. It would be presumptuous to say that Cook has a special place in their imagination and constructions of the past. He was one of numerous strangers who appeared on their shores. I quote from these texts, but with little commentary, mindful of the fact that they have been overshadowed by the work of Cook and his officers and ignored by historians. If there is a naiveté – or strategic essentialism or methodological double standard – in this, it is tied to the recognition that the force field of historical representation has for a long time drowned Native voices (or at least dressed them up as myth). I have used these Native stories mainly to unmask how Cook and his officers faced up to otherness. Yet, as I now want to go on to show, it is possible to delve some way into Nuu-chah-nulth ideas of kin, property, and society and thus explore in a slightly different way the fact that contact involved two parties.

To paraphrase one of Greg Dening's (and Walter Benjamin's) great concerns, I have not been trying to portray what *really* happened at Nootka Sound in

1778: I have been concerned with what *actually* happened within particular methodological and epistemological registers.[3] For me, the archival record of this encounter can be used to draw out the abbreviation, confinement, fracturing, and splitting of knowledge and meaning in geographies and histories that move in different directions, between Europe and British Columbia, and from the waters of Nootka Sound, to the rhetorical flourishes of editors such as Douglas, and back to the place where things actually happened, with observers who made Cook real in other ways.

Or to reiterate one of Foucault's central claims: "What is found at the historical origin of things is not the inviolable identity of their origin; it is the dissension of other things. It is disparity."[4]

PART 2

Geographies of Capital

Their fancy for many articles could be traced to a desire to imitate their somewhat more polished visitors, and the absurdity, if any there was, lay in the manner in which they used them. When attacked upon this point, they would dryly refer to some of our usages as equally absurd with their own. Talking one day upon such matters with Altadsee, a sarcastic old chief of the Hanslong tribe, I ridiculed the practice of covering their own and their childrens' garments with rows of brass & gilt buttons, & loading them with old keys, to be kept bright at a great expense of labour. "Why," said he, "the white men wear buttons." "True," I replied, "but they are useful to us: the fashion of our garments requires buttons to secure them." "Ah," said he, "perhaps it is so; but I could never discover the usefulness of half a dozen buttons upon your coat-tails: and, as for the waste of labour in scouring old keys, you are right; it is very foolish, and almost as ridiculous as the fashion, which I am told prevails in your country, of placing brass balls upon iron fences in front of your houses, to be polished every day & tarnished every night." "Truly," he added, "Eijets Hasdi & Hanslong Hasdi cootnanous coonug" ("White people & Hanslong people are equally foolish").

– MS. OF THREE LECTURES BY WILLIAM STURGIS,
DEALING WITH HIS VOYAGES (1846)

Introduction

The Native peoples of Nootka Sound were apparently sorry to see Cook's ships leave. They "sung us a parting song, flourishing the saws, swords, hatchets and other things they had got from us," James Burney reported.[1] They continued to trade as the *Resolution* and *Discovery* quit the sound, and Cook's officers thought that they wanted the ships to return.[2] And Cook made his own parting gesture:

> a Chief named ... who had some time before attached himself to me was one of the last who left us, before he went I made him up a small present and in return he present[ed] me with a Beaver skin [i.e., sea otter skin] of greater value, this occasioned me to make some addition to my present, on which he gave me the Beaver Cloak he had on, that I knew he set a value upon. And as I was desirous he should be no suffer[er] by his friendship and generosity to me, I made him a present of a New Broad Sword with a brass hilt which made him as happy as a prince.[3]

When James Hanna, a British trader, arrived at Nootka Sound in August 1785 in the brig *Sea Otter*, he was greeted by Natives chanting "Maakook" (trade).[4] According to a London newspaper, Hanna "entered into a friendly and commercial intercourse with the natives; but some difference about the barter of respective commodities arose," which culminated in a Native attack on the vessel. Native canoes approached the *Sea Otter*; "in one of which was a herald, who, standing up ... and within hearing of the European vessel, pronounced his reasons for war, and solemnly declared it; informing Capt. Hannay [*sic*], that they would attack him the next day, by a certain hour. Capt. Hannay put himself into the best posture of defense possible, and awaited the enemy. At the hour appointed, a fleet of prows appeared, and advanced to the vessel, pouring into her showers of arrows and darts." Hanna responded with musket-fire and small cannon, killing and wounding many people. By evening, however, trade had resumed; Hanna obtained a large cargo of furs and was invited to return the following year, the Natives "promising to provide furs for him."[5] Another newspaper account states that the Natives were "tempted" to attack "by the diminutive size of the vessel" (it was probably 50 to 60 tons, and 50 feet in length) but were "repulsed with considerable slaughter," being "unacquainted with the effects of firearms."[6]

The following year Alexander Walker, another British trader, gathered more details. The evening before the affray the Natives had traded with the *Sea Otter* "as usual" and relations were congenial, but Walker sensed that Hanna was not surprised by the attack the next day because he had been tipped off by a party of strangers who had been trading with the vessel. Walker concluded that Hanna had provoked the attack by firing on some Natives for "a petty theft," and he suggested that, "as an instance of the singular disposition of these People, the Battle was not long over, when the Savages who had been guilty of so recent an Act of perfidy, came again alongside, and offered their skins for Sale as if nothing had happened. The effects of this Engagement may in some Measure account for the extraordinary dread they expressed at our fire arms, – but the Secrecy and cunning with which they concealed the transaction [with Hanna] from us, forms a strong feature of their character."[7]

These two events, separated by only a few years but involving the same Native group, belong to different classes of interaction, observation, and truth. Cook singled out a chief, exchanged gifts, their value increasing in turns, and left the sound in an inflated atmosphere of conviviality. This encounter in some ways summarizes Cook's self-estimation as a European explorer.[8] Europeans and Natives had exchanged pieces of their cultures, and for Cook, perhaps, this event denoted the reciprocity that he thought had prevailed during his stay. The epistemological quandaries of Cook's officers seem distant from this final transaction at Nootka Sound. Hanna, on the other hand, was the first maritime fur trader on the Northwest Coast, and this encounter presages a different island of truth. We have only second-hand information about this event.[9] Hearsay was an integral feature of this business; it pointed to competition and commercial webs of uncertainty.

With the dawn of this maritime fur trade, Cook's mandate slips from view. Interaction was now driven by profit rather than science, appealed to the broker rather than the philosopher, and contact was charted on bank ledgers rather than on a great map of humankind. The work of explorers was used for strictly capitalist ends, and traders produced different kinds of knowledges and truths than Cook. Traders brought a large assortment of manufactured and semi-manufactured goods, and they made new ones as they became acquainted with

Native demands. They left the region with a much smaller range of commodities – principally furs – to trade in a niche of the world economy. Native peoples were dealt the (sometimes quite visible) hand of the market. Vessel masters juggled trading strategies rather than a scientific-humanitarian project.[10] Contact focused on the exchange of goods and "Trafficking" took on new, instrumental meanings. Few traders were specifically instructed to study Native life. Robert Haswell, sailing in 1788 with the *Columbia*, the first American vessel to trade on the coast, summarized the outlook of many of his cohorts: "a regular account of People manners and customs etca. of this vast coast is a task equell to the skill of an able Historian and what I am totally inadequate to."[11]

This phase of commercial interaction produced new histories, geographies, and genealogies. The world economy was stretched to the Northwest Coast, incorporating Native groups into a capitalist order of consumption and exchange. Yet the process of positioning these exchange relations in Native territories had a great bearing on the character of this capitalist project. The world economy was not planted or exemplified on the Northwest Coast. Such imagery of cultivation and display, which we see in Cook's voyages and Enlightenment thinking, pushes what traders and Natives sought from each other into a much too rigid interpretive corridor. As Marshall Sahlins argues generally about modern world history, "Western capital and commodities do not easily make their way by demonstration effects."[12] On the Northwest Coast, both Natives and traders fashioned geographies of inclusion and exclusion, and their different agendas creaked and groaned as they came into contact. I follow scholars of cross-cultural interaction who argue that a European global order was – and is – worlded in, rather than imposed on, fresh fields of accumulation and incorporation. Sahlins himself notes that "local people articulate with the dominant cultural order even as they take their distance from it, jiving to the world beat while making their own music." On the Northwest Coast the world economy had a staccato beat. The fur trade lasted from the 1780s to colonial times, but individual traders came and went, and the sea otter trade did not settle down in any one Native village or region for long. The staccato deployment of commercial capital from the Columbia River to Alaska brought the global trajectory of capitalism and its local arrangements into abrupt and vivid relief. Capital was embodied – visualized and concretized – in glaring ways, as traders and Natives engaged each other with weapons as well as harangues, and in murky ways, as they tried to fathom each other's intentions and actions. Outcomes were not preordained for either Natives or traders, yet particular patterns and processes can be discerned.

Part 2 considers the geography of the sea otter trade and its ramifications for Native groups along the west coast of Vancouver Island. I will not be dealing with an event like Cook's sojourn at Nootka Sound, but a process of engagement. Scholars of British Columbia have treated the fur trade as a historical benchmark from which to interpret (and sometimes judge) Native cultures and to contrast Native fortunes in pre-colonial and colonial times. If we are to move beyond non-Native views of the past and broach Native perspectives, then the maritime fur trade is our most substantial historical resource, for trade and traders constituted the bulk of what Native peoples saw of the West until the colonial period.

Chapter 6 focuses on commercial competition between traders and on how their projects were characterized by an economy of truth that was quite different than the one Cook exemplified. Traders generated self-serving stories about the trade, and I will note that some of their observations about Native peoples were mediated by fear anxiety. Yet we can find various forms of knowledge and shades of truth in traders' tales. Maritime fur traders also generated a valuable body of information about Native agendas and the make-up of the trade on different parts of the coast. Their observations about Native groups and places can be cross-referenced and combined with other historical materials (chiefly, for the part of the coast I am studying, Spanish records), ethnographic sources, and archaeological data to build up some fairly cogent pictures of the nature of Native-Western commercial interaction and the processes of sociopolitical change among Native groups. Following my discussion of what I call "the conflictual economy of truth" of the maritime fur trade, I contrast the dynamics of commercial contact at two of the earliest and most important trading locations on the coast: Nootka Sound and Clayoquot Sound.

In what follows I use the term "trader" – or, when the context seems to warrant it, "White" or "White trader" – as a shorthand for American and European maritime fur traders. I use the term "Native" when writing generally about Native peoples. "Trader" is a cumbersome expression, since Native peoples were also traders, yet this distinction between "trader" and "Native" signposts the fact that while traders came to the Pacific Northwest with one aim in mind (to trade furs), Native peoples had a much broader set of concerns and agendas, and did not pour all of their energies into the sea otter trade. "White" is a cumbersome word because the crews of fur trading vessels were drawn from many different parts of the world and because traders' observations were tinted by their national-cultural backgrounds. "White" is also a loaded word in that Native groups distinguished between traders from different countries (they called British traders "King George men" and American traders "Boston men"). But I still find "White" a more convenient label than "Europeans" or "Euroamericans." I use the terms "Native peoples" or "Native groups" rather than "First Nations" because contact between Whites and Natives in this region played a part in the formation of current First Nations boundaries and identities. I use the term "Indian" when writing indicatively through a White observer.

CHAPTER 6

The Conflictual Economy
of Truth of the
Maritime Fur Trade

The Savage, who is nevertheless dishonest, pretends to be Scrupulous, and
exact in his dealings.

– ALEXANDER WALKER,
ACCOUNT OF A VOYAGE TO THE NORTHWEST COAST (1786)

FROM COOK TO COMMERCE

In December 1787, William Bligh (master of the *Resolution* on Cook's third voyage) sailed for Tahiti to take breadfruit plants to the West Indies to feed negro
slaves. In January 1788, eleven British ships arrived at Botany Bay with a cargo
of convicts to establish a colony in Australia. And with much less publicity, in
the mid-1780s British merchants inaugurated a trade in sea otter furs with the
Native peoples of the Northwest Coast of North America. These were all attempts to "derive benefit" from Cook's "distant discoveries," as Bligh put it.[1]

Scholars have debated whether such developments were connected by a new
British imperial manifesto. Vincent Harlow's famous thesis about the emergence
of a "second British Empire" of trade now seems too schematic.[2] The British
prized international commerce, and between 1756 and 1783 the British began
to see their empire as a truly global phenomenon.[3] Yet commercial expansion
probably was not backed by a grand imperial project.[4] David Mackay argues
that after the American War of Independence, there was a haphazard and tentative search for alternatives to the "idealized economic network" that had been
based on the Atlantic Ocean.[5] The slave trade continued and British trade with
the New World soon bounced back to pre-war levels.[6] C.A. Bayly shows that late

73

eighteenth-century British imperialism was "in some places an era of the 'imperialism of free trade,' but there are as many examples of the 'imperialism of
monopoly' and chauvinist appropriation."[7] He argues that British and French imperialism were driven, to a considerable extent, by the imperatives of the fiscal-
military state, and he emphasizes that class and regional divisions within Britain,
and differences of opinion over the appropriate course of British overseas investment and expansion, were circumscribed by a new national-imperial sentiment.[8] During the eighteenth century, Kathleen Wilson argues, "the imperial
project – the 'empire of the sea' consisting of colonies and markets – was clearly
believed by contemporaries to maximise trade, liberty, prosperity and national
power, and thus appealed to a heterogeneous range of interests, grievances, and
aspirations at any given moment."[9] Commerce, especially, was prized by the nation. According to Britain's renowned compiler of global facts, Malachy
Postlethwayt, "the exercise of trade and commerce is soul of the whole British
Empire."[10]

The sea otter trade was a privately sponsored commercial response to the discovery made on Cook's third voyage that furs traded on the Northwest Coast
could be sold for a considerable profit in China. Some of the earliest merchants
in the trade were based in India and probably heard this news in Macao, where
Cook's crewmen had made their profitable transactions, but the message was
spread most directly by James King in the official account of Cook's voyage.[11]
Word also leaked to the United States of America before this account appeared.[12]
Indeed, the trade was not a solely British affair for long. American vessels from
New England (mainly from Boston) appeared on the Northwest Coast in the
late 1780s and by 1800 dominated the trade. Russians also traded along the
Alaskan coast, and a few French, Portuguese, and Spanish vessels ventured into
this new branch of commerce. Between the mid-1780s and early 1800s (the height
of the trade), there was an average of eleven trading vessels per year on the Northwest Coast.[13]

American and European merchants were trying to recover from the commercial upheavals created by the American War of Independence. The first British
traders in the business sailed from London and India, traded with Native groups
in the spring and summer, and then headed for Canton, the principal market for
furs. They were meant to be licensed by the English East India Company (EEIC),
which had an exclusive right to British trade with China, and by the South Sea
Company (SSC), which had an exclusive right to British trade in the Pacific.[14]
Some traders tried to circumvent these monopolies by sailing under the flags of
other nations, but the EEIC and the SSC dominated the Pacific sector of the
world economy in the eighteenth century.[15] At Canton, British traders dealt with
Chinese merchants through EEIC supercargoes (who charged a commission)
and received bills of exchange, which were recovered from the company's treasury in London.[16] The sea otter trade helped New England merchants to recover

from economic depression caused by the loss of colonial trade with Britain.[17] American traders, who were freed from these British monopolies in 1783, bargained with Hong for teas, silks, and porcelains, which they sold mainly in New England.[18]

Native fortunes were conditioned by capitalist logic. If furs and profits dried up in one location, then traders would move to another. When sea otters became extinct on parts of the Northwest Coast in the early 1800s, traders looked to exchange land furs and any other article they could profit by. In the 1780s and 1790s the west coast of Vancouver Island was one of the main areas of trade; by 1805 it had been largely abandoned by traders. Nootka Sound was the first and most important trading port, but few traders visited there after 1803.

I now consider traders' views of the sea otter business during the first few decades of commercial contact, and I then turn to Native agendas on the west coast of Vancouver Island. My account should not be taken as representative of the trade as a whole. The maritime fur trade lasted until the 1840s, underwent some significant changes after 1810, and stretched from Russian Alaska to the Columbia River.[19] Some general processes of Native-White interaction in this vast coastal region can be discerned, but there was also geographical variation in the way Native groups engaged traders, reflecting economic and political differences between Native groups.

ITINERATE GEOGRAPHIES

Traders viewed Native peoples as fickle savages who were locked in societies characterized by low levels of technological achievement and should naturally desire Western goods. Traders were very much concerned with how best to tap Native desire for goods.[20] "It is an incontrovertible fact," a prominent British merchant reported in 1790, as the trade was getting under way, "that in new discovered countries the natives are remarkably capricious; articles, in demand one day will be rejected the following; and both their fickleness and industry must be tempted by a variety of assortments."[21] Nicholas Thomas calls such formulations about the allure of Western goods "just-so" stories about White-Native contact – ways of essentializing interaction from a Western perspective, with trade as "the constitutive transaction" of cultural and colonial exchange.[22] "The central motif of this story is the gap between primitive tools and the manufactured things of white men: the magic and abundance of the latter are the source of asymmetry between powerless natives and dominant European colonizers."[23] The Indian was essentialized in European and American writing as the inferior Other of civilized life. Eve Kornfeld sketches the image of the Indian in the opening decades of the American Republic: "To do its cultural work for its [White] creators, the image of the Indian had to be flattened, reduced, simplified, and frozen. During the years of the early republic ... dominant

Americans saw only savagery and primitivism in the Other and almost completely effaced the variety and complexity of Indian cultures ... Even when intellectuals defended the Indians' potential for improvement or detected the noble savage among the many ignoble savages in their path, they still believed in the essential inferiority of primitive to civilized life."[24] American sea otter traders contributed to this imagery. Mary Malloy shows that writers such as James Fennimore Cooper found "a model for seafaring fiction ... in the factual narratives" of American trade in the Pacific, recycling traders' descriptions of savage and gullible Indians.[25]

Yet sea otter traders realized that the behaviour of Native peoples of the Northwest Coast did not conform entirely to these "just-so" stereotypes. Native groups wanted to trade, but they had specific wants and inspected traders' goods carefully. Traders were not always welcomed with open arms, and Native peoples did not necessarily look on Western goods as superior to their own. Traders struggled to impute a gulf between civilized and savage societies – between the peaks of Western achievement and the lowly life of the Indian – simply on the basis of their respective wares. To make their points about civilization and savagery, they resorted to arguments about the geographical circulation of capital and the generation of profit. Nor were these "just-so" stories about civilization and savagery their only terms of reference.

My basic claim about traders is that we cannot adequately assess the ways in which they viewed and dealt with Native peoples unless we treat the maritime fur trade as a heterogeneous and hierarchized space-economy – a space-economy that was at once embodied and reified; a space-economy that imbricated the cramped confines of merchant vessels, contact dynamics in and around Native villages, and a broader, more fluid, commercial geography in complex ways. The modes of interaction and representation that gave the maritime fur trade its distinctive texture were not simply underwritten by Western ideas about Indian savagery. Stereotypes of the Indian rogue and the Indian child sprang from different sorts of engagements with the world. Philosophers' representations of Native immaturity, and the equation of immaturity and savagery described by Thomas and Kornfeld, were conditioned, in important ways, by detachment from, and reflection on, contact zones such as the Northwest Coast – detachment through the protocols of science and through physical distance. By contrast, traders' inscriptions of superiority and inferiority, civility and barbarity, were drawn from the contact zone. Maritime fur traders' views of Native peoples were influenced by the micro-politics of shipboard life and the time-geography of trade. Representation was mediated by the durability of the contact relationships that traders established with Native peoples and by the way traders envisioned their own and Native involvement in the coastal trade and a global economy. In short, traders' accounts of commercial interaction were bound up with the way they imagined and produced space commercially. The economy of the maritime fur trade did not just amount to a bundle of trading locations and routes to profit. It was also an *imaginative space* stocked with commercial desire and cultural derision, where actions, meanings, and imputations tarried uneasily in different places and at a number of geographical scales.

The phrase "itinerate geographies" signposts three themes that criss-cross my argument. The first is that the trade was transient, moving from place to place as geographical knowledge of the coast grew, profits rose and fell, and as the plans of merchant houses changed. The Native peoples of Vancouver Island called traders "Tiyee awinna," or "travelling chiefs."[26] Many crew members of trade vessels were also itinerants. They came from the labouring classes and merchant marine, became conditioned to harsh regimes of shipboard discipline and the vagaries of nature, and had to endure the cramped, leaky, and unhealthy quarters of merchant vessels. Some of the first British traders on the coast had sailed with Cook, and as the trade developed, ships' mates became traders and some traders became financiers in Boston and London.[27] But few traders came to the coast more than twice. Maritime fur traders picked up some of the tricks and quirks of the trade by reading the accounts of their predecessors, but published texts describing the trade were few in number, even by the 1830s. Hoskins noted in his journal of the second voyage of the *Columbia* (one of the best documented trade ventures) that he left Boston in 1790 "without being able to procure the voyages of any of those preceeding navigators" and that the published account of Cook's third voyage gave "little or no information respecting the greater part of the trading coast"; he felt "subject to every inconvenience that can possibly attend a ship on an undiscovered coast."[28] Traders learned most on the coast itself, by word of mouth, in the face of competition, and with a world view that was shaped by life at sea. "There was too little space aboard the ship and too much space outside," Marcus Rediker writes in his dazzling account of the common sailor's lot in the eighteenth century. Sailors led a roving life. "Mobility, fluidity, and dispersion were intrinsic to the seaman's life," Rediker continues. "Seafaring culture necessarily took shape without firm geographic boundaries [apart from those of the ship] or stable residence." Life on merchant vessels was marked by incarceration on the ship for long periods, forced assimilation to discipline and control, and cultural ways (particularly lores about the sea, and distinct vocabularies and dialects) that were shaped by the basic relations of production of international commerce and an absence of family, church, and state. This was a self-contained world, and isolation heightened a sailor's awareness of the physical and symbolic uses of power and the importance of self-defence. Rediker builds up a picture of "a binding chain of linked limits: limited space, limited freedom, limited movement, limited sensory stimulation, and limited choices."[29] The world outside – Native movements around merchants,

Native freedom to come and go, not to mention their vibrant and intricate sensory world of painted faces, carved canoes, and long harangues – must have accentuated the sailor's sense of confinement and detachment from society.

Second, although the trade was transient, commercial interaction was thoroughly project-oriented. While traders vied with each other and Native groups for furs under intensely competitive conditions, the maritime fur trade was not quite the "series of disconnected and individual efforts" that F.W. Howay thought it was.[30] As sea otter pelts became scarcer, traders had to have a rough idea of where their competitors had been and would work in separate locations in order to be "economical in traffic," as one Boston financier put it.[31] In 1802, Sullivan Dorr, an American merchant in Canton, reported that the trade was "compleatly overdone" and that "the trade must be neglected for some years, unless the old and first adventurers unite and make a monopoly."[32] It was impossible for any single company or nation to monopolize the trade, but Dorr was right that, as competition rose and fur supplies fell because of Native over-hunting, merchants had to rethink their trading strategies. In the early nineteenth century Boston merchants such as Bryant and Sturgis devised corporate strategies, owning or fitting out a number of vessels and despatching them to different parts of the Pacific in search of new sources of profit.[33] This, too, affected traders' views of Native peoples. In the land-based fur trade, large corporate outfits such as the North West Company and the Hudson's Bay Company established forts, where fur traders were stationed for a number of years and gained experience with, and insights into, Native societies. Some maritime fur trade crews wintered on the coast near Native villages, but in general they had less experience with Native groups, and a more truncated understanding of Native ways, than did fort traders.

We should, of course, dismiss the view that Native peoples had "fickle" dispositions and that their demands and responses to traders were "whimsical."[34] Native groups dealt with traders according to their own set of economic, social, and political agendas and had their own forms of competition and collaboration. They were not marionettes of the global economy, and traders were not puppetmasters. Native peoples were neither awe-struck by "foreign" goods nor were they the dupes of capitalist development.[35] Capitalist relations of exchange did not have an indubitable capacity to corrupt or colonize Native economic and social arrangements. Native peoples incorporated Europeans and their goods into "their own system of the world," as Marshall Sahlins puts it.[36] The maritime fur trade was not a one-way traffic, with traders exploiting Natives, and it should not be studied in terms of White power and Native resistance; rather, the trade was characterized by relations of mutual appropriation and accommodation. The maritime fur trade connected Native fortunes to the capitalist world economy, but Native peoples had their own ways of bending commercial equations to their own advantage.

When these Native itineraries are tracked in particular areas (within and between specific groups), generalizations about early contact start to break down
and Native peoples begin to appear as partners in, rather than victims of, the
trade.[37] Native demands certainly changed over time and varied from group to
group, but to argue that they were "fickle" or "whimsical" is a Western fantasy
that misses the complicated logic behind Native tactics of trade. Indeed, traders'
self-assertive representations of civility and superiority – the ideological pistons
of European capitalism and imperialism – did not have hermetically sealed lives
of their own within traders' texts. They were brought into play by encounters
with these Native itineraries, were not always expressed straightforwardly or
confidently in traders' journals, and were, in part, retrospective journalistic codi-
fications of complicated (and often seemingly obscure) contact relationships.

And third, at the interface of these White and Native projects there was a
much more general and complex set of perceptions and equations about the
predictability and reliability of the Other – about whether the Native could trust
the trader, and vice versa, and about how commercial deals and guarantees might
be struck. William Sturgis (a prominent Boston merchant who traded on the
coast in the 1790s) recognized that traders were bent on "ultimate gain," but he
also understood that the traffic in furs could only partly be accounted for by
using Western economic formulae of supply and demand, price and profit.[38]
The trader's seemingly obvious quest for furs entailed its own conundrums and
smoke screens. Traders' and Natives' perceptions of each other were bound up
with the way goods were owned, given, exchanged, and circulated – with how
they were valued and used.[39]

"A commodity," Marx famously declared, "is a very strange thing, abounding
in metaphysical subtleties and theological niceties."[40] Marx's comment was based
on his rigorous observation of capitalism in Europe, of course, but it has obvious – and perhaps added – purchase in situations of cross-cultural commercial
exchange. Native and White participants in the maritime fur trade were not
simply accumulating wealth or extracting surplus value. They were also exchanging cultural perceptions of ownership, power, and prestige and dealing with subtleties and niceties that were often difficult to grasp. All that was solid could melt
into air – to trade on Marx's image of capitalist development in *The Communist
Manifesto* – because traders moved around the coast bartering with a Native
group one day and departing the next, and since Native peoples and White traders had different ways of evaluating commodities. Hard and fast distinctions
between want and fancy, gift and commodity, use value and exchange value (or
between "articles of value" and "articles of curiosity," as George Vancouver cat-
egorized goods) could fracture.[41] Whites and Natives became locked in a mael-
strom of cross-cultural signification and miscommunication. And this did not
apply solely to the Northwest Coast. "Circumstances and different countries alter the value of articles of merchandise," an American trader noted after trading

with peoples in different parts of the Pacific. "Hence things cannot always be estimated at their real value but at their price in the country they are in ... So unaccountable are the customs and fashions of different people!"[42]

These are my thematics. Substantively, there were two "itinerate geographies" embedded in the maritime fur trade. The first of these geographies was about *place*. Traders had to visit Native villages and trading places to get furs, and to achieve and maintain a good profit margin they had to attune themselves to the differences between Native groups – differences in the way furs and other goods were obtained, controlled, and handled in exchange. In effect, competition and the profit principle encouraged them to come to grips with Native agendas and geographies. Traders had to study Native peoples hard. Yet, in traders' writings, this acknowledgment of difference and specificity – this focus on place – often disintegrates into a heap of abstractions and stereotypes about Native peoples precisely because of traders' commercial objectives. Traders were interested foremost in the economic tide of events and frequently made little effort to connect commercial imperatives to Native social and political currents. Endlessly opportunistic, and without quite the time, energy, or talent to study and compare Native groups carefully, traders often accounted for their dealings with Native peoples by resorting to ad hoc statements about "the" Native mind and character. One French observer accused traders of offering little more than "conjectures" about Native societies.[43] The intricacies of Native economic and cultural geographies also became folded into more wholesale claims about "the market" for furs, "the coast" as a theatre of commercial interaction, and "Northwest policy." "The fur trade is inexhaustible wherever there are inhabitants," a British trader noted, rather optimistically, in the late 1780s, "and they (experience tells us) are not confined to any particular situation, but are scattered in tribes all along the coast."[44] In the first years of the business traders tended to visit many Native villages for short periods and sought new trade locations. As knowledge about the coast grew and competition rose, they started to stay longer in select locations.[45] Wherever and under whatever circumstances traders conducted their business, however, they had to size up a broader set of business tendencies.

Because of competition and opportunism, then, traders also worked with a much more anonymous and anomalous sense of *commercial space*.[46] They rarely expended all of their time, energy, or trade goods at one location. They had to be open to geographical exploration and attentive to new commercial possibilities. As they moved around the coast, they gradually filled in Cook's scanty map of the region, which pleased pundits and armchair geographers such as Alexander Dalrymple and Joseph Banks. On the eve of Vancouver's departure for the Pacific in 1791, Banks wrote to a British government minister extolling the virtues of the trade:

The Temptation of substituting conjecture for fact in laying down the shores of an unknown Country [sic] is so great, especially at times when ... it is difficult to approach the land, that few surveyors, I believe have wholly resisted it, but the present case, as every Creek on the Coast will be repeatedly examined by those in the collection of Furs, and as the merchant in consequence of the distance & danger of the voyage, find it necessary to employ seamen acquainted with all the modern improvement of navigation, no error that is made will long remain undetected.[47]

Geographical accuracy and error amounted quickly to profit or loss.[48]

As the trade developed, traders had to choose carefully where and how to trade. Joseph Ingraham grasped that one of the most basic decisions was whether to cruise the coast or sojourn in selected locations. "Cruising ... I adopted on my first arrival on the coast [1790], but I soon found it more to my advantage to remain awhile when in a good place. When cruising we went sometimes two or three days – nay once we were eight – without purchasing a skin; where while we were at anchor in Cummashawaa's [Cumshewa Inlet in the Queen Charlotte Islands] not a day passed but we purchased more or less skins."[49] His decision was not just influenced by the location of Native groups or how many furs they had. "[A] person is certainly in less danger at anchor in a good port than cruising among these isles where there are strong tides and sometimes heavy gales of wind."[50] Sturgis also understood the way merchant capital shuffled around the coast, and he knew that traders did not stay one step ahead of their competitors through single-handed enterprise alone. In 1799, he noted in his journal:

one after another are discovered the great resources of seaport tribes that inhabit this coast. Formerly all the skins that were collected were got at Nootkah, when some vessels pushing inland to the Northward of them, met that tribe on their trading expeditions. Panic struck at the discovery they scarcely made any exertions to keep the trade in their hands, and in one or two seasons sunk to nothing. It [the trade] was next transferred to the [Queen Charlotte] Islands who still keep a considerable share of it; but not half the skins are now got from them that formerly was, and we now have an evident proof that the greatest part of those they have are got from the Main[land].[51]

Traders learned a great deal from observing Native movements and trade patterns.

We can see from these passages that traders were not calm directors of capital whose trading strategies were set in Boston or London and applied mechanically to the Northwest Coast. They worked in a maze of commercial calculation, opportunity, and misfortune. "Prudence is doubtless requisite in all interprizes [sic]," noted Alexander Walker (ensign with the trading snows *Captain Cook* and *Experiment*, which reached Nootka Sound in June 1786), "but in such under-takings as ours, where so much is risked, the Execution should be managed with Spirit, and what would be rashness in other Situations, becomes in this case commendable. Much was hazarded in our Expedition, but a Game of Chance should be reduced as nearly to a certainty, as possible, and this could only be done by encreasing [sic] our Chances, or by dividing our Vessels."[52] Should trad-ers ply the coast in pairs but then run the risk of narrowing their profit margins by reaching fewer places? Or should they sail off in different directions and thereby run the risk of encountering dangerous shores and hostile Natives? Such choices influenced the way traders represented Native peoples and, contrary to Banks's observation, infused their geographies with conjecture as well as fact.

Traders entertained risk and anticipated danger. Today's chief, known to a trader by name and fêted as a dignitary, could become tomorrow's savage. Equally, for Native peoples, a trader could turn his guns on a Native village and become an instant enemy. The distinctions that traders and Native peoples noticed in the other – the trader's nationality, the group affiliations of Native peoples, along with distinctions of authority, social rank, and gender (i.e., particular constella-tions of subjectivity and power) could be washed away with the tide of events and the two groups end up looking on each other as foes. Traders learned to be on their guard and were often easily incited to violence.

The representation of place and difference could disintegrate into fractured abstractions. These concrete processes of interaction and abstract commercial imperatives made traders' accounts of their business with Native peoples at once hybrid and conflictual. As I will now show, this pirouette of Native places and commercial spaces gave the economy of truth of the maritime fur trade a hallu-cinatory quality. The panic that Sturgis described was built on a set of physical and psychical anxieties about how to deal with Native groups.

COMMERCIAL GAMES OF TRUTH AND FICTION

Merchants and financiers in London and Boston interviewed their traders on their return from the Pacific, and studied their journals, in order to gauge their successes and assess their commercial options.[53] Traders were no doubt asked to be honest, but their backers had to take much information on trust. In the mari-time fur trade the "game of truth and fiction," as Foucault glosses the idea of discourse, was mediated by competition and individualism.[54] Some of the first British traders tried to dissuade American traders from visiting the coast by claiming, verbally or in print, that the supply of furs had been exhausted, or that they had formed exclusive treaties with Native chiefs, or by representing a par-ticular Native group as hostile.[55] Many of the records of conflict between trading vessels and Native groups are third- or fourth-hand reports.[56] Some of the first traders also took advantage of the European public's enthusiasm for voyages of discovery and commerce, and they tried to enhance their personal emolument and public profile by exaggerating their achievements and highlighting their hardships. On all these counts, the British trader John Meares was the most notorious example. George Dixon, a British trader who had trained under Cook, was outraged by the way Meares described his geographical discoveries and commercial achievements in his *Voyages* (published in 1790) and embarked on a public diatribe, calling Meares's book "a confused heap of contradictions and misrepresentations."[57] And Robert Haswell reported that when Meares and his colleagues boarded the *Columbia* in September 1788 to discuss trade, "they fully employed themselves fabricating and rehursing vague and improvable tales relative to the coast of the vast danger attending its navigation [and] of the Monsterous Savage disposition of its inhabitants."[58] The Americans were certainly not saints either. One of Vancouver's officers observed that "the jealousies of trade" had taught Meares and the American trader Robert Gray of the *Columbia* "to play off their deceptions" against each other.[59]

But this game of truth and fiction was not just about competition; it was also cathartic. John Myers, who traded on the coast in the 1790s, captured this sentiment. "Life at every period seemed balanced in uncertainty," he wrote.[60] Traders compiled logs and journals of voyages for their employers. But they also used them to record their anxieties and justify their actions. They were instructed to be fair with Native peoples and to avoid violence. The owners of the American vessels *Columbia* and *Washington*, for example, hoped that Captain Kendrick would cultivate "the most inviolable harmony and friendship" with Native groups and told him that "no advantages may be taken of them in trading."[61] In 1789, British merchants impressed on Captain James Colnett of the *Argonaut* that violence was "not only destructive of the Commerce, but of every sentiment of humanity."[62] Given such instructions, when traders did resort to violence they must have felt some responsibility to explain the circumstances. Yet few records suggest that they were ever chastised by their backers for getting embroiled in conflicts. Traders documented Native threats and attacks in detail, and they described their retaliatory measures with bravado.

The Spanish explorer Dionisio Alcalá Galiano, who circumnavigated Vancouver Island in 1792, complained that traders had "set aside moral questions and resorted to force," and he declared: "If the governments of [trading] ships ... do not impose severe penalties on those who breach the laws of probity ... they cover themselves with the great opprobrium."[63] But why would Britain or the United States have been disgraced by the actions of their citizens in such distant waters? Merchants got official seals from their governments to secure the safe passage of their vessels through the waters of other countries, some traders claimed that their voyages enhanced the honour of their nations, and a few of the earliest traders were welcomed home as heroes.[64] But these were not state-sponsored voyages. Traders were "remote from the Laws & observation of

Society," as one religious-minded trader put it.[65] However undesirable and unfortunate, trickery and violence became part of ship life and trade with Native peoples, and traders were not expected to be humanitarians. If vessel owners wanted their captains be fair to Native peoples, it was largely because they did not want traders to jeopardize their investment.[66]

Thus, we cannot interpret how traders acted, what they wrote, and how they justified their actions simply by examining their instructions. Traders compiled their journals in the face of competition. The economy of truth of the maritime fur trade was riven with contingency and suspicion. Traders' journals are marked by a complex interplay of insight, presumption, and speculation about Native peoples.

Some traders approached Native peoples circumspectly. For instance, Captain Charles Bishop of the *Ruby*, which was on the coast in the mid-1790s, noted: "I cannot help observing how Cautious a Trader should be how he begins trade on his Arrival."[67] One had to assess the demeanour of each Native group before establishing prices or letting Native people near a vessel. Bishop claimed that Meares's *Voyages* was his textbook, but Meares presented himself as a swaggering adventurer who had approached Native peoples with great confidence and reaped great profits. Other traders cautioned their colleagues not to jump to conclusions about Native peoples. "Friendly intercourse" could easily be mistaken for "pretended humour," as Bernard Magee, a Boston trader, remarked in 1793; honesty could be malice in disguise.[68] William Shaler, another American trader, thought that merchant vessels should fire their guns as they approached Native villages in order to warn the inhabitants of their arrival and convince them of White superiority – a stock policy that many traders used.[69]

"Separated from the civilized world," as Sturgis explained, traders had to become "accustomed to rely on their own resources for protection and defense."[70] Most trading vessels were well-armed. Samuel Eliot Morrison documented some of the standard features of American trading vessels: "Besides swivel-guns on the bulwarks, they were armed with six to twenty cannon, kept well stocked with grape, langrange or canister; and provided with boarding nettings, muskets, pistols, cutlasses and boarding pikes. The quarterdecks were loopholed for musket fire, the hatches were veritable 'pill-boxes.'"[71] In short, traders took no chances; they were well-armed. But this did not prevent them from feeling vulnerable. When James Colnett anchored at Clayoquot Sound in November 1790 and questioned Native people about the whereabouts of some of his crew who had gone missing, he got some "confus'd stories" and started to speculate. "Being so long used to the Indians, and well acquainted with their Treachery and Cunning I began to be suspicious in my turn."[72] Had they drowned or been murdered? Colnett, like many other traders, described his anguish in detail: "My situation was desperate: short of Provisions, no Boat, Short Man'd, Season advanc'd for going to China, a leaky Ship."[73]

Traders, then, also projected their anxieties onto Native peoples. When the American vessel *Caroline* struck a sunken ledge in 1799, Captain Richard Cleveland noted that his situation "was now one of the most painful anxiety, no less from the prospect of losing our vessel and the rich cargo of furs we had collected with so much toil, than from the apprehension of being discovered in this defenceless state by any one of the hostile tribes by whom we were surrounded." Cleveland got himself into an "agonizing state of suspense, watching the horizon to discover if any savages were approaching."[74] There was no attack, and the vessel was repaired and went on its way, but Cleveland, like Colnett, felt the need to document such sentiments. They spoke to traders' suspicions about Native peoples and the problems they had navigating the coast.

When relations between the chiefs of Clayoquot Sound and the crew of the *Columbia* disintegrated in March 1792, John Hoskins wrote himself the following consoling note: "We have endeavoured to gain the good will of all ranks of people belonging to this tribe to instil into their minds noble and generous ideas of our nation and to efface from them all savage principles[.] [T]his in some respects we had the vanity to flatter ourselves was accomplished till this unfortunate period which puts it beyond a doubt that it is impossible for an honest honourable or gratefull principal ever to enter the breast of a savage."[75] This note was consoling because Hoskins sensed that his captain, Robert Gray, had inflamed tension between the two groups. Other traders, and particularly explorers not directly involved in the trade, understood where such platitudes came from. Most traders spent little time among Native peoples and had a superficial understanding of Native agendas. Vancouver stated that it was traders, rather than Native peoples, who often "fomented discords, and stirred up contentions."[76] George Hewitt, surgeon's mate on Vancouver's ship, noted that Kendrick was "one of the worst [traders] and ought to have been taken by Capt V – [Kendrick] ... declared he would fire at a village till they brought him 50 skins & this he intended to do every time he visited the N.W. Coast."[77] And Francois Péron, a French officer on the American trading vessel *Otter*, which was on the coast in 1796, observed that "the European sailors have exercised vengeances which are too severe as reprisals for some insult or for some surprise which they feel they have reason to complain of ... [and] some of them, after having welcomed the Indians with the appearance of friendship, wanted to take their peltries by force."[78] Even Sturgis, one of the most enlightened and insightful traders, suggested that trading relations were often volatile because it was "scarcely possible" to comprehend Native motivations or to interpret their "incongruous and seemingly conflicting statements."[79]

Could traders trust Natives? Did friendship preclude the possibility of attack? Maritime fur traders asked themselves such questions frequently, and it was they who used incongruous statements to capture their uncertainties. What did traders mean when they talked of the "pretended humour" of the Natives or the "savage dignity" of a chief?[80] Experience and insight were overlaid with "New Ideas, that naturally crowd in the Imagination; of the Savage Customs and Manners of the Indians," as Peter Puget, one of Vancouver's officers, noted upon stumbling across some severed heads in "Puget's Sound."[81] I quote Puget to highlight that this tension between observation and presumption, insight and imagination, was not peculiar to traders. The journals of Cook and his officers – indeed, those of any explorer or trader in non-European space during this era – trade on this tension. And, like Cook's officers, the Europeans and Americans involved in the maritime fur trade had different personalities and literary talents, and came from different backgrounds, all of which affected what they wrote. Cook's team distinguished "the Nootkans" from other Pacific peoples; maritime fur traders also compared different Native peoples and different parts of the Pacific. As James Gibson notes: "Shipmasters invariably remarked the stark (and welcome) contrast between the forbidding Northwest Coast – rainy and chilly and peopled by what they considered dirty, sullen, and hostile Indians – and the inviting Sandwich Islands, which were sunny and warm and inhabited by seemingly clean, cheerful, and friendly Polynesians."[82] Sturgis thought that many American traders formed an opinion of Northwest Coast Native societies "from the wretched, degraded remnants of the tribes who formerly occupied New England."[83]

Yet traders did not connect questions of representation to issues of scientific observation and epistemology to the extent that explorers did, and most of them probably did not expect that their journals would wind up in bookshops.[84] They were not operating within the framework of Enlightenment I discussed in Part 1. The mode of enunciation of the maritime fur trade was private, competitive, and vitriolic. "The general practice among traders on this coast is always to mislead competitors as far they can even at the expense of truth," one trader explained.[85] "Truth" meant different things to these traders than it did to Cook. Traders' truths about Native peoples were vexed, inward-looking platitudes that were conditioned by competition and fear.

The maritime fur trade was shot through with anxiety, deception, and hostility. We can neither understand the nature of traders' representations nor explain the mechanics of the trade by making clinical distinctions between fact and fiction, reality and illusion, and prejudice and fair-mindedness. Traders such as Meares had what Archibald Menzies (Vancouver's surgeon-botanist) described to Joseph Banks as a "fertile fancy" for truth: purposefully and sometimes unknowingly producing misleading statements, particularly about each other but also about Native peoples.[86] Their lines about the "savage ways" of the Indians were not simply rooted in a set of late eighteenth-century British and American ideas about non-Western societies. Hoskins's claim that it was "impossible for an honest honourable or gratefull principal ever to enter the breast of a savage," and other such blanket statements, were responses to the often illusory itinerate geographies I have sketched. Traders could not assume that Native peoples would view them as superiors. Native peoples played nuanced commercial games with traders. And Native attacks on trade vessels proved that Native peoples did not shy away from conflict just because the traders had greater firepower.

Traders presented "scenes of fear and desire."[87] This phrase comes from Homi Bhabha, who argues that we should not analyze Western discourses of the Other with a priori normative categories of truth or equality and then categorize statements as positive or negative. Such analyses fail to grasp the complexity and productivity of such discourses. Colonial discourses, particularly, he argues, were mediated by aggressive and narcissistic processes of identification that positioned the colonizer and the colonized in a cultural-racial-historical hierarchy. Bhabha has shown how stereotypical discourses entangled the colonizer and the colonized in a web of psychic, social, and imaginary relations. "The fetish or stereotype" is not a misrepresentation of reality or a distortion of the truth, he reasons, but "an arrested, fixated form of representation" characterized by "a repertoire of conflictual positions." The stereotype "gives access to an 'identity' which is predicated as much on mastery and pleasure as it is on anxiety and defence, for it is a form of multiple and contradictory belief in its recognition of difference and disavowal of it"; otherness is an object of both "desire and derision."[88] These conflictual positions do not necessarily impede or impoverish colonialism; this "mixing and splitting" of signification became a strategy of appropriation and mechanism of control: a way of articulating, visualizing, and legislating difference, justifying imperial expansion, and proving the necessity of colonial domination.[89] Bhabha's general point is that while the concept of fixity – the constitution of the colonial subject as "other" yet knowable, distant yet visible – is central to colonial discourse, representations of otherness are neither monolithic nor immortal. Statements about foreignness are tied to systems of enunciation that shift through time and over space in response to different needs.

Now this same mixing and splitting of signification can be found in the maritime fur trade. We can detect a "conflictual economy" of representation in traders' journals. Some of the first traders expected Native peoples to be gullible but soon discovered that they were astute traders. Yet "astuteness" was often translated as "cunning." The American merchant Sullivan Dorr, for example, informed his brother that "these cunning savages ... are great Merchant traders."[90] Some of the first traders thought that Native peoples would desire trinkets (by implication, "childish things") and would want "to imitate their somewhat more polished visitors" (as Sturgis noted), but he found that Native groups had very particular wants and desires. Yet single-mindedness was often translated as "audacity" or "insolence." "We found at our cost," Meares wrote, "that these people [of Vancouver Island] ... possessed all the cunning necessary to the gains of mercantile life."[91] And Walker noted: "The Savage, who is nevertheless dishonest, pretends to be Scrupulous, and exact in his dealings."[92] To return to Bhabha: many traders viewed Natives as "mystical, primitive, single-minded and yet the most worldly and accomplished of liars." Desire was split by derision; mastery was mixed with anxiety.

But this "repertoire of conflictual positions" in the maritime fur trade was obviously tied to a different system of enunciation than the ones Bhabha has in mind. He is interested foremost in the pronouncements of imperial thinkers, Orientalists, missionaries, and colonial administrators. As such he focuses on particular forms of address: the inscription of racial pre-eminence, national and cultural superiority, and forms of colonial paternalism/tutelage. He thinks of desire and fetishism mainly in psychoanalytical terms, and, as one critic charges, he tends to allot "ontological priority to the semiotic process" and is less interested in "the substance of the narrated event."[93] Bhabha discusses the command functions of colonial discourse – the complex ways in which colonial subjects are formed and placed under authority through language. He does not discuss cases such as the maritime fur trade, which was not wrapped up with an official imperial agenda, and where the machinations of desire and fetishism were modelled on the commodity and commercial relations of production rather than on empire. Bhabha's insights are important, but they need to be recontextualized on the Northwest Coast. These traders did not address Native peoples in any official colonial capacity, and most of them did not have a public audience in mind when they compiled their journals. Their concerns were "basic and personal," Mary Malloy argues. Traders invoked daily life at sea, memories of home, and the search for profits.[94] And Bhabha eschews discussion of conflict and physical antagonism, which were rife in the trade. So how might these traders' forms of address be conceptualized?

Michael Taussig's work offers some clues. He has traced these "scenes of fear and desire" beyond the stacks of the colonial library and found them at work in the Colombian jungle, in the Putumayo rubber boom at the beginning of the twentieth century, which brought together creole traders and Indians in a horrific danse macabre of torture and murder. Taussig looks at the efforts of various witnesses of the rubber trade to explain the atrocities to a British Select Committee.[95] Their testimony was characterized by an "intimate codependence of truth on illusion and myth on reality," mimicking the rubber trade itself, and the Select Committee struggled to understand the terror. British officials could not work out who was to blame for the violence. They sensed that the two groups were locked together in a commercial battle of fear and fantasy, where terror seemed to have a life of its own. Nor could they understand the mechanics of the rubber trade using the language of political economy. Terror, these witnesses seemed to relate, was more a "form of life" than a "utilitarian means of production." The Select Committee was left with two shady images: "the horror of the jungle and the horror of savagery." Or, as Taussig describes the terror in his characteristically ebullient prose, these "were in effect new rituals, rites of conquest and colony formation, mystiques of race and power, little dramas of civilization tailoring savagery which did not mix or homogenize ingredients from the two sides of the colonial divide but instead bound Indian understandings of white understandings of Indians to white understandings of Indian understandings of whites."[96]

Taussig shows how these witnesses populated the rubber boom with desire, fear, and horror, and he documents how these atrocities in the dark fringes of the capitalist-colonial world evaded categorization and analysis in the metropole. He thinks of the machinations of desire and derision in terms of complex, physical, and textured filaments of attraction and repulsion, fear and longing, that were based on the allure of the commodity and visions of profit. Presuppositions, imputations, meanings, and justifications shuffled uneasily between Colombia and London, and between the Indians and the traders themselves. Taussig asks us to "listen to these stories [presented to the Select Committee] neither as fiction nor as disguised signs of truth, but as real."[97] We might want to distinguish between the reality of the rubber boom and depictions of it, but "the disturbing thing is that the reality seeped through the pores of the depiction and by means of such seepage continued what such depictions were meant only to be about"; the forms of terror that the rubber traders devised "mirrored the horror of the savagery they both feared and fictionalized."[98]

What Taussig draws out, I think, is that space – in this case in the guise of the jungle/savagery – is not an inert plane on which colonial and commercial discourses unfold, but a material *and* imaginative medium through which desire and derision is visualized and articulated. He suggests that the Putamayo region was a conduit of enunciation as well as a site of commercial interaction; an imaginative, tropical space of chronic capitalist misadventure through which rubber traders and Indians encountered and fictionalized each other – both a figurative space that encapsulated the fetishism of the commodity and a thoroughly material space of torture and death.[99] There was no retreat from the horror of the jungle and savagery – no vantage point from which this canvas of terror could be pictured, surveyed, and rationalized. The facts of the rubber boom – the numbers killed or maimed for the price of so many tons of rubber – conjured up the terror but could not explain it.

The maritime fur trade was by no means as horrific as the Putumayo rubber boom, but Taussig's notion of "the real" might be extended to the Northwest Coast. When traders tried to summarize their transactions, they invoked two basic motifs: the *obstinacy* of the coast and the Indians, and the *absurdity* of the business. While trading around the northern end of Vancouver Island in June 1791, for instance, the crew of the *Columbia* were ordered not to offend the Natives, but contact over the ensuing weeks was filled with tension. Hoskins believed that the Indians were not given "umbrage," but he reflected: "No doubt it is too often the case that sailors ... from their ignorance of the [Native] language, either miscomprehend the natives, or the natives them; thus each deeming the other insulted, a quarrel ensues, and the officers who are on shore fall a sacrifice to it. [A]s well in civilized, so in savage governments; from small causes, great evils spring."[100] The stormy coast added a particular spray to these connections between "small causes" and "great evils." In 1791, the *Columbia* got into a number of precarious situations, and Hoskins noted that traders' fears about their own safety were "easier to be conceived than described."[101] Compounding these problems of navigation, the maritime fur trade also seemed to have its own economic logic. Sturgis used the phrase "absurdity" to capture the way traders and Native peoples fashioned hybrid and often volatile spaces of transaction. Traders conjured up *spaces of miscomprehension.* Ideas about the Indian that had clean lives in the Western imaginary – clean lives at home, where "Indians" were geographically as well as rhetorically distant from Whites – tarried nervously on a treacherous coast with muckier, physical encounters with difference.

Many traders wrote about the harshness of the coast. "Heavens knows what wilds of America are on our side of the Continent" Sturgis observed, "but I am sure on this [side] they may be called the wildest of the wild."[102] And Charles Bishop wrote of "this Savage coast."[103] There were few panoramas on the coast and little to please the eye of a weary trader. "No cultivated fields, no towns, no hamlets, or cottages enliven the prospect to a sailor as he views the land after a long voyage," Silas Holbrook wrote to his fellow Bostonians.[104] "The Country, as far as the Eye can penetrate," Alexander Walker despaired, "presents nothing to view, but a succession of Stupendenous and broken Mountains."[105]

Some traders remarked that Native life was stamped by this physical scene of wildness, danger, desolation, and deprivation. "Nature has implanted in him an extraordinary feeling and sagacity for his preservation against dangers to which he is incessantly exposed," Walker noted.

> It is this that creates so many unfavourable features of his Character. Always expecting injuries, and always exposed to danger, all his thoughts are employed about his own safety. He becomes suspicious, deceitful and treacherous ... The life of a Savage is mixed with uncertainty and privations: but its excitements and its habits are dear to him. Custom and ignorance are necessary in our Eyes to reconcile a Savage to his existence. How differently does he view his situation! Every attempt to reconcile him to the Ease and luxuries of civilized Life have failed. After enjoying them for a short time, and when he had the option of enjoying them for Ever, he has preferred all the hardships of his former state, and to cover himself again with the Skins of Wild Beasts.[106]

And in 1811 Robert Kemp asked his American readers to

Stop and Consider the lamentable fate of a sailor who is Exposed to the frozen Regions of the polar Cold ... [T]his is a Horrid Country for anay man to Exist in in my Opinion it is Neither fit for Habitation Cultivation nor Vegetation for any Human Being ... I have no idea of anay Misery more Extreme then what the Natives of his Country do absolutely suffer there Suffering Certainly are Adequate to the Crimes that they are daily guilty of they are a terrible Savage Inhuman Race of Beings as Ever Existed they have no Fortitude in bearing disappointments they have no Compassion nor Benelovence towards their Fellow Creatures they have no Sense of gratitude to Retaliate favours bestowed towards on them on the whole they are hard hearted [and] Revengeful in Every Sense of the word.[107]

This was not strictly geographical determinism. Was it the Indian or the trader who always expected "injuries" and was "exposed to danger"? Was it the life of "a Savage" or the life of the trader that was "mixed with uncertainty and privation"? Was it only Native peoples whose sufferings were "adequate" to their crimes? The Indian's preference for "the hardships of his former state" over "the Ease and luxuries of civilized Life" spoke to the absurdity of the business – the sense that traders did not always understand the ways in which Native peoples sized up goods.

It was the "horrid" coast in all of its manifestations – the cold and damp, dangerous navigation, shipboard discipline and deprivation, tyrannical captains, dangerous Natives, absurd trade relations – that made the sufferings of the maritime fur trade "real." Mary Malloy documents the violence of American traders towards their crews and Native peoples. Native peoples retaliated and ships' crews attempted mutiny.[108] There was no Archimedean point on the coast from which to survey and essentialize the trade – just an ensemble of sites and situations within the trade itself from which statements about the particular and the general, about place and space, could be articulated. Traders' representational tropes were mediated by physical and psychical difficulties.

To some extent, of course, traders tried to represent themselves on an axis of savagery and civilization by resorting to images of "home" and drawing stark contrasts. As some of the quotations above suggest, traders associated civilization with the welcoming, picturesque landscapes of England and New England (or the luxurious islands of the Pacific), and savagery with the hostile coast. The panorama versus the precipice. As Edward Said has argued, to some degree people and societies derive their identities negatively, "our" land being the counterpart of "theirs."[109] Yet often, he continues, "the sense in which someone feels himself to be not-foreign is based on a very unrigorous idea of what is 'out there,' beyond one's own territory. All kinds of suppositions, associations, and fictions appear to crowd the unfamiliar space outside one's own."[110] Maritime fur traders came to the Northwest Coast with "dark aspirations" of what was out there, as Holbrook put it. "It is utterly beyond my power to describe my present feelings," Ralph Haskins wrote in 1800 as he left Boston on the *Atahualpa*: "I have separated from my dearest Friends ... I have embarked on a voyage doubtful, and dangerous; which there is but little hopes of completing in less than three long years. Most of the time must be spent at sea, or among uncivilized Barbarians, whose treachery and savage ferocity are proverbially notorious. What a prospect!"[111]

But traders did not just look to home when they tried to impute difference and distance between themselves and Natives. They also turned to their own immediate, physical circumstances. They saw the coast and its Native inhabitants through Western eyes, but the contact process also raised personal and performative questions that needed to be answered. Traders may have considered themselves superiors, but how could such ideas be said to work on the ground, in Native space, when Native peoples did not necessarily see or treat them as such? "Home" was in some respects an empty abstraction for traders because Native peoples did not see them in their homes reaping the material benefits of their business on the coast.

Some traders claimed that they were treated like royalty by Native chiefs, and some Native chiefs, to be sure, were treated as such by traders. As I will show, the sea otter business entailed a complex set of negotiations between White and Native leaders. These bonds did not come about because the White man had an awe-inspiring presence; they were spurred by Native agendas. And a far more uncivilized world loitered around these high-level bonds. Here were crewmen cramped in dingy and unsanitary vessels exchanging goods such as iron bars and copper kettles that had been stripped of their Western "just-so" connotations. I think that Sturgis's story about the chief of the Hanslong tribe registering the absurdity of "placing brass balls on iron fences in front of your houses" (my epigraph for this chapter) points to traders' concerns over the way Natives saw them. How could traders demonstrate to Native peoples that they came from civilized societies when it was not apparent from the way they looked or lived? Could imaginary lines of difference be drawn across the trading process itself? I suggest that traders tried to draw imaginary lines separating self and other by "envisioning capital" in particular ways.

"ENVISIONING CAPITAL"

Susan Buck-Morss uses this phrase to argue that abstract concepts such as "economy" have to undergo a process of "representational mapping" before people can grasp their explanatory value and personal implications.[112] She discusses Adam Smith's way of picturing the relationship between the self-interested producer/consumer and the economy as a whole – especially his attempt to suggest to the individual that happiness is rooted in the restless pursuit of things.[113]

The "representational maps" that maritime fur traders drafted were by no means as sophisticated as Smith's. They were not trying to picture capitalism as a whole. But traders did mull over this question of how to picture their transactions.

Some traders appealed to notions of luxury and possession to mark their distance from Native peoples. Indians, on Walker's view, were people who could not quite hold on to "objects of comfort." Natives' seemingly "absurd" notions of demand and price, and the specific (or "whimsical") nature of their desires, were seen as characteristics of a savage society. Sturgis remarked that the influx of European goods "brought with it its concomitants – luxury and want of economy ... [T]he Indians, with that want of forethought natural to a people in an uncivilized state, did not reflect on the possibility of their supplies [of non-Native goods] hereafter being more limited and made no provision against future wants."[114] They would be rich one year but poor the next, having traded or consumed the goods they had obtained. Sturgis and Walker thought that the Indians of the coast were primitive because they did not know how to accumulate wealth and escape the bounds of necessity.

Still, traders found it difficult to explain why *their* desires were any more civilized than those of Native groups. How could traders claim that they enjoyed the comforts of material life and had escaped the realm of necessity when their crews were often starved or plagued with scurvy, dysentery, or rheumatic fever by the time they reached the coast and had to rely on Native groups to trade them fresh food? If the civility/comfort of White ways was not apparent from traders' apparel or decorum, then where might traders say it came from?

Traders tried to argue that they were superior merchants by emphasizing that Native peoples were ignorant of the global scale of the sea otter business and, hence, of the profit margins that could be obtained. Native peoples might regale themselves with stories of how they tricked a guileless trader, but they did not realize that once the trader had left the coast his cargo could still rise in value as furs were traded at Canton for tea, silks, and porcelain or for bills of exchange, and as these goods were shipped to London or Boston. The trader Myers wrote: "The canoes ... bringing the produce of Sea and Land, have a tendency to excite respect for man even in a savage state ... Here we procured a great number of Otter, Marten, and Beaver Skins. The articles we trafficked for them were trivial; but it should be considered that so ignorant were the inhabitants, that they readily parted with an Otter skin, for a small Iron spear, which on in China, produced us 80 dollars."[115] Native groups drove much harder bargains than this, and Myers's details are fanciful, even for the early years of the trade. But his general message – one that many traders bought into – was that the "comforts of life" afforded by the sea otter trade were not manifested on the coast itself; they were only revealed during this longer course of commercial transactions. They were revealed through the fetishistic structures of credit, debt, and indebtedness that characterize the capitalist mode of production and, Patrick Brantlinger has argued, nation- and empire-building.[116] "The articles hitherto employed in the purchase of America furs, &c. are in themselves but of small value, when compared with the prices which these furs obtain at China and other markets," John Meares declared; "their acquired value is of no trifling consideration."[117] Civilization was to be found at the end of this round trip (known as the "golden round") from London or Boston to the Northwest Coast, to Canton, and back home, where traders cashed in their cargoes and went out and bought a new suit of clothes and other "comforts." Civilization, on Meares's account, was beyond the scope of Native vision. "You," the Indian, are of trifling consideration because "I," the trader, know of other lands and riches. The irony, of course, which was not lost on many traders, was that Native peoples had their own circuits of commercial interaction and their own ways of enhancing the value of their goods through trade.

Traders, then, used images of the global nature of the sea otter business as "representational maps" with which to abstract themselves from the hardships and incongruities of commercial contact and to picture their lives as ultimately more comfortable than those of Native peoples. Sticking close to the object of their voyages, they tried to account for civility and savagery by thinking about their working lives at sea; by emphasizing that the maritime fur trade was a space-economy with different tiers; and by reassuring themselves that Native peoples had access to only a part of this commercial space.[118] Reminding himself that his objects of comfort had been gained from hard work and the occasional panic, Sturgis told a captive Boston audience that it would "give him more pleasure to look at a splendid sea-otter skin, than to examine half the pictures that are stuck up for exhibition, and puffed up by pretended connoisseurs."[119] His aesthetic was resolutely commercial and corporeal.

When the trade was discussed by people who were not involved in it, these notions of absurdity and obstinacy were often strained into harder-nosed statements that reflected dominant American and European views of Indians. American and British newspapers suggested that acts of Native violence were rooted in an essential and timeless difference between the Indian and the trader – the former, unpredictable and therefore savage, the latter honourable, daring, and civilized. Here, for example, is a stanza from a ballad titled *The Bold Northwestman*, published in Boston in the early nineteenth century, which dramatizes an attempt by a Native group of the Queen Charlotte Islands to seize the American brig *Washington* in June 1791:

I'd have you all take warning and always be ready,
For to suppress those savages of Northwest America;
For they are so desirous some vessel for to gain,
That they will never leave it off, till most of them are slain.[120]

This ballad echoes the sentiments of prominent late eighteenth-century American writers such as Timothy Dwight, who wrote about the Indian in his epic poem *Greenfield Hill* (1794):

> Fierce, dark, and jealous, is the exotic soul,
> That, cell'd in secret, rules the savage breast.
> There treacherous thoughts of gloomy vengeance roll,
> And deadly deeds of malice unconfess'd;
> The viper's poison rankling in its nest.[121]

In such texts the Westerner is prised away from the Indian and resituated in a more detached and axiomatic cultural realm of right and wrong, us and them. The world of the real (the harsh two-way world of commerce and these "representational maps" of possession, comfort, and deprivation) was transposed and simplified.

These processes of information circulation and reinscription aggravated the conflictual economy of truth of the maritime fur trade. Just as the British officials at the Select Committee on the Putumayo rubber boom struggled to explain the nature of the terror, so many European observers of the maritime fur trade struggled to understand the nature of Native-White interaction. When C.P. Claret Fleurieu (a distinguished naval historian who edited the journal of Etienne Marchand) tried to criticize traders' methods on moral grounds, he could not escape the complexities of the real – these "itinerate geographies" – and simply ended up with a set of questions and equivocations:

> Have ... [traders] never endeavoured to take an unfair advantage of the ignorance which they supposed in the Americans [Indians]? Have they, in the beginning, acted with the honesty, the sincerity which ought to be the basis of trade, especially of barter, and which is not always the basis of transactions between Europeans? In short, will they not deceive themselves still, when they imagine that they can do so with safety? ... I am not an apologist for savage people ... I am not examining here whether man be good, or whether he be wicked through his nature, nor what he may have lost or gained in the state of great societies; but let us not judge so precipitately, and without knowing them, the people of that unhappy AMERICA which has so much reason to complain of us.[122]

In other words, what did it mean to take unfair advantage? To buy the Indians' furs cheaply and sell them at a profit? To blow up Indian villages or take hostages? Were Indians being conned because they were ignorant of the real value of their goods? Was the trader deceiving himself when he thought he could trick Indians without impunity? Was there anything inherently sincere about barter? Or was honesty simply a wise commercial policy in light of the fact that Natives and traders did not fully understand each other's ways of transacting? In any case, who could tell when the Native or the trader was being honest? By the time Marchand got to the coast in 1791, Native peoples had many things to complain about and many reasons for looking on traders as inherently dishonest.

However hard Fleurieu and Marchand thought about the maritime fur trade, and however much they wanted to rationalize it for a European audience, they could not escape the knotted realm of desire and derision, mastery and anxiety, that characterized the trade.[123] The meddlesome coast, and the murky processes of interaction that went with the trade, could not be given a single meaning or purpose.

If these traders were appropriating Native life, then it was with these visions of capital and the physical and psychical lines of power that went with them. There were only a few spots on the coast – Nootka Sound was one of them – that traders knew well enough and visited frequently enough to feel comfortable with a particular Native chief or group. But even at Nootka Sound such relations lasted only until 1803, when the crew of the *Boston* was slaughtered. When John Jewitt (the armourer of the *Boston* who survived the massacre) reviewed the circumstances of the disaster in his journal, he noted that the Indians had not forgotten what Captain Hanna had done in 1785.[124]

It is with Hanna, then, that I will conclude this survey of maritime fur traders' conflictual economy of truth. His troubles at Nootka Sound encapsulate this hybrid realm of presumption, speculation, misunderstanding, and anxiety. Hanna was welcomed by the Natives of the sound, but "friendly" intercourse soon disintegrated into conflict. Hanna, it seems, expected an attack on his vessel; either a Native chief had declared war on him the day before or he had been tipped off by another Native group. But what was made of this conflict? In the newspaper reports it is treated as a trial of strength and a statement about the volatility and cunning of Native peoples. Yet the conflict was probably caused by some misunderstanding about trade. There was "some difference about the barter of respective commodities." Equally, Hanna may have incited the ire of the chief who declared war on him by trading with a rival Native group or, as Walker suggested, by shooting a Native person for a minor theft. But having introduced such possibilities, the newspaper reports, and Walker, retreat into platitudes about the Native character. The Natives, according to one of the accounts, were tempted to attack the vessel because of its size, as if to suggest that Native peoples were naturally aggressive. We do not learn what reasons the Native chief had for declaring war; it is likely that Hanna did not understand what he said. Then these correspondents were puzzled about why, so shortly after the attack, trade resumed as usual. Walker speculated that the Natives resumed trade in a mood of submission, having been overwhelmed and overawed by Hanna's firepower, and implied that these Natives did not sense that they had done anything wrong –

that they lived in a land of "perfidy." Walker also saw the Natives' secrecy about this event as a sign of cunning.

In effect, these assessments of Hanna's troubles play with mastery and fear. They dramatize this event and reveal the co-dependence of truth on illusion in the maritime fur trade. The trade was marked by trickery, miscomprehension, and violence. Quantifying such misdeeds, or looking at them within a broader historical perspective in order to make them seem more or less egregious, side-tracks our understanding of commercial engagement. As this founding encounter of the maritime fur trade intimates, representation became increasingly grounded in the geographical contours of the trade and the conditions of maritime life.

This was the agonistic side of the trade, and I have accentuated miscomprehension. I now want to return to traders' appreciation of place and to Native participation in the business along the west coast of Vancouver Island. For there is another way of assessing traders' pretensions: in terms of Native agendas, which can be partially interpreted from archaeological, ethnographic, and historical records.

CHAPTER 7

Native Power and Commercial Contact at Nootka Sound

In the interval between our arrival and the fifth of June [1788], a very brisk trade had been carried on for furs, and we had procured upwards of one hundred and forty sea otter skins. On our first arrival we had stipulated a certain price for every different kind of fur, according to its value; but in the whole business of this traffic they availed themselves of every advantage; and it was our interest, from the views of future benefit, to submit to any deviation they attempted to make from their original agreement.

– JOHN MEARES, *VOYAGES*

NODES, NETWORKS, AND HIERARCHIES

In 1792 John Hoskins wrote a memorandum on the trade for his Boston employers. The Natives of Nootka Sound, he noted, "will not sell a single Skin but for Copper or Muskits or Powder and Shot" and will place little value on iron goods except chisels. But between Cape Cook and Queen Charlotte Strait, "they like Iron the best." South of Nootka Sound "they esteem Chizzels very much," though "all of these places have the same liking for Copper and Muskets that they have at Nootka Sound." Turning to exchange rates, Hoskins noted that "the price of a skin at Nootka sound is ten Iron Chizzels, six inches square of sheet Copper or ten Copper Bangles, for a pistol four skins, for a Musket Six skins[,] for a pearl shell one Skin." Exchange rates were only slightly different at Clayoquot Sound, but they varied much more as one went south. At the mouth of the Strait of Juan de Fuca, a skin was worth five chisels or "a piece of copper as big as your

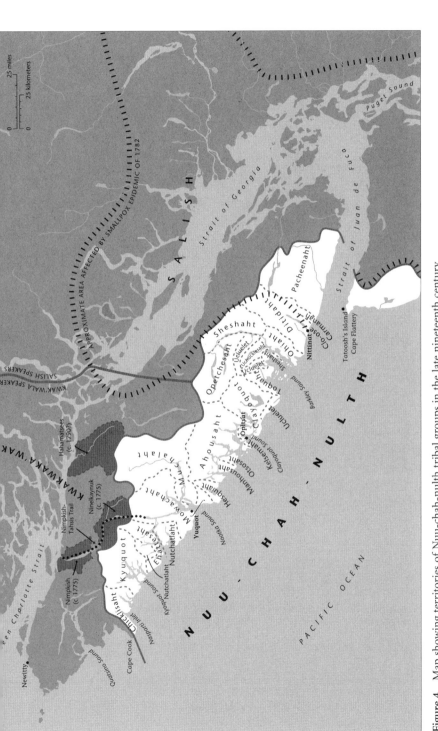

Figure 4 Map showing territories of Nuu-chah-nulth tribal groups in the late nineteenth century

Source: Adapted from Eugene Arima and John Dewhirst, "Nootkans of Vancouver Island," in William C. Sturevant, general ed., *Handbook of North American Indians,* vol. 7, 391-411; Robert Galois, *Kwakwaka'wakw settlements, 1775-1920* (Vancouver: UBC Press, 1994), 237-42, 305-20; Cole Harris, "Voices of smallpox around the Strait of Georgia," *The resettlement of British Columbia* (Vancouver: UBC Press, 1996), 19.

hand"; these Native people valued the clothes traders offered according to the size and number of buttons on them. Around Cape Flattery, Native groups wanted eight copper bangles for a skin and would offer eight skins for a musket (see Figure 4 for these localities).[1]

Written at the height of the trade, Hoskins's memorandum points to the dynamic and uneven commercial geography of the sea otter business around Vancouver Island. Native groups wanted different collections of commodities and established different prices for them. At Nootka Sound, the Natives were no longer "most desirous of iron" (more precisely "Chizzels," or cuttoes, which were plain iron bars that could be hammered, hot or cold, into tools or weapons), as Cook had reported.[2] Copper had become a major article of trade and a basic medium of inter-Native commerce.[3] Native groups also wanted firearms, and Gray and Hoskins stated that they had become "expert marksmen and exceedingly troublesome" with them.[4] There were elaborate and extensive Native trade networks in Native and non-Native goods as well as in slaves. In 1792 some traders told one of Vancouver's officers that they had identified articles possessed by the Natives of Cape Flattery and the Columbia River that they had sold to Natives north of the Queen Charlotte Islands.[5] A pewter basin stamped with "La Flovie V. Francais" (from the French vessel *La Flavie*), traded to Natives at Nootka Sound in late May 1792, was owned by the Nimpkish of "Cheslakees" village on the northeast coast of Vancouver Island when Vancouver's party visited them on 20 July 1792.[6] Thomas Manby, another of Vancouver's officers, was in no doubt that trade goods passed through many hands and that Native groups were very mobile: "Many of our commodities have found their way to situations far removed ... and if we understood them [the Natives] right, it is not uncommon for a trading party to make a voyage for one or two Moons."[7] As traders plied the coast, they started to appreciate the connections and differences between Native groups, and they got entangled in Native agendas and rivalries. Traders crossed Native networks of trade and power; they did not set them in motion.[8]

As I have indicated, it is difficult to generalize about the impact of the trade on Native groups. Historical records can be compared with archaeological and ethnographic materials to gain a fuller picture of early contact, but these three data sets contain different kinds of evidence, are mediated by different methodological problematics, and cannot easily be spliced together. These sources can be synthesized to a certain extent, however, and some degree of regional synthesis is warranted since the principal scholars of the trade – Howay and, more recently, James Gibson – have produced ageographical generalizations. Archaeologists and anthropologists are beginning to present more regionally nuanced pictures of Native life before and after contact, and I do not think that we can interpret Native participation in the trade fully unless we think about the time-geography I have just discussed.

The maritime fur trade was more short-lived on Vancouver Island than on other parts of the coast. By 1800, most traders headed for Newitty on the northern tip of Vancouver Island when they arrived on the coast, and from there they generally sailed north rather than south.[9] The trade was also concentrated in particular areas. I compare contact relations at Nootka Sound and Clayoquot Sound (the main centres of trade on Vancouver Island) and track their impact on outlying areas (roughly, from Brooks Peninsula to the Strait of Juan de Fuca) (see Figure 4). I will preface this regional geography by situating Nuu-chah-nulth agendas in a more holistic ethnographic context.

NUU-CHAH-NULTH SOCIOPOLITICAL ARRANGEMENTS

The "local group" was the basic unit of Nuu-chah-nulth social and political organization. The ethnographer Philip Drucker argued that social organization centred on "a family of chiefs who owned territorial rights, houses, and various other privileges," and who "bore a name, usually that of their 'place' (a site at their fishing ground where they 'belonged'), or sometimes that of a chief; and had a tradition, firmly believed, of descent from a common ancestor."[10] A local group was comprised of one or more family lines, or "ushtakamhl," each of which had its own house containing chiefs who were ranked according to their genealogical proximity to a common ancestor.[11] The chief of the most important family line led the local group, and a large ushtakamhl sometimes subdivided, with lesser chiefs building separate houses; that is, local groups were built on rank, hereditary ownership, and bonds of kinship, and their territories were demarcated on the landscape.[12] Drucker highlighted that the Nuu-chah-nulth "carried the concept of ownership to an incredible extreme. Not only rivers and fishing places close at hand, but the waters of the sea for miles offshore, the land, the houses, carvings on a house post, the right to marry in a certain way or the right to omit part of an ordinary marriage ceremony, names, songs, dances, medicines, and rituals, all were privately owned property."[13]

Native settlement at Yuquot in Nootka Sound dates back over 4,000 years, and Native peoples have lived on much of the west coast of Vancouver Island for thousands of years.[14] In the earliest centuries of Native settlement around Nootka Sound there were probably a number of small, independent local groups, each of which owned stretches of coastal or inland water where salmon ran, berry and root patches, and hunting grounds. The Nuu-chah-nulth fished, hunted, and collected fruits and vegetables in these territories at different times of the year, but they were primarily sea-oriented peoples who harvested marine life. Native territories became more clearly demarcated as the population of the region increased and groups competed over resource sites – especially fishing grounds.[15] The formalized concepts of ownership described by Drucker were probably in place for a number of centuries before contact.

An individual's social standing was bound up with the number and importance of the privileges he/she owned; privileges over tracts of land and water
were the most important. José Mariano Moziño (a Spanish botanist stationed at
Nootka Sound in 1792) named three "classes": chiefs, or *"taises,"* at the top of the
social ladder, who carried out "the duties of father of the families, of king, and
high priest"; a nobility of *"taiscatlati,"* or "brothers of the chief"; and *"meschimes,"*
or commoners, who were "not brothers or immediate relatives of the *tais.*"[16]
There was a fourth class, slaves, who were captured in wars and were owned and
traded by chiefs. The leader of the local group owned the group's resource territories, hereditary and ritual names, and privileges. Lesser chiefs owned rights to
resource procurement in particular areas and some ceremonial privileges. Commoners were only distantly related to the highest-ranking family line, and only a
chief could enhance their social status. Slaves were the chattel of their owners,
lived at their mercy, and had no rights.[17]

Clearly Nuu-chah-nulth societies were hierarchized. Yet certain responsibili-
ties came with the assumption of economic and ceremonial privileges.[18] Chiefs
relied on the members of the local group to work for them and help them fight
wars. In return for these favours, chiefs were responsible for coordinating the
activities of the local group and protecting the group's village(s) from attack.
Chiefs also had to provide for their families and relatives, and they were expected to reward group members for hard work and valour.[19] High-ranking chiefs
were usually the first to be offered food procured from the local group's resource
sites. Such offerings were an acknowledgment of rank and reaffirmed the social
relations of the group. Chiefs would then redistribute part of what they had
received at feasts given for their group and for visitors. High-ranking Native
people also confirmed and enhanced their status and authority through warfare
and by forming marriage and trade ties with other groups. In short, chiefly power
was performative as well as hereditary.[20]

This social system was conditioned by environmental factors. Native groups
instituted a division of labour, systems of exchange and redistribution, and social values (such as prestige) in order to cope with cycles of abundance and scarcity.[21] The feast (or potlatch) system was a basic social institution. As Wayne
Suttles explains: "a man's affinals are his allies against his importunate blood kin.
Perhaps a man can save better by giving to his affinals, who are honor-bound to
return the gifts when he needs them for potlatching, than by keeping his food
and wealth at home only to have it used up by his own blood kin, whom he is
honor-bound to support."[22] The local group would suffer if wealth was retained
in too few hands or if chiefs were too miserly. Chiefly beneficence was a method
of coping with environmental flux. In times of need, local groups also warred
with neighbours (absorbing new resource sites) or formed alliances with them.[23]

Drucker and Edward Sapir claimed that local groups were primarily kin communities based on bilateral descent.[24] Individuals could often choose to affiliate

with one of a number of groups because they could find relatives in a number of places.[25] Nuu-chah-nulth kinship networks permitted, and in a sense encouraged, individuals to shift residences and change their group affiliations. Local groups could be fairly fluid. People sometimes moved if the group they were with had been decimated by war or disease, but many chose to move. Since "class" was based on kinship – the social rank of one's parents and primogeniture – one's choice of residence would be influenced by genealogical factors. The Nuu-chah-nulth considered how closely they were related to a chiefly family, and they would usually want to live with a high-ranking family.[26]

People who were only distantly related to an important line of descent might change residence a number of times during their lives, and Drucker understood that they were often given minor privileges "in an effort to bind them more surely to their chiefs."[27] Indeed, Drucker got the impression from his informants "that there was a continual stream of people, mostly of low rank, pouring in and out of the houses."[28] When lower-rank people were thinking about where to live, they would have considered how generous their superiors had been. Chiefs who did not accumulate enough food or wealth to redistribute, or who were stingy, might lose followers.[29] Chiefs wanted to prevent this, of course, because if they lost followers they would not be able to exploit their economic privileges as effectively as possible. This being the case, Drucker claimed that "both the chief and his tenants knew that the former's effective performance of his role, his greatness, depended on the assistance of his tenants."[30]

There were aggregations of Native peoples that were larger than the local group: tribes (characterized by Drucker as two or more local groups sharing a common winter village) and confederacies (a collection of local groups or tribes sharing a summer village).[31] Native peoples united in these intergroup arrangements for a number of reasons: when one group dominated another militarily; for mutual protection; because of inter-marriage; and through mutual consent. Such arrangements lasted for varying lengths of time, and Drucker thought that there was "a very real feeling of solidarity" within them, even though they were not defined entirely by ties of kinship. The social and political integrity of the local group was not undermined as a result of these mergers, however.[32] Sapir explained that each local group retained "its own stock of legends, its distinctive privileges, its own house in the [confederate] village, its old village sites and distinctive fishing and hunting waters that were still remembered in detail by its members."[33] In short, kinship and hereditary rank were the basic organizing principles of Nuu-chah-nulth societies, and Native life along the west coast of Vancouver Island was socially and spatially dynamic.

Now what impact would these social relations have had on the sea otter trade? If Drucker and Sapir are right, then the wealth that traders injected into Native societies would have been perceived and controlled in particular ways. All Native people would have wanted to trade, for wealth was a form of prestige and a means of enhancing social standing. However, a small number of chiefs and their families owned the areas in which sea otters were caught and the waters in which traders anchored. Chiefs therefore controlled access to trade vessels and would have expected to gain most from the sea otter trade. Chiefs could handle the sea otter trade in a number of ways. The most direct way for them to accumulate wealth was by catching and trading sea otters themselves. They could also act as middlemen between traders and Native groups visiting their waters to trade. They could thereby enhance their personal prestige by giving more feasts and using their wealth to seal trade and marriage alliances. If chiefs were generous with their affiliates, then they might also consolidate their authority over the local group and attract more followers. Whether or not this was a viable strategy depended on a number of factors, the main one being the number of trade vessels and local groups involved in the trade. If, say, there were five vessels in a small area trading with five local groups in an area (i.e., among people who could probably find relatives in a number of places), then Native people who held few or unimportant privileges might choose to live with the chief who was doing the best business and redistributing the most wealth. Monopolization, seemingly, would best suit chiefs who could control the traffic in furs and keep their followers contented.

Monopolization was not the only or the most sensible option, however. Chiefs and their relatives could catch only a certain number of sea otters; if a number of trade vessels appeared in their waters at the same time, then they might run out of furs quickly and miss a trading opportunity. Chiefs could expand their economic horizons by trading or warring with other groups. It made equal sense for them to allow their followers to hunt or trade on their behalf. Chiefs would collect the wealth from these ventures and redistribute some of it, or they would allow their people to keep a portion of what they had traded. With this inclusionary strategy, chiefs might generate wealth while solidifying group affiliation. But by opening up the trade to the local group in these ways, chiefs could also lose a certain amount of control. They would have to gauge how much time and how many people could be devoted to the sea otter business without disrupting the resource procurement regimen of the group; Whites generally did not trade food. Local group members might hoard trade items or use them to attain a higher status in another village. Warfare also created social difficulties – especially divided loyalties – because of the geographical extensiveness of kin links.[34] If chiefs did not assess these possibilities, then their strategies of group inclusion and territorial expansion could become as self-defeating as monopolization.

These are abstract scenarios, but I suggest that they were all present in some shape or form in the maritime fur trade on Vancouver Island and that they were negotiated in different ways by the chiefs of Nootka Sound and Clayoquot Sound. Native agendas were also affected by the depletion of sea otter stocks and, in places, by the spread of disease. Nicholas Thomas has questioned the deployment of ethnographical reconstructions in the study of Native-White interaction because they tend to posit "an authentic indigenous form out of time."[35] And Richard White warns of the perils of ethnographic "upstreaming" – working with ideas and data collected decades and centuries after contact to interpret Native agendas; many ethnographies stress cultural continuity, if not an essential or timeless Indianness.[36] I accept these cautions but know, like Thomas and White, that we all upstream our data to some degree, that ethnographies feature in some Native invented traditions, and that by ignoring ethnographic material altogether we are thrown back onto the imperialisms and blinkers of the historical record. Drucker and Sapir knew that they were not recording a timeless Native past. They judged their ethnographic horizon to be the mid-to-late nineteenth century, and they worked with some historical records.[37] And Sapir, especially, sensed that his early twentieth-century Native interlocutors viewed him as a political intermediary as well as an ethnographer.[38] It is impossible to weigh up the theory-ladenness of their analyses, but these scholars were also chronicling social processes that traders encountered and, in part, observed.[39] I suspect that what both traders and these ethnographers picked up was a chiefly view of the world; it also seems that they were implicated in the elaboration of chiefly power. I work with their ideas and statements cautiously.

COMMERCIAL CONTACT AND CHIEFLY POWER AT NOOTKA SOUND

In 1786 James Strange (with the vessels *Captain Cook* and *Experiment*) named Yuquot "Friendly Harbour" (see Figure 5).[40] In spite of Hanna's troubles, the first traders to reach the sound regarded it as a safe harbour and a profitable trade location. They noted, as did Cook, that the Native groups of the sound had sharply defined territories and notions of property and that Native access to trading vessels was controlled by chiefs. This chiefly mediation was one of the main reasons why interaction was for the most part orderly. Native-White interaction was also calmed, if complicated, by the presence of a Spanish military garrison at Yuquot between 1790 and 1795. Spanish officials tried to keep the peace between Natives and traders and formed close ties with the chiefs of the sound, dining with them regularly, attending Native feasts, being invited to important Native events, using Native people as messengers and informants.[41] The American trader Joseph Ingraham suggested that the Native chiefs of the sound had been "polished" by the Spanish; the two groups engaged each other "with a great deal of ceremony – bowing, scraping, adieu senor."[42]

The Spanish explorer Alejandro Malaspina, who visited the Spanish garrison at Yuquot in August 1791, suggested that contact at Nootka Sound was harmonious: "Here the ship is surrounded by canoes, all with some goods for sale, all with the same desire for trade, all coming alongside confusedly in frail canoes, necessarily with frequent collisions, yet here is a silence, a harmony, an order which nothing can break. In the European ports to the contrary, scarcely do two boats alongside a ship touch each other, with any damage whatsoever, and instantly cries are heard from all sides and not infrequently an assault follows requiring the intervention of the Law."[43]

This image of harmony was perhaps a facade, however. Spanish officials used images of friendship and order for propaganda purposes in order to appease their bosses in New Spain and Madrid, who had instructed them to be beneficent towards Native peoples.[44] A Native chief told Malaspina that the Spanish were viewed with "vexation, coldness, and fear."[45] In 1789, Callicum, a chief of Tahsis Inlet, was killed by the Spanish official Don Estevan José Martínez. Maquinna, the highest-ranking chief at Yuquot, fled to Clayoquot Sound for a while in fear of his life, and he moved his people to Aoxsha, a few miles north of Yuquot (see Figure 5).[46] Meanwhile, Martínez billeted his garrison at Yuquot.[47]

This Spanish presence at Yuquot disrupted Maquinna's summer resource procurement regimen and his people began to starve.[48] And it seems that Spanish officials struggled to control their troops. Spain's five-year sojourn at Nootka Sound was peppered with incidents of violence. Spanish troops chased Native women for sex and took house boards from Native villages.[49]

Fur traders only viewed Nootka Sound a safe trading location in comparison with others on the coast, and they, too, assaulted Native peoples. For example, when James Colnett traded at the mouth of Muchalat Inlet in 1787, he became suspicious of Native trade motives and held a Native person hostage until he had a clearer picture of the situation.[50] The following summer William Douglas (one of Meares's associates) purportedly chased Native people up the sound and took provisions by force.[51] And according to Saavedra, the American trader Kendrick cannonaded a Native village on the east side of the sound in July 1791, killing 300 people.[52] British and American traders, and the Spanish, fabricated some stories of violence, and Native peoples, sensing the rivalry between these non-Native groups, also exaggerated reports of conflict for their own ends. But Native-White conflict at Nootka Sound was not fictional.[53] In 1905, Augustus Brabant, a Roman Catholic missionary, was told by Native peoples of the sound that their ancestors remembered what the Spanish and these traders had done. The Natives "had a bitter hatred for the white man since the Spanish fort," Brabant reported; "they suffered bad treatment from whites without taking revenge in fear that they might lose trade [from the British and Americans] & protection [from the Spanish]." After the Spanish left, few vessels visited Nootka Sound, and Chief Maquinna "became spiteful and vowed to plunder the next ship that came."[54] That ship was the *Boston*. Jewitt blamed "the melancholy disasters" that befell traders on "the imprudent conduct of some of the captains and the crews of the ships employed in this trade, in exasperating [Native people] ... by insulting, plundering, and even killing them on slight grounds."[55]

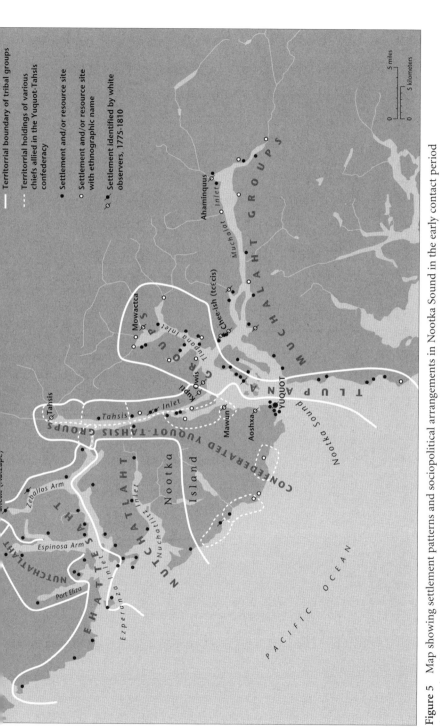

Figure 5 Map showing settlement patterns and sociopolitical arrangements in Nootka Sound in the early contact period

Source: Adapted in part from Philip Drucker, *The northern and central Nootkan tribes*, Smithsonian Institution of American Ethnology Bulletin 144 (Washington, DC: US Government Printing Office, 1951); Yvonne Marshall, "A political history of the Nuu-chah-nulth: A case study of the Mowachaht and Muchalaht tribes" (PhD diss., Department of Archaeology, Simon Fraser University, 1993).

Strange emphasized that he had avoided conflict, but this, he noted, "was more Owing to the Caution I took ... rather than to any Good disposition in them, not to attempt the Commission of Theft, which they were always ready to do whenever an Opportunity Offered."[56] Beneath this veneer of order there remained a level of apprehension and mistrust between traders and Native peoples. John Meares wrote glowingly about the Native chiefs of the sound but was disdainful of the general Native population, stating that "it had been very generally observed by us all that at times, their countenances told a very plain tale of a savage mind."[57]

These platitudes about Native peoples belong to the economy of representation I have outlined. At Nootka Sound, though, which pundits hoped would be the hearth of the sea otter business for many years, traders knew that to be successful they would have to try to understand Native ways.[58] Meares wrote: "We had not the time, even if we had possessed the ability, to have pursued the track of the philosopher and the naturalist. We had other objects before us; and all the knowledge we have obtained was, as it were, accidently acquired in pursuit them."[59] This "knowledge" was about how to trade furs, and since Native chiefs seemed to control the traffic, Meares and other traders mused about them in detail. Alexander Walker was another keen observer of Native social life. He supposed that Maquinna and Callicum were chiefs because they were "highly esteemed by their Countrymen," and continued:

> We were told, that they derived their consequence from the Number of their Male relations and connections. Several Families lived in each of their Houses, and these if we understood them correctly, were connected with them by ties of blood. Some of them fished and hunted for the benefit of their respective Chiefs; while others were ready to attend his Person. The whole composed one family of which the Chief was head. They deposited the joint fruits of their labours in the Chests of their leader, where it remained entirely at his disposal: But in some measure it must be considered as a joint stock, as the Chief was obliged to provide for the whole family.[60]

Walker judged that hereditary right and succession "was the acknowledged order of inheritance" at Nootka Sound, but he also noted that it was "evident that as obedience was voluntary, the exercise of authority must be limited and feeble. The Chiefs to ascertain [sic] extent would probably be elective, and their power would be in proportion to their Personal qualities."[61] Walker and Meares sensed that Native trade methods did not simply flow from some essential "disposition" – or "savage mind" – but were influenced by these "joint stock" economic and political relations.[62]

The chiefs of Nootka Sound apparently pursued an inclusionary contact strategy. Commoners as well as chiefly families participated in the trade. But the chiefs commanded the most furs, monitored the activities of their followers, and accumulated a disproportionate amount of wealth from the trade. When trade vessels visited the sound, especially before and after the Spanish occupation of Yuquot, they were met by many Natives who wanted to trade. Chiefs had the most furs, however, and dealt with vessel masters first.[63] Commoners often had little more than fresh fish to part with.[64] Walker recognized that Maquinna and Callicum were wealthier than anyone else at Yuquot because they employed their relatives as hunters, received tribute from strangers who wanted access to the *Captain Cook* and *Experiment*, and traded for furs with other groups.[65] And with wealth came personal prestige. Meares reported that when these chiefs returned to Yuquot in May 1788 after an expedition, they were received by their followers with fanfare and ceremony.[66]

Traders looked to strike trading relationships with such chiefs. On Vancouver Island, as in other parts of the Pacific, the proffering of presents was an important feature of Native-White interaction. Traders such as Colnett, who had been trained by Cook, grasped the importance of seeking out Native dignitaries when he arrived at a new place and offering some object in order to ingratiate himself, appease Native suspicions, or entice Native groups to trade. Colnett offered grenadiers' caps. The chiefs of the sound usually reciprocated, and traders were sometimes invited ashore for a feast on their arrival. Meares emphasized that Maquinna and Callicum expected to exchange presents before trade commenced.[67] These chiefs accepted many different articles as presents, but they wanted copper sheet and ear-rings, broadcloth and blankets, guns, and powder and shot the most;[68] that is, they took as presents items that they also wanted in trade. Jewitt judged that Native chiefs regarded these presents as an acknowledgment of their status and authority.[69]

Walker and Meares also ascertained that Maquinna and Callicum were ranked differently and performed different duties. When Strange and Walker visited Yuquot and stopped at Callicum's house first, thinking that he was the more important chief, Maquinna was "highly offended at the preference" and explained that he was served by far more people. "Enumerating every thing esteemed valuable at Nootka Arrows, Canoes, Iron, Copper, Skins, he asserted that in all these he was richer than Kurrighum," Walker noted.[70] Once this relationship was understood, Strange tried to encourage Maquinna "to part with everything for furs" and promised the chief that his vessels would return to Nootka Sound "with more Copper and Iron than his house would contain."[71] Meares observed that the districts of Nootka Sound were "more immediately under ... [Maquinna's] command" than Callicum's but that, between them, the dominions of these two chiefs extended as far north as Cape Scott.[72] Meares also noted that Maquinna possessed many slaves.[73] Callicum hunted and collected furs to sell to the vessels and managed the traffic of Native groups visiting the sound.[74] Maquinna entertained the captains of trading vessels, oversaw village affairs at Yuquot, and supervised his people's dealings with traders.[75]

These chiefly relations of power may have made contact at Nootka Sound safe, but they did not entirely satisfy traders. My epigraph from Meares points to traders' equivocations over the contact process. The Natives of Nootka Sound, he declared, "stipulated a certain price for every different kind of fur, according to its value; but in the whole business of this traffic they availed themselves of every advantage; and it was our interest, from the views of future benefit, to submit to any deviation they attempted to make from their original agreement"; and, after a short time, "they changed the whole order of their traffic with us; and instead of common barter, according to the distinct value of the articles exchanged, the whole of our mercantile dealings was carried on by making reciprocal presents."[76] Meares could not determine the reason for this switch and was not sure whether he was being tricked or if these Native peoples simply misunderstood his concept of value.

Walker used stronger words to convey his confusions. The Natives of Yuquot "showed great inconstancy in their desires after different commodities," he noted, "an article being one Day in high estimation, and the next totally despised"; and they used "a thousand little arts" to inflate the value of their goods.[77] Exchange rates fluctuated more as one ventured into the sound.[78] Natives would trade metal goods such as copper kettles, only to turn them into personal ornaments.[79] They would show great interest in certain articles but refuse to trade for them. They sometimes ceased trading after obtaining a certain number of goods, even though they still had furs or other items in their canoes. They would pay great attention to the ships one day and ignore them the next.[80] James Strange wondered why most of the Indians seemed to think that his vessels had visited the sound solely to obtain food.[81] Walker did not understand how Native peoples distinguished between utility and fashion. "They give and receive what is useful," he remarked; yet "profit and conveniency yield, not unseldom even in this state, to vanity."[82] And as the French trader Camille de Roquefeuil remarked in 1818, the Native's vanity case contained a mixture of the old and the new: "a comb, some necklasses and ear-rings, a mirror, some down to serve as powder, and several little bags, with black, white, and red dust."[83]

None of this quite made sense to traders. At Nootka Sound, it was the hybridity and seeming irrationality of these exchange processes and notions of value, rather than the actions of chiefs such as Maquinna and Callicum, that prompted frustration and anxiety. "Among savages," Walker declared, struggling to fathom Native trade methods, "the greatest ferocity, and an extraordinary suavity of manners, follow close Upon each other."[84] For him, the Natives of Yuquot had unpredictable standards of trade: they were generous, sincere, and kind one minute but selfish, savage, and rude the next; they were fair traders one minute but devious and secretive the next. Walker hammered home his message by informing his readers that the South Sea Islanders, "who are Cannibals, guilty of Murdering their Children ... are at the same time distinguished by their mild, social and hospitable disposition."[85] By the end of his stay at Nootka Sound, Walker was convinced that Maquinna and Callicum, who appeared initially to be competitors, had conspired to deceive their visitors.[86] And Strange suspected that acts of theft were committed "with the Connivance & perhaps at the special Command" of these chiefs.[87] Meares and Colnett were less discriminating with their accusations, calling the Native peoples of the sound fickle and indolent.[88]

These frustrations were compounded by issues of cannibalism and sexual licence. Most late eighteenth-century European explorers and traders looked for signs of cannibalism when they were in unfamiliar territory; it was seen as a litmus test of savagery and cultural difference.[89] Maritime fur traders and Spanish officials tried to determine whether the Natives of Nootka Sound were cannibals, and Native chiefs, cognizant of this form of enquiry, toyed with White fears. The Spanish bought children from Maquinna for sheets of copper under the impression that he would have otherwise devoured them.[90] And Captain Péron, who was at Nootka Sound in 1796, reported that when he questioned Maquinna about a six-year-old he was carrying around, the chief responded: "I plan to have him for my supper."[91] Native men also frustrated sailors by toying with their licentiousness. The prostitution of Native women to the crews of trade vessels was much less common on Vancouver Island than in other parts of the Pacific, and most of the Nuu-chah-nulth women who were prostituted probably came from the slave population.[92] Spanish sources suggest that sailors' attempts to tempt or bribe the women of Nootka Sound into prostitution were mostly rejected.[93] However, Walker noted that Native men "never made any scruple of bartering for their Women ... and that with much obscenity, but they could never be prevailed upon to bring the affair to a conclusion. It evidently appeared, that all they designed was to raise a laugh against us (or to get something from us.)"[94]

Traders were most concerned about the exchange process, however, and their confusions about Native trade methods encouraged them to be defensive. Native chiefs were invited aboard trade vessels, but business with the general Native population was usually conducted over the side of a ship. In spite of his putative friendship with Maquinna and Callicum, Meares remained unsure about Native motives and judged it prudent "to inform them of our power, by explaining the force we possessed, and the mode of applying it." He wished "to operate on their fears as well as their gratitude."[95] Strange fired a musket at a canoe to convince the Natives of his superiority.[96] Walker suggested that such tricks worked at Yuquot, arguing that the Natives' "apparent acquiescence and assistance in seconding our business, was owing to the vicinity of the Ships, and their conviction that the Village, their property, their canoes, and their Persons, were wholly under our power."[97] But Native groups in other parts of the sound did not seem overawed by traders' cannons or firearms, and they were more contemptuous with visitors.[98]

At Nootka Sound, as elsewhere, traders invoked scenes of desire and anxiety. Yet because Nootka Sound was described in detail, it is possible to interrogate these White representations and get at Native itineraries. Commercial interaction can be reassessed in terms of chiefly relations of power as well as in terms of Native competition and collaboration.

NATIVE COMPETITION AND CHIEFLY POWER

First, the "inconstancy" of Native demands may have been a reflection of Native competition. A number of Native groups traded at Yuquot, and they may each have established different prices for trade goods. Traders sometimes struggled to distinguish the members of different Native groups. Variations in Native demand and prices between different villages was also affected by inter-group trade. Walker, for instance, noted that as he advanced up the sound, the prices of furs became more exorbitant and that Native peoples possessed such a quantity of beads, traded from other groups in the sound, and that "they offered them to us in derision."[99]

Second, traders did not receive assistance at Yuquot simply because Natives were afraid of their swivel guns or muskets. More reasonably, this Native group sought to control the trade of Nootka Sound and did not want to drive traders away by being unfriendly. Furthermore, a British merchant noted that if British traders had been able to use their guns to impress the Natives of the sound, then this advantage was lost after Martínez arrested Colnett and Meares in 1789 (see Chapter 10 for a discussion of this incident). "The Indians, hitherto, had been impressed with an idea that no human force could oppose, much less conquer Britain, but having lately been witness to its humiliation, they will naturally become estranged, and lose that reverence and admiration which they entertained for the power, superiority and protection of its subjects. In their future mutual intercourse and traffic, there will be on each side, more diffidence and distrust, and the proprietors precautions for their own safety and defence, must increase their stationary force and expenditure."[100] Don Juan Francisco de la Bodega y Quadra, the leading Spanish official at Yuquot in the summer of 1792, noted that American and British traders arrived at Nootka Sound "on a war footing ... and not even the least of these is free from the dread of being attacked by the Indians."[101] Martínez's actions surely contributed to Native irreverence towards traders, but the Spaniard did not create this aura of estrangement. Before 1789 there were signs that Native groups knew how to play off traders against each other.

Third, the terms under which Native people traded with vessels were dictated by particular chiefs. Maquinna and Callicum may have authorized commoners to sell only a certain type and number of goods. Strange's comment that the people of Yuquot thought that the *Captain Cook* and *Experiment* had come for sustenance perhaps indicates that he dealt with commoners who had few furs to trade or were only permitted to sell food. Colnett's difficulties in procuring furs from Native groups in Muchalat groups may have stemmed from Maquinna's increasing dominance over Native access to furs and trade vessels visiting the sound during the first few years of trade.[102] On the other hand, Maquinna and other chiefs may not have wanted to exclude their followers and other Native groups from trading altogether. Galiano understood that these chiefs were "masters of the life and labour of their mischismis, distributing work to them and having whatever they require at their disposal"; but he also noticed that the loyalty of the commoners arose from the chief's interest in their well being.[103] Yvonne Marshall argues that under the *ha hoolthe* and *tupati* system of chiefly rights, commoners would have procured food for chiefs, which was then given or sold to traders.[104] Commoners may have become resentful of their chief if he gave or sold too much to traders and did not keep enough to distribute to his followers to thank them for their services. And commoners had more to worry about than access to trade vessels. John MacKay, who was left at Nootka Sound by Strange to observe Native life, stated that soon after the *Captain Cook* and *Experiment* departed, Maquinna had a big feast, invited several hundred people from neighbouring local groups, and distributed large quantities of dried salmon.[105] MacKay did not state whether the people of Yuquot were invited, but Malaspina reported that during MacKay's fourteen-month residence at Nootka Sound there was a great scarcity of food.[106] Possibly, Maquinna had given away too many winter provisions to these visiting Natives.

Finally, incidents of theft are difficult to interpret, but it is unlikely that they were foremost a chiefly strategy. Galiano claimed that Maquinna knew that traders and the Spanish were highly sensitive about theft and instituted "rigorous penalties" to dissuade his people from stealing.[107] More likely, theft was a form of Native rivalry. Traders rarely recorded who, precisely, stole from their vessels, but Natives from beyond Nootka Sound may have poached more goods than Maquinna's people under the presumption that their own villages were safe from traders' guns.[108] Drucker noted that instances of theft among Native peoples were frowned upon and rare, but that the same social sanctions did not apply to non-Native property.[109]

These are just possibilities, but they conform with the ethnographic context I have sketched. We can do a great deal with Walker's observation that the Native groups of Nootka Sound viewed trading vessels as "enormous bulk[s] of wealth."[110] The Native tricks that traders wrote about were, more properly, strategies for gaining and managing this wealth. What these early traders sensed, though never discussed at length, was that the Native groups of Nootka Sound were enmeshed in a complex and shifting set of collaborative and competitive relationships. As elsewhere in North America and the Pacific, Native agendas that pre-dated contact took on new twists because wealth was injected into particular locations and was controlled by certain chiefs.

Such agendas are difficult to discern but should not be discounted. The attack on the *Boston* is a case in point. It was not simply an act of revenge – or an act of "savage eloquence," as one newspaper described the event.[111] It was also about chiefly power and prestige.[112] The number of trade vessels visiting the sound dropped dramatically between 1795 and 1803. Jewitt sensed that without trade goods, Maquinna found it increasingly difficult to maintain his status. Maquinna looked on the wealth of the *Boston* as a means of regaining his influence. Jewitt's life was spared because he was an armourer and therefore useful to the chief.[113] He "was very proud of his new acquisition," Jewitt reported, and within a few days of the attack a great number of canoes from twenty or so Native groups assembled at Yuquot, expecting to trade and feast.[114] Maquinna apparently gave away many spoils of war – 100 muskets, 100 looking glasses, 400 yards of cloth, 20 casks of powder, and many other articles – in order to reaffirm his chiefly status in the eyes of these other groups.[115] Presents were also distributed to the people of Yuquot. Maquinna's reasoning in 1803 was probably more compli-cated than this, but these details about the *Boston* suggest that to understand the impact of the trade at Nootka Sound we need to consider questions of prestige. Chiefly status was not inviolable. At Nootka Sound, the maritime fur trade posed a series of opportunities and challenges for chiefs, their followers, and groups from other areas seeking power and influence.

CHIEFLY POWER AND PRESTIGE

American, British, and Spanish visitors to Nootka Sound identified a number of chiefs. Apart from Maquinna and Callicum, Meares dealt with Hannape, an Ehattesaht chief.[116] Hannape's daughter, Hestoquatto, was married to Maquinna.[117] Kendrick and Gray usually anchored at the village of Mawun (see Figure 5), where they had dealings with Clahquakinnah.[118] Galiano encountered Quicomacsia, another chief living at Mawun, who married the daughter of Chief Natzape in 1791, assuming the name Ouicsiocomic.[119] Saavedra identified Guadazapé as Maquinna's brother.[120] The Malaspina expedition had frequent dealings with Natzape, who was either an Ehattesaht or Nimpkish chief; a Span-ish chart shows that he owned a village and territory at the head of Zeballos Inlet.[121] Natzape was married to the daughter of a Nimpkish chief and probably had economic and ceremonial privileges on the west and east coasts of Vancou-ver Island.[122] According to Saavedra, Quicomacsia was Hannape's son (and there-fore Maquinna's brother-in-law) and succeeded his father around 1792.[123] Natzape's sister was one of Maquinna's four wives. Maquinna was also married to Y-ya-tintla-no, the daughter of Wickaninish (the highest-ranking chief of

Clayoquot Sound).[124] Galiano named Tlupananul and Cicomacsia as "heads of tribes."[125] This former chief, from Tlupana Inlet, formed close ties with the Spanish.[126] Officers with the Malaspina expedition thought that Tlupananul had previously been called Callicum; Saavedra figured that he was the uncle of Maquinna and Quicomacsia.[127] The Spanish also dealt with Naneguiyus (a son of Hannape and a brother-in-law of Maquinna, who acted closely with Natzape), Tlaparanalh, and Apecos, and he thought that Hannape was the father of both Natzape and Tlupananul.[128] Hereditary names were passed from father to son, and individual chiefs assumed different names as they grew older, married, and gained new privileges.[129]

In other words, there was a maze of marriages and alliances at Nootka Sound. Yvonne Marshall, an archaeologist, argues that there were three power blocks, or intergroup collectivities, around Nootka Sound during this period. Maquinna, Callicum, and Clahquakinnah were each the highest ranking chiefs of their own lineages and were also, respectively, the three highest ranking chiefs of a Yuquot-Tahsis confederacy comprised of seven or eight groups (see Figure 5). Tlupananul was the highest ranking chief of a number of local groups that lived most of the year in Tlupana Inlet; these groups also had rights on Bligh Island and Hesquiat Peninsula. Hannape was the highest ranked chief of a number of Ehattesaht groups that lived around Zeballos Arm and Espinosa Inlet.[130] Some Nutchatlaht groups of Nuchatlitz Inlet shared summer and winter residences, but it does not seem that they constituted a power block during this period. In Muchalat Inlet and on Hesquiat Peninsula, there were a number of independent groups.[131]

When, how, and why these different social and political arrangements came about has been the subject of much speculation. Different local groups give different accounts, and there are a number of conflicting ethnographic histories.[132] Marshall's account of group politics is the most recent and detailed. She argues that Native origin and family stories (she works mainly with those in volume 11 of Edward Curtis's *North American Indian* [1916]), as well as archaeological evidence, show that lineages and local groups around Nootka Sound cherished both sovereign autonomy and political alliance.[133] She claims that there was a constantly shifting balance of power in the sound before contact and during the early contact period that reflected a basic tension "between marrying out, forming alliances and therefore sharing power, and marrying in, consolidating local power and building a sovereign, autonomous power base."[134] And she thinks that when Cook arrived in the sound, four different sets of political arrangements co-existed. First, there were independent local groups whose economic, social, and political life was rooted in particular places, usually at the mouth of a salmon stream. Second, there were alliances of two or more "inside groups" living in the inlets. Third, there were alliances of two or more "outside groups" living on the coastal fringe of the sound. These alliances were often characterized by multi-lineage villages, encouraged group identification with a chief and lineage rather than a place, and led to the formation of collectivities that had access to both coastal and inland resources. Chiefs were also expected to widen their social connections through marriage alliances. And fourth, the Yuquot-Tahsis confederacy, which Marshall thinks was formed 300 to 400 years before contact and synthesized this tension between autonomy and alliance, was a large, ranked political structure. The groups in this confederacy derived their names from chiefs and lineages rather than places. They wintered in Tahsis Inlet and spent the summer and fall at Yuquot, where the chiefs of different lineages had their own houses and feast seats.[135] Drucker's interpretation of tribal and chiefly territories is depicted in Figure 5.

During the early contact period, Native itineraries at Nootka Sound were characterized by chiefly rivalry, the consolidation of pre-existing Native trade links, the formation of new trade and marriage ties, and a proliferation of Native warfare. The Yuquot-Tahsis confederacy became a powerful trading block, Maquinna and other chiefs became wealthy and enhanced their authority by widening their economic and social connections, and the local groups of the confederacy looked on trade goods as primary sources of prestige.

Just as Cook experienced, the Native peoples of the sound were territorial in their dealings with Whites and competed over the sea otter trade. Walker explained that Native peoples "completely identified themselves with their Country, and claimed every thing that appertained to it as their peculiar Possession."[136] Natives ushered traders to their villages, where they tried to monopolize the traffic.[137] Ingraham reported that these Native groups were jealous of each other and that the stronger tribes (such as Maquinna's) tried to rob the weaker ones of their goods, even within the sight of trade vessels.[138] He also suggested that the people of Yuquot had more muskets than other groups in the sound and asked Captain Gray not to sell firearms to anyone else.[139]

Traders sometimes treated these sharply defined Native territories as cocoons, hoping that they would form close trade ties with a particular group and secure a promise from a chief to supply furs on a yearly basis.[140] In his *Plan for Promoting the Fur Trade* (1789), Alexander Dalrymple encouraged traders to go to Nootka Sound because the Indians were known for their "Probity and Honour," having stood true to their promise to Hanna in 1785 to keep their furs until he returned the following year.[141] But traders and their backers soon realized that they could not put too much store by these Native promises, and in the summer of 1792, when over fifteen trade vessels visited the sound, Quadra noted that traders had "taken precautions against becoming rivals of each other," either fanning out around the sound or working in pairs and dividing their furs.[142] Traders were expected to capitulate to Native protocol and Native chiefs were prepared to push their luck with vessel masters. Native leaders sometimes made promises to specific traders in order to discourage them from visiting other villages. Chiefs also withheld their furs until a number of vessels had visited the sound and they had a full picture of what goods different traders had and what prices they were asking. In 1791, Ingraham thought that Kendrick was being deceived by the people of Mawun: they said "they had plenty of skins for him and they would not sell to anyone else ... [They were] very fond of Captain Kendrick for he ever treated them with great kindness; but I believe their view for wishing to see him at present was to dispose of their skins at an exorbitant price which none but Captain Kendrick would give."[143]

It is difficult to establish the veracity of traders statements about furs. As I argued in Chapter 6, they lied to each other. Bell reported that at Nootka Sound it was "very difficult ... to come at the truth of what numbers of skins ships collected; for the Masters of them and their mates & ships company ... seldom agree in their accounts of their quantity on board, many of them, and often, varying hundreds of skins."[144] Dalrymple was probably too uncritical of Native honour; Walker reported that in July 1786, Strange traded over 500 skins, and when Hanna arrived in the sound (on his second voyage) a few weeks later, he procured only 150 or so skins.[145] Yet if traders could not trust Native promises, it was not because Native demands and trade methods were whimsical. Peeping through traders' lies and confusions about the exchange process at Nootka Sound is the idea that the trade was heavily influenced by Native as well as White competition.

These commercial dynamics were complicated by Native attitudes towards status. The chiefs of Nootka Sound did not just view trade vessels as bulks of wealth; they also treated their relationships with traders and the Spanish as ways of gaining prestige. These political dynamics became most evident in the spring and summer of 1792, when Quadra arrived at Yuquot. He tried to work out how the chiefs of the sound were ranked, and he picked out Maquinna for special attention. Maquinna "always occupies the first place when he dines at my table," Quadra remarked; "I myself take the trouble of waiting on him, and he makes a lot of my friendship and much appreciates my visits to his rancherias" at Mawun, Kupti, and Tahsis (see Figure 5).[146] Maquinna responded in kind, entertaining the Spaniard as well as Vancouver's party when they visited in 1792 and 1794. Marshall interprets this scenario in ethnographic terms:

> Quadra's hospitality, especially the importance he attached to rituals involving the serving of food, the attention he paid to placing people at his table according to rank, and his policy of housing high ranking guests in his own quarters, again placing each one according to their rank, closely paralleled local notions of what constituted appropriate chiefly behaviour. Paramount among chiefly virtues was hospitality, and in particular, lavish generosity with food. Quadra's behaviour was of a kind that would earn a local chief his people's respect and approval. But more

importantly, it was the kind of behaviour that established the correctness of a chief's position in the eyes of other chiefs and commoners. It demonstrated that a chief's inherited right to hold an exalted rank was indeed valid.[147]

Maquinna temporarily put aside the indignities he had suffered at the hands of the Spanish and used his dealings with Quadra to consolidate his authority among his people and neighbouring groups. This friendship was not simply a spell of calm in a stormy contact process. As with other aspects of Native-White inter-action, it was rooted in the structures of Nuu-chah-nulth life – in the performa-tive facets of chiefly power.

Quadra's favouritism towards Maquinna was challenged by other chiefs, par-ticularly those who were not formally ranked in the Yuquot-Tahsis confederacy. The "vanity of enobling themselves over the others is the principal topic of con-versation of the taises," Galiano noted in May 1792.[148] Quicomacsia, in his twen-ties and perhaps eager to expand his influence, invited Galiano's crew to Mawun, where he held a dance for them, distributed gifts, and boasted about his mar-riage alliance with the Nimpkish, claiming repeatedly that it gave him precedence over Maquinna.[149] Tlupananul, though an elderly man, also tried to ingratiate himself to the Spanish. Galiano stated that "equalizing two fingers of his hand," this chief "said to us that he was Cococoa [similar to] Macuina. We did not observe that they had the least respect for each other."[150] In 1791, Tlupananul received Malaspina's party at the mouth of the sound and gave a long speech that Tomás de Suria (the Spanish pilot who recorded it) thought was designed to wrest the Spanish away from Maquinna's influence:

Do not believe that my years can serve as an obstacle to serve you in what you may be pleased to order me to do. Although you may marvel and believe me a barbarian, I am not ignorant of the inviolable laws of friendship. They inspire me to tell you not to confide in nor feel safe from the dissimulated perfidity of Macuina. I tell you that he is crafty and overbearing and he looks on you with hatred and abhorrence. He shortly meditates dislodging you from this place which you have founded in our dominion, but he cannot do it while Tlupanamibo lives, who, being experienced in this double-crossing game, will know how to oppose it as I have his malign projects to the present.[151]

These chiefs offered friendship and services to the Spanish, and both of them feasted with Quadra.[152]

Neither Quadra nor Maquinna were convinced by such appeals, however. Maquinna kept his special place at Quadra's table. When Quadra and Vancouver feasted at Tahsis in September 1792, Maquinna made a speech in which he com-pared himself only to Wickaninish of Clayoquot Sound, thereby implying that the other chiefs of the sound were of lower birth than he.[153] According to

Archibald Menzies, dinner was served up "in a manner that made us forget that we were in such a remote corner, under the humble roof of a Nootka Chief." Maquinna deported himself like a king, and Menzies surmised that these other chiefs were his dependents.[154]

Maquinna seemingly exercised a good deal of agency in his dealings with Spanish and British officials, acting as a go-between and consultant but always with his interests and those of his followers foremost in mind.[155] Quadra's attention to Native detail helped Maquinna to enhance his status, and the Spanish were not able to dictate to him or any other chiefs. Christon Archer argues that "the small Spanish garrison at Yuquot became the hostage of Native activities and of the rivalries among the different Nootka tribes."[156] Because of misunderstandings and minor conflicts between the Spanish and Native peoples, in 1793 Spanish commanders banned their troops from leaving Yuquot or visiting Native settlements without official permission.

We should not stretch this image of Native rivalry too far, however. The chiefs of Nootka Sound may have used foreigners to compete for status, but this did not rule out the need for Native collaboration. These chiefs knew that there were fewer sea otters at Nootka Sound than at Clayoquot Sound and on other parts of the coast. To make the most out of the trade, Maquinna had to gather furs from other groups and widen his social connections, as I will now explain.

NATIVE COLLABORATION AND THE YUQUOT-TAHSIS CONFEDERACY

In 1786, Walker reported that Nutchatlaht people from the north end of Nootka Island and around Nuchatlitz Inlet traded at Nootka Sound.[157] Jewitt noted that by the early 1800s, Ehattesaht people were supplying Maquinna with many furs and other Native goods, and that the marriage ties between Hannape's family and Maquinna's had forged this commercial link.[158] Maquinna also had strong commercial ties with Clayoquot and Nimpkish peoples. In 1789, Martínez noted that the groups of Nootka Sound traded with nine villages to the north and another nine to the south – from Kyuquot Sound to the Strait of Juan de Fuca.[159] These connections were still in place when Jewitt was captured.[160]

The groups of Nootka Sound also warred with other groups for furs and slaves. Contrary to the vitriolic tone of his speech to Malaspina, de Suria judged that Tlupananul had friendly ties with the groups of Yuquot and acted as "head of the army" in Maquinna's military campaigns.[161] While chiefs were trained to lead the local group and learned the protocols of appropriate chiefly behaviour, they often were not trained specifically to fight wars. That honour was usually bestowed on lesser chiefs.[162]

Of the 107 or so trade vessels that visited the Northwest Coast between 1785 and 1795, around 70 traded at Nootka Sound.[163] All of the Native groups of the sound could benefit from the trade, even if a large portion of the business was channelled through Yuquot and Maquinna's hands. And fewer vessels would have visited Yuquot had there been protracted Native warfare in the vicinity. There was great Native rivalry, but the groups of the western part of the sound did not jettison peace for short-term gain. Internecine warfare would have caused political instability and made Native villages vulnerable to attack and/or colonization by neighbouring groups. Maquinna was not a monarch but what Marshall calls an "umbrella chief" – a figure of exalted status but one who shared power with his confederate chiefs.[164]

Marshall claims that Maquinna's politics at Nootka Sound during this period were marked by consensus and diplomacy. This became most evident, she claims, in 1792, when violence broke out between the Natives of Neah Bay, led by Chief Tatoosh, and the Spanish commander Salvador Fidalgo. A Spanish pilot was killed by Tatoosh's people and Fidalgo retaliated by killing eight Natives.[165] Tatoosh appealed to Chiefs Wickaninish and Hanna, his relatives at Clayoquot Sound, to avenge Fidalgo's actions. Wickaninish had his own reasons for revenge: his people and village had been fired at a number of times by American and British traders. Marshall thinks that a plot was hatched by these three chiefs to expel both traders and the Spanish from the coast. They appealed to Maquinna to join their cause, and his vote of confidence was crucial because of his rank, wealth, and prestige. Maquinna chose not to sever his links with the Spanish and did not want to curtail the fur trade. Marshall argues that a general war between Whites and Natives would have undermined Maquinna's position, and she claims that his dealings with traders and the Spanish prove that he treated conflict as a last resort. As Marshall interprets Maquinna's decision, "to go against the call for united action would be to gamble with possible annihilation. If Maquinna opposed the planned action but did not gain the support of other chiefs, Wickaninish would not only attack the Europeans but also treat Maquinna as their ally and pursue his destruction. At stake was not only who would decide how the Europeans and their trade were to be managed but also who could command the greatest influence and highest status – Maquinna or Wickaninish."[166] Maquinna invited Hanna to Nootka Sound for a meeting and defused the plot.

Autonomy versus alliance; conflict or consensus? Marshall illustrates that these tensions were played out both regionally and locally. Decisions made by powerful chiefs such as Maquinna and Wickaninish affected the plans of other groups. Rumours and reports, imputations and implications, travelled quickly between Native villages. Native chiefs performed their own pirouette of place and space (or locale and region). Traders imagined that the Native groups of Vancouver Island lived on the fringes of the global economy, but Native peoples had their own canons of desire, derision, and power. Their attitudes towards traders were mediated by complex issues of Native fellowship and chiefly prestige.

Marshall emphasizes that Maquinna's exalted position was built on peaceful interaction with Whites, and she uses his dealings with Quadra to suggest that the roots of present-day Nuu-chah-nulth politics lay "in long-established political structures and practices which valued the sharing of power, diplomacy, and consensus."[167] Marshall's attempt to show that Native dealings with traders and the Spanish were rational and strategic is noble, but this conclusion about Mowachaht politics is maybe too revisionist. She overlooks the aggressive policies that Maquinna and the Yuquot-Tahsis confederacy adopted towards other Native groups, especially before the Spanish occupied Yuquot, in order to ensure that Nootka Sound remained a centre of trade.[168]

In 1792, Moziño sensed that there had been about two centuries of warfare between the groups of Nootka Sound and the "Tlaumases," being "all nations that live on the other shore of the sea."[169] More specifically, he reported that Maquinna's father (possibly the chief who exchanged presents with Cook) died in 1778 in a war against this group.[170] Roquefeuil recorded that young Maquinna avenged his father's death at the hands of the "Tahumasses ... in a terrible manner."[171] In July 1786, Maquinna introduced Strange to a war chief of Nootka Sound named Clamata who had "personally slain Eight and twenty of the Enemy within the last Ten Moons" (around nine months); that is, shortly after Hanna had left the sound.[172] Walker noted that the people of Yuquot "were fond of speaking of their Enemies, who, according to their account, were very numerous, and frequently employed in making War."[173] According to Meares, in August 1788 Maquinna and Callicum were preparing for an expedition against an enemy "more powerful, numerous and savage than themselves" who had attacked a village about sixty miles north of Nootka Sound that was under the jurisdiction of Maquinna's grandmother.[174] Meares claimed that Maquinna and Callicum borrowed firearms from him, killed about thirty people in battle, and seized "a great-booty of sea-otter skins."[175] And in November 1788, Kendrick learned that the people of Yuquot were at war with a Native group from the east side of the sound, probably Muchalat Inlet.[176] By 1791, Maquinna had more muskets than any other chief in the area, and Saavedra thought that he had traded many of them from Kendrick.[177]

This information is sketchy, but the timing of these events is noteworthy. The first two instances of prolonged contact with Whites on Vancouver Island, in 1778 and 1785, were seemingly followed by Native conflict. The maritime fur trade probably inflamed old grievances and encouraged new conflicts. Native groups were probably fighting over furs, sea otter territories, and access to trade goods. Chiefs also hoped to capture slaves.

We should not read too much into these references to firearms. Haswell thought that the Natives of Nootka Sound had added guns to their traditional weaponry of bows and arrows, spears, daggers, and stone axes, but the muskets Native people received were probably not very accurate or reliable.[178] In 1794, Saavedra was informed that only twenty of the many muskets Kendrick had traded to Wickaninish in 1791 still worked.[179] The evidence concerning the use of guns by Native peoples is contradictory, but the chiefs of Nootka Sound, it seems, clung to tried and tested war methods: surprise attacks at night or dawn with blades and clubs. Caamaño reported that the Natives of Yuquot wanted firearms in order to intimidate rivals rather than to wage war, and, contradicting Hoskin's remark about Native marksmanship, the Spaniard claimed that "the [Nootka Sound] Indian who dares to discharge them is very rare, and even the one who does attempt to it turns his head to one side, and closes his eyes."[180] These chiefs may have viewed firearms more as prestige goods – icons of wealth and power – than as war weapons.

Now Folan has speculated that the "Tlaumases" were the N-La', a Nutchatlaht group from around Nuchatlitz Inlet, and that a Yuquot war song recorded by Jewitt may have described their defeat at the hands of Yuquot people.[181] In addition, when Walker visited Nuchatlitz Inlet he saw many people he had seen at Yuquot, noted that they were poorer than the people of the sound, and implied that they were vassals of Maquinna.[182] But Folan's interpretation can be questioned. Jewitt distinguished between the "Neu-chad-lits" (or Nutchatlaht), the Klahars (who lived at Yuquot, had been conquered by Maquinna, and whom Folan identifies as the "Tlaumases"), and the "Newchemasses" (or Nimpkish, on traders' and Spanish understanding). Jewitt claimed that the Newchemasses were "a very savage nation ... who come from a great way to the northward, and from some distance inland," who spoke a different language than the Nootkans but one well understood by the people of Nootka Sound.[183] And given Moziño's description, it is unlikely that the Tlaumases were a Nutchatlaht group.

Robert Galois has presented some tantalizing material with which to think about the identity of the Tlaumases and to interpret Nuu-chah-nulth involvement with Kwak'wala-speaking peoples. In the late eighteenth and early nineteenth centuries, he argues, Kwakwaka'wakw sociopolitical space was fairly volatile, especially around Cape Mudge and Quatsino Sound.[184] During this period the Hahamatsees, a Lekwiltok group, took control of Salmon River, having either moved south from Nimpkish River or moved north from the interior (see Figure 4).[185] Galois suggests that, prior to contact, the area between Quatsino Sound and Cape Cook was controlled by Nuu-chah-nulth peoples. This region was taken over (probably) by the Klaskino, who either captured it or merged with a Nuu-chah-nulth group just before or around the time of contact.[186]

It is difficult to know how traders heard Native sounds and determined a spelling, but, superficially, "Tlaumases"/"Tahumasses" does not sound like a Nuu-chah-nulth tribal name because it does not contain the first person singular or plural clauses -art/at/it(s), -lat/let/lit(s), or -quot/quat(s) commonly used by traders to designate Nuu-chah-nulth groups. And superficially, Hahamatsees is the only Kwakwaka'wakw group name resembling those given in Moziño's and Roquefeuil's interpretations. It is also possible that the war Maquinna and Callicum fought sixty miles north of Nootka Sound (the Cape Cook area) in 1788 was to avenge a Klaskino incursion.

I am speculating, but my interpretation of Nuu-chah-nulth ties and conflict with Kwakwaka'wakw groups can be supported. Franz Boas recorded the details of an "early war" involving the Nimpkish and Nuu-chah-nulth groups (though he did not ascertain a date), and he noted that there had been a number of Nuu-chah-nulth incursions into Kwakwaka'wakw lands over the years.[187] When Cook arrived at Nootka Sound, the main avenue of trade between the west and east coasts of Vancouver Island was between Tahsis Inlet and the Nimpkish River (see Figure 4). Natzape told Malaspina that he traversed this route quite regularly and had met Cook as a youth of thirteen or fourteen years of age. Malaspina claimed that Natzape "preserved very well in his memory various events of that expedition. The house and rancheria visited by Captain Cook were those of Calacan [Callicum]. He recognized a portrait of the Captain; he named without aid Captain Clerke, and asserted his belief that Lieutenant King was the son of Captain Cook."[188] More to the point, Natzape informed Malaspina that "the hands, heads and bones presented aboard the Resolution, were nothing more than the remains of his enemies."[189] Galois does not give any evidence of warfare involving the Nimpkish or the Ninelkaynuk (their neighbours living around Woss Lake) at this time (see Figure 4), and we have no other sources with which to check Malaspina's story, but putting these fragments together, I suggest that around 1778 groups from Nootka Sound and the Nimpkish River were at war with some other Kwakwaka'wakw group called the Tlaumases/Tahumasses for control of the Tahsis-Nimpkish trail.[190] After Cook's visit, these Nootka Sound and Nimpkish groups may have stepped up their expeditions against the Tlaumases in order to protect their mutual trading interests.

Ethnographers have emphasized that warfare was an integral, if probably only sporadic, feature of pre-contact Nuu-chah-nulth life, and what Walker heard implies as much.[191] Scholars have ascribed a number of motives for war; revenge and economic gain are the reasons that have been given most often by Nuu-chah-nulth informants.[192] These wars of the 1770s and 1780s were seemingly fought for basically these reasons. But something else is striking about them: they were not internecine conflicts: they were between Nuu-chah-nulth and Kwakwaka'wakw groups. This was certainly not a general pattern along the west coast of Vancouver Island. Groups around Clayoquot Sound and Barkley Sound fought between themselves before and after contact, as I will document. Maquinna and Callicum, on the other hand, fought with groups quite far to the north and northeast of Nootka Sound. Nor do these late eighteenth-century wars imply that the chiefs of Nootka Sound had a master plan to annex and control distant territories; rather, it seems that Nootka Sound groups fought these wars to consolidate their trading interests with the Nimpkish and to widen the economic berth of the Yuquot-Tahsis confederacy.

This scenario makes sense if we recall the marriage and trade connections between chiefly families in and around Nootka Sound. Malaspina noted that the chiefs of the sound were interrelated "either by accident, or by regulation, or by convenience derived possibly from previous bloody wars," and estimated that Maquinna's influence stretched to the Nimpkish River.[193] Meares reported that Maquinna was the chief of four villages to the north of the sound and four villages to the south.[194] And, trusting Maquinna's testimony, Meares characterized the area from Cape Cook to Nootka Sound as a huge extended family: "From him we learned that there were several very populous villages to the Northward, entrusted to the government of the principal female relations of Maquilla and Callicum; such as grandmothers, mothers, aunts sisters &c ... and several other villages were assigned to the direction of other relations, all of which were ready to join, as occasion required, for the support of their mutual safety, and to yield a ready obedience to the summons of the sovereign chief."[195] We do not know when or how, precisely, these connections came about, and Maquinna and Meares were likely exaggerating their extent. Nonetheless, it seems to me that Meares got the gist of Maquinna's approach to the maritime fur trade. From the mid-1780s to the early 1800s, Maquinna widened his commercial horizon through inter-marriage, trade, and warfare. The Yuquot-Tahsis confederacy also became more tight-knit through inter-marriage and military liaison. The marriage alliances documented above facilitated inter-group trade and made warfare with neighbouring Nuu-chah-nulth groups an unwise policy. If Drucker is right in stating that Nuu-chah-nulth peoples had relatives in a number of places, it is unlikely that the chiefs of Nootka Sound could have waged war on their neighbours without creating divided loyalties. Meares noted that, "from political motives," Maquinna had married out his female relatives rather than his brothers and sons, some of whom had no doubt been trained as war chiefs and may have threatened his power had they assumed leadership roles in villages distant from his direct supervision.[196]

In part because of these policies, many Native groups came to trade at Nootka Sound, and Maquinna relied on his neighbours to supply him with furs. The inhabitants of Yuquot ran out of furs to sell within three weeks of the arrival of the *Captain Cook* and *Experiment*. Walker noted that Callicum made a number of trips to the south, and Maquinna's agents "swept the Coast a great way to the Northward" to trade.[197] And furs and trade goods changed hands quickly. Given the number of vessels that had traded in the sound between 1778 and 1788, Meares was surprised to find on his arrival that the inhabitants were "totally destitute of European articles" and wondered about the "manner they had contrived ... to dissipate their treasures."[198] Archaeologists have since found few

remains of Western goods in the layer of midden at Yuquot dated to early contact. John Dewhirst notes that this can be explained, in part, by the fact that the
mostly wooden and metal items traded by Whites would have disintegrated over
time. But archaeologists have also used this evidence, and their examination of
Native tools, to suggest that Nuu-chah-nulth technology remained basically
unchanged during the early contact period. Few Western goods were adopted by
Native peoples for practical purposes. Most of them were traded for furs and as
prestige goods or used as ornaments.[199]

The Yuquot-Tahsis groups traded many of the Western goods they obtained
from Whites to the Nimpkish for furs. The Nimpkish were probably Maquinna's
greatest trade partners during the early contact period and especially in the 1790s,
when the fur trade was at its peak but sea otters were vanishing from Nootka
Sound itself.[200] According to Quadra, the Nimpkish were the best fur trappers
on Vancouver Island, and the importance of the Tahsis-Nimpkish trail was noted
by many observers.[201] Malaspina claimed that the Nimpkish supplied about 6,000
sea otter furs per year to Nootka Sound, and Chief Natzape drew him a map
showing the "two great lagoons" (Nimpkish Lake and Woss Lake) where they
captured the sea otter.[202]

In 1790, Caamaño observed that copper was the principal article of traffic
with the Nimpkish, who "were very anxious for it."[203] Copper was highly valued
by the Tlingit, Tsimshian, Haida, and Kwakwaka'wakw, who manufactured it
into breastplates and collars that were used as currency and status emblems.[204]
Spanish Monterey shells and muskets were also cherished by the Nimpkish. When
Vancouver's party visited the Nimpkish village of "Cheslakees" in July 1792, they
discovered that the inhabitants understood the Nootkan language, viewed
Maquinna as a "great chief," were "well versed with the principles of trade," and
possessed many trade goods, including about 100 muskets, most of them of
Spanish manufacture.[205] "Their commercial intercourse with the Natives of
Nootka ... was pretty evident from their own account," Menzies explained, "for
they assured us of having received from thence most of the Articles of European
Manufactory in their possession."[206] Both Vancouver and Galiano noted that the
Nimpkish were much less shy with Europeans than were the Native people they
met just thirty miles south, suggesting that cross-island traffic and interaction
was tightly focused along the Tahsis-Nimpkish trail.[207]

It was via these trading routes that Maquinna and the other chiefs of Nootka
Sound became wealthy. According to Moziño, Cook inaugurated a "memorable
epoch" for them: "The natives believed they had succeeded in unloading their
merchandise at a very advantageous price. In effect they had ... tripled their
capital by means of the copper which, leaving the hands of the Nootkans, began
to disperse itself throughout almost all the Archipelago."[208] And so it would remain as long as Nootka Sound remained a main centre of White commerce and

other Native groups had less frequent contact with White traders. Native groups did not need a global economy to enhance the value of their goods; they profited by the variegated nature of their own commercial environment. On Moziño's logic, the three sheets of copper that a chief of Nootka Sound got from a trader for one sea otter fur could be sold to the Nimpkish for three sea otter furs; those three Nimpkish furs might have been procured from another group for one sheet of copper; and so forth.

But Maquinna did not triple his capital for long. He did not monopolize this Nimpkish traffic. By 1790, if not before, the Nimpkish were trading directly with the Spanish for guns, copper, and shells.[209] And when Jewitt was at Nootka Sound, the Nimpkish arrived to trade without any furs.[210] In 1818, Roquefeuil was told that since the late 1790s, Maquinna had been selling most of his furs to the Chicklisaht of Nasparti Bay (Cape Cook), which was visited occasionally by traders. As the maritime fur trade wound down at Nootka Sound, Maquinna struggled to retain his status and influence. He had incorporated Western goods (especially guns and copper) into the Native prestige and trading system, and without them he slipped in importance in the eyes of his neighbours. He tried to ameliorate economic hardship by focusing the energies of his local group on salmon fishing and whaling.[211] And he became less vulnerable politically when Tlupananul was given a house site and feast seat at Yuquot in the mid-to-late 1790s, forming what anthropologists call the Mowachaht confederacy.[212] As the Yuquot, Tahsis, and Tlupana Inlet groups allied, the more loosely allied groups of Muchalat Inlet became vulnerable to Mowachaht attack and colonization. During the nineteenth century a number of wars broke out over salmon streams in Muchalat Inlet. We do not know when, precisely, these wars started, but according to Augustus Brabant, they continued on and off until 1874.[213] While Jewitt was at Nootka Sound, Maquinna also went to war with a Barkley Sound group.[214]

REGIONAL EFFECTS OF THE TRADE

The maritime fur trade at Nootka Sound was connected to a much broader space of Native calculation and aggrandizement. Questions of value and wealth were overlaid with the politics and symbolism of kin, status, and territoriality. In aggregate terms, the maritime fur trade exacerbated inequalities of wealth between the Native groups of central and northern Vancouver Island. In relative terms, however, things were more complicated. Groups that had infrequent contact with Whites, or had limited access to trade goods, could balance out inequality by forming trade and marriage alliances with wealthier groups. The fur trade also exacerbated inequalities of wealth within local groups. Maquinna and the other chiefs of Nootka Sound amassed a disproportionate amount of their wealth and influence from the fur trade, and they enhanced their status through marriage and trade alliances as well as warfare. And we have seen that these chiefs specified and supervised the conditions under which their followers participated in the trade. In 1912, C.F. Newcombe was told by a Mowachaht informant that, following the seizure of the *Boston*, Maquinna was stingy with his followers and wanted to keep everything for himself.[215] This contradicts Jewitt's observations, but taken together, these two pieces of evidence imply that Natives were sensitive about the spoils of the trade. There is also some suggestion that Maquinna and Callicum gave away a large number of trade goods and foodstuffs to visiting Native groups at the feast they held after the departure of the *Captain Cook* and *Experiment*, depleting precious winter provisions.

These references to the distribution of provisions and trade goods raise important questions about the effect of the trade on Native groups. Did this Native enthusiasm for trade with Whites affect Native procurement strategies, settlement patterns, and technologies? John Dewhirst has argued that Native groups on the west coast of Vancouver Island probably used outside and inside environmental settings on a seasonal basis prior to contact. And on the basis of excavations of the midden at Yuquot, he claimed that Nootkan cultural patterns (especially tool technology) did not change greatly from 1,000 years before contact to the late nineteenth century.[216] On the other hand, Richard Inglis and James Haggarty have suggested that pre-contact Native subsistence and settlement patterns changed dramatically during the early years of contact and that the Native seasonal round at Nootka Sound was a post-contact phenomenon. When the maritime fur trade started, the chiefs of outside groups, such as Maquinna, sought to become port managers and had to reschedule their resource procurement strategies if they were to devote the summers months to trading with Whites. They exchanged trade goods for foodstuffs and furs with their neighbours, and they developed a subsistence cycle that would not interfere with the sea otter trade. Inglis and Haggarty think that Cook observed independent local groups operating within small resource territories, whereas Jewitt described a ranked sociopolitical confederacy and a seasonal round. In short, Jewitt observed Native groups that had undergone intense change over twenty-five years.[217]

Dewhirst was too quick to generalize about Nuu-chah-nulth cultural patterns from his Yuquot data. There have been other archaeological site surveys and digs on Vancouver Island since he wrote in 1980, and these show that the trade had a very disruptive impact on subsistence and settlement patterns in some areas.[218] Inglis and Haggarty pinpointed the relationship between trade and changing subsistence strategies at Nootka Sound, but their reading of the early historical record is partial. Cook and some of his officers, Strange, Meares, and Haswell, all pointed to the existence of a seasonal cycle of resource procurement and habitation.[219] More recently, Marshall has argued that an inside-outside seasonal cycle was in place at Nootka Sound well before contact but that the maritime fur trade encouraged the outside groups of the sound to focus more on the procurement of inside resources. This was obviously the case with Maquinna's people because Yuquot was occupied by the Spanish for six years.[220] Outside resources, especially whales, were harvested in greater numbers again after the trade declined.[221]

Local group dynamics at Nootka Sound are difficult to interpret, but population data suggest that Yuquot grew during the early years of contact. Population estimates vary greatly, but if we rely on the counts made by Cook's team in 1778 and Jewitt's figures for 1803, the summer population of Yuquot grew from around 400 to 700 to about 1,500 during the first 25 years of contact, and the number of dwellings at the site doubled.[222] Marshall argues that settlement patterns in the Nootka Sound area were stable during the first few decades of contact. No major pre-contact settlements were abandoned, and no new large settlements were established; rather, there was a growth in the intensity and extent of occupation at major settlements such as Yuquot, Tahsis, and Kupti.[223] What we do not know is how many of these extra people hailed from local groups in the sound and how many were slaves.[224] Since wealth was a form of status, lesser chiefs, and the chiefs of villages who were not ranked in the Yuquot-Tahsis confederacy, were able to enhance their social standing by giving more feasts and exchanging trade goods in return for prized ceremonial privileges and access to resource sites. But the situation of Native commoners is unclear. Natives with distant kin ties to the chiefly families of the Yuquot-Tahsis confederacy may have moved to places such as Yuquot. But equally, if chiefs such as Maquinna were stingy with their followers, commoners may have remained at the villages they lived in prior to contact. Given the Native trade and marriage alliances documented above, it seems likely that the maritime fur trade encouraged individual mobility between local groups, and the image of transiency that Drucker picked up from his informants may have been a post-contact phenomenon.

In all, we are left with a series of impressions about changes in subsistence and settlement patterns at Nootka Sound rather than clear facts. Likewise, there is little evidence with which to assess the impact of this commercial focus on Nootka Sound on Nuu-chah-nulth economic and political geographies to the north of the sound. Nutchatlaht, Ehattesaht, Kyuquot, and Chicklisaht people traded with the Natives of Yuquot during the early years of contact, but these northern Nuu-chah-nulth were visited only sporadically by traders.

Colnett visited Chicklisaht territory in 1787, and Robert Gray visited "Columbia's Cove" on the north side of Nasparti Inlet in the summers of 1791 and 1792.[225] John Boit (who had sailed with Gray) returned to this inlet in the summer of 1795 as captain of the American vessel *Union*. And a few other traders visited the area in the 1790s. But Nasparti was only a minor port of call, and it was established for the sake of convenience during the Spanish occupation of

Yuquot. Gray was suspicious of the Natives of the inlet, and in May 1792, following a dispute about trade, he fired at them.[226] A week later a delegation of Chicklisaht people arrived at Nootka Sound to ask Quadra to tend to their wounded and to punish Gray; the American had apparently killed seven Natives and taken furs by force.[227] Boit thought that these Natives were more hospitable when he visited in 1795, but he exhausted their supply of furs within a few days.[228]

Few traders visited Kyuquot Sound, and the one detailed account we have of commercial contact there speaks directly to traders' distrust of Native peoples. Joseph Ingraham reached this sound in the seventy-ton brigantine *Hope* in July 1792. After trading at a couple of villages at the mouth of the sound, he ventured further into Kyuquot territory and, suspicious of Native intentions, took two Natives with him as hostages. Within a few hours, the *Hope* was surrounded by fifteen canoes. Judging that the Natives planned to attack his vessel, Ingraham fired warning shots over the canoes, but they kept coming. So he fired directly at the Natives, driving them away. With this trading opportunity bungled, he made a speedy exit for Nootka Sound.[229] Ingraham, like many traders in small vessels, approached unfamiliar territory very cautiously and often expected the worst.

Because contact with Whites was sporadic, the fur trade probably had a minimal effect on the social geography of these northern Nuu-chah-nulth groups. There have been no major archaeological surveys in this area of Vancouver Island, so the interpretative possibilities are limited. Nevertheless, I have not found any ethnographic or historical evidence of social disruption due to disease or warfare among these groups during the late eighteenth century. Maquinna may have partially colonized the region, as Meares suggested, but Drucker believed that Kyuquot people lived in a confederacy of four tribes uniting fourteen local groups that had been stable for a considerable time.[230] Chicklisaht geography was likely affected more by the incursions of Kwak'wala-speaking groups than by contact with Whites – although such incursions may have been related to the fur trade.

Closer to Nootka Sound, matters were more complicated. Drucker thought that Nutchatlaht groupings were formed from the leftovers of Mowachaht and Ehattesaht unions, and as some of the above documentation implies, the Nutchatlaht living around Nootka Island may have been dominated by Maquinna.[231] Traders visited Ehattesaht territory quite frequently, and these people had ancient and ongoing ties with the Yuquot-Tahsis groups and the Nimpkish. Hannape and Natzape were seemingly important and powerful chiefs.

In Nootka Sound itself, I have been arguing, the contact process was influenced by chiefly relations of power and prestige, competition and collaboration. Traders became incorporated into Native practices of power that anchored the sea otter trade in specific ways. We can see different notions of competition and profit in these Native agendas. And when we try to appreciate these Native agendas, other formulations of place and space appear. To Native peoples, traders did not represent the world economy or a capitalist system. Traders carried great bulks of wealth and prestige, and they entered Native orders of inclusion and exclusion. Yet if Nootka Sound was a premier trading place, it was still part of the agonistic commercial space I have described. Traders would only go there if it was profitable, and their observations about Native agendas were, after all, a means to an end – profit. Native peoples became connected to a shifting coastal space-economy and international division of labour. If Native chiefs became dependent on the trade and prized Western goods such as iron bars, copper kettles, guns, and other trade items, then it was because they were useful; they were incorporated into their own systems of superiority. Western goods were material additions to established Native practices of exchange and consumption. The chiefs of Nootka Sound began to rely on them as sources of power.

As traders found new trading locations, geographical relations of Native power twisted and turned. As the traders' quick abandonment of Nootka Sound and Maquinna's attack on the *Boston* illustrate, Native geographies became more agonistic. And as the Nuu-chah-nulth plan (discussed by Marshall) to take control of the trade implies, Native groups began to see links between themselves that were not solely defined by kinship. Chiefs such as Maquinna distinguished between Spanish, British, and American traders, but we also sense that he – and Native peoples generally – perceived these strangers as a collective, non-Native Other.

CHAPTER 8

The Spatial Politics of Exchange at Clayoquot Sound

We ... had sufficient reason to remain in a state of preparation against the
possibility of that mischief which it was in his [Wickaninish's] power to do
us, and which opportunity might tempt him to employ.

– JOHN MEARES, *VOYAGES* (1790)

"WICKANINISH'S SOUND"

Contact relations and Native agendas at Clayoquot Sound were different than
those at Nootka Sound and can be summarized more easily. The first trader to
reach this sound, Captain Charles Barkley of the *Imperial Eagle* in 1787, named
it "Wickinanish's Sound" after Chief Wickaninish, who seemed to possess "great
authority" there.[1] In the late 1780s and the 1790s the area between Meares Island to Barkley Sound became increasingly dominated by Wickaninish and his
family (see Figure 6). He expanded his influence over neighbouring groups
through warfare and the institution of a tribute system, and he monopolized
commerce with traders in Clayoquot Sound. Traders discovered that there was a
large supply of furs in the region and understood that they had to go through
Wickaninish to get them.

At Clayoquot Sound, traders had entered a recently amalgamated Native space.
In pre-contact times the sound was inhabited by between eleven and seventeen
local groups of varying size, influence, and degrees of autonomy.[2] The three
most important groups were probably the Clayoquot, a large family that owned
the villages of Tla'ohw on Clayoquot Arm (their ancestral home) and Ohqmin
on Kennedy River, lived part of the year at Ya'hlapis, and had fishing and whal-

ing rights around Echachis Island; the Hohpitshaht, whose ancestral settlement was Hophitsh, and who also lived at Echachist in the summer and probably at Opitsat during the winter; and the Hisau'istaht, who owned the villages of Esowista and Kanoowis and probably controlled much of Tofino Inlet (see Figure 6). There were a series of conflicts in the sound in pre-contact times, but the most decisive war occurred a few years (or decades) before contact. The Clayoquot, allied with three or four other local groups, wiped out the Hisau'istaht. After the war, Clayoquot Chief Ya'aihlstohsmahhlneh (who later took the name Wickaninish) redistributed Hisau'istaht territories, names, and privileges to his relatives and war allies, and the local groups of the region began to live together at Opitsat during the winter.[3] The eleven families of the Clayoquot group each had a house at Opitsat. Smaller local groups probably had one or two houses each in the village. Native informants state that there were between thirty and forty lineage houses at the village in the early contact period, over two-thirds of which belonged to offshoot lineages of the Clayoquot and surrounding groups that had allied with the Clayoquot in the war.[4] Meares named the area around Opitsat "Port Cox" and depicted seventeen houses on his 1788 map of the village – built, he said, with "a greater share of ... rude magnificence" than any he had seen.[5] By 1791, the Spanish explorer Francisco Eliza estimated that about 2,500 people lived at the village.[6] In 1792, Boit counted over 200 houses there.[7] If we trust these figures, Opitsat grew enormously during the first few years of contact with Whites; by the 1790s it was the largest Native settlement on the west coast of Vancouver Island.

These wars and amalgamations gave Wickaninish an influence over the contact process that was almost unparalleled along the coast. He was not an umbrella chief like Maquinna, but a patriarch whose large family and allies owned rich inside and outside resource territories. When Meares first encountered the Clayoquot at Nootka Sound in June 1788, he noted that they were "superbly dressed in furs of the highest estimation" and had a "thriving appearance."[8] He subsequently judged that their opulence stemmed from the abundance of whales around Clayoquot Sound.[9] The Clayoquot groups had a large resource base, were probably more self-sufficient than their Yuquot-Tahsis neighbours, and did not have to adjust their annual round because a foreign force was lodged on their territory. As such, Wickaninish was able to dictate the timing and terms of commerce to traders; he largely expected them to work around his seasonal schedule.

Archaeologists and ethnographers have suggested that before the Clayoquot-Hisau'istaht war, these Clayoquot groups used Ohqmin as their winter village.[10] In the fall they pursued salmon through the Kennedy River system to spawning grounds at the head of Clayoquot Arm, where their ancestral home was located. While wintering at Ohqmin, they relied on stores of dried fish and whale oil. In

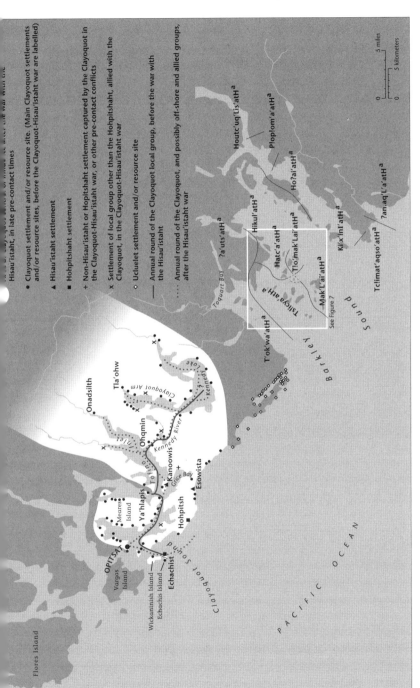

Figure 6 Map showing settlement patterns and sociopolitical arrangements in Clayoquot Sound and in tribal territories in Barkley Sound in the late pre-contact period

Source: Adapted from Arcas Associates, "Patterns of settlement of the Ahousaht (Kelsemaht) and Clayoquot bands," unpublished report, Vancouver and Kamloops, 1989 (Clayoquot Sound); Richard I. Inglis and James C. Haggarty, "Pacific Rim National Park: Ethnographic history," unpublished report to Parks Canada, Calgary, 1986, (Ucluelet and Barkley Sound).

the spring they moved to Ya'hlapis. During the summer some people moved to Echachist to fish and hunt whales. Following the war, new outside and inside resource areas were added to this basic territorial pattern (see Figure 6). This annual cycle can be discerned from traders' observations. In the fall many Clayoquot people stayed at Kanoowis on Indian Island (previously Hisau'istaht territory) and around early October moved to Ohqmin and fished for salmon in the Kennedy River system. They moved to Opitsat in December, where they wintered. In the spring they moved to Echachist and other outside villages, where they stayed during the summer to fish and hunt sea mammals.[11] Meares gives a vivid description of the preparations they made for their gravitation back towards Ohqmin in late summer:

> The inhabitants ... were busily employed in packing up fish in mats, securing the roes of them in bladders, cutting whales into slices, and melting down blubber into oil, which they poured into seal-skins. All this mighty preparation was the provident spirit of catering for the winter: and the incredible quantities of these various provisions which our people saw collected, promised, at least, that famine would not be an evil of the approaching season.
>
> On these shores the winter is the happy portion of the year which is appropriated to luxury and ease; nor are they ever aroused into action, but to take some of those enormous whales, which, at that season, frequent their seas, in order to feast any of the neighbouring chiefs who may come to visit them.[12]

Commerce with traders virtually ceased at these busy times in the annual round.

At Clayoquot Sound, as at Nootka Sound, chiefs dictated the terms of group participation in the fur trade. Traders were usually offered little more than fresh food by Native commoners.[13] Wickaninish, his family, and chosen attendants controlled the traffic in furs. When the *Columbia* entered the sound in June 1791, Gray was ushered to Wickaninish, who opened trade negotiations. Hoskins noted that trade commenced "first with Wickananish's father, then with the other Chiefs in succession."[14] If commoners got to trade at all, it was after Wickaninish's entourage had finished. Meares suggested that Native groups visiting the sound usually had to pay tribute to Wickaninish for the privilege of bartering with trade vessels, and there are indications that some groups from the south were refused access altogether.[15]

This sociopolitical hierarchy, which probably had become more formalized and extenuated as a result of the Clayoquot-Hisau'istaht war, was reflected in feast arrangements at Opitsat. Wickaninish's house took centre stage in the village, and traders usually met other Clayoquot chiefs through him. He lived in "a great house adorned with columns of huge figures which hold up three large pine timbers, as long as ninety feet and thick in proportion," one Spanish explorer recorded. "The entrance is a figure the mouth of which is a door. More than one hundred persons besides the king live in it."[16] Meares was invited inside this huge house in July 1788 and claimed that he met over 800 people "divided into groupes, according to their respective offices, which had their distinctive places assigned them."[17]

Traders had different experiences with Wickaninish. Charles Bishop of the *Ruby* declared that he was "one of the most esay People" he ever knew. "He Prides himself on having but one Word in a Barter: he Throws the Skins before you ... [and says] I want such an Article; if you object, they are taken back into the Canoe and not offered again. A Stranger not knowing this Whim of his, would loose many skins."[18] The crew of the *Columbia* had a more frustrating time. When they first reached the sound in August 1788, they were received cordially by Wickaninish and trade prospects looked good. But Haswell noted that while the chief and his family came with many skins, "greatly to our mortification there was nothing in our vessel except muskits [which] would perchace one of them [and] that was an article we were not supplied with having scarce armes enough for our defence."[19] Wickaninish also demanded copper, but the *Columbia* had little of it either and left the sound empty handed.

These experiences point to Wickaninish's policy towards traders: he tried to get them to accept his prices, and traders did little business unless they took stock of his desires.[20] Wickaninish, like Maquinna, amassed a great deal of wealth from the trade. By attending feasts, traders acknowledged his power and thereby confirmed his status in the eyes of his followers and would-be challengers.[21] Wickaninish expected traders to participate in his world of power and prestige. There is hardly any suggestion in traders' journals that Wickaninish's followers were disgruntled with his handling of the trade or that other Clayoquot Sound chiefs challenged his supremacy.[22] He distributed large quantities of provisions and trade goods at feasts, thus consolidating his prestige by being generous with his relatives, allies, and followers.

SPATIAL POLITICS OF EXCHANGE

Traders felt threatened by Wickaninish's power, however, and took defensive measures. Meares declared that

the subjects of [Wickaninish] ... appeared to be far less civilized than our friends at Nootka; we therefore proportionably encreased our precautions. Their numbers were very considerable, and the boldness they discovered in all their transactions with us, gave us reason to believe, that any relaxation of our vigilance might tempt them to a conduct which would produce disagreeable consequences to us all ... We ... had sufficient reason to remain in a state of preparation against the possibility of that mischief which it was in his [Wickaninish's] power to do us, and which opportunity might tempt him to employ.[23]

Here again are some of the main elements of traders' vexed appreciation of place. Traders studied Wickaninish and appreciated the way he controlled Native affairs in the sound, but they never trusted him fully and recorded their physical anxieties with expressions about Native temptation and opportunism. The entrance to Clayoquot Sound is narrow, and traders could be detected easily by Native villagers. On passing into the sound, traders would have seen Opitsat straight ahead and, on many accounts, a large number of canoes approaching. Colnett, who was more narrow-minded and suspicious of Native peoples than were many traders, fired at Opitsat in December 1790 under the impression that a group of Clayoquot, who had attempted to board the *Argonaut*, had been instructed by their chief to capture the vessel.[24] Traders also took precautions because Wickaninish turned a blind eye to Native thefts from trade vessels. Kendrick and Gray built a bulwark around the *Washington* in 1789 after a cannon was stolen.[25] Pieces of equipment were also stolen from the *Gustavas III* while it was in the sound in 1791.[26]

But the exchange process itself was the biggest source of Native-White tension. Despite his defensiveness, Meares was sensitive to the ceremonial trappings of Native-White interaction, looked to attach himself to Native dignitaries, and sensed that present-giving was an integral part of the contact process at Clayoquot Sound. When he first reached the sound in June 1788, he was invited to a feast at Opitsat, where he presented Wickaninish with "a great variety of articles," including blankets and copper kettles; Meares suggested that the chief prized them highly. Fifty men then stepped in to the middle of Wickaninish's house, each displaying a six-foot-long sea otter skin, and remained still while Wickaninish informed Meares that the skins were "the return he proposed to make for our present."[27] "Our royal host appeared entirely satisfied with our homage," Meares noted, "and we ... were equally pleased with his magnificence."[28] One wonders whether Meares understood Native languages as well as he claimed, but we do get a good sense from him (and the Spanish) that Wickaninish used foreigners to bolster his status and would not negotiate exchange rates or trade regularly with vessels until such "homage" had been paid.[29]

Traders who did not pay as much attention to this prestation system gathered fewer furs. When the *Columbia* returned to the sound in June 1791, loaded with copper and muskets, Wickaninish and his family went on board but "appear'd quite indifferent about trading; rather wishing to receive our articles of traffic as presents."[30] Gray was reluctant to exchange presents, however, because he thought that they "would cost much dearer than if the skins were purchased," and he declined some of Wickaninish's invitations to attend some important events at Opitsat.[31] This evidently irritated the chief, and tension between the two groups mounted.

In June 1791, a Hawaiian boy named Ottoo deserted the *Columbia*, and Gray held one of Wickaninish's brothers hostage until he was returned.[32] Gray's actions seemed to be forgotten when the *Columbia* anchored at Clayoquot Sound for the winter three months later. Hoskins and Boit feasted at Opitsat, and in January 1792 they witnessed an important potlatch at which Wickaninish's twelve-year-old son assumed his father's name and chiefly privileges.[33] And Clayoquot chiefs dined regularly on the *Columbia*. Trouble was never far from the surface, though. In October 1791, one of Wickaninish's brothers tried to take Gray's "great coat"; other thefts occurred over the next few months.[34] Then, on 18 February 1792, Gray thought he had uncovered a Native plot to massacre his crew. Ottoo admitted to Gray that one of Wickaninish's brothers promised to make him a great chief if he would wet the firearms, small cannon, swivel guns, and powder on the *Columbia*. Hoskins became convinced that Ottoo's story was true when Wickaninish and his brothers started to inspect the *Columbia* carefully and ask detailed questions about the seaworthiness of the *Adventure*, a sloop Gray was building on the shore.[35] Native people approached the *Columbia* and the *Adventure* over the following two days in war canoes, making "the most dreadfull shrieks and whoops," and Haswell claimed that Wickaninish had over 200 firearms and plenty of ammunition. But Gray had taken adequate precautions and no attack transpired.[36]

After Ottoo's revelation, Hoskins noted that "it was not revenge for any injury they had received for which they were seeking[;] it was alone to possess themselves of our property which to them appeared immense."[37] But then on 20 February, Wickaninish and one of his brothers visited the *Columbia* "with the most specious shew of friendship" and presented a sea otter cape and two skins. "[T]hese Captain Gray took from them," Hoskins recounted, "and told them to go to Yethlure and Yeklan to whom a musket and cloth cootsack [coat] had been sent for their pay[.] [T]hese chiefs were then ordered to depart and never to return again on pain of death." Hoskins then thought that Gray had overreacted to the rumoured Native plot: his captain's dismissal of Wickaninish had "effectively shut up our source of trade ... and we now have no longer a right to expect to be able to procure any more skins from this tribe who as yet have done us no farther injury than alarm us."[38] Finally, Gray destroyed Opitsat as he was leaving the sound at the end of March in retaliation for the insults he thought he had endured.[39] Fortunately, the village was deserted at the time.

This is a classic example of the way contact relations could disintegrate over the course of a few weeks or months – one that was repeated many times on the Northwest Coast. Mutual suspicion and contempt did not disappear as Natives and traders grew familiar with each other. Contact relations often became pricklier the longer a trader stayed in one place. Gray's destruction of Opitsat stemmed from his general distrust of Native peoples, but Wickaninish may have intended to attack his crew. Indeed, Yvonne Marshall hypothesizes that Wickaninish did plan to take the *Adventure*, and the *Argonaut* before that, in order to enter the fur trade himself.[40] This is certainly credible, for by the late 1780s Clayoquot chiefs were using sails to power their canoes, and in 1793 and again in 1795 Wickaninish tried to purchase a schooner from traders.[41] But it does not fully explain why tension grew.

Traders' violent actions were remembered differently by Clayoquot people and were reported differently by other traders. When Magee of the *Jefferson* reached the sound in 1793, Wickaninish's brothers told him that contact relations had disintegrated because traders had not observed Native protocol and that Native frustration had reached fever pitch over Gray's "loan of a coat of war" to Wickaninish (probably the transaction on 20 February noted by Hoskins).[42] Gray did not treat this transaction as a loan; Clayoquot people reported that Gray was unhappy with the number of furs he had received for the coat and threatened to shoot one of Wickaninish's brothers unless more furs were brought in recompense.[43] Drucker claimed that there was a "vagueness as to the values" Nuu-chah-nulth groups attributed to wealth goods such as furs and blankets and that "there was no concept of borrowing and lending, and even less, of loans at interest." And, indeed, the Nuu-chah-nulth were vague, at least in comparison with Kawkwaka'wakw groups and with the elaborate systems of exchange, wealth complexes, and permutations of debt that characterized societies and polities in the Pacific Islands during this period.[44] There were "rough standards" of barter, Drucker observed, "but each exchange was arrived at as an individual case."[45] Now Drucker was a good student of Native social life, but he was a poor student of material culture. While some Nuu-chah-nulth groups may not have worked with concepts of borrowing and lending, Wickaninish evidently did, especially in his dealings with traders.

The violence did not stop there. In August 1792, William Brown, master of the British vessel *Butterworth*, told Ingraham that Clayoquot Natives had attacked his crew "without any cause of provocation," killing one person and wounding two others.[46] But Ingraham again got a different picture from Magee, who had been on the scene: "He said the English sailors landed at a village in order to rob the natives and actually cut several skins off the natives' backs."[47] Armed conflict broke out, which Magee quelled by firing a cannon into the air. Magee learned more about this violent affair when he returned to Clayoquot Sound the following year, and he described how the actions of Colnett, Gray, and Brown had affected contact relations.

We were visited ... by a number of women & children belonging to the family of Wicananish as well as by two of his brothers, to all of whome [we] paid particular attention while on board, presenting them with various trifling articles to thire fancy with regard to Commencing a trade with the Cheeff ... Tatootchicsettle said that his brother [Wickaninish] would not come on board for that purpose unless two of the officers of the ship would go on shore to remain till his return from the ship and being assented to the[y] immediately sent a message to thire brother to acquaint

him thereof & mention the various articles with which it was proposed to affect a
trade ... [I]n the afternoon the messenger returned with [the] answer that Wicananish
should not come on board, upon which the brother proposed that we should send
the 3rd officer with another to wait upon him & know from himself respecting the
prosecution of any business with him ... [The] docter went down to the village in a
Canoe carrying a few small presents. [R]eturning on board in the evening [he] reported that having had a Conference with his Majesty & being courteously & civily
treated by him & those around him[,] he [Wickaninish] informed them that ... he
should not come on board this or any other vessel whatever for the futer, giving the
reason his having being insulted & his people fired upon & several of them killed,
among which were his brother & two Cheeffs, by the people belonging to an English ship visiting that place the last season Commanded by Capt Brown who not
having received such a number of Skins from him as to be esteemed a sufficient
Complementary return to the present he had made him, of his own will had thought
fit to extr[ac]t them by sending his boat armed & which attacked him at his village.
[He] also mentioned a further instance of Capt Gray of Boston ... [H]e did not
Conceive it safe for to trust his own person on any vessel ... he could not but be
apprehensive some advantage would be taken upon him by some unknown stranger
to his people's hurt. [H]e seemed to have amassed Confidence in Capt Kendrick ...
believed that Capt Roberts was his friend and ment no hurt to him, but observed
that if he were to trust one he might all. [He] was willing if he [we] would send his
Copper and Cloth &c to the village to trade thire if agreable & his brother should
remain on board while we were trading.[48]

I relate these stories mindful of traders' conflictual economy of truth, but I
think this nexus of documentation relating to Clayoquot Sound allows us to
build up a reasonable impression of Wickaninish's approach to traders. This
passage from Magee points to the ebb and flow of contact relations at Clayoquot
Sound in the early 1790s and suggests that misunderstanding and conflict was
rooted in the exchange process and appreciation of Native protocol.

In Nuu-chah-nulth societies, rank and status were acknowledged and confirmed through the giving and receiving of goods, and Native leaders expected
traders to conform to these values. The form and quantity of goods given, and
whether any return was expected, depended on the type of relationship being
forged or renewed. Marriage alliances were often expensive, and the size of a
dowry varied according the relative rank and status of the transacting parties. In
1793, Wickaninish told Magee that he had very few skins because he had "exposed of his whole stock in the purchase of a young wife & alliance from
Maquinna."[49] In presenting a large dowry, Wickaninish may have been acknowledging that he was "not considered as equal in rank to Maquilla" – the observation being Meares's.[50] The negotiation of Native-White trading relationships
could also involve the exchange of a large number of presents, as Meares's case

illustrates. Wickaninish treated such exchanges as ways of establishing political and commercial bonds with traders for the duration of their stay. Meares sensed that these bonds had to be reaffirmed each time he returned to Clayoquot Sound. He presented Wickaninish with copper kettles and twelve brass-hilted swords when he returned to Opitsat in August 1788, and a "brisk trade" then commenced.[51]

Other traders were reluctant to follow Meares's lead and became frustrated by this logic of present-giving. They thought it a Native ruse. Clayoquot Sound, like other trading locations on the coast, was a space of miscomprehension where traders' fears and (mis)perceptions of Native agendas sat uneasily with Native expectations of Whites. I tried to explain traders' confusions over the exchange process at Nootka Sound in terms of Native rivalry and collaboration. At Clayoquot Sound, on the other hand, tension and conflict should be interpreted in terms of this prestation system.

Goods had phantasmagoric qualities. A "coat of war," of trifling value relative to Gray's grander commercial scheme, heightened tension and led to the *Columbia*'s premature departure from the sound. A copper kettle, again of trifling value in Meares's grand scheme of things but given as a present and apparently highly prized by Wickaninish, facilitated trade. Exchange relations were emblematic of power relations – of the facility to use objects to establish and hold together social relationships. The power to exchange lay at the threshold of the forms of power that chiefs and traders exercised over their constitutive groups. The successful exchange of furs and kettles substantiated routinized facets of sanction and domination – the disciplinary power invested in vessel masters by their financiers to control a vessel's cargo, supervise the daily tasks of crew members, and punish transgressions of a stipulated code of conduct; or the power bestowed on a chief by primogeniture and rank, and the power invested in him by a larger kin community, to coordinate the seasonal round, handle the community's furs, and police interaction with foreigners. The authoritativeness of Meares's and Wickaninish's power to exchange rested on these social relations of power. Yet there was a fine line between power based on social sanction and power that entailed domination – or between the performative search for prestige and the demonstrative exercise of power. Wickaninish and Meares supported each other's taste for prestige by exchanging presents, but their followers and crew would not sanction their dominion over the exchange process unless they could see that their interests were being considered. In Drucker's view, Native peoples based such judgements on social notions of generosity. Wickaninish's monopolistic strategy apparently worked because he redistributed many of the articles he got from traders.[52] The crews of trade vessels probably sized up whether they could trade privately with Natives behind their captain's back as well as whether their captain ensured that they got adequate provisions. Captains took these concerns seriously. Meares's crew attempted mutiny a number of times.[53]

Native concepts of value and exchange were not as vague or individualized as Drucker claimed; rather, value was corporeal and liminal: it stemmed from physical and imaginative processes of exchange. Goods carried alienable social and political identities, and exchange prices and relations were as stable or unstable as the socially sanctioned relations of power that underpinned the way Native and White leaders matched their demands and desires. The officers of the *Columbia* were critical of Gray for overstepping the bounds of Native protocol and taking matters into his own hands. Meares realized that the way he operated in Native space had just as much bearing on his profit margins as the use he could make of the "golden round."

These relations of prestige and power, sanction and domination – of performance and appropriation in exchange – were also acutely spatialized. The matching of demands involved the negotiation of social space. In times of calm, the trade vessel and the chief's house were spaces where Natives and Whites witnessed each other's ways, inspected each other's goods, and negotiated each other's fortunes. In times of tension or conflict, they were transformed into bastions of safety in unpredictable waters. Physical and imaginary lines dividing self and other became starker and less negotiable, as the passage from Magee suggests. A chief checked how many guns a trading party had as it approached his village. Watchmen stationed on the quarterdeck of a trade vessel peered into shadows for signs of approaching canoes. Hostages were exchanged like pawns in a more rarefied and bloody game of contact. The ship and the Native village were transformed from spaces of mutual exploration into containers of power. Wickaninish knew traders by name and discriminated between them, but once the threshold of abuse had been crossed he was forced to think of them as one – as unknown quantities. He still wanted copper and cloth, but the contact relationship was reduced to an exchange of bodies under pain of death. Natives and Whites became more proprietorial about their goods and spaces. There was little in the contact process more basic than this recourse to hostage-taking and violence. In the maritime fur trade the entanglement of bodies, spaces, and objects was volatile.

Meares also documented the ebb and flow of contact relations at Clayoquot Sound, and he pointed to the way objects and spaces took on different properties and connotations in times of peace and tension. His "state of preparation" against a Native attack in June 1788

was considered by the chief as distrust in his friendship, gave him great offence, and occasioned a short coolness between us ... Wicananish observed that whenever he paid us a visit the great cabin was decorated with arms, and that several blunderbusses, &c. were placed on the deck; and not only left the ship in great anger, but refused to trade with us himself, and forbade his people from bringing us any supplies or fish or vegetable. It was not, however, by any means, our interest that things should remain in this unpleasant, as well as inconvenient situation; it was therefore thought prudent to pay him a visit of peace on the following day; when, by the conciliating present of a sword, with a brass handle, and a large copper dish, the treaty of friendship was renewed; and this restoration of good humour was confirmed by a present of five beautiful otter skins, a fat doe, and supply of fish for the crew. The generosity, as well as the friendly conduct of the chief, on this occasion, seemed to demand an extraordinary exertion of acknowledgement on ours; and we made him happy beyond expression, by adding to his regalia a pistol and two charges of powder; a present which he had long solicited.[54]

Traders and Native chiefs had to exert themselves to maintain pleasant and convenient contact relations; they opened and closed their domiciles as events turned.

Traders continued to visit Clayoquot Sound because Wickaninish had more furs than other chiefs on Vancouver Island, but the area became known as a volatile space of interaction.[55] The trickery and violence that went with the trade culminated in the Clayoquot attack on John Jacob Astor's vessel the *Tonquin* in 1811. Most of the crew were slaughtered, and one of the survivors blew up the vessel the following day, killing over 100 Natives as they plundered the decks. Contemporaries saw this event as a leitmotif of Indian savagery, and the Clayoquot were held to be the most warlike Native group on Vancouver Island. There are many different accounts of what happened, and American and Canadian journalists, collectors, and scholars have written more about the *Tonquin* disaster than any other single event in early British Columbian history.[56] I do not want to discuss this event in any detail here, but I will note that many accounts imply that the disaster was sparked, again, by a misunderstanding over trade. According to a number of contemporary observers, there was a dispute over trade prices, an important Native chief became "insolent" towards a trader, and the trader struck him with a sea otter pelt. White commentators viewed the Native attack as a cold-blooded act of revenge.[57] A Native account collected by W.E. Banfield in the 1850s provides a slightly different assessment: an old Indian named Wookamis annoyed the chief trader of the vessel because he asked for an extra present after a trade deal had been struck; he may have received fewer presents from the trader than he expected or was trying his luck.[58] In sum, when traders and commentators tried to account for conflict at Clayoquot Sound, they generally lapsed into remarks about Indian savagery and did not see abuse of the Native prestation system as a primary source of tension. The Native accounts collected by Magee and Banfield, on the other hand, suggest that the giving and receiving of presents was integral to the way Clayoquot people engaged foreigners and was one of their main sources of irritation with traders.

WICKANINISH AND BARKLEY SOUND

But there was more to Wickaninish's involvement in the fur trade than his dealings with traders. He also competed with neighbouring chiefs and extended his sway beyond the sound. Traders had to pass Vargas Island (Ahousaht territory) to get to Opitsat, and in the late 1780s there was a complex set of negotiations between Wickaninish and Ahousaht chiefs Hanna and Detooche over trade privileges on the outside coast of Clayoquot Sound. They argued over access to trade vessels and the order in which they should trade.[59] The Ahousaht were an autonomous group and seemed to have peaceful relations with the Clayoquot during the early contact period. A Clayoquot-Ahousaht war would have caused political instability in the region and pushed traders away. Wickaninish also had marriage ties with Maquinna and Hannape, and Chief Tatoosh of Cape Flattery.[60] When Wickaninish's people visited Nootka Sound to trade, they were granted freer access to trade vessels than were other visiting groups.[61] Maquinna and Tatoosh were not given free reign to trade at Clayoquot, but they were certainly welcomed and feasted by Wickaninish.

Wickaninish adopted a more aggressive policy towards groups immediately south of Clayoquot Sound, however. Between 1789 and 1793 the Native peoples of Barkley Sound refused to sell their furs to traders, saying that they were to be collected by Wickaninish.[62] Clayoquot chiefs visited the American vessel *Jefferson* regularly while it wintered at the head of Toquart Bay in 1793-94; they collected furs from Barkley Sound groups to trade to Magee.[63] And in 1795, Captain Bishop of the *Ruby* ascertained that the Native groups of Ucluelet Arm were "subject" to the Clayoquot. Bishop traded only two of the fifty furs promised him by Ucluelet chief Hyhocus and was told that the remainder had been disposed of to Wickaninish, their "sovereign."[64]

Wickaninish extorted furs from these groups and dominated the west side of Barkley Sound. When a crew member of the *Jefferson* was murdered in Toquart harbour by Natives from "Seshart" (Ts!icya'atHa people) in October 1793, Wickaninish advised the captain to take two Native lives in retaliation and added that he had "been under the necessity himself to kill forty of them not long since on acc[oun]t of thire obstenate & troublesome disposition ... that the[y] paid him little tribute."[65] There is also evidence that Wickaninish used the firearms and ammunition he traded from Gray to check the growing influence of the Hatc'a'atHa (Jewitt's A-y-charts) in Barkley Sound. The Hatc'a'atHa fought and defeated the T!o'mak'Lai'atHa and two other Barkley Sound groups, probably just before contact, after a dispute over territorial jurisdiction.[66] Then the Hatc'a'atHa fought with the T'ok'wa'atHa (Toquart). The Ucluelets joined in the conflict when a Hatc'a'atHa killed a Ucluelet, having mistaken him for a T'ok'wa'atHa. The Ucluelet raided with spears and swords. Then the Clayoquot sided with the Ucluelet and joined the war. "They said that the Hachaa Tribe was bad and had killed a Clayoquot," Alex Thomas (one of Edward Sapir's Native fieldworkers) was told in 1914 by Kwishanishim, a Ucluelet informant. "The Clayoquots had got guns ... The Hachaa learned that the Clayoquots had guns. They laughed at them. They said they were only for frightening and that they could not kill. The Clayoquots never raided twice, but always wiped out the enemy in a single raid, because they knew how to fight"; after the raid "no one was left of the Hachaa."[67] This war probably started in April 1792. In January 1792, Boit noted that Clayoquot chiefs "had been telling us for some time that they was going to war with a distant tribe and wish'd for us to lend them Musketts and Ammunition."[68] A month later there was gunfire around Opitsat, and Chief Tootoocheetticus (one of Wickaninish's brothers) informed Hoskins that his people were preparing for a war against "a tribe not far distant called Hichahats [Hatc'a'atHa] who had not of late in every respect paid them that homage which they thought due to so great a nation," and that he had been teaching his people how to fire muskets.[69] Haswell was told that the Clayoquot wanted guns – and, if we pursue Marshall's logic, a vessel as well – to attack the village of Highshakt.[70] Kwishanishim's account implies that the Clayoquot had used guns before to intimidate their neighbours, and it also suggests that Wickaninish's sway over the west side of Barkley Sound was resisted. This war against the Hatc'a'atHa probably lasted for around ten years, for when Jewitt met Wickaninish at Nootka Sound in 1803, the chief informed him that he had just been at war with the "Ah-char-arts" and had killed 150 of them.[71]

Traders discerned only the edges of these Native relations around Barkley Sound, but they sensed that Wickaninish effectively controlled the region. "He lives in a state of magnificence much superior to any of his neighbours, and [is] both loved and dreaded by the other chiefs," Meares observed. "His subjects, as he himself informed us, amounted to about thirteen thousand people": 4,000 in Clayoquot Sound; 2,000 around Ucluelet Arm and Barkley Sound; and 7,000 people further south.[72] Meares did not spell out what he meant by "subject," and we do not know where he got his figures from, but he used such phrases and "facts" to draw out the difference between Wickaninish's and Maquinna's approach to the maritime fur trade. The historical and ethnographic record suggests that Wickaninish did not form trade or marriage ties with these Barkley Sound groups and, therefore, did not have to worry about creating divided loyalties in times of conflict. He had peaceful trade ties with the Native groups of Cape Flattery and Nittinat, and groups to the north, but he was ruthless with his Barkley Sound neighbours, instituting a tribute system.[73]

Wickaninish took advantage of the fact that Barkley Sound was a highly volatile region. During the eighteenth century there were a series of wars and amalgamations between Native groups of various sizes in and around the Broken

Group Islands. By the late eighteenth century, there were probably five main local groups in the central and western part of the sound: the T'ok'wa'atHa (Toquart); the Ts!icya'atHa (Sheshart); the MakL'ai'atHa; the T!o'mak'Lai'atHa; and the Hatc'a'atHa (Haachaht) (see Figures 6 and 7). Warfare between these groups and their neighbours proliferated in the early contact period and lasted until the 1850s, when an amalgamated Sheshart tribe established itself in the Broken Group Islands.[74] In the 1840s and 1850s slaves were also captured in Barkley Sound by Clallam, Makah, Pacheenaht, and Ditidaht groups and sold in Port San Juan, the fledgling town of Victoria, and Cape Flattery.[75]

Richard Inglis and James Haggarty, who conducted an archaeological survey of Barkley Sound and have synthesized most of the ethnographic data on the region, show that there were intense and violent inter-Native conflicts in Barkley Sound between the late eighteenth and mid-nineteenth centuries, and they hypothesize that the maritime fur trade was one of the principal catalysts. The Ahousaht, Clayoquot, Ucluelet, these five Barkley Sound groups, the Ohiaht on the east side of Barkley Sound, and the Ditidaht to the south, all trying to make the most out of the trade, focused their competitive and destructive energies on Barkley Sound. Native contact with traders was quite sporadic in the sound itself, but there was a large population of sea otters. There was great competition between the T'ok'wa'atHa, Ts!icya'atHa, and Hatc'a'atHa over trade with the *Jefferson* in 1793-94, such as these groups managed it behind Wickaninish's back. The Ts!icya'atHa, like the Hatc'a'atHa, also became embroiled in conflict with the Clayoquot and Ucluelet during the 1790s. And in 1793, Ts!icya'atHa villages were attacked by the Oanayit'atHa, a Ditidaht group, and by the *Jefferson*.[76] The Ts!icya'atHa abandoned the region in the early nineteenth century; their territories were occupied by the Ahousaht and Ucluelet until "The long war in Barkley Sound," which broke out around 1830 and was started by a Ts!icya'atHa raid on the Ucluelet (see Figure 7).[77] When Hamilton Moffatt, a Hudson's Bay Company trader, visited the west coast of Vancouver Island in the late 1840s, he reported that there was warfare among most of the tribes; and when George Blenkinsop toured Barkley Sound for the Canadian Department of Indian Affairs in 1874, he observed numerous deserted villages in Barkley Sound and noted that many people had perished because of frequent wars with the Clayoquot.[78]

These wars entailed depopulation and profound settlement change, and they probably became more destructive as firearms became more available. In the late nineteenth century Augustus Brabant was told by Native people that some Barkley Sound groups decided to exterminate the Clayoquot after the *Tonquin* disaster, believing they had few warriors left, but the Clayoquot, known for their ingenuity, dressed their women in war robes to scare off aggressors.[79] There were attacks on the Clayoquot, however. According to a story heard by an American pioneer in the mid-nineteenth century, two White survivors of the *Tonquin*

disaster, a blacksmith and his father, who were captured by the Clayoquot, operated two cannons recovered from the vessel in a war that "sprang up ... [with] a
neighbouring tribe" in 1813 – probably Barkley Sound people.[80]

   If we trust the statements of Meares and Eliza, and Blenkinsop's 1874 census,
the Native population of the Barkley Sound region fell by about 90 percent during the first 100 years of contact, from 9,000 to 10,000 people to less than 1,000.[81]
These are general estimates, of course, but they give a vivid impression of significant Native depopulation. Between the mid-1850s and 1870s, much of this
devastation was caused by smallpox, measles, dysentery, and scrofula (tubercu-
losis of the lymph glands), which spread along the coast of Vancouver Island.
Inglis and Haggarty suggest that warfare was the principal cause of depopulation in the late eighteenth and early nineteenth centuries. A Hudson's Bay Company census taken sometime between the early 1840s and early 1850s gives a
Native population of 2,770 between Port San Juan and Ahousaht territory, including 379 Clayoquot people, 215 Ucluelet people, and 392 Ohiaht people, but
only 31 Toquart people and 119 Sheshart people.[82] These figures imply that there
had been great population decline in Barkley Sound before the spread of disease. They are echoed in William Banfield's 1859 census of the male adult population of the region, which gives 190 Clayoquot men, 120 Ucluelet men, and 175
Ohiaht men, but only 11 Toquart men and 16 Sheshart men. Banfield also noted
that some of the tribes between Barkley Sound and Port San Juan were "slave or
tributary tribes" to Clayoquot, Nootka, Kyuquot, and Ahousaht groups.[83] Inglis
and Haggarty argue that the Broken Group Islands were abandoned around the
time of contact because of inter-Native conflict and that tribal boundaries
changed markedly. There were probably many more large Native settlements in
Barkley Sound in pre-contact times than the few that traders and Spanish explorers counted in the late eighteenth century (see Figure 7).[84]

   How much of this warfare can be attributed to the presence of traders and the
influx of trade goods and firearms is open to debate. The Native war stories
collected by Sapir and his workers in the 1910s contain few references to Whites
or the fur trade, but this does not necessarily mean that the maritime fur trade
did not ignite or inflame Native grievances. Barkley Sound was never a major
centre of Native-White trade, but it remained a region of intense inter-Native
conflict into the nineteenth century, in part because of the uneven geographical
distribution of wealth flowing from the fur trade. Wickaninish pillaged furs from
Barkley Sound using the firearms he had traded.[85]

   Traders visited other fairly large Native settlements in Ditidaht and Pacheenaht
territory but did not sail far into the Strait of Juan de Fuca until the 1820s, when
Hudson's Bay Company traders started to venture into the Strait of Georgia to
trade. Between 1785 and the 1810s, the maritime fur trade effectively stopped at
Tatoosh's Island, Cape Flattery, where there was a large Native settlement (see
Figure 4). Meares, Charles Duncan, Gray, and other traders visited Cape Flattery

- ● Main village site and/or defensive site
- X Village identified by traders
- + Sheshart village, attacked by *Jefferson,* 1793
- ▬ ▬ ▬ Group boundary

⟵ Cycle of raids and group amalgamations, in Broken Group Islands, affecting Sheshart before the long war in Barkley Sound, as hypothesized by Inglis and Haggarty (1986)

① Hatc'a'atHᵃ take territory of T!o'mak'Lai'atHᵃ by his'ōk't

② Hatc'a'atHᵃ warred with Mak'LᵋaiᵋatHᵃ, and almost wiped them out

③ Mak'LᵋaiᵋatHa joined Ts!icya'atHᵃ

④ Hatc'a'atHᵃ fought T'ok'wa'atHᵃ, either having taken NácᵋasᵋatHᵃ territory as his'ōk't, or after the Ts!icya'atHᵃ had conquered the NácᵋasᵋatHᵃ, and come into conflict with the T'ok'wa'atHᵃ

⑤ But before the long war in Barkley Sound, in the early nineteenth century, this region was controlled by Ucluelets, who gained it from the Hatc'a'atHᵃ or Ts!icya'atHᵃ

⑥ Ts!icya'atHᵃ fought with the Ahousahts

Figure 7 Map showing main settlement and/or defensive sites, and sociopolitical arrangements in the Broken Group Islands, Central Barkley Sound in the late pre-contact period
Source: Adapted from Richard I. Inglis and James C. Haggarty, "Pacific Rim National Park: Ethnographic history," unpublished report to Parks Canada, Calgary, 1986.

a number of times, but they found Chiefs Tatoosh (of Tatoosh's Island) and Cassacan (of Nittinat) difficult to deal with, and some trade vessels were attacked by Natives in this area.[86] Spanish explorers ventured farther into the Strait of Juan de Fuca in the early 1790s, noting that the Natives were warlike and daring, that most of them had not met Whites before, and that there were many signs of Native warfare.[87]

As Vancouver and Galiano sailed into the Strait of Georgia in 1792, they encountered small groups of people living in scattered locations and discovered a stark, horrific reality: the ravages of smallpox. "The smallpox most have had," Peter Puget noted, "and most terribly pitted they are; indeed many have lost their Eyes, & no Doubt it has raged with uncommon Inveteracy among them."[88] Galiano noticed abandoned villages.[89] Cole Harris has argued that a smallpox epidemic swept the Strait of Georgia region in 1782, devastating Native populations (see Figure 4).[90] This epidemic seemingly spread as far west as Nittinat, the home of Chief Cassacan, who had a pock-marked face, and maybe as far north as Cape Mudge at the northern end of the Strait of Georgia. Tatoosh's people of Cape Flattery were spared from the disease, however, and it touched neither Nootka Sound nor Clayoquot Sound.

Given the amount of Native traffic along the west coast of Vancouver Island, the geographical reach of this epidemic is intriguing. There are no references to smallpox or measles in the historical or ethnographic record pertaining to Vancouver Island north of Nittinat in the late eighteenth century. In 1845, Roderick Finlayson, a Hudson's Bay Company factor at Fort Victoria, noted that there had only been "trifling intercourse" between Cape Flattery groups and those on the west coast of Vancouver Island before the 1840s.[91] Yet maritime fur traders reported that Wickaninish's brothers visited Cape Flattery regularly, that Tatoosh and Cassacan visited Barkley Sound and Clayoquot Sound to trade and capture slaves, and that Tatoosh collected furs from groups living along the Strait of Juan de Fuca.[92] This raises many questions, among them whether these Native trade patterns were post-1785 creations.

GEOGRAPHIES OF TRADE

At Nootka Sound the maritime fur trade encouraged the consolidation of pre-existing trade routes – principally the Nimpkish-Tahsis Trail – as well as the elaboration of others to the north and south. But what about Clayoquot Sound and Barkley Sound? The archaeological and ethnographic data presented by Arcas Associates and by Inglis and Haggarty suggest that whether at peace or war, local groups operated within fairly small resource territories in pre-contact times. Native inter-connectedness seemed to grow as a result of the Clayoquot-Hisau'istaht war, the wars involving the Ts!icya'atHa and the Hatc'a'atHa, and

Clayoquot and Ucluelet intervention in Barkley Sound around the time of contact. The maritime fur trade bolstered Wickaninish's power and probably encouraged the Clayoquot to become more mobile. Traders' focus on Clayoquot Sound, and the likelihood that a smallpox epidemic had devastated the Strait of Georgia region, probably also encouraged southern Nuu-chah-nulth groups to venture north more frequently to trade. The fur trade was superimposed on processes of territorial change that had probably been under way for a number of decades before contact, and it encouraged the reformulation of Native trade patterns.

Wickaninish's dominance, and the geography of Clayoquot Sound, also gives us a good view of the spatiality of exchange. Trade vessels were vulnerable islands in Native waters. Traders could not hide in Clayoquot Sound, and violence led to more violence. Wickaninish wanted guns and powder, and as firearms changed hands, a ship's arsenal looked less threatening to Native peoples. Power flowed through particular spatial conduits – the quarterdeck, the ship's side netting, the Native longhouse, and the passage between ship and shore. Cultural sanction and brute force, familiarity and estrangement, were bound up in jagged ways in these spaces. Routines of interaction erupted into violence; violence gathered its own routines. Literary-minded scholars discuss how, in encounters with otherness, people fall back on the basic texts of their culture – on stark ethnocentrisms. At Clayoquot Sound, traders' basic texts were the spaces they lived in. They gave their experiences textual form, and traders such as Meares played on the theatricality of cultural and material exchange, but it was on the ropes, at the forecastle, in the longboat, and at entrance to a Native longhouse that dramas and plots unfolded and characters emerged. The metaphorical realm of commercial contact, where allegories of profit headed back to London and Boston, emanated from these spaces.

CHAPTER 9

Regional Geographies of Accommodation and Appropriation

Until recently there were basically two theses about the impact of the maritime fur trade on Native-White relations in British Columbia. The first, marked by the colonialist paradigm of thought sketched in Part 1, was that the trade marked the beginning of the end for Native peoples. F.W. Howay argued that the trade was "of a predatory character and best constituted unequal trade with a primitive people" – "merely a looting of the coast."[1] Drucker recycled Howay's views in his popular book *Indians of the Northwest Coast*, arguing that maritime fur traders "had no interest in cultivating the good will of the natives."[2] And in a more general article on Native-White contact in North America, Edward Sapir argued that the influx of Western goods caused "the fading away of genuine [Native] cultures." Native people, he proclaimed, "slipped out of the warm embrace of culture into the cold air of fragmentary existence."[3] Salvage ethnography was spurred on by this nineteenth-century Western ideology of Native cultural decline and fragmentation.

Howay's views, particularly, were tied to the assumption that Native peoples lived in unchanging societies – and "in harmony with [their] maritime environment," as a latter day historian has finished his thought – and that regardless of traders' actions, Western commodities could only dislocate Native societies.[4] Such notions stemmed from the idea that Native groups suffered because of their fatal attraction to Western goods; that they were victims of their own innocent, short-sighted desire to trade. These scholars denied that Native peoples had much control over the terms of trade. Their arguments helped to justify the Indian reserve system; they took the sting out of formal colonialism by rooting Native dislocation and dependence on Whites in a pre-colonial past. Howay, a judge, was perhaps contrasting the violence of the maritime fur trade with a colonial order based on the rule of law.

This formulation was first questioned fully in 1947 by Joyce Wike, a political scientist, who argued that the maritime fur trade facilitated an efflorescence "of prevailing [Native] cultural emphases and directions."[5] Her thesis has been developed most forcefully and consistently by Robin Fisher. Over the last twenty years Fisher has held that "the cultural balance sheet, like the trade itself, was evenly weighed during the early years of contact."[6] He maintains that Native peoples "met the maritime fur trade and molded it to serve their ends."[7] The two groups established a "mutually beneficial" relationship, Native societies were enriched through trade, and Native chiefs controlled the traffic.[8]

This second thesis, popularly known as the enrichment thesis, challenges images of Native dislocation and the metanarrative of White invasion that informs much twentieth-century historical literature on the impact of European trade on the peoples of the Pacific. Fisher grapples with questions of Native agency, Western domination, and cultural continuity and change among Indigenous peoples. Nicholas Thomas is one of the most sophisticated exponents of this style of inquiry, and he argues that

> although the ultimately exploitative character of the global economy can hardly be overlooked, an analysis which makes dominance and extraction central to intersocial exchange from its beginnings will frequently misconstrue power relations which did not, in fact, entail the subordination of native people. The character of early contact was often such that foreigners were in no position to enforce their demands; consequently local terms of trade often had to be acceded to ... The partial intransigence of indigenous societies in the face of both imperialism's sheer violence and its more subtle ploys must thus be recognised.[9]

Fisher would agree with this intellectual agenda, but he has tended to invoke it didactically rather than to work through it empirically. He focuses on chiefly control of the trade at places such as Nootka Sound and Clayoquot Sound to support his argument but ignores the more diffuse geographical ramifications of the trade on intra-group and inter-tribal relations. Chiefs such as Maquinna and Wickaninnish obviously did have a powerful influence on the contact process, but to what extent did they exercise such power at the expense of their followers and neighbours? And is "enrichment" the best concept and adjective with which to assess the nature of change among Native groups? Conceptually, this thesis assumes that trade goods had some automatic value to Native peoples. And it imputes Western values of accumulation and material progress to judge whether the trade – and Native-Western contact more generally – was good or bad for Native peoples. Empirically, the thesis is too general to account for the historical-geographical variation of Native demands and the uneven geography of Native participation in the trade.

Wike in fact shed doubt on the utility of the enrichment thesis for the study of early contact in the Northwest Coast in an article published in 1958, and she called for more research.[10] Over the last ten to fifteen years it has become increasingly clear that the earliest phase of contact was marked by intense social change and geographical disruption among some Native groups. Fisher underestimated the scale and impact of warfare and disease.[11] We now have a much more intricate and variegated image of contact, conflict, and change than what is allowed for in the enrichment thesis. The maritime fur trade fostered myriad alliances and oppositions, and probably entailed far more mechanisms of change than can be recovered. When looked at geographically and analyzed with questions of power in mind, questions of Native agency and social change become much more complex, and coastal generalizations about "the cultural balance sheet" of contact (itself a Western economic metaphor that reifies the corporeal dimensions of the trade) become more difficult to sustain.

But some general points about the maritime fur trade can be made. First, Native villages and regions became important, if fleeting, centres of trade in a coastal space-economy and capitalist world economy. The meaning and character of maritime fur trade changes when it is studied at these different scales. Analysis of contact dynamics at places such Nootka Sound and Clayoquot Sound can provide a vivid picture of how Natives and Westerners were situated in, and handled, the world economy. The trade juxtaposed different systems of the world. Natives and Westerners objectified each other because each had a limited, commercial interest in the other. If this made for a "mutually beneficial" contact relationship, then it was a volatile relationship that drew out cultural differences. For chiefs such as Maquinna and Wickaninish, trade vessels were enormous bulks of wealth that could generate prestige. Traders became pawns in Native strategies of power, and Western goods moved through Native circuits of social reproduction: kin networks and feast systems. Traders, on the other hand, worked at the fringes of the world economy, where Western systems of moral regulation and the trappings of civilization were a long way off, and displayed the stark logic of capitalist accumulation. Take what you can, and do what you have to do, to generate a profit: these were traders' basic mottoes; the Northwest Coast recommended itself to them in few other ways. For Western pundits such as Alexander Dalrymple, the coast was a distant and profitable arena of commodity exchange in an emerging system of free trade.

Traders often found it difficult to gauge profits from the exchange process, however. They had to negotiate with, and often fought with, Native groups for furs. The "just-so" stories of commercial and cultural exchange that Thomas has criticized, and the representational maps that traders drew to abstract themselves from the harshness of the coast and their accession to Native ways, belonged to Western imaginative geographies of commerce that diffused the impact of Native "subtle ploys" on capitalist expansion and attempted to pin heterogeneity to a great map of Western homogenization and commodification. The Western metaphorization of Native-White commercial contact as an exchange between unequals licensed Western attitudes of dominance and formulations of Indian primitivism. Yet in the maritime fur trade cultural superiority was assumed and imputed by both Natives and traders. Native peoples did not see the world economy, and a White presence was not yet fenced off by picket fences. Trade vessels and Native villages were bastions of power and islands of cultural difference. Wealth did not simply consist in a stock of goods, and the accumulation of wealth should not be toted up on a balance sheet. Material relations of accumulation and exchange were social relations, and these social relations were grounded in volatile and shifting projects of trade.

While Native chiefs exercised a good deal of control over the exchange process in their own areas, they could not control traders' movements. When the maritime fur trade is studied at regional scale, as a coastal encounter, and at a global scale, Native agency is cast in a different light. Native-Western interaction was circumscribed by the capitalist logic of creative destruction. The intensity and unevenness of the trade along the coast had important implications for Native groups. As they incorporated traders into their worlds of wealth, competition, and prestige, they were being absorbed into a capitalist space-economy of fixity and motion. Individual traders may not have always understood how they generated profit. They were often confused about the exchange process and often lied to one another about their successes. That many trade ventures were one- or two-time affairs suggests that many financiers were not confident about the long-term viability of the trade. But these White confusions and concerns show up the rapaciousness of the trade. Native centres of contact came and went with traders and, at a greater distance, with changing patterns of merchant investment on the Northwest Coast and in other parts of the world. Traders abandoned places such as Nootka Sound and Clayoquot Sound as soon as profits dried up, and commercial contact was often stripped down to the bare essentials of force. Howay and Drucker made these points, of course. We should accept them, but without their cultural baggage and with a sensitivity to the geographical dynamics of capitalism. Traders looted the coast, but this point should not be used to suggest that Native peoples were the dupes of capitalist expansion, for this denigrates the use that they made of traders and their goods. Still, the logic of capital compromised some Native projects and encouraged others. If capitalism works through a set of tensions between place and space, agglomeration and dispersal, monopoly and competition, as geographers such as David Harvey insist, then these conceptual couplets had different expressions in different parts of the world.[12] When tracked from the West, the maritime fur trade stands for commercial competition, capitalist dispersal, and the creation of the Pacific as a space of Western commercial interest and Native-Western exchange. When we look at the deployment of these capitalist energies along the coast, capitalism does not lose its meaningfulness as a geographically dynamic totality; rather, we see how it adapts to details and takes on particular forms. The capitalist tension between spatial concentration and dispersal was effected along the coast in a specific guise. Traders had to valorize Native places and to consider Native differences. The structures of fixed investment that tied capital to place were not physical infrastructures, such as factories, machinery, or rail networks, but Native chiefs. Chiefs were traders' main means of exchange, and they had to be studied and appeased. Yet traders were always looking for new spaces of exchange.

Second, then, Native patterns of interaction and power were altered significantly by the maritime fur trade. Native peoples became familiar with Westerners and probably came into more frequent and geographically extensive contact with each other because of the trade. Native centre-periphery relationships shifted as sea otter populations dwindled, Natives and traders came into conflict, and commercial capital moved around the coast. This commercial focus on Native places encouraged the concentration of Native people within particular villages, and the concentration of wealth, prestige, and influence in the hands of the chiefs who owned these villages. There is ample evidence to suggest that Yuquot and Opitsat grew considerably in the first decade or so of contact and that the two chiefs of these villages, Maquinna and Wickaninish, respectively, enhanced their power.

These Native processes of concentration had various ramifications within and between Native areas. Maquinna had a great influence over the fur trade at Nootka Sound, but he did not monopolize it. Traders and the Spanish encountered complex and shifting relations of competition and collaboration that were bound up with the social and political organization and alliance of local groups. Traders crossed inland and coastal resource sites that were owned by particular families, and Native competition over access to trade vessels and resource sites entailed a reworking of Native rights and privileges through marriage, trade, and conflict. At Clayoquot Sound, on the other hand, Native power was renegotiated over a larger area. Archaeological and ethnographic data suggest that there had been an amalgamation of local groups in Clayoquot Sound before traders arrived and that Wickaninish's family had become dominant. Wickaninish's control over the sea otter trade was more encompassing than Maquinna's, and Opitsat, the Clayoquot seat of power, was the principal node of trade. Maquinna pursued a fairly inclusionary strategy towards the trade, allowing his followers and neighbouring groups some access to trade vessels, whereas Wickaninish gained a monopoly.

These two chiefly strategies had different implications for surrounding Native groups. As the sea otter population of Nootka Sound dwindled more rapidly than that of Clayoquot Sound, Maquinna and other chiefs looked to the north and east for supplies. At Nootka Sound, Native competition and

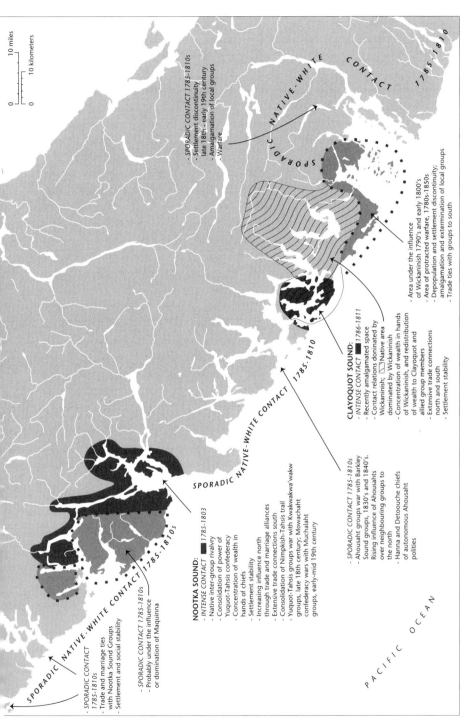

NOOTKA SOUND:
- *INTENSE CONTACT* ■ *1785-1803*
- Native inter-group rivalry
- Consolidation of power of Yuquot-Tahsis confederacy
- Concentration of wealth in hands of chiefs
- Settlement stability
- Increasing influence north through trade and marriage alliances
- Extensive trade connections south
- Consolidation of Nimpkish-Tahsis trail
- Yuquot-Tahsis groups war with Kwakwakwa'wakw groups, late 18th century; Mowachaht confederacy wars with Muchalaht groups, early-mid 19th century

- *SPORADIC CONTACT 1785-1810s*
- Ahousaht groups war with Barkley Sound groups, 1830's and 1840's.
- Rising influence of Ahousahts over neighbouring groups to the north
- Hanna and Detoouche chiefs of autonomous Ahousaht polities

CLAYOQUOT SOUND:
- *INTENSE CONTACT* ■ *1786-1811*
- Recently amalgamated space
- Contact relations dominated by Wickaninish; ▨ Native area dominated by Wickaninish
- Concentration of wealth in hands of Wickaninish, and redistribution of wealth to Clayoquot and allied group members
- Extensive trade connections north and south
- Settlement stability

- Area under the influence of Wickaninish 1790's and early 1800's
- Area of protracted warfare, 1780s-1850s
- Depopulation and settlement discontinuity; amalgamation and extermination of local groups
- Trade ties with groups to south

- *SPORADIC CONTACT 1785-1810s*
- Probably under the influence or domination of Maquinna

- *SPORADIC CONTACT 1785-1810s*
- Trade and marriage ties with Nootka Sound Groups
- Settlement and social stability

- *SPORADIC CONTACT 1785-1810s*
- Settlement discontinuity late 18th - early 19th century
- Amalgamation of local groups
- Warfare

SPORADIC NATIVE-WHITE CONTACT 1785-1810

SPORADIC NATIVE-WHITE CONTACT 1785-1810s

NATIVE-WHITE CONTACT 1785-1810

PACIFIC OCEAN

0   10 miles
0   10 kilometers

Figure 8   The geography of contact and the impact of the maritime fur trade on Native groups on the west coast of Vancouver Island, 1785-1810s

collaboration was characterized by trade and marriage alliances within the sound and to the north. It was also possibly marked by wars and alliances between Native groups of Nootka Sound and Nimpkish people. Yet if Maquinna and other chiefs managed to make Nootka Sound a core of Native power, their influence over surrounding groups seemed to wane quickly when traders quit the area in the mid-1790s. By contrast, the consolidation and expansion of Clayoquot power over neighbouring groups was violent and thoroughgoing. Wickaninish sought a Native tribute system and achieved more unbridled influence beyond his own locality than any chief of Nootka Sound could effect beyond theirs. This expansion of Clayoquot power probably helped Wickaninish to ameliorate the decline in Native-Western trade around Clayoquot Sound from the late 1790s.

I have depicted these Native relationships of power in Figure 8. Along the west coast of Vancouver Island, wealth flowed into some Native areas and bypassed others, making some Native groups powerful and others vulnerable to colonization. And the effect of the trade on Native material culture was not egalitarian. Some chiefs, such as Wickaninish, distributed many trade goods to their followers, but chiefly agendas also exacerbated inequalities of wealth within Native groups because Native people did not have equal access to traders. The sociopolitical dynamics of Native participation in the trade were geographical dynamics. Around the time of contact there was an intensification of Native territorial struggle. Native tribal territories were extended, subdivided, and amalgamated, and some Native groups were colonized or wiped out by other Native groups. Native geographies on Vancouver Island had been rearranged in important ways by the time colonists arrived in Victoria in the 1850s and Governor Douglas sent William Banfield to Barkley Sound to take a census of the Native population.

So third, generalizations about the impact of the trade on Native groups should be built up geographically as well as temporally, around the interconnections and cleavages between Native peoples through trade and marriage, disease and warfare. These points hold for the coast as a whole, but details and patterns of Native change no doubt varied within and between Native regions. My synthesis of developments on the west coast of Vancouver Island might be used to round out extant generalizations about Native change in this region but maybe not in others.[13] Inglis and Haggarty have proposed that on Vancouver Island, "contact with Euro-Americans at the end of the eighteenth century resulted in immediate and profound changes to economic patterns and to socio-political and settlement patterns for groups at the trading centres. In areas peripheral to this intensive contact changes were likely less radical and the traditional patterns persisted."[14] I agree with their last point, but Yvonne Marshall and Arcas Associates have shown that at Nootka Sound and Clayoquot Sound there was settlement stability and a consolidation of socio-political structures during the era of the maritime fur trade. Indeed, Inglis's and Haggarty's own analysis suggests that the most profound changes in subsistence and settlement patterns, and socio-political structures, occurred in areas immediately adjacent to main centres of trade, such as Barkley Sound. Marshall argues that "greater changes probably occurred among those groups who maintained small sovereign polities than among those who developed more complex sovereign and confederate polities."[15] Small polities, such as the groups of Barkley Sound, became destabilized because of the actions of powerful chiefs such as Wickaninish. But should we deduce the likelihood and extent of change on the basis of levels of sociopolitical sophistication, as Marshall implies? Such a model is attentive to the importance of kinship relations in Nuu-chah-nulth life, but it downplays issues of brute material power and logistical-political issues raised by depopulation due to warfare.

How the spread of disease affected the logistics of Native territorial change on the west coast of Vancouver Island is less clear. Some epidemics, spreading from the plains and Central America, reached the Northwest Coast before explorers and traders. Other diseases came with contact. We do not know whether the Native groups of the Northwest Coast had been hooked into North American circuits of European disease before the 1770s. One wonders about the extent to which Native groups associated disease with the presence of foreigners, but we do know that these diseases did not have a blanket impact. They affected some groups severely and bypassed others, thereby affecting the geography of Native interaction. Native populations on the west coast of Vancouver Island were not affected by smallpox until the mid-nineteenth century. Theoretically, the smallpox epidemic of 1782, which swept the Gulf of Georgia, would have made surviving Native groups vulnerable to the incursions of Native groups to the north. Galois has shown that between the 1770s and 1850s, Lekwiltok groups expanded south into the Strait of Georgia and raided for slaves further afield.[16] But the situation around the Strait of Juan de Fuca remains unclear. Few maritime fur traders ventured into the Gulf of Georgia (so there is little information to go on), and those few recognized the influence of Chief Tatoosh of Cape Flattery. Tatoosh's people may have been the main beneficiaries of Native depopulation in this area, though by the early 1840s Cowichan groups were also strong.

Fourth, I have argued that the cultural processes influencing these patterns of change should also be conceptualized in geographical terms. Debate about the impact of the trade on Native groups has been underpinned by ageographical and dualistic concepts of stability versus change, and directed versus undirected change. What has been missing from this debate is any sustained analysis of the geographical fabrication of power relations – a sensitivity to the spatial bases and strategies of power that Natives and traders could or did forge. Tension and violence between Natives and traders was influenced by the time-geography of the trade and by how contact was worked out in particular sites (ships and Native villages, especially). Traders' views of Native peoples were not rooted in an unbendable body of Western assumptions about Indians. Their representational practices were acutely spatialized and mediated by the physical and psychical dynamics of face-to-face contact. They came to the coast with a short capitalist fuse, were mobile, and wrote about the absurdity of the business. Native strategies of power flowed from detailed local knowledges of rights and privileges over land and water that had deep ancestral roots and broad kin dimensions. While the trade probably made Native groups more mobile, in places such as Nootka Sound and Clayoquot Sound, where these ancestral and kin relations were not compromised by disease, the accumulation and redistribution of wealth was anchored in Native spaces of possession. Traders got into trouble when they violated the Native protocols of rank and prestige that were grounded in these spaces. Traders did not seek to settle Native land, but there was still an intense competition over space. Native peoples threatened and attacked trade vessels when Native boundaries of tolerance were crossed. In the longer term, it seems, Native-Western violence and inter-Native warfare sprang from an increasing Native reliance on Western goods as sources of prestige.

What I have not been able to broach, mainly because the matter is obscured in the historical and ethnographic record, is the spiritual dimensions of Native familiarity with traders. What were the connections between Native material and spiritual life? Are such categories spurious? Drucker used these categories and largely separated them, discussing them in different chapters of his published ethnography of central and northern Nuu-chah-nulth tribes. More recently, scholars such as Fisher and Marshall have offered materialist interpretations of Native-White interaction. I am partly bound by this tradition of scholarship. While Native ideas of property and prestige were obviously different than traders', we tend to assert this difference but to avoid discussion of what these Native ideas consisted of or whether they were altered by contact. The tenor of my argument is that traders quickly lost the supernatural connotations that we see in the Native accounts of Cook's arrival at Nootka Sound and were treated in more instrumental ways. But this is not to say that Natives viewed traders in Western material terms. Native ideas of rank and kinship, right and privilege, were rooted in family myth and origin stories that linked natural, human, and supernatural forces. At the face of contact, as it was recorded by traders, however, these forces are less evident than the social spaces of mutual desire and fear that characterized interaction.

The historical and ethnographic record has a strong materialist slant. Edward Sapir and his fieldworkers recorded numerous family origin stories, myths, and legends, but Sapir did not conceptualize the connections between the material and spiritual realms of Native life in his published essays. Nor did he consider the impact of contact on Native peoples. This demonstrates the disciplinary limits of inquiry in salvage ethnography, for Sapir's correspondence shows that when he reached Vancouver Island in 1910, he realized that a timeless, traditional

Native past was both unrecoverable and a dubious ethnographic construct. He discovered that Native life in Barkley Sound was stamped by wars and movements that predated and postdated contact. In October 1914, Sapir wrote to his fieldworker Alex Thomas: "I shall be quite pleased to get the war story that you refer to, also any other stories that you may be able to obtain. Now that the great European war is on, perhaps the Indians will be particularly eager to shell out with information about old time war customs ... Of course we know that old Indians often do better when they tell things of their own accord than when they are bothered by precise questions which they do not always understand."[17] It did not take a war in Europe to jog Native memories, however. Native peoples had their own long history of warfare (Sapir and his fieldworkers simply had not asked much about it before) – a tumultuous history, in which traders, for all of their bravado, were only partially implicated.

This undermines the colonialist paradigm that holds that it was Whites who instituted and drove change among Native groups. On the other hand, commercial contact with Whites did constitute a threshold for Native peoples. The maritime fur trade affected the nature and intensity of change among Native groups. More and new goods circulated through the Native feast system, and Native land was reterritorialized.

These four summary points about the maritime fur trade raise questions about the politics of scholarship at a period when Native/non-Native relations in British Columbia are tense. Will this documented history of Native warfare and disease be used to rejuvenate older colonial tenets: that contact *was* mortal for Native peoples and that colonists *did* settle a largely empty land? And will this history of ongoing territorial realignment among Native groups be used to criticize Native claims about traditional lands? The problem, of course, is with the categories and agendas imposed on the past. Court judgements about Native title to land are premised on a geography of fixity and make little room for Native social or geographical dynamism. Native groups have to show that they had stable and static cultural-geographical identities at the time of contact. The courts associate notions of Native tradition and authenticity – Indianness – with deep temporal roots in the land; postcontact shifts in Native social and territorial organization are viewed as an abandonment of Indianness. Such views thin our understanding of the past – or overwhelm it with dichotomies of Western/modernity/dynamism and Native/tradition/stasis that come from a later era. These dichotomies had an ambivalent and fledgling career in traders' texts. Traders found it difficult to impute a timeless or essential gulf between Western civilization and Indian savagery on the basis of commodity exchange. Now, though, criticism of these geographical formulations of Native rootedness and stasis may throw up thorny political and cultural issues. If Native groups stress territorial continuity in the courts, then it is partly because they have been forced to operate within legal language games in order to have their grievances addressed.

Nuu-chah-nulth groups have not been involved in long court trials, but would Clayoquot people or Barkley Sound people, say, include this history of warfare in litigation? I am not suggesting that Native peoples have not had, and do not still feel, close bonds with the land; rather, I am suggesting that we need to re-think what we mean by authenticity and whether Native rights should be configured around ideas of cultural-geographical fixity. I hope my analysis of the west coast of Vancouver Island broadens discussion of notions of tradition, continuity, and change.

Finally, Cook and these maritime fur traders produced different islands of truth. They generated knowledge in different ways and used it for different ends. Cook's economy of truth was yoked to a broader Enlightenment world view that grappled with the powers of observation and possibilities of comparison and classification. Cook and his crew did not simply generate partial truths; they also reflected on the problematic of truth production as such. Their observa-tions and reports were informed by, and fed into, epistemological quandaries about the nature of observation and synthesis, and the relationship between a viewing subject and an object world. And the knowledge they created was scru-tinized and validated by institutions of power and learning such as the Admi-ralty and the Royal Society as well as by a broader public culture. Maritime fur traders also generated partial truths, but theirs were of a different order than Cook's. Fur traders were capitalists, and the knowledges they produced were assessed mainly by merchants and traders themselves. The dynamics of truth production in these two projects of exploration and trade were quite distinct.

We will see shortly that traders' observations and texts had an ambivalent status in political and institutional circles. Traders' claims and testimony about the Northwest Coast became implicated in processes of imperial aggrandize-ment (the British Government reacted quickly to traders' reports of abuse at the hands of the Spanish), yet traders' texts were shaped to a considerable extent by their capitalist aims and methods, and by the intricate and volatile deployment of commercial capital on the coast. The knowledges that they produced did not easily lend themselves to imperial projects of power and inscription that worked with protocols of mapping, classification, and quantification. Traders did not make space visible and legible in a straightforward way. Traders' tales were vexed and introverted stories about the traffic between people and, particularly, be-tween people and things. When politicians used such stories to draw links be-tween capitalism and empire, they generally overlooked what traders said or wrote about the details of the contact process. They looked instead for grand, synthetic statements about profit margins and the potential of the coast. Politi-cians did not have to trust traders' reports to find them useful or important; yet to find them useful, politicians had to strip them down and rework them. If commercial knowledge was to serve state power, it needed to be made combin-able and transposable – it needed to be reviewed and reordered. Explorers and scientists surely helped to picture "the planet appropriated and deployed from a unified, European perspective," as Mary Louise Pratt suggests, but these processes of redeployment started to fray when traders actually started to follow in explorers' footsteps. If the relations between truth and power opened up by Cook's voyages were circumscribed by a planetary consciousness, then those developed by maritime fur traders were based on strategies and tactics of appropriation and accommodation that did not simply incorporate the coast into a capitalist world order or European consciousness.

Yet as the maritime fur trade developed, a more abstract geography did begin to emerge: an imperial geography that deflated the materiality and physicality of the contact process and that worked through definitively European rather than Native corridors of power. If we should stress Native attachment to land amidst these details of Native territorial change, then it is partly because this distant imperial outreach had a more decisive and divisive impact on Western views of the Northwest Coast than did the maritime fur trade. Part 3 considers this impact and the emergence of a formal colonial presence on the coast.

PART 3

Circulating Knowledge and Power

There are some unquestionably who know our [Vancouver] Island by name alone and recognise in it an almost mythical locality.

– J.R. ANDERSON, "NOTES AND COMMENTS ON EARLY DAYS AND EVENTS IN BRITISH COLUMBIA, WASHINGTON, AND OREGON" (1878)

Introduction

When Edward Belcher, a British explorer, reached Nootka Sound in September 1837, he found few signs of Native-White interaction and imagined that the place looked much as it had before Cook arrived. "At first I doubted my senses," he noted, "that so small a space could have occupied so much type."[1] Belcher was alluding to the fact that Nootka Sound had become an elaborate textual space, described numerous times and for different purposes from Cook on. As I have implied, the maritime fur trade did not develop in a geopolitical vacuum. The Spanish assumed that they had exclusive rights of sovereignty over the Pacific littoral of the Americas by virtue of treaties and conventions stretching back to 1493. Worried initially about Russian advances south from (what is now) Alaska, and then about the implications of Cook's reconnaissance for British trade and dominion in the region, the Spanish sent officials to Nootka Sound to stake their claim to the barely charted Northwest Coast. Between May and July 1789, four British trade vessels were seized by Estevan Martínez (Spain's commander at Nootka Sound) as legal prizes, and two of them were taken to Spanish naval headquarters in Alta California, where their captains were imprisoned for working in Spanish waters. When this news reached Britain, a diplomatic dispute ensued that almost culminated in war. Commercial expansion fanned the flames of national and imperial rivalry. The world economy was not just a commercial network; it was also an international political system of assumed rights and privileges that had developed in tandem with the growth of European knowledge about the non-European world and the development of the European state system. Circuits of capital were entangled with networks of imperial signification.[2] This burst of commercial and geopolitical interest in the

Northwest Coast did not prompt colonial intervention or have immediate territorial implications for Native peoples. But we should not underestimate the ideological import of the maritime fur trade and, especially, the Nootka Sound Crisis in the formation of imperialist ideas and assumptions about Native peoples. Colonialism does not start with occupation alone, and it does not work solely on land; it also works with images and representations, with imaginative geographies that precede, and to a degree anticipate, colonialism.[3]

Between 1790 and the 1840s imperial aggrandizement over the Northwest Coast laid some of the legal and ideological groundwork for the colonization of Vancouver Island and British Columbia in the second half of the nineteenth century. A good deal has been written about the geopolitical disputes over Nootka sound and the Oregon Territory. I do not want to rehearse all of the intricate facts relating to these disputes. Rather, I am interested in the connection between the production of geographical knowledge about the Northwest Coast and the creation of imperial space. My review of the primary sources and secondary literature emphasizes the links between mapping, geopolitics, and empire. I seek to show that these disputes were marked by processes of abstraction and point to the appropriation of Native land and life. The trading propensities of Native groups and the tricky business of making contact, which were of utmost concern to fur traders, barely made it into the heap of diplomatic correspondence over Nootka or the Oregon Territory. Legal arguments about sovereignty and a convoluted set of international political relations were of paramount importance in this imperial outreach. The physicality of Native-White contact described in Parts 1 and 2 became buried beneath the imperial paperwork of politicians and diplomats, and the Northwest Coast was gradually turned into a geopolitical shell.

The British explorer George Vancouver played an important role in the creation of this shell. Following the Nootka Sound Crisis he was sent to the coast to conduct a more exhaustive survey than Cook had managed, to settle (once and for all) dispute about the existence of the Northwest Passage, and to negotiate with Spanish officials at Nootka Sound over the restoration of British property that Martinez had seized. Vancouver's diplomacy achieved little, but his charts became important geopolitical tools during the Oregon boundary dispute. His reconnaissance was invoked by British politicians to foil American territorial claims to the coastal region around the 49th parallel, and his map of Vancouver Island implied an alluring colonial future. In the 1870s, J.R. Anderson, the son of a Hudson's Bay Company fur trader, suggested that British speculators and colonists recognized Vancouver Island "by name alone" and viewed it as "an almost mythical locality" – as a largely empty land that was up for grabs.[4] Anderson's father, Alexander, complained that these geographical impressions contributed to a number of "alluring fictions" about Native peoples: that British colonists tended to exaggerate Indian treachery, truncate traders' appreciation of Native agendas, and regard Indians either as bloodthirsty savages or as primitives who had barely scratched the land and who could easily be pushed aside.[5]

Part 3 explores colonial Vancouver Island's imperial inheritance. I track these processes of abstraction across international space and sketch some of the main boundary-making procedures and place-holding tactics that went with them. European and American politicians sought a space of summation – an imperial map of who owned what and where, an inventory of the commercial and geopolitical value of the vast region west of the Rockies. The work of explorers and traders was abbreviated, rationalized, and used to support a set of territorial claims. The scientific-humanitarian mandate that gave Cook's sojourn at Nootka Sound its vibrancy, and the spatial strategies of commerce that mediated the maritime fur trade – that is, the means by which Natives and Whites *encountered* each other on the Northwest Coast in the late eighteenth century – became encompassed by geopolitical forces that operated at a distance from Native peoples. A set of imperial equations were superimposed on the contact process, and a more divisive set of connections between power and space began to emerge.

CHAPTER 10

The Ledger, the Map, and
British Imperial Vision

British subjects trading under the protection of the British flag ... have an
unquestionable Right to a free and undisturbed enjoyment of the Benefits
of Commerce, Navigation and Fishery [in the Pacific], and also [to] the
Possession of such Establishments as they may form, with the consent of
the Natives, in such places unoccupied by other European Nations.

– DUKE OF LEEDS TO ANTHONY MERRY, 4 MAY 1790

SHUFFLES IN THE CABINET

In January 1790, the British Cabinet learned from Britain's chargé d'affaires in
Madrid, Anthony Merry, that a Spanish military officer, Estevan Martínez, had
seized a British vessel at Nootka Sound as a legal prize.[1] According to Merry,
Spanish ministers thought that the British planned to establish a settlement at
Nootka Sound and that the viceroy of Mexico had sent Martínez to Nootka
Sound to safeguard Spain's imperial claim to a barely charted or policed region
that American and British traders were venturing to in increasing numbers to
trade for sea otter furs. Merry's report was based on rumours, but Britain's foreign secretary, the duke of Leeds, responded to it quickly.[2] Merry was instructed
to gather more precise information, and Leeds urged him to be "very cautious
[in conversation] of giving even a hint which may be construed into a derelic-
tion of our right to visit for the purposes of trade, or to make a settlement in the
District in question; to which we undoubtedly have a complete right, to be asserted and maintained with a proper degree of vigour, should circumstances
make such an assertion necessary."[3] Leeds also wrote to Spain's ambassador to

168

London, the marquis del Campo de Alange, arguing that Martínez's "violent" act "must be disposed of in a way to satisfy the injured Honour of the British Crown before any discussion of the point of right to the particular place in question can be agitated."[4] Campo de Alange informed the British that the vessel had been seized because its commander planned to take possession of Spanish territory "in the name of the British King," and he urged "His Britannic Majesty ... [to] punish such undertakings in a manner to restrain his subjects from ... [visiting] lands which have been occupied and frequented by the Spaniards for so many years."[5] Britain and Spain each made formal protests over an obscure place and incident using a pointed language of national honour and territorial rights, and over the next few months this scuffle at Nootka Sound escalated into an international crisis.

Leeds thought that it was the "unanimous sense" of the British Cabinet that the incident should be treated with "a high hand," but William Pitt, first minister of the Cabinet, was agitated by the aggressive tone of Leeds's letter to Campo de Alange and started to manage the affair himself.[6] Pitt demanded the restitution of the British vessel and compensation for the insult, but he also suggested that both courts should seek more information before making declarations about territorial issues.[7] Neither country wanted war.[8] This diplomatic affray unfolded in a complicated international situation. Britain and Spain had been imperial rivals for centuries, of course, and were at war frequently between 1739 and 1783. But Anglo-Spanish relations improved after 1784, and British diplomats thought that Spain's first minister, the conte de Floridablanca, wanted to keep Spain out of expensive and troublesome alliances with other European powers until the political ramifications of the French Revolution became clearer. Yet in 1790, King Carlos the Fourth of Spain still hoped that he could revive the Bourbon Family Compact with France (Britain's other great rival) in times of international crisis. Pitt was troubled by the possibility of a Franco-Spanish military alliance against Britain. He also understood that Prussia, Britain's main ally during this period, was unenthusiastic about assisting Britain if war broke out.[9]

Pitt and Floridablanca were acutely aware that if the incident at Nootka Sound was not treated cautiously, then it might trigger a wider political crisis in Europe, for no individual European state was strong enough, militarily or financially, to be able to ignore the maze of fleeting international alliances and conflicts that enveloped late eighteenth-century Europe.[10] Thus, while Britain and Spain wanted peace, the two countries remained suspicious of each other, took precautions, and began to assess the possible reverberations of Martínez's actions. In April 1790, Spain explained its case to France and approached Austria, Russia, and Sweden to negotiate an alliance against Britain.[11] Spanish defences in the West Indies were strengthened, and Spain started to fit out ships of the line.[12] Floridablanca tried to convince Merry that Spain was arming against France, but the British Cabinet watched this Spanish naval build up carefully and took heed of Merry's despatch of 29 March, which stated that Floridablanca maintained that the British viewed the incident at Nootka Sound as "a ground for quarrelling."[13]

This diplomatic dispute prompted the British Cabinet to review British commercial activity in the Pacific. The Cabinet knew that the British whale and seal fishery in the south Pacific posed a considerable threat to Spain's commercial monopoly over the Pacific littoral of South America, and Pitt's sense that the incident at Nootka Sound presented a chance for Britain to enhance its position in South America was heightened on 14 February, when he met with a Spanish American agitator, Francisco de Miranda, who had a grand plan for overthrowing Spanish rule and forming a federation of independent states that would trade with Britain.[14] Then, in late February, the Cabinet endorsed an Admiralty plan to send a naval expedition to Nootka Sound to establish a British trade post and assess the value of the sea otter trade.[15] The commanders of the expedition were about to sail at the end of April when the plan was shelved due to the revelations of John Meares.[16]

Meares arrived in England from Macao in early April and presented Britain's home secretary, William Grenville, with a detailed memorial describing Martínez's actions and the sea otter trade.[17] He stated that four British vessels belonging to a British company (in which he was a principal investor), and commanded by former British navy officers, had been arrested and that their crews had been imprisoned and abused by the Spanish. Three of these vessels had been arrested as legal prizes, and two of them had been escorted to San Blas, where their commanders had to explain to a Spanish court why they had been trading in Spanish waters.[18] Meares also noted that Martínez had claimed formal possession of Nootka Sound for Spain in June 1790.

British citizens had been bruised and insulted. But Meares did not stop there. What grabbed Grenville's attention, and subsequently altered the nature of the dispute, was Meares's claim that he had bought spots of land on the coast and had erected a small building at Nootka Sound a year before Martínez arrived:

That your Memorialist, immediately on his Arrival in Nootka Sound, purchased from Maquilla, the Chief of the District contiguous to and surrounding that Place, a Spot of Ground, whereon he built a House for his occasional Residence, as well as for the more convenient Pursuit of his Trade with the Natives, and hoisted the British Colours thereon ... That during the absence of your Memorialist from Nootka Sound, he obtained from *Wickananish*, the Chief of the District surrounding Port Cox and Port Effingham ... in consequence of considerable Presents, the Promise of a *free and exclusive Trade with the Natives of the District*, and also his Permission to build any Storehouses, or other Edifices, which he might judge necessary; that he also acquired the same Privilege of exclusive Trade from *Tatouche*, the Chief of the Country bordering on the Straits of *Juan de Fuca*, and purchased from him a Tract of Land within the said Strait, which One of your Memorialist's Officers took Possession of in the King's Name, calling the same *Tatouche*, in honour of the Chief.

That the *Iphigenia* [one of Meares's vessels], in her Progress to the Southward, also visited several Ports, and in consequence of Presents to the Chiefs of the Country, her Commander had Assurances given to him of not only a free Access, but of an exclusive Trade upon that Coast, no other European Vessel having been there before her.[19]

This information dishevelled Spain's claim to exclusive sovereignty and put British rights to trade and settle in the region on firmer ground. For at the core of Britain's understanding of the Law of Nations was the formulation that "Discovery alone, not followed by Actual Occupation and Establishment, can never be admitted as giving any Right to the Exclusion of Other Nations," as Leeds expressed it.[20] I will return to this formulation below. Here the point is that Leeds thought that Martínez had acted illegally because Meares had provided Britain with prior rights to the sound.

Meares's memorial was largely self-serving. Looking for notoriety and compensation for Martínez's assault on his company, he exaggerated his losses and the brutality of the affair and misled the government about his activities.[21] But with no other British information to go on, Meares's claims were treated seriously and incited indignation towards the Spanish. Leeds learned from Campo de Alange that "the British vessel" taken to San Blas had been restored, but Meares showed that Spain had concealed the extent of the insult. And after studying Meares's memorial, Leeds and Pitt also became dissatisfied with the reason Campo de Alange had given for the restoration of the vessel: that Spain was being courteous to Britain because the British trader arrested by Martínez was evidently "ignorant" of Spain's "exclusive rights of sovereignty" over the region.[22] The aspersive implication here was that Britain should have acknowledged such rights and instructed British traders to steer clear of Spanish territory. The Cabinet maintained that these rights were simply alleged.

British ministers acted quickly on Meares's information, and this diplomatic affray over insult and injury developed into a full-fledged dispute about territorial rights. On 30 April, King George the Third approved a Cabinet decision to demand "immediate and adequate satisfaction for the outrages committed" by the Spanish: financial compensation for Meares and his associates, acknowledgment that Martínez had acted illegally, and an admission that British rights to the region had not been erased.[23] At the start of May, the Navy Board was ordered to fit out forty ships of the line and organize a press for sailors in order to back Britain's demand.[24] And over the next few weeks the Admiralty sent circular letters to British colonial officials in America, Asia, and the Mediterranean, alerting them that war could be on the horizon, and despatched spy vessels to assess the state of the Spanish fleet.[25] Meanwhile, military strategists advised the Cabinet on how to coordinate a naval onslaught on Spain's colonies on the Caribbean coast, and Pitt met with Miranda on 6 May to gauge how much support Britain could expect in Spanish America if war broke out.[26] Britain tried to gain the allegiance of Vermont separatists and Kentucky pioneers, Grenville's reasoning being that if war with Spain focused on the Caribbean, then the former might prevent the United States from allying with Spain (and could defend British military posts in North America), and the latter might support a British military campaign for control of the Mississippi delta.[27]

As these preparations involved a great mobilization of people and resources, the details of this dispute could not be kept secret any longer. The Navy Board's press of 4 May apparently took the country by surprise.[28] The following day the government published Meares's memorial, and Pitt and Leeds read the king's message on Nootka Sound in Parliament.[29] And on 6 May Pitt asked the House of Commons for £1 million to finance Britain's military preparations and debated the Nootka issue with the Opposition.[30] He was reported as stating that between January and March Spain had made

> the most absurd and exorbitant [claim about sovereignty] that could well be imagined, a claim which [Britain] ... had never heard of before, which was indefinite in its extent, and which originated in no treaty, nor formal establishment of a colony, nor rested on any of those grounds on which claims of sovereignty, navigation, and commerce usually rested. If that claim were given way to, it must deprive this country of the means of excluding his majesty's subjects from an infant trade, the future extension of which could not but be essentially beneficial to the commercial interests of Great Britain.[31]

These sentiments were echoed in despatches to Merry at the beginning of May. Leeds stated that while the king would prevent his subjects from "interfering with the Just and Acknowledged Rights" of Spain, Britain could not accept Spain's claim to exclusive sovereignty over the Northwest Coast.[32] Merry was briefed about Meares's memorial and told to impress on Floridablanca that "British subjects trading under the protection of the British flag ... have an unquestionable Right to a free and undisturbed enjoyment of the Benefits of Commerce, Navigation and Fishery [in the Pacific], and also [to] the Possession of such Establishments as they may form, with the consent of the Natives, in such places unoccupied by other European Nations."[33]

The Cabinet wanted to resolve the dispute peacefully. Campo de Alange was told that Britain's military preparations were defensive measures, and Pitt decided to replace Merry with a more experienced diplomat, Alleyne Fitzherbert. Fitzherbert was appointed ambassador to Spain and instructed to assure Floridablanca that Britain wanted to do justice to the interests of both countries.[34]

But these overtures were in many respects diplomatic foils. Britain and Spain were now at loggerheads over the spoils of navigation and commerce in the Pacific.

The Nootka Crisis dragged on through the summer of 1790, generating a flurry of diplomatic activity in Europe, and Britain spent over £2 million on its military preparations.[35] Spain continued to seek the assistance of France and other European powers, and British diplomats tried to ensure that France remained neutral in the dispute.[36] Territorial rights were not discussed until late August, after Spain had signed a declaration agreeing to reparations, and a settlement was not reached until the end of October, when Spain, without allies in Europe, dropped its claim to exclusive sovereignty.[37] The Nootka Convention granted both Britain and Spain the right to navigate, trade, and settle on the Northwest Coast.[38]

In essence, Britain's navy was much stronger than Spain's, and the Spanish knew that they could not win a war without allies. Spain failed to rejuvenate the Bourbon Family Compact with Louis the Sixteenth of France and could not secure the support of any other European court. Floridablanca reasoned that a few concessions over trade and navigation in the marchlands of the Spanish Empire had prevented a catastrophic war.[39] The Convention rested on Britain's military superiority, and the Cabinet's stand over Nootka Sound was conditioned by political factors. Pitt was entering an election year, and if his firm handling of the dispute had an important bearing on his election victory, as some argued, it was because international commerce was central to British identity and well-being. The Nootka Sound Crisis also points to some of the main features of European geopolitics and imperialism at the end of the eighteenth century. It may have struck Europe as "a bolt from the blue," as one of Pitt's biographers remarked, but it was also a striking example of the way European powers projected the non-European world through their own national prisms of rivalry and conflict.[40] Martínez's actions reignited long-standing Anglo-Spanish competition over the New World, and the diplomatic dispute became wrapped up with a larger body of political reaction in Britain to the French Revolution.[41]. Britain, Spain, and France also viewed European reaction to the dispute as a test of the strength and durability of the Triple Alliance. In brief, Nootka Sound was roped into European geopolitics, and this crisis reoriented Britain's engagement with the Northwest Coast.

The British viewed Nootka Sound as an important territorial marker of international commerce. Europe's age of revolution reaffirmed that the economic and political strength, and national self-consciousness, of European states was bound up with commercial and imperial forces that spanned the globe.[42] Europe drew a large part of its wealth from the rest of the world, and inter-state competition over markets and resources induced territorial conflict within and beyond Europe. European powers considered themselves to be what Jean

Comaroff and John Comaroff call "polities on a world map": nation-states whose identities were mediated, to varying degrees, by the way they had explored, carved up, and exploited the world.[43] European geopolitical relations were regulated, in part, by diplomats who standardized procedures of address; developed tit-for-tat formulae for offsetting the estrangement of states; and appealed to treaties, conventions, proclamations, and philosophical and legal texts concerning the nature of sovereignty (collectively known as the Law of Nations) to resolve international disputes.[44] But diplomats often failed to prevent wars, and European states interpreted the Law of Nations in different ways.[45] Michael Mann aptly describes late eighteenth-century Europe as "a multi-power-actor-civilization embodying an inherent contradiction: geopolitically highly competitive unto war, yet regulated by common norms. Eighteenth-century war [in and beyond Europe] became more destructive and costly, yet also more profitable for the Great Powers [Britain, France, Russia, and Spain] and also partly regulated by transnational institutions and by multistate diplomacy."[46] Nootka Sound was transposed into this European setting and reconstructed as an object of both national and imperial concern. Martínez's actions concerned the British Cabinet, as I will now illustrate, because of the material and ideological importance of overseas trade to Britons.

BRITISH IMPERIAL VISION

In eighteenth-century Britain, commerce, nationalism, and imperialism were intertwined. As Linda Colley has spelled out: "the claim that trade was the muscle and the soul of Great Britain, both the source of its greatness and the nursery of patriots, was abundantly echoed in the poetry, drama, novels, newspapers, tracts, parliamentary speeches, private correspondence, even the sermons of the time."[47] Britain's commercial community was highly segmented, of course, and land had by no means been eclipsed as a main source of government revenue or social prestige, but Colley argues that "this cult of trade crossed party divisions, just as it crossed social boundaries."[48] And it crossed the oceans with traders such as Meares. Commerce was central to Britain's wealth and identity as a European actor and imperial power. During the eighteenth century, customs and excise duties made up between 60 and 70 percent of British government revenue, the ratio of exports to national income climbed from around 8 to between 15 and 18 percent, the import ratio hovered between 11 and 16 percent, and creditors were highly sensitive to fluctuations in international trade.[49] Domestic and international traders supplied the state with much of the revenue it needed to defend the nation from foreign invasion and domestic insurrection (which would upset business), and to expand Britain's infrastructure and regulate business practices. Equally, Britain's military successes overseas opened up new markets and sources of raw materials and encouraged new forms of trade. Patrick O'Brien argues that Britons from a variety of backgrounds shared the conviction that international commerce and national prestige were intimately connected and that both "depended on the use of force, backed up by a skilful deployment of diplomacy in order to make and to retain economic gains at the expense of their major rivals."[50]

This "cult of trade" was rooted in mercantilist doctrines. The basic British mercantilist view was that national prestige was relative to the proportion of wealth controlled by different states. Before Adam Smith's arguments about the benefits of free markets started to influence British economic and foreign policy towards the end of the eighteenth century, Britain maintained that the monopolization of international trade through imperial expansion was the best way to enhance British wealth and prestige.[51] Many scholars have stressed that mercantilism was a project of enumeration.[52] For example, Kathleen Wilson notes that British mercantilism was characterized by "counting, measuring, and assessing national wealth numerically against that of other nations"; there was a fascination with "the moveable products of imperialist accumulation."[53] The daily and periodical press produced scores of calculations about imports and exports, output and profits, and charted the movement of ships, stocks, prices, and domestic and colonial merchandise. Wilson estimates that through the eighteenth century about one-third of news items in London newspapers contained some discussion of imperial affairs.

It was these mercantilist connections between government and trade, credit and debt, war and commercial expansion, and naval strength and national prestige – in short, the imbrications of what John Brewer has called Britain's "fiscal-military state" – as much as any point of law that made the incident at Nootka Sound an important national issue.[54] The Cabinet did not seek "unqualified satisfaction" from Spain simply because it thought that Martínez had acted illegally. More profoundly, Spain had insulted the British nation because Meares and his cohorts were considered to be *public* agents – bearers of Britain's commercial soul. Alexander Dalrymple highlighted that "the Insult and Injury was publick" and that "the Satisfaction and Atonement must [therefore] be publick!"; he and other commentators demanded that Spain make a formal apology to *all* Britons.[55] There were intricate, symbiotic relationships between king, country, and a wider world of British trade and settlement. James Boswell satirized the connections between commerce, state rivalry, and nationhood at a banquet that was held at the Guildhall in London to install John Boydell as the new lord mayor of London on 7 November 1790 – the day that the Convention with Spain was published. He wrote a ballad for the occasion, entitled, "William Pitt, the Grocer of London." The third and fourth stanzas read:

> Though fleets in vain-boasting hostility ride,
> Still BRITAIN is queen of the main;

> The secret well kept now comes forth with due pride;
> And lo! a Convention with Spain!
>
> Too noble to brag, as we're never afraid,
> 'Tis enough that we've had a good pull.
> There's a GROCER OF LONDON who watches our trade,
> And takes care of th'estate of JOHN BULL.[56]

Pitt's handling of the Nootka Crisis was stamped by a ruthless determination to protect Britain's international trading interests.[57]

The Nootka Crisis also brought the Pacific within political realms of commercial-imperial calculation. It exemplified Britain's ledger-book imperial mentality. Spain posed a threat to Britain's economic stability, and Martínez's actions prompted Britain to weigh up its interests in the Pacific. On the one hand, the king's message of 5 May caused "much alarm and [a] falling of stocks" in London, and it caused one wry, if concerned, Opposition pamphleteer to ask whether it was "a wise measure to go to war with half of Europe for the sake of the fur trade of Nootka Sound."[58] This crisis raised practical as well as ideological questions about whether British commerce in the Pacific was large enough to warrant an expensive war.[59] Britain's National Debt was a major worry, but commentators did not just worry about the reverberations of the dispute in Europe or on the British economy. In June 1790 Bland Burges (under-secretary of state at the Foreign Office) warned Leeds that "before we know where we are, we shall have the Americans, and possibly the Russians on our backs" and that if Britain were defeated in a naval war, "we [would] lose the Canada Forts and possibly something still more essential."[60] On the other hand, Pitt argued in the Commons that the dispute presented a window of commercial and imperial opportunity. Fitzherbert reported that Floridablanca was convinced that Britain's demand for satisfaction was underpinned by "a real design of making ourselves Masters of the Trade of Mexico – that our Southern Whale-Fishery covered a like design against Peru & Chili, and as to our Colony at Botany-Bay, that it must necessarily have been founded with a view of seconding these designs & of adding to our other conquests that of the Philippines."[61]

Floridablanca was a gifted and insightful politician. He sensed that Pitt's approach to this dispute was heavily influenced by the prospect of gaining access to the resources and extensive markets of Spanish America. This prospect was articulated most emphatically by Henry Dundas (treasurer of the navy in 1790, home secretary in 1791, and one of the principal architects of British commercial policy in the 1790s) in a Commons debate on the Convention with Spain in December 1790. "The spirit of the nation was roused" over Nootka Sound, he declared, to vindicate its honour, and to assert an equal right with Spain to occupancy, trade, and navigation in those parts. Whatever settlement we had at Nootka, every thing was restored according to circumstances, either in land or pecuniary compensation. So much as to reparation. But it had been asked, what had we for the security of our settlement? Was there any precise line of demarcation drawn as a boundary? No. This was impracticable; as we were not contending for a few miles, but a large world ... This country would not be limited in its market. Its wealth was founded upon the skill of our manufacturers, and the adventures of our merchants. These raised our armaments, and rendered us formidable in the scale of nations. Our prosperity was the admiration and envy of the world ... We do not insist on any right to invade the colonial rights of other nations, in order to extend our commerce; but the spirit of commercial adventure in this country is unbounded.[62]

Britain would not be limited in its market. Nootka Sound was viewed as a doorway leading to a large world of profit, as this cartoon (Figure 9), *Billy and Harry Fishing For Whales* (published by William Holland in December 1790), also illustrates. Dundas steers the boat while Pitt, revelling in the settlement with Spain, fishes hefty bags of sterling and some small fry out of the South Sea. The Pacific is depicted as an accessible and lucrative space, and Pitt and Dundas are there protecting British commerce, filling state coffers, and taking this part of the world out of Spain's imperial clutches. Under Pitt, Margaret Steven suggests, "the whalers

Figure 9   William Pitt, Henry Dundas, and Britain's ledger book imperial mentality
Source: William Holland, *Billy and Harry fishing for whales,* London, 1790. Courtesy National Archives of Canada, C-137926.

of the southern fishery enjoyed an indulgence that has few parallels in British economic history."[63] The Convention with Spain protected their interests and those of British sea otter traders. This political similitude of commerce, money, and power in British thinking was echoed by one of Meares's associates, John Cadman Etches, who argued that "the vigorous and the tender shoots of diverging commerce should be fostered and protected, with the same scrupulous vigilance as its bank paper, or its national stock."[64]

As Dundas suggested, Britain's commercial soul was fuelled by the "adventures" of British explorers and traders. And as Kathleen Wilson argues, this equation of commerce and nationhood should be seen "within the context of extensive cartographic mania over the colonies."[65] "In the fashion of his age," Ehrman notes, "Pitt was a great reader of maps."[66] He kept four sets of maps at his Downing Street study (including maps of the fabled Northwest Passage and of the Pacific), and a large section of his personal library was devoted to international trade. He collected colonial dictionaries, gazetteers of commerce, navigation pilots, and books of exploration and trade.[67] The Board of Trade, Home Office, and India Board also kept enormous collections of commercial records. During the Nootka Crisis, Pitt and his colleagues turned to Aaron Arrowsmith's *Chart of the World on Mercator's Projection* (published in January 1790, which collated European discoveries in the Pacific up to 1780) in order to chart the activities of British traders and to assess Spain's territorial claims. They also turned to trade statistics and universal registers and dictionaries of commerce in order to plot connections between Britain's disparate international business ventures. And they consulted traders such as Meares. Pitt and his colleagues had a large general knowledge of international commerce and were interested in patterns of trade and business trajectories.[68] They viewed Nootka Sound through the lexicons of the ledger and the map.

The synoptic quality of British commercial thinking about the Pacific is highlighted in John Meares's interview with the Committee of Trade and Plantations in May 1790. Meares was asked general questions about the sea otter trade. What was "the highest and lowest latitude of successful commerce" on the Northwest Coast? How long did it take to get from Canton to the Sandwich Islands, and from there to Nootka? What were the chief "objects of commerce" and "articles of barter" in the trade? Was the Native population of the region large enough to make the demand for British manufactures "considerable"? How much competition did Meares suffer from American traders? Was the Asian market for furs large enough to keep the business profitable, and were there any trade posts in the western Pacific that Britain did not know about? Meares was also asked whether the sea otter trade and whaling trade could be combined, whether there was any prospect of developing a trade between Japan and India, whether North American ginseng could be sold in China, and about what the government could do to bolster British business in the region.[69] The committee wanted a general picture of the value and potential of the sea otter trade rather than a detailed account of how to conduct it. At several points in the interview, Meares suggested that issues of value and profit were mediated by Native demand and competition, and the relationships that traders could forge with Native chiefs. But the committee kept pressing him with general questions. The sea otter trade was being repositioned as a cog in a global wheel of commerce. The British Cabinet was not interested in the intricacies or mechanics of the contact process: it was after simpler patterns and equations.

When the diplomatic negotiations turned to territorial questions, the Foreign Office turned to Alexander Dalrymple (hydrographer to the East India Company and then the Admiralty) for a fuller understanding of the history of exploration and trade in the Pacific and the legitimacy of Spanish claims.[70] Dalrymple was one of the principal custodians of geographical knowledge about North America and the Pacific. He supplied Leeds with maps, compendia of information about Spanish America, and two pamphlets that he published about the dispute in May and June 1790.[71] "In Disputes concerning Geographical Limits," Dalrymple argued in one pamphlet (aiming, perhaps, to draw attention to his own geographical expertise), "The Proper Authorities to consult are *Geographers*; for although a *Map* may not be considered as *conclusive*, it must be admitted as *presumptive, testimony* of a *fact*."[72]

Spain's memorial of 13 June, which was delivered to all foreign ambassadors in Madrid, stated: "The vast extent of the Spanish territories, navigation, and dominion on the continent of America, the islands and adjacent Seas in the South Seas appears by documents, Laws, Schedules, particular orders, discoveries and formal acts of possession."[73] Leeds did not discuss the empirical merits of this memorial until after Spain had agreed to reparations on 24 July, and when he finally did, in a long despatch to Fitzherbert on 17 August about how to negotiate territorial questions (a despatch that the ambassador noted was almost "more voluminous than Postlethwayt's Dictionary"), he treated the texts that Dalrymple had sent him as proof that Spain's claim to exclusive sovereignty was vague and insupportable.[74] Leeds enclosed copies of Meares's *Memorial*, two Spanish works on the history of California, Dalrymple's pamphlets, and Arrowsmith's *Chart* for Fitzherbert to study, and he emphasized two points: first, that on "the most Authentic Map published in different Countries previous to the late Discoveries" of the 1780s (i.e., Arrowsmith's), "the Whole Coast, north of the Peninsula of California, is laid down as Unknown to Europeans, and cannot therefore be reasonably supposed to be settled by Spain"; and second, that "in a *Noticia de California*, said to be published in 1757 by Authority of the Spanish Government, their knowledge of the America[n] Coast is expressly stated not to go beyond California."[75] In other words, to Leeds's knowledge, Spain's first and only settlement north of California was at Nootka Sound, and Meares had apparently bought land there before Martínez took formal possession. The geographical parameters of the dispute now became more precise. In Pitt's eyes, Spain could only reasonably claim sovereignty over the coastal area between the latitudes of 40°N and 45°S – thus leaving the sea otter trade and South Sea fishery intact.

Ehrman rehearses the global scope of the Cabinet's commercial vision during this period: "In the middle eighties its thoughts were directed to snatching the Atlantic trade from the Americans; by the early nineties it was also envisaging a new pattern of commerce in the East, from the Pacific coast of America to the South Sea Islands and Canton."[76] And Edmund Burke captured the way Britain and Spain abstracted the Pacific from an imperial standpoint, writing to the earl of Charlemont on 25 May 1790:

> I do by no means bel[ie]ve that Spain had serious Intentions of making war upon us, because I do not see what serious Object she could have in risquing it upon offensive principles. I do indeed apprehend, that if she thought we had formed a Systematick Scheme of a connected chain of establishments, beginning at Staten Island, and ending at Nootka Sound, and by a Port in Sandwich Islands commencing a regular establishment in the South Sea, that Court would rather put every thing to hazard, rather than suffer a Line of circumvallation to be drawn about their Colonies.[77]

These modes of vision, inquiry, and argument were not simply practical means of connecting the incident at Nootka Sound to a broader set of issues, or of distilling the details and implications of the dispute into a manageable set of claims. They were also ways of constructing the Pacific, and reconstructing the contact process, from imperial perspectives. Politicians and diplomats viewed the Pacific as a set of geographical co-ordinates and trade statistics that revealed the boundaries of European knowledge and the pulse of European capital. Edward Said has called such representational practices acts of "geographical violence": ways of seizing and devouring space from a distance.[78] Britain and Spain were objectifying the Pacific as a space to be delineated and carved up. The itinerate commercial geographies that I discussed in Part 2 were brought within a different order of inquiry.

These ways of constructing the Pacific were mediated by the rationalist currents of eighteenth-century thought. Texts such as Dalrymple's *Historical Collection of Voyages*, Malachy Postlethwayt's *Universal Dictionary of Trade and Commerce*, and Arrowsmith's *Chart* belong to the international project of "universal" knowledge – the attempt to picture the world as a systematic totality, to arrange it as an object of intellectual inquiry, to collate the way it had been encountered, and to classify its diversity, richness, and potential.[79] Such texts organized the world into useful patterns that could be used for a variety of ends. As scholars such as John Brewer have demonstrated, this project had a particular cast in Britain.[80] British authors of "universal" dictionaries and registers aimed to demonstrate the affinity between accurate empirical knowledge about the peoples, resources, and commerce of the world and Britain's national well-being. British authors aimed to "profess" to the public "the essence of all the books of Geography, voyages, & travels ever published" in order to reveal the connections between what was "beneficial" to the nation and "delightful" to the intellect, as two late eighteenth-century British chroniclers put it.[81]

Brewer argues that these projects of "universal knowledge" made knowledge useful to the individual and the state and were thus experiments in how to turn knowledge into power.[82] The expansion of Britain's state apparatus during the eighteenth century was bolstered by the development of a new form of knowledge – what Brewer terms "useful knowledge": bodies of descriptive and statistical information about the regions of the world, European affairs, domestic and international trade, government revenue and expenditure, social conditions, and so forth. "If Britain were to play a major part on the grand stage of European strategy," Brewer notes, "information about the diplomatic and military plans of her rivals was needed. If a new duty was required to fund another government loan, some knowledge or informed prediction of its return was necessary."[83] And as the state grew, the public called for more information about its activities. In eighteenth-century Britain, there was a proliferation of government departments, information agencies, and lobby groups.[84] These systems of data collection and compendia of "useful knowledge" were important to politicians and the public "as constructs, ways of ordering knowledge," and ways of "bring[ing] the world to order."[85] Scholars such as Bernard Cohn and Nicholas Dirks have shown that the creation and ordering of cultural difference through projects of classification and enumeration was central to the expansion and consolidation of British power in India in the late-eighteenth century. "Colonial knowledge both enabled conquest and was produced by it," Dirks argues. "In certain important ways, knowledge was what colonialism was all about. Cultural forms in societies newly classified as 'traditional' were reconstructed and transformed by and through this knowledge, which created new categories and oppositions between colonizers and colonized, Europe and Asia, modern and traditional, West and East."[86] The knowledge derived from Meares and Dalrymple allowed the Cabinet to think in terms of "systematick schemes" and "lines of circumvallation," as Burke put it. The ledger and the map were the technical matrices through which Britain ordered the Pacific as a commercial arena and a space of European sovereignty.

As Brewer suggests, then, and as Michel Foucault showed in more conceptual terms, these modes of vision and inquiry – these constructions of the world – induced regular effects of power. Foucault connected the development of "useful knowledge" to a specifically governmental form of political rationality. Government departments such as the Excise Commission and Home Office, disciplines such as political arithmetic and, eventually, political economy, and compendia of commercial data and tracts about how to administer social and political affairs were among a panoply of "institutions, procedures, analyses and reflections" that established new "fields" of state intervention and methods for examining and managing them in their "depths and details."[87]

By extension, my argument that the Northwest Coast was brought to order through the political rationalization of cartographic and commercial information should not be viewed simply as a discursive counterpoint to my discussion of the contact process. For the ledger and the map were also tools of power. The British used them to *assert* themselves in the world (to establish the Pacific as a field of possession and intervention) and to *insert* the Northwest Coast into European rationalist discourse (a view of the world, as Sudipta Kiviraj has pointed out, that "is clear, precise, instrumentalist, technical, scientific, effective, true and above all [deemed] beneficial to all who came in contact with it, both the rulers and the subjects").[88] The British Cabinet related the activities of private traders to national commercial policy. Monopoly and profit were recontextualized as imperial right, and folded into Britain's assertion of imperial right was the equation of private prosperity and national honour.[89] National honour was circumscribed by a rationalist, instrumentalist view of the world that legitimized imperialism and colonialism. In short, the modes of calculation and representational maps that maritime fur traders worked with were recontextualized and abstracted. Traders such as Meares had to attune themselves to Native ways in order to make a profit. In a different location, politicians such as Leeds used the ledger and the map to fashion a geopolitical space that Native peoples could not manipulate and to claim the right to hold it for a future generation of British settlers. The Nootka Crisis laid some of the groundwork for the colonial disposal of land to British settlers in the second half of the nineteenth century in that it ushered in European ideas about imperial possession and private property. In the colonial period, these ideas were deemed to be the backbone of an orderly colonial society.

The Nootka Crisis was shaped by strategies of accumulation and calculation that exceeded the political details of the dispute. Pitt and the British Cabinet familiarized themselves with far-off places and events in partial and propitious ways. David Philip Miller explores these issues in a more general vein, drawing on the work of Bruno Latour: "If voyages of exploration could dispatch or bring back to Europe measurements of latitude and longitude; charts of coastlines, harbors and seaways; collections of flora and fauna; depictions of people; and accounts of their languages, then future emissaries could deal from a position of strength with the places and peoples encountered on subsequent occasions. What Latour calls a 'cycle of accumulation' is set up, in which useful knowledge is accumulated at the 'center,' each new voyage both drawing on that stock of knowledge and contributing to it."[90] This was not easily achieved. Particularity had to be generalized in some way; there had to be a code of translation. Latour argues that the foreign and distant had be to be made "mobile," "stable," and "combinable." "Mobility" was achieved most thoroughly. Geographical features, natural specimens, and human artefacts were rendered mobile through processes of abstraction – through cartographic inscription and practices of naming, classification, tabulation, and illustration. We saw in Part 1 that the stability and combination of information was beset with epistemological and methodological problems. Miller adds that the division of information into private and public collections was a further obstacle to the combination of information. Yet the general representational mechanisms of appropriation – or centring – that Miller and Latour explore help us to interpret the Nootka Crisis. Leeds used information provided by Dalrymple. The Committee of Trade and Plantations worked with Meares. Politicians sought to collate private and public knowledge, and the ledger and the map belonged to what Miller calls the "submarine base" of abstraction that characterized late eighteenth-century British imperial vision.

We might say that Britain's approach to the Pacific was mediated by two rationalities of power. A calculus of governmental rationality, which was characterized by the centring of particular types of knowledge for political ends and was disciplinary in orientation, was superimposed on an older power of imperial assertion that was shaped by models of sovereignty and the philosophy of mercantilism. The types of information derived from Meares and Dalrymple were folded into a mode of power that targeted space rather than people, tied the Pacific to ideas about the national good, and, as I will now argue, filtered out issues of Native territoriality.

BRITAIN, SPAIN, AND THE LAW OF NATIONS

At the core of the Nootka Crisis was a centuries-old disagreement between Britain and Spain about the nature of European sovereignty in the New World, and in this dispute both countries drew on a rarefied body of ideas, images, and facts to support their views of sovereignty. I have sketched how the British Cabinet pushed its case with a small number of seemingly definitive facts that came to hand. Let me now say something more about Spain.

Floridablanca argued that the "vast extent and limits" of the Spanish Empire "were clearly laid down and authenticated by a variety of documents, laws and formal acts of possession": Pope Alexander the Sixth's *Inter Caetera* of 4 May 1493, which granted to Ferdinand and Isabella, and their heirs and successors, all discovered or unknown lands that were not already occupied by another Christian prince west of the meridian 100 leagues west of the Azores; Article 8 of the Treaty of Utrecht, 1713, between Britain and Spain, which confirmed the "vast extent" of Spanish dominion in America; and formal acts of possession-taking on the Northwest Coast between 1774 and 1789, which proved that Spain had "preserved here possession entire."[91] Furthermore, the viceroy of Mexico claimed that Martínez's right to treat British vessels as legal prizes was based on a Spanish Royal *Cedula* of 1692 (and the Anglo-Spanish Treaty of Madrid of 1670, to which the *Cedula* referred), which stated that British subjects "shall not sail unto, and trade in the havens and places which the Catholic King holdeth," and implied that Spain had "true and just" dominion over the Pacific coast north of California; and on a peremptory Royal Order of 1776, which authorized Spanish officials to "detain, take prisoner and prosecute by law whatsoever foreign vessel should arrive in our ports" in the Pacific.[92] Spanish politicians invoked a variety of texts, authorities, and acts; so much so that Dalrymple and Leeds argued that Spain had to scramble to find enough evidence to support its position and that its territorial claims were contradictory.[93]

The British, by contrast, rooted questions of sovereignty in strictures about occupation.[94] "Whatever the Pretensions may be, which Spain may think herself justified to advance with respect to Nootka Sound founded either on an alleged prior Discovery or on the Application of the general Words of formal Treaties to that Place," Leeds wrote to Fitzherbert on 5 July 1790, "it is clear that she had not such an established Possession and Acknowledged Dominion there [before mid-June 1789], as could alone justify the Seizure of the British Vessels [from late May to mid-July]. A Right to proceed in that manner in the First Instance, could, according to the Law of Nations, result only from a Right of Territory, manifested by open Possession, and by the actual exercise of His Catholick Majesty's Authority, and this confirmed by an express or tacit Acknowledgment of other Nations."[95] Leeds did not deviate from this position over the ensuing months. The British challenged the validity of Papal Bulls and considered acts of discovery and symbolic acts of possession-taking (marking one's discoveries with crosses or royal banners and exchanging presents with Native peoples) insufficient grounds for establishing sovereignty.[96] Leeds insisted that the "general words" of treaties did not create clear territorial rights. Sovereignty could only stem from "open Possession," and Meares provided the British with a handy memorial.

Patricia Seed has suggested that from the sixteenth century onwards, "the primary symbolism of the English conception of sovereignty was architectural."[97] Sovereignty was founded on the erection of permanent dwellings. "Because their concept of dominion was bound up with residence on the land and with the nearly synonymous use of 'possession' and 'property,'" Seed continues, "the English believed that symbolic manifestations [of possession-taking] ... functioned merely as mnemonic devices, or at best as navigational beacons."[98] To Leeds, rights of ownership stemmed from de facto possession and the cultivation/improvement of land. Such ideas about the nature of property were enshrined in John Locke's *Two Treatises on Government*, British common law, and a body of imperial precepts and precedents. It was these ideas that made Meares's memorial influential. He abandoned his dwelling at Nootka Sound but made it clear that he intended to reoccupy the building and possibly build trade posts on the other spots of land he said he had bought. Leeds admitted that the two silver spoons that Martínez stated were stolen in 1774 and returned to him by Natives of Nootka Sound in 1789 were tangible evidence that the Spanish had discovered the sound before Cook, but Leeds denied that this, or any other acts of discovery or evidence of contact with Native peoples, gave Spain any *exclusive* territorial rights to the region. Leaving "a few trifling articles with the Natives," he argued, did not amount to sovereignty.[99] In addition, Daines Barrington, who published an account of Hezeta's 1775 voyage in England in 1781, noted that Spain's alleged rights to the coast were "flimsy" because this region was peopled by Natives who lived in permanent dwellings and because Natives pulled down the crosses planted by the Spaniard.[100] Finally, Leeds disputed Spain's recourse to the Treaty of Madrid and the Treaty of Utrecht, noting that Spain had never occupied the vast majority of the territories mentioned in these international agreements.[101]

Britain and Spain invoked incommensurable discourses on sovereignty. The British emphasized the primacy of planting and argued that physical manifestations of possession were more authoritative than words and tacit actions. The British drew on Meares's memorial and Dalrymple's information to hedge the vast and ancient limits of the Spanish Empire. Spain, on the other hand, invoked ideas of imperial continuity and adjacency. Floridablanca drew on narratives of possession and (Amerindian and European) acquiescence that came from what Jose Rabasa has called "a thesaurus of New World motifs" – from a range of Spanish inscriptions (or inventions) of the New World.[102] The Pacific littoral of Americas, Floridablanca suggested, had been made Spanish by a treasury of entitlements that stretched back over three centuries and covered the region entirely. He was concerned with the longevity of the Spanish Empire, and the authority and effectivity of languages of imperial prestige, rather than with the density and scope of Spanish occupation and control. Britain and Spain were at loggerheads over how imperial space was created.

At another level, however, neither Britain nor Spain questioned Europe's right to sovereignty over Native land. Leeds and Floridablanca worked out of an intrinsically Eurocentric discourse about the underlying right of civilized nations to impose themselves on uncivilized ones. Britain stressed that Meares had bought and built on land "with the consent of the Natives."[103] In Leeds's eyes, this made Britain's case morally stronger than Spain's. Native consent was an important trope of imperial legitimation, but as Anthony Pagden has shown, it was also a duplicitous one. Pagden argues that while Europeans were acutely aware that "some kind of claim to the legitimate possession of the lands of 'aboriginal peoples' was a necessary condition of successful occupation," legal and philosophical debate about such matters were informed and fuelled by assumptions about European superiority.[104]

This clause about taking land with the consent of the Natives did not cause Leeds to admit that Native peoples had sovereignty over their lands in any internationally acceptable legal sense of the term. In 1938, the authors of *Creation of Rights of Sovereignty*, one of the classic texts on European methods of possession-taking, came to the following conclusion, which reflects Leeds's silence on the question of Native sovereignty:

> Since the European states considered that ownership could be ascertained without reference to the acts of natives, it is apparent that they did not consider the natives as having anything in the nature of sovereignty that had to be respected. On the other hand, possession, as distinguished from ownership, was to be determined by the actual situation on the spot, and the acts of the natives were to be considered, not as having legal significance in the sense of a transfer of a recognized title, but merely as facts that showed the actual situation as to possession.[105]

More recently, the legal historian Leslie Green has argued that at the end of the eighteenth century, "international law did not recognise the aboriginal inhabitants of ... newly discovered territories as having any legal rights that were good as against those who 'discovered' and settled in their territories."[106] Native peoples were deemed to be "the subjects of the [European] ruler exercising sovereignty over the territory. As such they enjoyed no rights that international law would recognise."[107]

These are controversial claims, but they reflect the tenor of the Nootka Crisis. Floridablanca questioned the veracity of Meares's memorial, but neither he nor Leeds were interested in the nature of Meares's dealings with Native peoples. Leeds simply used this clause about Native consent to support Britain's diplomatic case, and Britain's demand for satisfaction was strengthened by the fact that other European observers, including Floridablanca, acknowledged that Meares had occupied Nootka Sound before Martínez. When Meares was interviewed by Britain's Privy Council in 1791, he spoke of how he had exchanged gifts with Chief Maquinna. But politicians were not concerned with issues of cultural negotiation. The notes they made in the margins of Meares's testimony highlight where he had erected his buildings but not how he had come into possession of land.[108] The Privy Council was not interested in such fine details. All Meares had to do was show that he had occupied some land. Neither Britain nor Spain investigated Meares's land purchases, and, if we follow Green, then the veracity of Meares's story about these purchases was inconsequential from a legal point of view. The way Native chiefs regarded Meares and his land purchases were filtered out of these legal-imperial equations.

Dalrymple's pamphlet *The Spanish Pretensions Fairly Discussed* exemplifies this siphoning off of issues of Native consent and points to a broader set of tensions in this dispute. "I shall not despair," he wrote, when Universal Commerce shall invigorate the hand of Industry, by supplying the mutual Wants, and maintaining the Common-Rights of ALL MANKIND; instead of the *Lives* and *Property* of the PEOPLE being sported away; at the caprice of a Fool! or a Tyrant!

The fundamental Principles of the Law of Nations, are *Justice* and *common Interest:* In former times, when Ignorance prevailed, and narrow prejudices, ever consequent to Ignorance, the Law of Nations was not extended to *Infidels* or *Pagans*; who were then considered, by *Christians*, as free Objects of Injury and Oppression; but in these enlightened Times, The Catholic King has no hesitation in concluding Treaties with Mahometans, with whom, by the absurd Oaths of ancient Bigotry, He was engaged to perpetual Warfare.

... Common Sense must evince that Europeans, visiting Countries *already inhabited*, can acquire *no right* in *Such Countries* but from the *good will* of the *Friendly Inhabitants*, or by *Conquest* of *Those* who are *Aggressors* in *Acts* of *Injury:* nor can the right of Conquest be justly extended, when Acts of Injury, in the Natives, can be construed to proceed from *fear* of the *Strangers*, or from *mistake*: In either case, Both Parties being equally culpable, though no criminality in either; the European in not sufficiently explaining his peaceable intentions, and the Native in not readily apprehending those intentions.[109]

It was the legitimacy of European sovereignty and methods of possession-taking that concerned Dalrymple, not Native title to land. European sovereignty over the non-European world and European superiority over Natives were not in dispute. Patricia Seed has shown how colonial rule "was initiated through largely symbolic practices – planting crosses, standards, banners and coats of arms – marching in processions, picking up dirt, measuring the stars, drawing maps, speaking certain words, or remaining silent."[110] Britain, France, Holland, Portugal, and Spain developed different styles of possession-taking, and each country claimed that its own method was the most acceptable. Native peoples were variously configured in such proceedings, as active participants, witnesses, and as irrelevant. Dalrymple was historicizing some of these differences. He was suggesting that Spain's old ceremony of possession-taking – the sixteenth-century *Requirement*, which was read before Native peoples in the New World, imploring them to recognize the superiority of Christianity (and particularly Spanish Catholicism) or be warred on – had been overtaken by enlightened "justice" and "common interest." It was Europe's peaceful intentions that now had to be recognized by the Natives; European sovereignty could no longer be based on Native fear of strangers. Dalrymple realized that Spain had not taken Nootka Sound by force, but he also suggested that it had not attempted to cultivate the good will of the Natives. Meares had. More specifically, he had cultivated the "invigorating hand of commerce" (i.e., property in its commercial and landed guises).

Dalrymple's discussion of Spain's "pretensions" encapsulates some of the main themes of my argument about the imperial refashioning of the Northwest Coast. He chained the physicality of Native-White interaction – that embodied world of apprehension, fear, and mistakes – to a set of European ideas about civilization, sovereignty, and empire.[111] In Dalrymple's mind, Spain's imperial methods were rooted in tyranny, whereas Britain's were based on the development of "mutual wants" and "common-rights" – on the enlightened, liberal principles of "universal commerce" that characterized Britain's national soul. Spanish imperial despotism had been fuelled by the Pope and was littered with "acts of injury," whereas the interests of "all mankind" were only truly served by that "just" mixture of liberty and commerce that British traders and colonists took overseas. Fostering the "good will of the Friendly Inhabitants" – or taking land with the consent of the Natives – was not an admission of Native rights to land but a demonstration of Britain's approach to the world: its peaceful, beneficent development of universal commerce. The land deals supposedly struck by Meares proved that Britain was a peaceable nation, and they were evidence that Native peoples around the world had entered into mutually beneficial trading relationships with British merchants. Martínez's actions, Dalrymple implied, stemmed from the "narrow prejudices" of an older imperial world. We can now say that Dalrymple's "enlightened" views about Natives were mediated by an apparatus of appropriation – a discourse of sovereignty that licensed intervention. In 1790 Dalrymple and Leeds used the Law of Nations as a rhetorical whip with which to beat Spain's claims to exclusive sovereignty. "Among Nations, ignorant of Letters and the Diplomatic Rules of Europe," Dalrymple concluded, "Treaties of Amity cannot be executed according to European Forms."[112] He meant that while treaties of amity in the form of land purchases from Native chiefs could be used to ground *Britain's* right to trade and settle in the Pacific, Native peoples themselves did not have any legal rights to the soil because they did not act according to European rules.

In the Nootka Crisis, then, the details of exploration and commercial contact were reworked into European legal and geopolitical codes. The Nootka Convention did not fix precise imperial boundaries, but politicians raised the idea, albeit vaguely at this point, that Native peoples might one day be subjects of European rule. The Law of Nations was built by Europeans for Europeans. Britain did not colonize the coast immediately after the Convention with Spain. Pitt turned his attention to events in central Europe and the affairs of the Triple Alliance, the details of compensation and the restoration of British property took another five years to work out, and the British Cabinet decided to wait for the results of Vancouver's survey before deciding whether Britain should take up its hard-won right to trade and settle on the coast. It was the Oregon Treaty rather than the Nootka Convention that marked the beginnings of formal colonialism on the Northwest Coast, and it was the settlement of the region by

American and British emigrants, rather than simply ideas about sovereignty, that transformed Native fortunes. Yet the Nootka Crisis inaugurated the absorption of the coast into the British imperial imagination and pointed to the sequestration of Native land and life.

We can see in the work of Leeds and Floridablanca, and Dalrymple and the Committee of Trade and Plantations, the productivity of discourse. Detailed information about the Pacific was organized into useful patterns, and the categories of private trade and national honour, profit and imperial right, monopoly and sovereignty that organized these patterns transformed Britain's approach to the Northwest Coast. There was nothing inevitable about this transition from commerce to imperialism, or the modulation of imperial sovereignty into colonial rule. It is upon the production of an imperial context within which Vancouver Island, the Northwest Coast, and the Pacific could be re-imagined and dealt with from afar that we should focus on. The Nootka Crisis set up and clarified a process of abstraction that was initially hinted at by Cook – not Cook the writer, but Cook the cartographer. His scanty map of the coast imposed a cartographic order on the coast that was at odds with the fluidities of contact. This and other maps fuelled an imperial imagination that ran with rarefied images of regions like the Northwest Coast and operated with particular brands of knowledge. Soon after the Nootka Crisis, George Vancouver was sent to the coast to fill in Cook's map.

CHAPTER 11

Circumscribing
Vancouver Island

VANCOUVER'S ISLAND

The Nootka Crisis prompted the British Cabinet to seek more precise information about the Northwest Coast, and George Vancouver was Britain's emissary
to the region. He was instructed to negotiate with Spain's official at Nootka Sound,
Juan Francisco de la Bodega y Quadra, over the restoration of Meares's property,
but the main aim of his voyage was to conduct an exhaustive cartographic survey of the coast up the latitude 60° north and end speculation about the existence of a Northwest Passage. His diplomatic mission achieved little, but he
conducted a meticulous survey in the 330-ton ship *Discovery* and 131-ton brig
Chatham. Vancouver circumnavigated the island that bears his name in the summer of 1792 and left the coast after two more arduous survey seasons, having in
his mind "set aside every opinion of a *north-west passage* ... existing between the
North Pacific, and the interior of the American continent, within the limits of
our researches."[1] Upon the conclusion of his reconnaissance in October 1794,
Vancouver's botanist and surgeon, Archibald Menzies, reported to his sponsor,
Sir Joseph Banks, that "no task was ever executed with more assiduity & perse-
vering zeal, than the intricate examination of this coast."[2]

This notion that Vancouver and his party truly sorted out the geography of
the Northwest Coast was reiterated by nineteenth-century commentators and
has been upheld by a host of scholars. After visiting the region in the mid-1820s,
the Scottish naturalist John Scouler reported that he had nothing to add to Vancouver's map and that "the admirable surveys of that navigator have rendered
the numerous islands and complicated inlets of the N.W. coast of America familiar to the geographers of Europe."[3] Another naturalist, Berthold Seeman, who
toured the Pacific in the mid-1840s, noted that "no accurate information [of the
Northwest Coast] ... begins previous to Vancouver, who ... examined the whole

190

with scientific accuracy. His work is still referred to for its agreeable truthfulness."[4] Vancouver's work was not bettered until the late 1850s, when G.H. Richards led a six-year survey for the British Admiralty.[5] This century, J.C. Beaglehole maintained that "Vancouver's systematic and painstaking survey ranks with the most distinguished work of the kind ever done" – a remark cited approvingly by W. Kaye Lamb, who re-edited Vancouver's journals for the Hakluyt Society of London.[6]

Vancouver's achievement, so these remarks suggest, was that he separated geographical fact from fiction – that he discovered a good portion of the spatial reality of the coast and forged a more accurate and thorough cartographic relation with it than his contemporaries. Glyndwr Williams writes: "This exact, meticulous explorer found his satisfaction in producing charts of such accuracy that they were used for more than a century after his death."[7] And in their introduction to a recent collection of essays, *From Maps to Metaphors: The Pacific World of George Vancouver*, which stemmed from a conference that was held in 1992 to mark the bicentenary of Vancouver's arrival on the coast, Robin Fisher and Hugh Johnston suggest that "Vancouver could be said to have discovered the northwest coast of North America, for it was he who established that it was a continuous line, unbroken by any passage to the Atlantic."[8]

Such images mimic Vancouver's own sense of his survey. He wrote in his published account of the voyage (1798): "Although the ardour of the present age, to discover and delineate the true geography of the earth, had been rewarded with uncommon and unexpected success, particularly by the perservering exertions of this great man [Captain Cook] ... all was not completed."[9] Vancouver sailed on Cook's second and third voyages, and he knew that the illustrious navigator had not explored much of the Northwest Coast.[10] Vancouver noted that the "very detached and broken region that lies before so large a portion of this coast, rendered a minute examination altogether unavoidable," and he figured that his team had conducted "an accurate survey" and "dispassionate investigation of the truth."[11] "It was with infinite satisfaction," he concluded, "that I saw, amongst the officers and young gentlemen of the quarter-deck, some who, with little instruction, would soon be enabled to construct charts, take plans of bays and harbours, draw landscapes, and make faithful representations of the several headlands, coasts, and countries, which we might discover."[12]

This rhetoric of accuracy, exactitude, and faithful geographical representation, invoked by Vancouver and recycled by scholars, is underwritten by the idea that Vancouver's team charted in a more or less truthful way a geography that was waiting to be discovered; that they made a closer copy of reality than any previous surveyors. Scholars of Vancouver's voyage have not considered the recent critical literature on the history of cartography, which posits a set of links between maps, knowledge, and power. "Whether a map is produced under the banner of cartographic science – as most official maps have been [and

Vancouver's were] – or whether it is an overt propaganda exercise," Brian Harley argued in 1988, "it cannot escape involvement in the process by which power is deployed." Maps often "'desocialise' the territory they represent," he continues, to the degree that "decisions about the exercise of power are removed from the realm of immediate face-to-face contacts."[13]

This, roughly, I suggest, is what Vancouver's cartography encouraged. He was not simply engaged in a veridical search for an anticipated geographical reality. Nor did he simply unfurl the geographical truth about the Northwest Coast in a progressive fashion – starting at the Strait of Juan de Fuca (which some European pundits thought led to the Northwest Passage) and finishing his survey at "Point Conclusion" on Baranof Island – as the recent literature on his survey suggests. As accurately, Vancouver created a geography, and his geography had imperial connotations.[14] His cartography facilitated geopolitical processes of appropriation that worked at a distance from Native peoples. He papered over the intersubjective spaces of interaction created by the maritime fur trade and reinvented the island that bears his name. His cartography became connected to Western formulae of sovereignty that worked around Native geopolitical dynamics. In my view, Vancouver's achievements should be assessed in the light of the concepts and methods that he brought to bear on the Northwest Coast and in relation to the imperial and colonial legacies of his survey.

Fisher and Johnston argue that we should not hold Vancouver responsible for the way his survey was used for imperial ends and is now seen by some Native groups and non-Native sympathizers as a part of the narrative of colonialism. They acknowledge that "to map an area is to appropriate it" and that "Vancouver's charts of the northwest coast were a part of the process of economic exploitation and, eventually, cultural disruption"; but they emphasize that "appropriation did not begin or end with Vancouver," and they criticize the representation of Native history "as a straight and unrelieved downhill run from 1492 to the present day." They single out Ronald Wright's *Stolen Continents* (published in 1992, the quincentenary year of Columbus's discovery of the New World) for special criticism. This and other "fatal impact" narratives are organized around themes of cultural misunderstanding and collision, and they emphasize the blanket insidiousness of Western representations of Native peoples and land. Such narratives may give us "a politically palatable version of the past," Fisher and Johnston note, but they overlook "periods and places of cooperation and accommodation between Natives and newcomers." Bringing these historiographical issues to bear on the Vancouver bicentenary, they argue:

> There is no denying the oppression and suffering of the Native peoples of the Pacific region, and around the globe, from the time of the their first encounter with Europeans, but as non-Natives strive to write the so-called "history of the other side" they sometimes forget their own. The achievements of explorers are

downplayed. Certainly for Vancouver the wheel had come full circle by 1992 as, once again, he was disparaged or ignored, just as he had been in the years after he returned from his voyage. The bicentennial of his coming to the northwest coast did not receive the same recognition as the Cook bicentennial had ... One reason was an increased consciousness among civic politicians and the public of Native issues and Native perspectives. A Vancouver event no longer seemed appropriate. But laundering history for public consumption does not lead to better understanding of the past. History must constantly be reinterpreted, but ought not be denied.[15]

I have a number of criticisms of the way Fisher and Johnston represent Vancouver's voyage. First, while they acknowledge that there are links between maps and power, issues of appropriation are barely broached in *From Maps to Metaphors* and other recent volumes on European exploration in the North Pacific.[16] Recent writing on Vancouver shies away from questions of power rather than delves into them. Second, implicit in this oversight is the notion that representations of space – and particularly cartographic representations – have only a minor bearing on the formation of imperial attitudes and colonial practices. This is especially apparent in Fisher's work. He regards face-to-face processes of interaction as the principal generators of change and measures of cultural appropriation and accommodation. In *From Maps to Metaphors*, Fisher and Johnston emphasize that Vancouver had largely friendly dealings with Native peoples and that his survey work depended on their "tacit compliance." The suggestion here, I think, is that Vancouver should be situated in the economy of cultural accommodation that Fisher thinks characterized the pre-colonial era of contact as a whole. Vancouver went about his business quietly and competently. His "information was used, and misused, by *others* to develop their own conceptions of the Pacific world."[17] Fisher, Johnston, and other historians have given Vancouver a congenial reputation in the history of contact and colonialism. His global – imperial – reputation, they suggest, lies elsewhere, with others.

Ironically, in depoliticizing Vancouver's voyage, and focusing on the accuracy of his cartography, scholars have cut a set of links between maps, imperial power, and regional identity that were forged by British Columbians earlier this century, albeit in a colonialist vein. In the summer of 1792 the Spanish explorers Galiano and Valdés were also searching for the Northwest Passage, and they accompanied Vancouver through the Strait of Georgia. The British and Spanish explorers shared information, and to acknowledge such participation, and the purpose of his diplomatic mission at Nootka Sound, Vancouver, at Quadra's request, named the region he had surveyed "the island of QUADRA and VANCOUVER."[18] In addition, in 1790 Meares informed the Foreign Office that the American trader Gray had sailed "a considerable distance" into the Strait of Juan de Fuca in 1789 and "arrive[d] at an open Channel or Sea, [and] did reenter the Pacific Ocean between the Latitudes of 54° and 55° North, having completely ascertained that Nootka Sound, and all the lands adjacent, to be an archipelago of Islands, and not the Continent of America."[19] This left some scholars of British Columbia confused about who deserved the accolade "true discoverer" of Vancouver Island. C.F. Newcombe tried to set the record straight. In his memoir, *The First Circumnavigation of Vancouver Island*, published in 1914, he argued that Vancouver deserved the accolade. "The earliest stages in the progressive discovery of the inner channels of Vancouver Island were reached entirely by British ships," he declared, and Vancouver's "sketches and charts were of such a reliable nature that the names bestowed on various places are still in use upon the maps of the present day."[20] Newcombe was sloughing off the influence of nineteenth-century American explorers on the toponymy of the Puget Sound region as well as Spain's hand in the exploration of the coast. And F.W. Howay wrote of the meeting between Vancouver and the Spanish explorers in the Gulf of Georgia: "It was the meeting of destinies, the dawn of British rule, the setting of Spanish glory."[21]

These authors were pointing to the imperial dimensions of cartography and geographical exploration. G.M. Sproat thought that Vancouver's circumnavigation was "the outstanding historic occurrence" in the early history of British Columbia because it caused American politicians to admit that Britain had sovereignty over Vancouver Island, which, he continued, "was empty but for savage tribes."[22] Other scholars were bent on preventing the names bestowed by explorers and pioneers from being taken off the map by the Geographic Board of Canada. E.O.S. Scholefield argued that they were vital "links in the chain" between the past and the present.[23] And a reviewer of Captain John Walbran's *British Columbia Coast Names* (1909, and still the definitive work on the subject), noted that "names are in a sense an epitome of the history of the country. If they are aboriginal in their origin they are always, either historical or descriptive, for the idea of a name, as something apart from the thing to which it was applied, does not seem to have suggested itself to the North American Indian."[24]

These early custodians of British Columbia's past recognized that Vancouver created "something apart from the thing to which it was applied": a cartographic and toponymic totality that was deployed for political purposes connected Vancouver Island to a broader imperial horizon and underwrote British Columbia's colonial history. More specifically, Vancouver made Vancouver Island British rather than Spanish, American, or Native.[25] These scholars pieced together something of Vancouver's contribution to empire and saw him as a founding father like Cook. Recent writing on Vancouver, by contrast, tends to downplay these themes and gives us little sense of how or why his maps were turned into metaphors of power. How did his voyage become implicated in these "other" processes of use and misuse? Fisher works with the view that the splitting of cultural perspectives on the past into "our own history" and the history "of the other side" stemmed from the breakdown of cultural accommodation during the colonial period. I want to argue that Vancouver's cartography played an important role in this splitting of perspectives. In the 1790s processes of cultural accommodation were circumscribed by relations of territorial appropriation. I will suggest that a critical emphasis on issues of appropriation and power in Vancouver's survey and its legacies does not necessarily amount to a "laundering" of history for the present; rather, Vancouver's cartography helps us to clarify how this transition from "contact" to "conflict" came about and prompts us to reconsider what comes to pass when formal colonialism begins.

In this chapter I explore how Vancouver produced his chart of the Northwest Coast and discuss why it was insidious. The following two chapters will consider how his survey and cartography became entangled with wider processes of imperial fashioning and projects of colonial development.

Vancouver's "Combinatory Calculus"

Vancouver's surveying instructions, which were prepared for the Home Office by Major James Rennell (who had a great hand in the mapping of India), Sir Joseph Banks, and William Bligh, were far more detailed than any Cook had been given, and they reveal the great emphasis that the British government placed on the cartographic aspects of his mission.

> It is judged necessary, in order that future Surveyors may profit to the fullest Extent, by your Discoveries & Operations; & that they may be able to Appreciate the Authorities on which the Geography of the several Portions of the Coast rest; that those Authorities should not only be pointedly marked in your Chart but that a Register should also be kept in the Nature of a *Log Survey Book* ... so that, in Cases where you have not been able, either from Weather or Accidents to compleat the Trigonometrical or Observational Process, others may be enabled to compleat what you have begun, without the Delay of going through the whole Process anew.[26]

With regard to charting, Vancouver was told that

> every principal object whose position is either wholly or even thro' Accident only partially and incompletely determined shall have that position marked by a dot (.) & the mode by which it was so determined shall be described by adding as many of the following Marks as may serve to express it.
> *   a Position determined by Celestial Observation ...
> ⊕   Longitude of Time Keeper
> ⊖   Latitude by Observation
> ○   Lat. by Account

△   By Intersection of Bearings, with 2 or more broken lines ...
⊙   Surveying Stations of the Day, Month & Year to be added ...
═══ Measured bases ...[27]

And, with regard to illustrating the charts, "It is suggested that significant and Characteristic Names should be given, on the spot of the several Objects that form the Sound Marks; in which case, if named with Judgment the Name would convey some portion of information to succeeding Navigators and Surveyors."[28] Vancouver had another set of instructions from the Admiralty, which outlined his diplomatic objectives but also impressed on him that his principal goal was to acquire "a more complete knowledge" of the coast.[29] This was a different mission than that of Cook's third voyage. Vancouver, like other British explorers sponsored by the Admiralty during this period, was told to observe people and nature and to avoid collisions with Native peoples. But it was Archibald Menzies who was chiefly responsible for describing "the present state & comparative degree of Civilization of the [Native] Inhabitants" and collecting botanical specimens.[30] Menzies was counselled by Joseph Banks; Vancouver and his officers were meant to focus on surveying.[31]

At the heart of Vancouver's surveying instructions, and his introduction to his account of his transactions, was the idea that he should produce a conclusive and, hence, authoritative geography. The British government hoped that he would render the geography of the coast "compleat" and instructed him to chart the "authorities" on which his geography rested – his own discoveries and those of others. "The benefit that Government will derive from this mode of surveying is that the Employment of conjecture [especially about the Northwest Passage] will be rendered impossible," Banks wrote to Grenville.[32] Vancouver added that, because the region was so "detached and broken,"

> I have considered it essential to the illustration of our survey, to state very exactly not only the track of the vessels when navigating these regions, but likewise those of the boats when so employed ... The perusal of these parts of our voyage to persons not particularly interested, I am conscious will afford but little entertainment; yet I have been induced to give a detailed account, instead of an abstract, of our proceedings, for the purpose of illustrating the charts accompanying this journal: of shewing the manner in which our time day by day had been employed; and, for the additional purpose, of making the history of our transactions on the north-west coast of America, *as conclusive as possible.*[33]

Vancouver sought a finite space – a calculable geography – and was determined to show how he had mapped it. He discussed the techniques and physical toils involved in his work and the ways in which he arrived at a conclusion. His charts and log survey book were meant to describe his physical, cognitive, and optical

route through spaces that were at once real and technical, geographical and ana-
logical. Headlands, inlets, bays, tides, beaches, and horizons were simultaneously spotted and measured, discovered, and brought into spatial existence by a
cartographic method.

Vancouver and his team used a set of methods and instruments to draw together space and to depict it on a uniform plane – a scale map. They worked
with what William Boelhower calls "a combinatory calculus."[34] Boelhower discusses the mapping of the eastern seaboard of North America up to the nineteenth century, but his arguments about scale maps have a more general purchase.
Vancouver's survey work, I take Boelhower to suggest, revolved around his "physical and cognitive mobility across an open series of heterogeneous spaces," and
his charts were attempts "to weave such infinite variety into a unified discourse."[35]
Vancouver used different techniques and types of equipment to connect up the
dots on his charts: chronometers and lunar observations for establishing longitude at sea; gunther chains for measuring bases in areas with long stretches of
beach; triangulation stations on shore for determining the angle of a bay or
headland in relation to the sun; sextants, compasses, long lines, and the turning
points of a long boat when determining the size of an inlet; and compass bearings taken from "ship stations" to judge the distance between prominent coastal
features. The combination of methods and tools used at specific points was influenced by the weather and the physical terrain.[36] Vancouver judged that his
team had "completely explored every turning" of Puget Sound. This survey was
successful because there was much flat land in the area and triangulation bases
could be established at regular intervals.[37] And he noted that there were "a sufficient number of stopping places" in Johnstone Strait "to answer all our [survey-
ing] purposes."[38] But Vancouver could not obtain an accurate latitude for the
head of Jervis Inlet and other locations because of low cloud.[39] Vancouver's island was produced from Vancouver's intricate and heterogeneous passage between his survey log book, journal, and charts.[40] "At the centre of the map is not
geography *in se*," Boelhower declares, "but the eye of the cartographer."[41]

Vancouver's eyes, of course, were not just fixed on distances and angles. He
looked for *safe* anchorages, *deep* harbours, and *fertile* tracts of land as well as
that elusive water passage into the interior. And he was instructed to bestow
appropriate names. Vancouver was meant to characterize the region's potential
and make it characteristically British. One the one hand, he was a representative
of George the Third and was meant to stamp his geography "British" and describe its main features. Like many other explorers on state-sponsored voyages,
he named many of his findings after royal, aristocratic, military, and political
figures: "The Gulf of Georgia" after the king; "Bute's Canal" after the Earl of
Bute; "Grenville Channel" after the home secretary. And he bestowed the name
"Possession Sound" at the opening of Puget Sound to signify where he claimed
formal possession of the Gulf of Georgia region for Britain. Vancouver then

described the landscapes to which such names had been fixed. For instance, he considered the area around Possession Sound to be of "a rich fertile mould" and, from an agricultural point of view, "capable of high improvement" – a "most lovely country" with commodious harbours.[42] As he moved north during the summer, however, he discovered that the "country presented a very different aspect from that which we have been accustomed to behold further south" – steep, rugged rocks with small bays and "herbage of a dull colour."[43]

However, like Cook, Vancouver also sought to capture his experience of exploration in his journal and on his charts. On the other hand, then, he bestowed names that signified the physical and technological aspects of surveying, and the particular circumstances of his voyage at different points in time. He named "Puget's Sound" and "Johnstone's Strait" after two of his most hard-working officers. He bestowed names such as "Desolation Sound" because he considered it a "gloomy place" that "afforded not a single prospect that was pleasing to the eye," and "Observatory Inlet" (on the Nass River) because he reckoned that the time his party spent there in July 1793 was "essential for correcting our former survey."[44] His writing about landscape was also tempered by the purpose and duration of his work. He noted that Johnstone Strait was "infinitely more grateful" than Desolation Sound; but he also found it grateful, no doubt, because it was the passage that led him to the discovery that Vancouver Island is an island.[45] And as his exhausting survey dragged on, Vancouver became less enthusiastic about the coast. He wrote to the Admiralty Board in December 1793: "The country we have passed through in general this summer appears incapable of being appropriated to any other use than the abode of the few uncouth inhabitants it at present contains."[46] By the end of the third survey season he was desperate to quit "these remote and uncouth parts."[47]

In short, Vancouver tried to intersperse the physicality, technicality, and official nature of his voyage in his journal and on his charts. One can follow his path around Vancouver Island from "Port Discovery" (which he bestowed to mark the arrival of his aptly named ship in uncharted waters), to "Admiralty Inlet" (bestowed, in part, to signify its commodious harbours), to "Port Townsend" (after the marquis of that name, who became commander of British forces in Quebec after General Wolfe's death). Or one can follow him from "Jervis Inlet" (named after an admiral), to "Upwood Point" (named "in remembrance of an early friendship"), and on through parts of the Strait of Georgia where Spanish explorers had bestowed names.[48] His charts represent the spatial relations of exploration. His journal describes the circumstances under which he had made his discoveries: the weather, the instruments used, his mood, and his expectations and disappointments. Vancouver produced a unified geographical discourse that was at once personal and national, corporeal and imperial. Overall, he framed the Northwest Coast as a distinctively British and scientific domain.

Yet as scholars such as Boelhower argue, cartographic systems of representation are not as stable or uniform as they appear. We can reveal the arbitrariness of their claims to universality and completeness by searching for their "blind spots," or erasures and closures.[49] Maps can be "deconstructed" in a number of ways. In Vancouver's case, I think, it is the differences between his journal, published in 1798 in three quarto volumes, and some of the engraved charts in the folio atlas that accompanied this text, that reveal such "blind spots."[50]

Consider Figure 10: the southern portion of Vancouver's *Chart Shewing Part of the Coast of N.W. America* (45º30'-52º15' latitude – 230º30'-238º30' longitude), which was produced by four renowned engravers who were employed by the Admiralty and whose work was supervised by Vancouver and the Admiralty's hydrographer, Alexander Dalrymple. The engravers worked with draft summary charts prepared by two of Vancouver's officers, Joseph Baker and Edward Roberts, and these drafts had been prepared from more detailed manuscript charts. This *Chart*, and a smaller one depicting the coast from 28 to 63 degrees latitude and 205 to 245 degrees longitude, rationalizes Vancouver's reconnaissance of 1792 in particular ways.[51] There was not the space on the published charts to include all of the information that Vancouver's team had generated. Only aspects of Vancouver's cartography were emphasized, and, as far as it is possible to know, the engravers highlighted those aspects that Vancouver deemed important and that the Admiralty approved of.[52]

On this chart, Vancouver Island's intricate shoreline is circumscribed by the jagged track of Vancouver's vessels. There is a double message in Vancouver's statement that the purpose of representing the tracks of his vessels on his charts was to make the history of his transactions "as conclusive as possible." The island is named "Quadra and Vancouver's Island," but the fact that Vancouver circumnavigated it stands out. The polynominalism of the Nootka Convention, and Vancouver's meeting with Quadra, is acknowledged but circumvented. By 1825, Hudson's Bay Company fur traders and British politicians were referring to the island simply as "Vancouver's Island." In 1792, Vancouver despatched two of his officers to Britain with manuscript maps of the coast that included much information from Spanish charts, and the engraved chart states that those parts of the coastline "not shaded" had been derived from Spanish authorities. Vancouver's noted that he drew on the important survey work done in the region by the Spanish explorers Quimper, Fidalgo, and Eliza in 1790 and 1791, received assistance from Galiano and Valdés in 1792, and felt obliged to mention Spanish names.[53] But the engraved chart retains only sixteen of the numerous names bestowed on the island by Spanish explorers.[54]

Nor does this chart give much indication of maritime fur traders' cartographic endeavours, or of the contact process, or of a Native presence. Vancouver discussed his dealings with traders and Natives in his journal, and he noted that

A CHART

shewing part of the

COAST OF N.W. AMERICA,

with the tracks of His MAJESTY's Sloop

DISCOVERY and Armed Tender CHATHAM ;

Commanded by GEORGE VANCOUVER Esq. and prepared

under his immediate inspection by Lieut. Joseph Baker in which

the Continental Shore has been traced and determined from

Lat. 30°..2' and Long. 236°..7' to Lat. 56°..45' and Long. 231°..21'

at the different periods shewn by the Tracks.

The parts not shaded are taken from Spanish Authorities

drawn the 14th. of April. Northward ? their return southward

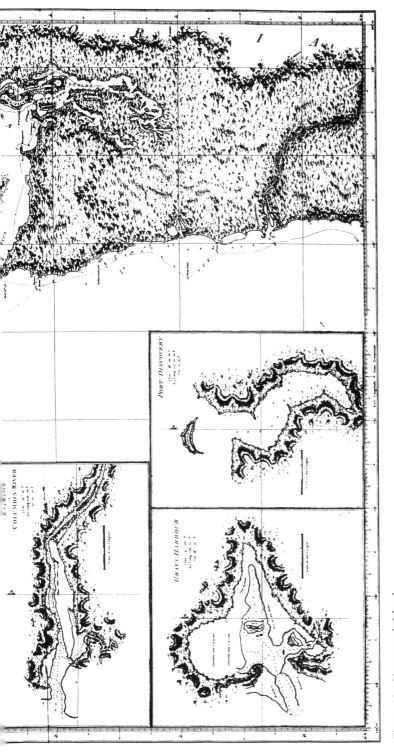

Figure 10 Vancouver's Island.

Source: John Warner, *A chart showing part of the coast of n.w. America with the tracks of his majesty's sloop Discovery and the armed tender Chatham commanded by George Vancouver ... in George Vancouver, A voyage of discovery to the north Pacific Ocean and round the world ...* (London: G.G. and J. Robinson and J. Edwards, 1798), plate 5. Courtesy Special Collections and University Archives Division, University of British Columbia Library.

he valued the charts produced by a number of British traders. But he dismissed most fur traders as "adventurers" who "had neither the means, nor the leisure ... for amassing any certain geographical information," and he declared that he did not trust Native testimony about the geography of the region.[55] As significant, Figure 10 does not fully represent the fact that Vancouver spotted many Native villages and came into contact with many Native peoples. It depicts only a handful of Native place names, and all but one of these – Cheslakees – was recorded by other explorers.

The absence of point symbols for land topography on this chart, and the fact that the tiny crosses dotting the coastline appear only on the sea side of the shoreline (depicting sunken ledges and rocks), suggests that Vancouver saw his cartography as a record of maritime surveying. Dalrymple also saw Vancouver's work in this way. Little is known about Dalrymple's involvement in this particular project, but Andrew Cook has shown that he devised a set of conventions for engraving sea charts. Cook thinks that the engravers' decoration used to fill the interior of the island and the coastal fringe of the mainland was there to help the viewer distinguish sea from land on a coast where Vancouver had to chart intricate passages and fjords.[56]

The Admiralty's engravers produced a chart that displays the technical skill of the British Admiralty but hardly anything of the contact process. In effect, this chart suppresses the idea that the Spanish had mapped the region, that Vancouver had traversed Native space, and that Native peoples and traders were in close proximity of each other's ways. It occludes the vibrancy of contact and the complex Native territorial and political arrangements that were described, in part, by fur traders. Vancouver's cartography subverts the commercial and corporeal connections between place and space that gave the early contact period its colour, and re-presents the coast as a lifeless, unified, objective spatial environment dotted with names that refer mainly to the power of science and the geographical reach of the British Admiralty. An abridged version of this chart, which appeared with the 1801 (corrected) octavio edition of Vancouver's voyage, retains even fewer signs of a Spanish, Native, or Western commercial presence but highlights Vancouver's route around the island and a handful of Vancouver's more significant names.

Two of the principal scholars of Vancouver's voyage, Andrew David and W. Kaye Lamb, have noted that Vancouver distrusted Spanish maps, but they are puzzled by his drastic cartographic abbreviation of Spanish exploration on the west coast of Vancouver Island.[57] Vancouver did not explain his motives. And these scholars have not discussed the representation of Native geographies in the engraved chart of Vancouver Island. Such puzzles and abbreviations add to the metonymic effect of Vancouver's cartography. The Admiralty's engravers inserted Vancouver Island into what Boelhower calls a system of "global circulation" characterized by the "combinatory passion of the scale map." It was with the rise of scale cartography, he argues, that maps "truly" became icons of nation-building and imperial expansion because they instituted a series of distinctions between the global and the local, line and image, place and passage. In the eighteenth and nineteenth centuries, Boelhower claims, the scale map became an icon of the American state's "sheer passage" across the continent: "Global circulation over the continental territory was ... the categorical imperative of nation-building. But if the global-route-line becomes the dominant factor of the cartographic text, then the local-place-image becomes mere context. At the global level – that is, on the abstract surface of the scale map – context disappears, place is no longer important."[58] This was a passage purportedly without obstacles – a passage premised on what Rabasa calls a "systematic forgetfulness" of prior inscriptions on the land.[59]

Boelhower's distinctions are probably too acute. Vancouver was not making context disappear; rather, he was producing a cartographic text and context. He fashioned a cartographic space with a selection of old and new lines, names, and passages, and he emphasized his – and Britain's – presence. Yet Boelhower is right to emphasize the global combinatory calculus of scientific cartography. For Vancouver worked towards the order of discourse that informed the Nootka Crisis. In fixing Vancouver Island on a grid of latitude and longitude, imposing British names, and representing his own achievements, he was rendering the island stable and combinable. David Turnbull argues that the "power of maps lies not merely in their accuracy or their correspondence with reality. It lies in their having incorporated a set of conventions that make them combinable in one central place, enabling the accumulation of both power and knowledge at that centre."[60] Maps are simultaneously practical tools, ways of ordering and disciplining space, and discourses through which people come to take particular conceptions of space for granted. Navigators found Vancouver's charts useful, and politicians could use them to locate the activities of British traders and size up the potential of the coast. Map-makers such as Arrowsmith had new cartographic details to work with on their maps of the Pacific and North America. In fashioning Vancouver Island as a cartographic shell – representing it in intricate but faint outline – Vancouver contributed to an imaginative geography that recontextualized the Northwest Coast from imperial vantage points. I will go on to show that the "compleat" picture that figures such as Grenville and Banks were looking for had imperial overtones. Vancouver shaped what Harley has called an "anticipatory geography" of colonialism.[61]

I have been suggesting that Vancouver's achievements should be assessed in the light of his surveying practices (which unified space), his naming practices (which personified Vancouver Island as British), and the categorical connections he made with the coast. He achieved both an intimacy with and detachment from the coast that reflected a broader confidence in his ability to know the world as a geometric totality and represent it accurately. He distinguished his work from the "fallacious speculations" of theoretical geographers and corrected the work of others who had been on the coast.

This, roughly, is what went into the production of this cartographic space. Vancouver started to desocialize the coast by opening up a conceptual gap between contact and cartography. As I now want to show, his cartography provided an objective link between exploration and empire. British politicians, speculators, and colonists invoked his survey as a basic link between British interest in the Northwest Coast and British power over it. They embellished and redefined the space of appropriation that Vancouver had fashioned.

CHAPTER 12

Delineating the Oregon Territory

"Have you any claim," said I [John Quincy Adams], "to the mouth of the Columbia River?"

"Why, do you not know," replied he [Stratford Canning], "that we have a claim?"

"I do not know," said I, "what you claim nor what you do not claim. You claim India; you claim Africa; you claim-"

"Perhaps," said he, "a piece of the moon."

"No," said I, "I have not heard you claim exclusively any part of the moon; but there is not a spot on this habitable globe that I could affirm you do not claim; and there is none which you may not with as much color of right as you can have to the Columbia River or its mouth."

"And how far would you consider," said he, "this exclusion of right to extend?"

"To all the shores of the South Sea," said I. "We know of no right you have there."

"Suppose," said he, "Great Britain should undertake to make a settlement there; would you object to it?"

"I have no doubt we should," said I.

– MEMOIRS OF JOHN QUINCY ADAMS (1825)

CARTOGRAPHIES OF NATIONAL HONOUR

As this humorous encounter between John Quincy Adams (then US Secretary of State) and Stratford Canning (Britain's minister in Washington) suggests, the Anglo-American dispute over the Oregon Territory also reduced Western-Native engagement on the Northwest Coast to a set of territorial claims that turned around questions of national honour and opportunity.[1] As with the Nootka Crisis, American and British statesmen made locational details speak to grander visions of empire and nationhood. The derivation of rights of sovereignty from facts of discovery and occupation were at the core of both disputes. But there were basic differences between these two geopolitical processes. The Nootka Crisis evolved at the interface of British mercantilism and Spain's American empire, and it spiralled into the international maze of European revolution. The Oregon boundary dispute, on the other hand, evolved at the interface of two land empires and involved visions of permanent occupation. Howard Jones and Donald Rakestraw show that between the Webster-Ashburton Treaty of 1842, which fixed the British-American border in northeast America, and the Oregon Treaty of 1846, "free-spirited Americans converged on the [Oregon] territory while equally unruly and outspoken statesmen on both sides of the Atlantic transformed the distant territory into the flashpoint of another war-threatening crisis."[2] An expanding American Republic encountered an old, recalcitrant imperial partner. For Americans, the continental destiny of the US and the twilight of Europe's presence in the New World was at hand. For the British, Anglo-American colonial wounds were re-opened and Britain's imperial philosophy of commerce, Protestantism and liberty, was juxtaposed with American ideas of manifest destiny. I am interested in the ways in which the geopolitical and cartographic nexus created by the Nootka Crisis and Vancouver's survey figured in the Oregon boundary dispute, and how, in turn, this dispute shaped Western appreciation of the Northwest Coast.

The first full round of negotiations, held in London in 1818, were prompted by political bickering in the United States over the transfer of the American trade post Astoria at the mouth of the Columbia River to British traders in 1813 but were used mainly to consolidate the provisions of past treaties.[3] The convention resulting from these negotiations fixed a boundary from Lake of the Woods (now on the Minnesota/Ontario border) along the 49th parallel to the Rockies, granted joint occupancy of the Oregon Territory for ten years, but left questions of title in the region in abeyance.[4] European and American diplomats had considered the 49th parallel west from the Great Lakes to be an appropriate boundary separating British and French territory in North America for much of the eighteenth century, but this boundary had never been instituted in any treaty or convention. In 1818, British diplomats wanted to ratify this boundary because the cartographic wisdom at this time was that the headwaters of the Mississippi River lay above 49°N, and British traders could thereby claim the right to descend the river to the Gulf of Mexico.[5] Henry Popple's *Map of the British Empire in America* (1732), which shows the 49th parallel bisecting the Mississippi River, was still considered accurate in 1818; the headwaters of the Mississippi were not discovered to lie below 49°N until 1823.[6]

The diplomats at these 1818 negotiations drew on geopolitical ideas stemming from the Anglo-French Treaty of Utrecht of 1713, which adjudicated commercial competition between the two nations around Hudson Bay. This treaty did not establish a British-French border in the region; it ruled that an Anglo-French commission would determine a border at a later date. This commission met in Paris in 1719. It did not fix a border either, but the idea that the 49th parallel west from Lake of the Woods was an appropriate boundary dividing British and French territory as far as they extended was clearly stated in instructions to Britain's commissioners and became a British diplomatic assumption.[7] Nor did the United States formally dispute this assumption when it acquired France's American possessions in the Louisiana Purchase of 1803. While trying to stretch this boundary to the Rockies in 1818, American diplomats Albert Gallatin and Richard Rush simply refused to grant Britain rights to descend the Mississippi and, looking beyond the mountains, suggested to Adams that "there was no reason why, if the countries extended their claims Westward the same line should not be continued to the Pacific."[8]

The idea that the 49th parallel was an appropriate boundary did not just rest on British diplomatic assumptions, however. The boundary was also engraved on British, American, and French maps published from 1751 onwards, such as Jean Palairet's *Map of North America* (1765). Yet the eighteenth-century cartography of North America was quite varied. There were maps that divided British and French territory around Hudson Bay much higher than 49°N – most notably John Mitchell's *Map of the British and French Dominions in North America* (1755), which was respected by scholars and politicians on both sides of the Atlantic.[9] And other famous maps, such as Aaron Arrowsmith's *Map Exhibiting all the New Discoveries in the Interior Parts of North America* (1795; additions to 1818) did not depict any boundaries west of the Great Lakes.[10] Why did not United States diplomats appeal to Mitchell's map to argue for a boundary west from Lake of the Woods that would run higher than 49 degrees? Gallatin gave the following explanation:

> As this [the 49th parallel] had been assumed many years before, as a positive fact, and had never been contradicted, I also assumed it as such and did not thoroughly investigate the subject ... It appears very extraordinary that any geographer or mapmaker should have invented the dividing line, with such specific details, without

having sufficient grounds for believing that it had been thus determined by the
Commissioners under the treaty of Utrecht ... [and] there is no apparent motive, if
the assertion was known by the British negotiators not to be founded in fact, why
they should not have at once denied it.[11]

It seems that Gallatin and the other diplomats viewed maps as honest, transparent depictions of an assumed geopolitical order. Palairet's map represented
eighteenth-century diplomatic wisdom. Mitchell's map did not encourage dispute because it did not represent this wisdom and gave no geopolitical prec-
edent for the existence of other boundaries.[12]

In the negotiations of 1818 cartography and diplomacy, image and assumed
reality, were tightly bound. The idea of the 49th parallel as an appropriate boundary and the maps depicting this border reinforced one another. Questions of
cartographic competence and propaganda were sidelined. These diplomats were
concerned with the classification of signs (the identity of words and maps) rather
than with the historical and political context of their production or the suitabil-
ity of establishing a line of latitude as a border. They worked in short-hand, with
diplomatic and cartographic texts that reduced the exploration and occupation
of the continent to a simple set of geopolitical coordinates and precedents, and
they used such texts to strive for a quick territorial settlement. The British explorer David Thompson, who traversed and mapped much of northwest America
between 1787 and 1797, and established a number of trade routes and posts in
the Columbia River region for the North West Company between 1807 and 1812,
complained that "the British ministry appear to consider and prefer general lines
for Boundaries in the wilderness of North America in preference to Lines more
in detail, as if Mountains, Hills and Rivers would assume the form [of] place
position and course intended by a general line."[13] Nevertheless, when Gallatin
suggested that the 49th parallel might be stretched from the Rockies to the Pacific, the British objected because the boundary would bisect the British fur trade,
which was focused on the lower reaches of the Columbia River and the upper
reaches of the Fraser River, and was connected by an elaborate system of brigade
trails and water routes.[14]

The British only hinted at a general boundary – the Columbia River. The United
States proposed the 49th parallel, but it was unacceptable to the British. Looking
for a compromise, Gallatin and Rush turned again to maps – in this instance, a
map in an anonymous pamphlet published in 1817 (but since credited to Simon
McGillivray of the North West Company) showing a river purportedly used by
British traders emptying into Puget Sound (see Figure 11).[15] On the basis of this
map, Gallatin proposed a line which, after crossing the Columbia at 49°N,
"should deviate so far southwardly as to leave within the British claim all

Figure 11 McGillivray's fictitious Caledonia River

Source: A map of America, between latitudes 10 and 70 north, and longitudes 80 and 150 west, exhibiting the principal trading stations of the North West Company, in [Simon McGillivray], *Notice respecting the boundary ...* (London: B. M'Millan, 1817). Courtesy Special Collections and University Archives Division, University of British Columbia Library.

waters emptying into the sound called the Gulf of Georgia."[16] Lord Castlereagh, Britain's foreign secretary, accepted Gallatin's logic but rejected the proposal. McGillivray may have simply confused his fictitious Caledonia River with some smaller streams in the area, but we might also suggest that he was playing a confidence trick on diplomats. Just as eighteenth-century maps depicting the 49th parallel reinforced diplomatic wisdom, so McGillivray may have thought that his map would reinforce the idea that British traders used the Caledonia River. Neither Gallatin nor Castlereagh consulted any explorers or traders to verify whether the river existed.

This is how the 49th parallel became lodged in the Oregon negotiations. These diplomats were trying to reconstruct, albeit in a rudimentary fashion at this stage, an authoritative history of boundary-making precedents, and they based such a history on a sequence of diplomatic and cartographic "facts."[17] They were trying to work out what Benedict Anderson has neatly termed (in relation to nineteenth-century Thailand) the "property-history" of the North American continent west of the Great Lakes – a space that Britain and the United States claimed they owned but which had not been formally segmented.[18]

Diplomats' willingness to divide up the continent in this way points to recent arguments about the cartographic grain of nation-states. Scholars such as Richard Helgerson have tried to show that the status of the state as a unified space that governments and citizens could visualize as their land was conditioned by the arrival of the state as a territorially defined entity and actor. Cartography was central to the advent of the state as a nation-state. The state needed to be given its own distinctive space – it needed to be mapped, Helgerson argues – before it could become a fully constituted national space and field of state intervention. Gallatin started to create this effect in 1818. The state began to appear in what Adams called "the Western deserts" of North America in the form of a geometric division of political jurisdiction.[19]

Yet it was a tentative effect, and by 1826 Anglo-American debate about the boundary had a slightly different quality. Jones and Rakestraw show that between 1818 and 1826, "America's appetite for preserving territory for Republican virtue ... increased."[20] In 1819, Adams concluded a treaty with the Spanish that extended the US border from Texas to the Pacific at 42°N, and in 1824 he struck an agreement with the Russians that limited their territorial pretensions south of what is now Alaska; and Adams told Rush, his negotiator in London, that the US would reject any British "application of colonial principles of exclusion" to the region between California and Alaska.[21] Adams was touting President James Monroe's position that the Americas were "off limits to Europe."[22] In 1825-26, and more fully in 1845-46, when the dispute reached a crisis point, the US was not seeking an Anglo-American balance of power in North America; rather, it was determined to prevent any foreign power interfering with its advance across the continent.

ANNALS OF DISCOVERY AND OCCUPATION

When British and US diplomats negotiated in 1826, they confronted the details of discovery and occupation. They turned to the testimony of people with first-hand knowledge of the Oregon Territory. Their mental political geography of North America had faltered at the Rockies. These negotiations revolved around the nature of local empirical knowledge about the Oregon Territory, and what linked local knowledge to diplomacy was the way the territory had been, and might be, produced: where explorers had gone, where traders were placed, and where new commercial outlets might be anchored. Diplomats pushed aside the work of map-makers and focused on how knowledge of the Oregon Territory had been acquired.

George Canning (Britain's foreign secretary in 1826) prompted the negotiations for two main reasons: first, because he was irritated by the build up of the US Navy in the Pacific and by American plans to establish a military post in the Oregon Territory;[23] second, and perhaps more important, because he had been lobbied by the Hudson's Bay Company. The company absorbed the North West Company in 1821 and established the Columbia Department west of the Rockies as part of a major commercial expansion.[24] George Simpson, the head of the company's operations in North America, toured the region in 1824-25 and reported to headquarters in London that it had enormous economic potential. In December 1825, Sir John Pelly, the governor of the company, appealed to Canning to secure British territorial rights to the Cordillera, noting that "the free navigation" of the Columbia River was essential to the company's lucrative business on the Pacific.[25] By 1826, the company had thirteen establishments scattered between the lower Columbia River and the headwaters of the Fraser River; if the 49th parallel was adopted as the boundary, then their spatial economy would effectively be undermined.

Issues of occupation, and the Hudson's Bay Company's monopoly over the fur trade west of the Rockies, reoriented the nature of this dispute. Gallatin was sent back to London to negotiate with Britain's restaffed, empire-conscious Foreign Office.[26] In debate, he emphasized that the United States had exclusive title to the area between the 49th parallel and the Columbia River by virtue of discoveries made by American explorers and traders. Britain, on the other hand, emphasized the issue of occupation and argued that the United States had no right of sovereignty over any of the Oregon Territory. In November 1826, Gallatin wrote to Henry Clay (who had replaced Adams as secretary of state): "the general ground assumed by the British plenipotentiaries is that ... mere discovery without occupation constitutes no title."[27]

These positions were drawn, in part, from circumstance. The American sea otter trader Robert Gray had beaten Vancouver past the mouth of the Columbia River in 1792 (the river was named after his vessel). Farther north, Britain,

Russia, Spain, and the US had shared in the exploration of the coast, British traders such as Thompson had mapped the interior, and American traders had used the interior of the Oregon Territory for only a few years.[28] United States sovereignty was therefore harder to prove. And in 1826, the Hudson's Bay Company's headquarters west of the Rockies were at Fort Vancouver on the

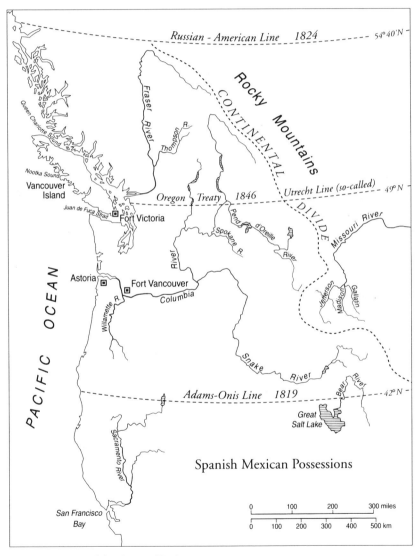

Figure 12   Map of the Oregon Territory

Columbia – so named in March 1825, Simpson noted, "to identify our claim to the Soil and Trade with [Vancouver's] ... discovery of the River and the Coast on behalf of Gt Britain."[29]

British and United States diplomats grounded their respective claims by rationalizing the activities of explorers and traders in particular ways. As the British saw it, Vancouver's survey diminished American claims to the Oregon Territory because he had been despatched to the region by the British government and had sought to separate geographical fact from fiction. As Gallatin saw it, the United States had a strong title to the Columbia River because Gray had discovered its mouth, and Lewis and Clark had descended the River from one of its sources under the patronage of President Jefferson, in 1805. Britain rejected the idea that Gray had given the United States any solid title to the lower Columbia on the grounds that he was a private trader and that his discovery was "a lucky adventure" rather than a scientific reconnaissance of the river, as was William Broughton's (one of Vancouver's officers) survey shortly thereafter.[30] This is how H.U. Addington, undersecretary of state at the Foreign Office, summarized Britain's position for Canning in May 1826:

> The American title *proper* [to the Columbia], on which by far the greatest stress is laid [by the United States], is founded on the expeditions of *Gray*, and of *Lewis*, and *Clarke*, to that Country; but more especially of the first, Gray, a *private trader*, and sailing in a private Merchant Vessel ...
>
> Great Britain proceeds to oppose to the names of the Adventurers above-mentioned those of *Meares, Cook*, and *Vancouver*, all sent on publick expeditions fitted out by their Government; but especially the latter, who, in 1792, explored most minutely every part of the Coast in question, and took formal possession of it in the name of Great Britain.[31]

Similarly, when Britain tried to base a claim to the coast south of the 49th parallel on the "prior discoveries" of Meares in 1788, the United States argued that there was nothing scientific or intentional about Meares's foray into the Columbia River region. Meares had his eyes set on the Strait of Juan de Fuca. Or, as Gallatin caustically remarked: "Meeres [sic] had given names [on the Oregon coast] indicative of his total failure [to find the Strait] – Cape Disappointment and Deception Bay."[32] In other words, both countries emphasized that the most significant feats of territorial appropriation were those based on scientific intention and state sanction.

But while Britain and the United States agreed about the authoritativeness of official surveys, they disagreed about the nature of sovereignty. Addington summarized the United States' view of Gray's discovery as well as Britain's reaction to it.

> After, in the first place, denying the validity of this private act of occupation ... [we secondly reject] the American doctrine, that the occupation of one point on a River gives, *ipso facto*, to the Occupant an exclusive title to the whole extent of the Country watered by that River and it Tributaries ... If the American claim *proper* [derived from Gray] be insisted on, Great Britain can equally shew a superior right to The United States over the same Country, inasmuch as a commissioned Navigator of her own [Vancouver], fitted out on the publick account, first took actual possession of the River and Territory in dispute, in the name of his Sovereign; Her Traders first frequented the vicinity of that Country, and She has, without interruption, continued in uncontested possession of it since 1810, thereby adding to the right of discovery and possession, that derived from Use, Occupancy, and Settlement.[33]

As Gallatin grasped, Britain objected strongly to this American "doctrine" about discovery because it had a peculiarly architectural notion of title and sovereignty. "The whole of this [British] doctrine," Gallatin noted, "which excludes titles derived from prior discovery and substitutes occupancy, rests on the Nootka Convention ... Actual occupancy and regard to mutual convenience are therefore the only bases of any arrangement ... of a boundary" that Britain would accept.[34]

The United States, on the other hand, maintained that acts of discovery were important because they signified an *intention* to settle and govern. Gallatin implied that the British had simply occupied the Oregon Territory to traffic with the Indians – that they would be transient rather than permanent dwellers – while Gray had found and preserved American title for a future republic. "The United States claimed a natural extension of their territory to the Pacific Ocean," Gallatin observed, "on the ground of contiguity and population which gave them a better right to the adjacent unoccupied land than could be set up by any other Nation ... How much more natural and stronger the claim when made by a Nation, whose population extended to the central parts of the Continent, and whose dominions were by all acknowledged to extend to the Stony Mountains."[35] The United States thought that the principle of contiguity was clearly established in the Law of Nations and that successive British governments had referred to it in imperial proclamations made between 1580 and 1732. Gallatin also remarked that the "point of occupancy," on which Britain rested its case, "was solely owing to that westwardly expansion of their trading settlements of Hudson's Bay."[36]

The United States pursued this argument about its "natural" right to expand westwards up to 1846. It was part of what became known as the doctrine of manifest destiny. But Britain would not accept such ideas, and Hudson's Bay Company officials thought that this principle of contiguity was ridiculous. In 1826, Simpson pointed out that the United States showed no intention of occupying the Oregon Territory.[37] And when American settlers did venture over the Rockies in the early 1840s, and the United States started to agitate the question of American title over the whole of the Oregon Territory more forcefully, James Douglas, who was then a company trader at Fort Vancouver, emphasized that it was British traders, not American settlers, who were the first and bona fide occupants of the region. "If you chance to overlook a ditch on your estate and I should be the first person to stumble into it, does that simple accident invest me with any right of propriety in your broad acres?" he asked.[38] Or as Adam Thom, a Hudson's Bay Company lawyer, put it to Simpson in 1842: "The Americans would claim whole kingdoms for the sake of a harbour or even a mooring post."[39]

Britain and the United States articulated different conceptual positions and constructed the Oregon Territory as an exclusively Anglo-American space of geopolitical dispute. In the process the issue of Native title to land was sidelined. In 1845, Henry Howells, a British philanthropist, reminded Britain's foreign secretary that "the Oregon Territory ... is occupied by about one hundred and fifty thousand Indians who inherit it from their ancestors; to whom, therefore, it rightfully belongs, and not in equity to either of the nations claiming the same."[40] But such issues had effectively been buried much earlier. Gallatin commented on the protocol of his second meeting with British ministers in 1826:

Mr Huskisson said that it would be lamentable that, in this age, two such Nations as the United States and Great Britain should be drawn to a rupture on such subject as the uncultivated wilds of the North West Coast. But the honour and dignity of both Countries must be respected, and the mutual convenience of both parties should also be consulted. He then objected to the straight line which we proposed [the 49th parallel to the Pacific] as having no regard to such convenience, and observed particularly that its cutting off the southern portion of Quadra & Vancouver's Island ... was quite inadmissible.[41]

Huskisson highlighted Vancouver's survey and the imperial baggage that went with it: that the Northwest Coast was an austere, "uncultivated" (and, by implication, empty) region, foreign to the dignified world of metropolitan diplomacy and culture, but a region that Vancouver had nevertheless mapped and claimed for Britain. Because Vancouver had replaced traders' vague descriptions of this "wild" land with precise cartographic lines, general boundary lines across the region would not do justice to the issue of convenience. Huskisson and Gallatin attempted to divide a geographical space that had already been prised away from Native groups by a cartographic apparatus of representation.

The diplomats at the 1826 negotiations failed to establish a border, and the joint occupancy agreement was renewed. The boundary issue did not start to rumble again until the late 1830s, when US Senator Lewis Linn cancelled a political campaign to get Van Buren's government to promote American claims to the Oregon Territory. By the early 1840s American settlers had occupied Hudson's Bay Company's lands around the Columbia River and sought to organize a government. Political debate about the Oregon Territory was intricate, swayed the on-off boundary negotiations that took place in Washington between 1843 and 1846, and caused great public excitement in Britain and the United States. The details of the dispute were pronounced in American Congressional debates and discussed in the American and British press. The boundary question was bound up with national and imperial agendas. The United States connected the region to the continental destiny of the American Republic, while Britain viewed the region in a more utilitarian light.

When American and British politicians met in the summer of 1842 to negotiate a northeastern boundary, Anglo-American relations were extremely tense. The Canadian rebellions of 1837 against the British Crown, British military activity around Niagara Falls, and Anglo-American differences over the slave trade prompted calls for the protection of national honour on both sides of the Atlantic. Britain feared the spread of American republicanism into Canada and, following the Emancipation Act, 1833, which abolished slavery in the British Empire, pushed the US to end its slave trade. Americans in Maine and New York were concerned about Britain's military presence in Canada, and politicians in the American South resented Britain's interference with American slave vessels. The two nations still had strong commercial ties, however, and recognized that war would create economic havoc.[42] The US Congress grappled with a maze of Republican and Democratic political differences. Meanwhile, Britain was grappling with the changing nature and coherence of the British Empire – especially its commitment to free trade, its relationship with Upper and Lower Canada, and the consolidation of the Hudson's Bay Company's power west of the Rockies.

The Oregon Territory was drawn into this diffuse Anglo-American realm of conflict, and in the 1840s it became viewed as an outpost of American westward expansion. Following the Webster-Ashburton Treaty, the US embarked on what David Pletcher has called a "diplomacy of annexation."[43] During the 1840s, American power was shored up in Texas and California, and in 1845 Democratic president James Polk, who harboured the interests of expansion-minded Southern politicians, announced that "no future European colony or dominion shall, with our consent, be planted or established on any part of the North American continent."[44] This was a bolder public declaration of the ideas that Adams and Rush had worked with in the 1820s. Such sentiments were padded out by the American press and prompted the Duke of Wellingon, Britain's war veteran, to declare: "the Democratic Party throughout the World is inimical to this country. The reason is, that our system is essentially conservative: that the freedom of the subject is founded upon law and order; which provides at the same time for the conservation of person, property, privileges, honor and character; and the institutions of the country. Democracy abroad looks for plunder; which cannot exist with our system. Wherever a democratical influence or even a democratical Press exists, we must expect to find enemies."[45] War loomed and

Lord Aberdeen, Britain's foreign secretary, debated the Oregon issue in the Commons, reassuring Parliament that "our honour is a substantial property that we can certainly never neglect."[46] Britain would not let American missionaries and troops simply walk into the Oregon Territory. The Hudson's Bay Company pressed the British government to protect its trading interests, and the Cabinet decided to despatch a secret naval expedition to the region to assess its strategic potential.[47] "The only hope for a settlement favourable to Great Britain," John Galbraith has argued, "was to precipitate a crisis while the Hudson's Bay Company remained in physical control of most of the territory and before the Oregon fever prevented any American government from accepting a boundary south of the 49 parallel."[48]

In October 1843, Abel Upshur (then US secretary of state) noted that previous rounds of negotiations had "very nearly exhausted the argument," but politicians and diplomats proceeded to interpret past treaties more vigorously and to look for a "civilised settlement."[48] US politicians John Calhoun and James Buchanan presented their nation's territorial claims in great detail. They explained how principles of continuity could be derived from acts of discovery and occupation. Explorers who discovered part of an island, they reasoned, could claim "the whole," and those who discovered the source of a river could claim "the entire region drained by it." They added that the US had a good claim to all the lands west of the Mississippi between the latitudes 42° and 54°40' north by virtue of international treaties and conventions that stretched back to the Peace of Paris (1763). Calhoun and Buchanan then claimed that the US had assumed all of France's and Spain's claims to the American continent and the Pacific. In short, with the Oregon Territory now delimited by two lines of latitudes, these politicians concentrated on how American jurisdiction might fill this imperial shell to its geographical limits. Britain's minister plenipotentiary to Washington, Richard Packenham, thought that the claim that the US derived from France was "good for nothing" and that the rights that the US inherited from Spain were hedged by the stipulations of the Nootka Convention.[50]

During this final set of negotiations, different logics of imperial appropriation – the power and scope of treaties, the cartographic austerity of the 49th parallel, and more intricate geographies of sovereignty that could be derived from explorers' and traders' discoveries and activities – started to clash. The Oregon Territory had become what Aberdeen called thoroughly "litigated ground," and Buchanan noted that this dispute now turned around "irresistible inferences" and "superadded titles." The region had been covered with layers of imperial meaning and assertion that stemmed from a range of facts, precedents, precepts, images, and ideas.

At another level, however (and to repeat what I said about the Nootka Crisis), this dispute boiled down to just a few grand images, practices, and debating points: "civilized" nations imposing themselves on "uncivilized" ones; the separation of issues of contact and questions of sovereignty in the evaluation of territorial claims; the authority of scientific exploration and the mimetic power of maps; and the status of Gray and Vancouver's expedition as "true" discoverers of the Columbia. Britain and the US claimed rights over a region that they deemed to be "settled only by savages," as Upshur put it, and politicians depicted themselves as enlightened peacemakers who were bringing wild land under the aegis of reason and the state.

In July 1845, Buchanan observed:

> If the discovery of the mouth of a river [Gray], followed up within a reasonable time by ... first exploration [Lewis and Clark] ... do not constitute a title to the territory drained by its waters in the nation performing these acts, then the principles consecrated by the practice of civilized nations ever since the discovery of the New World must have lost its force. These principles were necessary to preserve the peace of the world. Had they not been enforced in practice clashing claims to newly-discovered territory and perpetual strife among the nations would have been the inevitable result.[51]

Buchanan implied that this dispute was now about the nature of diplomacy itself. He established a historical geography of "consecrated" principles and practices and worked towards a "civilized" settlement.

But behind this rhetoric of reason and peace, of course, there were utilitarian affairs of state. Buchanan's model of imperial enlightenment – his geopolitical textualization of a vast region – was encompassed by American expansionist energy. American pioneers were pouring into the Willamette Valley south of the Columbia, and US Senators declared that their interests would be protected at any price. Ultimately, Britain was willing to give up the Columbia River if it retained Vancouver Island, where the company established a trade post (Fort Victoria) in 1843 as part of a major reorganization of its business on the Pacific.[52]

Some British politicians thought that Aberdeen was an ineffectual foreign secretary. And as these two cartoons (Figure 13) from London's *Punch* magazine (January-June 1846) illustrate, the British still considered the United States to be a rebellious sibling and viewed Polk as a trickster.[53] Pletcher argues that Polk lacked the primary quality of a diplomat, "the ability to appreciate a foreign people's hopes," and saw Britain as a "thieving bully."[54] In the United States public debate about Oregon was high-spirited. Gallatin observed that by 1845, the territorial issue had become "one of feeling rather than of right."[55] By 1845, a stream of information about Oregon was flowing back east. Extracts from emigrants' letters home were published in newspapers and journals. Editors superimposed their own commentary on these raw vignettes, and British and American journalists entered into a war of words. In lieu of a boundary settlement, and in an attempt to legitimize Polk's pronouncements, American writers

"WHAT? YOU YOUNG YANKEE-NOODLE, STRIKE YOUR
OWN FATHER!"

YOUNG YANKEE-NOODLE TEACHING GRANDMOTHER
BRITANNIA TO SUCK EGGS

Figure 13   James Polk and John Bull at loggerheads over the Oregon Territory, 1846
Source: Punch, vol. X (January-June 1846). Courtesy Special Collections and University Archives
Division, University of British Columbia Library.

devised an elaborate rhetoric of American right and destiny.[56] Some agitated for
war against Britain. Gallatin, Calhoun, and the American newspaper *Niles' Weekly
Register* spoke for those who wanted peace or who at least thought that Britain
would not threaten war. In 1843, Calhoun proposed a policy of "wise & masterly
inactivity" – swamping Britain's claim to Oregon and the Hudson's Bay Company's trading districts by encouraging Americans to emigrate to the region.[57] James
Douglas acknowledged Calhoun's influence on American attitudes, writing to
Simpson in October 1843: "It would appear from the rush of emigration to this
quarter [in 1843], that his words have produced their effect and there can be no
doubt about the final success of the plan, if the country remains open a few
years longer ... An American population will never willingly submit to British
domination, and it would be ruinous and hopeless to enforce obedience on a
disaffected people."[58] And Gallatin published some sobering letters in the American *National Intelligencer* explaining the nature of the dispute and suggesting
that it did not merit war.[59] Other American commentators described the Hudson's Bay Company as a rapacious, violent monopoly – as an enemy of civilized
living based on permanent agricultural settlement, competitive markets, and
individual liberty backed by federal institutions. Oregon had a rhetorical place
in the Union before it had US institutions, and in the summer of 1843 American
pioneers organized a provisional government.

Spirits also ran high in Britain. In the spring of 1845 the *Times* declared that
"the territory of Oregon will never be wrested from the British Crown, but by

war," and it admonished the "ill regulated, overbearing, and aggressive spirit of the American democracy."[60] But during the summer of 1845 the Oregon issue was overshadowed by the Irish potato famine and splits in Prime Minister Robert Peel's Cabinet over the Corn Laws. Aberdeen, who remained foreign secretary through this period of political crisis, saw the territorial issue in an instrumental light. He took advantage of Oregon's obscurity in the public mind to secretly promote a press campaign debasing the utility of the region and suggesting that territorial concession need not entail a loss of national honour.[61] "The real strength of public opinion is arrayed against a belligerent policy," the *Times* (under Aberdeen's influence) tried to persuade its readers in January 1846.[62] Other commentators and journalists supported Aberdeen's position. In 1845, the *Edinburgh Review* described the Oregon Territory as an "unprofitable incumberence" and "unfit ... by situation, soil, and climate, for profitable settlement," and the London *Examiner* called the region "a mere hunting ground."[63]

By April 1846, the question of national honour hinged mainly on Britain's retention of Vancouver Island as an anchor in a British Empire based increasingly on free trade. Pakenham renewed negotiations in Washington and successfully defended the diplomatic position he had established a year before: "In 1792, Vancouver ... circumnavigated the island which now bears his name; and here we have ... as complete a case of discovery, exploration, and settlement, as can well be presented, giving to Great Britain, in any arrangement that may be made with regard to the territory in dispute, the strongest possible claim to the exclusive possession of that island."[64] Vancouver's survey had become entangled with a broader anticipatory geography of colonialism that was now shaped by the reoccupation and commercial development of the Oregon Territory as well as by imperial inscriptions of it from afar. British and American politicians broadened the gap between contact and cartography that Vancouver had opened up. They extrapolated ideas of sovereignty from his meticulous examination of the coast and whittled the dynamics of contact down to simpler calculations about profit and the imperial potential of huge tracts of land. By 1845, they had to work out questions of jurisdiction because the Oregon Territory was being filled by Americans who had very different ideas about its future than did fur traders. Richard Mackie has shown that a declining fur trade and the development of profitable export industries "were the background to Simpson's 1842 decision to realign the company's business to the resource-rich northern region." The 1840s, he continues, ended "a thirty-year period during which the British fur traders effectively controlled the non-Native commerce of the coastal and interior districts between California and Russian America." Both Aberdeen and Simpson thought that the adoption of the 49th parallel as the international border would leave the Hudson's Bay Company with "a viable economy." As Mackie summarizes the geographical reorientation of the company's commercial strategies in the Cordillera between 1824 and 1842:

While Fort Vancouver reflected Simpson's 1824-5 plans for the department, Fort Victoria mirrored the experience of the intervening two decades and his new plans. The fur trades of the Columbia and Fraser drainages figured prominently in the 1820s. Terminus of the York Factory Express and the interior fur brigades, Fort Vancouver was built near the end of the transcontinental trade route ... [and was] accessible from the lower Columbia.

Fort Victoria, on the other hand, was a Pacific depot, accessible to the Company's new deep-sea commerce from Oahu, Sitka, and San Francisco, as well as from London. Access to the Pacific was immediate: there was no hazardous and time-consuming river to cross [at the mouth of the Columbia]. The new post was to be the base of an ocean-borne commerce with Pacific markets.[65]

The Hudson's Bay Company was no longer as dependent on the drainage systems that emptied into the Pacific.

Britain and the US compromised in June 1846. In Britain, the repeal of the Corn Laws had become a much more important national issue than the Oregon Territory. And the US Senate endorsed the Oregon Treaty mindful of the fact that Britain's Tory government was tottering and that a Whig government would likely appoint a foreign secretary who was bent more on threatening war to protect national honour than on preserving peace – Lord Palmerston. In 1846, the US was also at war with Mexico and worried about Britain's reaction to its expansionist policies.

The Oregon Treaty confirmed what John Quincy Adams had suggested in 1823 was "pointed out by the finger of nature": that the United States had a continental destiny and that British influence in the Americas had natural limits.[66] It established a geopolitical space that was fundamentally at odds with the way the region had been explored and developed by fur traders up to the 1840s. The 49th parallel cut the Hudson's Bay Company's vast Columbia Department in half, but by 1846 the Hudson's Bay Company was no longer quite as reliant on the fur trade, and the new border solidified the commercial changes that Simpson was putting in place. Hudson's Bay Company strategies of power and profit-making – strategies of Native-Western accommodation and conflict, the establishment of forts that were bastions of non-Native power in a Native world, brigade trails along rivers and across mountain ranges that linked the Northwest Coast to an outside world, and processes of economic diversification that made the company's business on the Pacific profitable – would continue on Vancouver Island. Yet the space of Western sovereignty that encompassed and was grafted on to Native territories and the fur trade facilitated the erosion of these dynamics of contact and the emergence of a new order. Over the next few decades colonists moved on to Native land, Natives were placed on reserves, and Native peoples were granted a subordinate place in new colonial projects.

The Oregon Treaty was obviously more than an agreement that looked to the future. It was a rationalization of sixty years of spatial experience – an attempt to press a range of geographical meanings onto a map that solidified who owned what and where. The Oregon boundary dispute as a whole shows that distinctions between fact and fiction, truth and error, are made rather than given. Britain and the US fashioned the Oregon Territory in distinctive ways. The Nootka Crisis and the Oregon dispute reveal the importance of commerce in British imperialism. Britain advanced territorial claims that were geared to access to markets and trade locations. In 1790, it was private traders such as Meares who were the key players. In the Oregon dispute it was the occupation of the Cordillera by British traders working with corporate capital that informed Canning's elaboration of principles of occupation. But the British ran into a philosophy of annexation. Occupation, in Britain's commercial sense of the term, proved less compelling than settlement. American settlers did not use the Oregon Territory in the same way as British fur traders. The thousands of Americans who settled south of the Columbia River effectively turned part of the geopolitical shell that Britain had nurtured into an American place. Britain's commercial and imperial place-holding tactics gave way to American colonization and led to war with Native groups. Britain responded to this American presence by colonizing Vancouver Island.

More conceptually, the Oregon Territory was not an inert plane over which a geopolitical drama unfolded. It was actively fashioned through a concatenation of diplomatic arguments about discovery and occupation as well as by competing national outlooks. In the process the work of explorers and traders, and the different relationships they had forged with Native peoples, was encompassed by imperial discourses about sovereignty and national discourses about honour and destiny. At root, the Oregon boundary dispute, like the Nootka Crisis, points to the geographical violence of imperialism: the creation and deployment of representational practices through which Native land is appropriated, and the realm of Native-White contact is abstracted away, to the point where territory actually *becomes* non-Native, competing Native claims to the soil are seen only dimly, if at all, and territory is emptied of its prior significations and seen as an empty shell awaiting development. "The Oregon territory is a subject of curiosity for two reasons," a reviewer for *The Gentleman's Magazine* wrote in 1845: "The one, from its forming at present a point of dispute ... as to the right of possession. Secondly, because it is said to be the only remaining portion of the globe where there lies an unoccupied territory, suitable to receive the emigration from populous countries."[67] This reviewer probably would not have written this forty or sixty years before. In the 1840s momentous decisions about the Northwest Coast were taken, and they barely considered Native peoples.

Vancouver's survey played an important role in this transformation. We cannot hold him personally responsible for the ways in which his survey was used by others, but the imperial geography that he helped to fashion would not have taken the precise form it did without Vancouver's map and the nature of his survey. To borrow and embellish one of Jody Berland's formulations, Vancouver contributed to the production of colonial space "as traversed space; not [simply] the empty landscape of a wilderness, or geometrical, abstractly quantifiable space, but space that has been mapped and shaped by specific imperial forms of knowledge and interest."[68] Vancouver Island had become important to the British for psychological reasons as well as practical ones. It symbolized an imperial history that was inaugurated in 1790. Vancouver's mandate and achievements snaked through a body of imperial ideas, conventions, and representations that had brought the Northwest Coast into the fold of empire. The Oregon Territory was pressed into sovereignty by politicians, traders, and settlers, but American and British claims to the soil were made up from partial and propitious bodies of knowledge that facilitated the accumulation of power at the centre. Vancouver did not exercise power over the space he mapped so much as he lent others, at a later date, the capacity to exercise it through his cartography and survey. He embellished a system of abstraction that was initially and tentatively put in place for the British by Cook. Henry Roberts's general chart of Cook's reconnaissance depicts the coast with a thin line and leaves the vast region between the coast and Hudson Bay blank, much to Roberts's annoyance. Dalrymple and Banks played a crucial role in the engraving of these charts. It was they who persuaded the Admiralty to exclude the Hudson's Bay Company's interior discoveries from this map and highlight only Cook's endeavours.[69] Banks and Dalrymple viewed Cook's map as a record of exploration. As such they rubbed out what others had discovered but Cook had not seen. Yet the blank spaces of the interior can also be viewed as an invitation to further adventure and as part of a theoretical geography of imperial appropriation. As I will suggest shortly, colonists turned the blanks spaces on Cook's and especially Vancouver's map into seductive landscapes of colonial adventure and opportunity.

I want to turn finally, then, to how these practices framed the colonisation of Vancouver in the 1850s and 1860s.

CHAPTER 13

Mythical Localities

Among the questions asked of me are – Where is Vancouver Island? How
can I get there? And what is the best season to arrive? Vancouver's Island
will be found where Vancouver "laid it down," – on the north-west coast of
America ...

– LETTER TO THE LONDON *TIMES*, 13 JANUARY 1862

In September 1846, Britain's colonial secretary, Earl Grey, worried about "the
encroaching spirit of the US" and deemed it important to strengthen Britain's
hold on Vancouver Island "by encouraging a settlement upon it of B[riti]sh subjects."[1] The British Cabinet entertained a number of colonization schemes, and
the one it accepted – that of the Hudson's Bay Company – was based on detailed
knowledge of the Cordillera and an enterprising grasp of its commercial potential.[2] Other schemes were put forward, however, that were based on the abstract
geographical impressions of the region that had been generated over the previous sixty years.[3] The most far-fetched scheme was sketched by Theodore Cordua
(a British speculator) in 1852, three years after the company had taken the colonial reins. He proposed to divide the island into twelve districts, named: England, Scotland, Ireland, North and South Germany, Holland, Belgium, Sweden,
Poland, Hungary, New Helvetia, and France.[4] While ludicrous, Cordua's scheme
underlines what was at stake in the colonization of Vancouver Island: the region
had been constructed as an absolute, unoccupied, and divisible imperial space.
The coast had been charted in detail, British names had been imposed, and British sovereignty over the island was assumed.

John Dunn gained many years of experience with Native peoples as a British
fur trader, but when he assessed the value of the Oregon Territory for a Western

audience in the 1840s, he stripped the landscape of its Native significations and described Vancouver Island as "a perfect network," a "labyrinth of bays, sounds, inlets, creeks, and harbours – promontories, islands, and land tongues, with ... countless sinuosities of land and water" – as a rationalized geographic space.[5] And Charles Forbes introduced his 1862 essay *Vancouver Island: Its Resources and Capabilities as a Colony* with this image:

> Who will not recall, with delight, the early feelings and associations of his boyhood, when glancing at the chart, he sees, that under yonder rugged mountains like Nootka and Clayoquot, names well remembered, but over the reality of which, from the remoteness of the scene, a certain mystery seemed to hang, graphically described though the places were, by Cook and Vancouver. The romance and the mystery have now however alike given way to a hopeful reality, and the Emigrant sees before him in that mountain range, the rocky pillars and stony butresses of the land of his adoption – a land full of promise and hope ... [T]he field is still unoccupied, still open, calling for the labour of man, to regulate its wild luxurance, and develop its latent wealth.[6]

Vancouver, especially, had described the edges of colonial space in graphic detail, but he had also rendered the interior remote and mysterious. The area behind Nootka and Clayoquot, and the land beyond the coastal fringe of the mainland that Vancouver had named New Hanover and New Georgia, was a field of wild luxuriance – an unoccupied domain – "calling for the labour of man."

Some British commentators complained about the austerity and partiality of such images. For example, two years before Forbes wrote his essay, George Hills, the first Anglican bishop of British Columbia, moaned that explorers such as Cook and Vancouver had only "surrounded the country ... with a visionary romantic interest of no practical use."[7] Yet Hills could not quell the colonial romance associated with Vancouver's labours. In 1862 Reginald Pidcock maintained that colonists had an "eager desire" to see the colony as a beautiful new home, and Matthew Macfie added: "None will grudge to the gallant explorer [Vancouver] the honour which so righteously attaches to his name in being associated with a colony that bids fair to become, as years advance, one of the brightest jewels in the British crown."[8]

Colonists were not simply attracted to Vancouver Island by Vancouver's gallantry, of course. There were diverse motivations for emigration. The Hudson's Bay Company contracted poor English and Scottish labourers to work on its farms on the south end of the island. Independent colonists and wealthier emigrants brought capital, bought property, and looked to elevate their social standing overseas. Nevertheless, most colonists knew little about Vancouver Island when they left Britain. When the Hudson's Bay Company recruited J.S. Helmcken as surgeon, he asked, "Where on earth is Vancouver Island?" He was told: "It is in the Pacific – here it is on the map." Helmcken thought he was "going to a wild country."[9] As a correspondent helpfully answered a query in the London *Times* concerning the location of Britain's new colony: "Vancouver's Island will be found where Vancouver 'laid it down.'"

There was ignorance and anxiety as well as romance, then, and ignorance bred anxiety. On reading the company's advertisements for the colony in the London press in 1849, a prospective emigrant wrote for information about the land allocation system and asked whether the Natives scalped colonists.[10] And Charles Bayley recalled that in the early 1850s British ships arriving at Victoria, the colonial capital, were "surrounded by ... canoes filled with Indians in all sorts of grotesque dress and many of them in a nude state which to the eyes of our passengers was anything but agreeable. One young lady burst into tears at the sight."[11] Native groups from different parts of the coast congregated in Victoria to trade. The company's advertisements did not highlight either this Native presence or the fact that Fort Victoria was built on Songhees land. Colonists responded to the Native people who lived in their midst in a variety ways. Some colonists noted that it was best to "purchase" the Natives' friendship by hiring them as labourers, and commentators noted that Native-White relations on the Hudson's Bay Company's farms were cordial.[12] Other settlers looked down on these White farmers and had no interest in dealing with Native people.[13] Colonial officials reported that the sight of large numbers of Native people put colonists in a "state of alarm."[14] And a Hudson's Bay Company official noted that the "predatory habits of the natives ... checked the extension of white settlements along the coast."[15]

These real and imagined forms of colonial contact both displaced Native peoples from the territorial scene and degraded their presence in it. Vancouver's cartography became entangled with a broader set of ideas and assumptions about wilderness, savagery, and private property that were ingrained in the British imagination and a wider Western culture of empire. Vancouver obviously did not create the attitudes towards land and Native peoples that colonists arrived with, and it is not easy to work out precisely how these attitudes and expectations were formed – what people had heard or read, why they left Britain and what they intended to do overseas, and how their perceptions were influenced by issues of class, gender, or ethnicity. But as this range of opinion and observation suggests, Vancouver's map – and, we might surmise, cartography more generally – reflected and consolidated colonists' views of this region. The names Cook and Vancouver formed an important point of introduction to the island, and colonists derived a theoretical geography from their endeavours. We see in these early views of Britain's new colony the development of powers of association that extenuated and reshaped imperial inscriptions of this part of the world. Vancouver Island became tied to a wider culture of empire through a set of colonialist habits of thought and strategies of representation that encompassed far-flung parts of the world, but Vancouver, especially, had given these habits and strategies a local texture and incited colonial projects that perpetuated the marginalization of Native groups.

Hills suggested that "so distant, wild, and difficult of access did [the interior of Vancouver Island and the mainland] ... appear to be that men habitually regarded it as only suited for the last refuge of the Indian with such animals as delight in wild freedom and desolation."[16] Explorers such as Vancouver had imputed a series of spatial distinctions: between the domesticated outskirts of space (domesticated because they had come under the cartographer's gaze) and the unmapped wilds of the interior (as untamed as the Indians); between the dots on the map linking up the coastline and the cartographic blankness of the interior. It was in such blank-mysterious-wild spaces that colonists placed the Indian and situated their dreams of colonial lucre.

Some White observers were sensitive to Native views of colonists. For example, Richard Mayne, a British naval officer, reported that Native peoples thought that "whites had no business" on their land, but that many Native groups realized that these foreigners were permanent settlers and hoped they would become trade partners.[17] But many colonists viewed Native peoples as denizens of the forest, "still in a primitive state," with no respect for property and out of place in "civilized" towns such as Victoria.[18] They also viewed the interior as a promethean space of colonial fantasy and advancement where "the indolent, contented, savage, must give ... [the] place to the busteling sons of civilisation and Toil."[19]

These were gross stereotypes of the Indian and bumptious constructions of colonial opportunity, but they were compelling and productive. "Regarding the interior [of Vancouver Island] ... absurd notions prevailed," the British explorer-naturalist Robert Brown noted in 1868, "and for long the Colonists (in the face of all geographical analogy) flattered themselves that rich prairies would be found embossemed amid wooded mountains in that mystical interior."[20] The act of simply "surrounding the country," as Vancouver had done, was enough to encourage colonial schemes based on little practical knowledge of the region and little regard for its Aboriginal inhabitants. J.R. Anderson captured this range of sentiments in 1878: "there are some unquestionably who know our Island by name alone," he declared, "and recognise in it an almost mythical locality.[21]

Brown was one of the first non-Natives to bring "light geographical," as he put it, to the interior of Vancouver Island.[22] He led the Vancouver Island Exploring Expedition in 1864 and wrote in his diary on his birthday in 1865 that he had achieved "colonial fame at 23" for doing so.[23] He proclaimed that "a diligent naturalist does better when he visits a country after another because he has then a sort of frame-work to weave his labours around."[24] Vancouver had provided that framework, but Brown noted that "a country is not 'worked out' because so

and so had been there."[25] By the 1860s, exploration was tied to colonial development – Brown was searching for new resources and areas of settlement – and
explorers, surveyors, and settlers began to realize that the geography of Vancouver Island was much more variegated than Vancouver's "frame-work" of it. In
the 1860s one British colonist acknowledged that there was still "a touch of the
Robinson Crusoe romance" in colonial life on Vancouver Island but suggested
that the land was not as bountiful as he had been led to believe.[26] Other colonists
moaned that British newspapers had exaggerated the potential of the colony.[27]
And Hudson's Bay Company officials had doubts about the value of the colony.[28]
The south end of the island – the first area to be colonized – was strewn with
rock and swamp, making farming difficult.

Emigrants' hopes of a better life on Vancouver Island were not just framed by
these imaginative geographies of wealth and wilderness. They were also conditioned by colonial land policy. The Colonial Office and Hudson's Bay Company
worked with Edward Gibbon Wakefield's formulations about "systematic colonisation."[29] In 1849, Archibald Barclay (the company's secretary) informed James
Douglas (the company's chief factor at Fort Victoria) that "the object of every
sound system of colonization should be, not to reorganise Society on a new
basis, which is simply absurd, but to transfer to the new country whatever is
most valuable, and most approved in the institutions of the old, so that Society
may, as far as possible consist of the same classes, united together by the same
ties, and having the same relative duties to perform in the one country as in the
other."[30] Douglas was instructed to institute a "reasonable" price for land (£1
per acre) in order to prevent land speculation and to encourage the
recomposition of Britain's class system overseas. He was to use 90 percent of
the income from land sales to build a colonial infrastructure and to make the
colony self-sufficient. This, in outline, was Wakefield's system, and it was the
cornerstone of the Charter of Grant (January 1849), which made the Hudson's
Bay Company the colonial proprietors of Vancouver Island.

These strictures were opposed by both settlers and Vancouver Island's colonial officials. Land was cheaper or free south of the 49th parallel, some early
emigrants left the colony for the California goldfields, and independent settlers
on Vancouver Island complained that Hudson's Bay Company personnel had
bought most the prime land in the Victoria district before they arrived.[31] Joseph
Pemberton, the colonial surveyor from 1851 to 1864, had to cope with "hills,
thickly Timbered valleys, Swamps and Lakes" and asked for "discretionary powers" in devising a land policy that was attuned to such mixed terrain.[32]

Some of the details of land allocation changed over the 1850s, but Wakefieldian
principles prevailed.[33] Pemberton is an intriguing figure in these arguments over
land policy. In his 1860 book, *Facts and Figures Relating to Vancouver Island and
British Columbia*, he argued that the conditions of the charter had almost stopped
settlement. But he also tried to promote the colony in Britain, defended the

Hudson's Bay Company's record as colonial proprietors, and criticized those colonists "who hold that rulers at a distance are necessarily imperfectly informed." Pemberton suggested that the Colonial Office had an "intimate knowledge of circumstances and places in these colonies" and that Wakefield's ideas were important and viable. Yet much of the rest of his book demonstrates how little the Colonial Office knew about the region and how much it relied on the company and officials such as Pemberton to adapt metropolitan directives to colonial conditions.[34]

The Colonial Office scrutinized land policy, colonial finances, and constitutional matters in Britain's settler colonies, but Native policy was often deemed a local – peripheral – issue. This metropolitan-colonial division of responsibility is especially apparent on Vancouver Island. James Douglas was appointed governor in 1851, in part because of his long experience with Native peoples, and the colonial secretary quickly informed him that "the mode of dealing with the Native Tribes is a point which I must leave to your own discretion, trusting to your disposition to cultivate friendly relations with them."[35] Hudson's Bay Company officials reiterated the point.[36]

The Colonial Office touched on the treatment of Native peoples intermittently through the 1850s – and the charter included a short clause about protecting the "welfare" of the Natives. But it hardly broached Native rights to land.[37] It was Douglas who prompted discussion of Native rights, and the company and the Colonial Office usually replied to his detailed reports on Native affairs with short notes of "approbation."[38] Barclay instructed him "to confer with the Chiefs of the tribes" over the sale of land to the company and "to consider the natives as the rightful possessors of such lands only as they occupied by cultivation, or had houses built on, at the time when the Island came under the undivided sovereignty of Great Britain in 1846. All other land is to be regarded as waste, and applicable to the purposes of colonization."[39] Barclay cited a British Select Committee report on the New Zealand Company, which stated that Native peoples had "a right to occupancy only ... until they establish among themselves a settled form of government, and subjugate the ground." Between April 1850 and February 1851, Douglas concluded eleven "treaties" with Native groups of south Vancouver Island, buying "the whole of their lands ... with the exception of Village sites, and enclosed fields," mainly with blankets and for around £500 (only a few more pounds than were spent on surveying equipment at this time).[40]

Colonial Vancouver Island had a specific place in a shifting British imperial world. In the first half of the nineteenth century Britain turned towards policies of free trade, and colonial rebellions and British-Native conflict in its settler colonies made the Colonial Office more attentive to the structure and diversity of metropolitan-colonial relationships. British politicians worried about the size and cost of empire, and "colonial reformers" such as Wakefield called for thoroughgoing changes in imperial administration.[41] In his famous

Lectures on Colonization and Colonies (1841, 2nd ed. 1865), Herman Merivale, a professor of political economy and permanent undersecretary at the Colonial Office from 1847 to 1859, argued that colonial governments should aim to protect and civilize Natives peoples but noted that in "preliminary dealings with savages" Native policy should stem from "tact, prudence, and firmness in each separate emergency."[42] Colonial secretaries told Douglas to treat Native peoples with kindness and respect, but in the 1850s the Colonial Office was more concerned about the threat of American encroachment, and the institution of an ordered system of settlement and economic development, than with Native questions.[43] Political contingencies and faith in Douglas's tact with Native peoples were married to an underlying faith in the legitimacy of colonialism.

The colony of Vancouver Island developed within this imperial context. New metropolitan schemes, colonial projects, and cultural discourses were superimposed on the imperial framework I have tracked, and in the 1850s Vancouver Island's distance from Britain took on new cultural and political proportions. The Colonial Office managed a far-flung and variegated empire, and colonial governors had considerable leeway to manage colonial affairs as they saw fit and to use their colonial despatches to shape metropolitan understandings of what was taking place in the colonies. The processes of imperial marginalization that took hold of the Northwest Coast and Vancouver Island between 1790 and the 1840s were grounded in the 1850s in a sovereign-cadastral system of power. The British colonized a region that it knew only in outline from cartographic lines and that it had constructed with principles of sovereignty. Douglas and Pemberton implemented a land policy that was premised on the idea that Vancouver Island was now the Queen's land.[44] And the platitudes of British writers such as D.G.F. Macdonald, who warned prospective colonists that they were "waited for by the crafty, bloodthirsty and implacable savage," were not simply rooted in a metropolitan racist ideology.[45] They were inflected by notions of colonial opportunity and constraint that stemmed from Vancouver's labours, the Hudson's Bay Company's advertisements, and colonial land policy. They were wrapped up in a local scene as well as in a Western imperial mindset. A.C. Anderson, a British fur trader, stressed the importance of these local relationships in colonial constructions of the island. Colonists' "misapprehensions" about Indians, he noted, stemmed from "the disappointment of over-sanguine hopes" and their "exaggeration of minor difficulties."[46] Colonists did not view Native peoples as fur traders did – as trade partners – but as obstacles to colonial plenitude, and they looked to Douglas to promote and protect their interests.

Douglas declared that "the first end and object of Government, is to obtain for its subjects, protection of life and property."[47] Native "depredations" on colonial land and life were not tolerated. Douglas advocated "moderate" judicial methods – punishment "as the law directs [with trials] and the justice of the case requires." He assured Native peoples that he would arrest only the "real" offenders and not punish whole tribes for their crimes, but the rule of law over Native peoples was marked by summary justice and military violence that was designed to give them "a proper idea of our capacity of inflicting punishment for offences." Douglas noted that he used "the greatest possible display of force for the sake of effect." British gunboats bombarded Native villages, marines marched into Native districts, Natives found guilty of murder were hanged before their tribe, and Douglas lectured Native peoples about their relationship with the Queen. These spectacles of power, Douglas suggested, were "calculated to make a deep impression" on Native minds, and on many accounts they did.[48] One naval officer reported that the Natives of Nanaimo thought that colonists were "like themselves in different tribes & that we belong to the 'Angry or Fighting' tribe," and he noted that Native groups feared gunboats.[49] These military tactics were derived from the land-based fur trade, but they were now used to demonstrate to Native peoples the centrality of private property in the colonial order of things and the futility of "resisting the Queen's authority."[50] Douglas remarked on the "solemnity" of such military spectacles. They were tactics of terror – measures of dissuasion – that were supposed to temper Native "excitements" and prevent the "pain of [Douglas] carrying fire and sword" into Native territories.[51] Such tactics boosted colonists' confidence in their property and were bolstered by naval visits to Native communities and military parades through Victoria that were designed to make Native people "sensible that they are not unwatched," as Douglas put it to a British naval commander, and to prevent collisions between Natives and settlers.[52]

These were ways of exercising British sovereignty. Douglas displayed the power of a distant monarch. More broadly, he policed a colonial landscape that was circumscribed by the imperial endeavours that preceded formal colonialism. Native peoples were granted a subsidiary place in a colonial region that was "applicable" to colonization – a space of British sovereignty and a domain of civilization. Native peoples would not be permitted to live in this space on equal terms with Whites unless they lived by the rule of law, in the judgement of God, and according to the ways of civilization. In the meantime, Douglas explained in 1857, in typically prosaic terms, "It is well for us that the Almighty has put the fear of intelligence upon all the beasts of the fields or ignorant races of men, or we should be swept away by the flood of barbarism."[53] These tactics of power did not change until the 1860s, when they were accompanied by a systematic Indian reserve policy and a more regularized, disciplinary system of power spearheaded by missionaries and Indian agents began to be put in place.

Simon Ryan's discussion of how explorers constructed Australia helps us to contextualize the colonial construction of Vancouver Island:

The imperial endeavour encourages the construction of space as a universal, mensurable and divisible entity, for this is the self-legitimising view of the world ...

Constructing a monolithic space, on the other hand, allows imperialism to hierarchise the use of space to its own advantage. In imperial ideology the Aborigines do not have a different space to that of the explorers; rather, they under-utilise the space imperialism understands as absolute ... The explorers are ostensibly at the vanguard of the establishment of a colonial space ... inserting all objects into the coordinates of Cartesian space.[54]

While "the imperial endeavour" universalized space in Cartesian terms, it was not monolithic. Different regions were fashioned in different ways. Colonial spaces had local as well as metropolitan imperial identities. If Vancouver Island was a mythical locality, then it had much to do with Vancouver's vanguard depiction of the region, the Oregon Treaty, and their influence on colonists' expectations. But Ryan correctly points to a broader set of imperial tendencies. Colonialism on Vancouver Island was induced and legitimized by a Cartesian apparatus of sovereignty. Native peoples became repositioned in a rationalized, cartographic space that had been constructed in absolute terms: a space created by explorers and politicians for settlers and colonial administrators. Embedded in Pemberton's survey work and Douglas's "treaties" was the self-legitimizing view that Native peoples underutilized "Crown" land. Colonists' dealings with Native peoples were encompassed by an imperial geography that had global coordinates and a local form.

Let me end this story about the imperial fashioning and colonial construction of Vancouver Island by clarifying my position. Native peoples were not dispossessed by international treaties or maps, and the geopolitical disputes over Nootka and Oregon did not specify how the colony should be settled or administered. Native peoples were stripped of large resource territories and placed on reserves by a colonial apparatus of power, and Vancouver Island was colonized because British politicians deemed it necessary, the Hudson's Bay Company wanted to preserve its business in the Pacific, and it was judged that the new colony would attract emigrants from different backgrounds. Nor am I trying to imply that the whole scene of colonizing power can be loaded on to Vancouver or imperial inscriptions of territory or models of sovereignty. Of course it cannot. Colonial views of land and Natives and the territory of Vancouver Island did not simply stem from cartography, and colonialism is not just a system of representational violence. Colonialism is a landed project of power. The intricate story of how this imperial domain was turned into colonial space is beyond the purview of this book. Yet I do think that these colonial forces and this prior imperial outreach were interlocking. I have tried to show how much had changed before colonial intervention. Consideration of this imperial outreach prompts us to reconsider the moment of colonialism.

CHAPTER 14

Conclusion:
The Loss of Locality

At the conference held in Vancouver in 1992 to mark the bicentenary of Vancouver's survey, Chief Philip Joe of the Squamish Nation reminded the audience that Native and White histories "have been inexorably intertwined, but recalled from different perspectives." Chief Joe related his people's story of their meeting with Vancouver in Howe Sound. Vancouver shared his molasses and biscuits, Chief Joe said, and the Squamish reciprocated, sharing their resources with the Whites who came in the wake of the "floating islands." They named the site where they met the explorer *Whul-whul-LAY-ton* – "Whiteman place."[1]

Islands of Truth has considered how Westerners came to know Vancouver Island over the first seventy or so years of contact, charted something of the changing make-up of the island as a Native domain, and tracked some of the ways in which the meeting of Natives and non-Natives came to be viewed over time. Chief Joe puts the past and its relations with the present in a generous light. Natives and non-Natives did not simply share resources. Between the 1770s and 1850s Native groups competed over the floating islands that came to their shores, traders worked with a capitalist logic of competition, and Western explorers and politicians brought Native space in empire. Then, in the second half of the nineteenth century, land and resources were taken away from Native peoples.

Before the colonial period, Native peoples encountered one mode of Western expansion – profit-sensitive traders working in an expanding world economy – and incorporated traders and their goods into their own worlds of collaboration, competition, and conflict. When the Hudson's Bay Company established Fort Victoria in 1843, Native groups from the coast and interior came to trade and knew Westerners as traders. In the 1850s, however, the town became the fulcrum of a colonial order that brought Native peoples into contact with a system of Western dominance of which they had only seen the edges but that had been encroaching on their territories for over six decades. Colonial officials worked with a philosophy of private property and rhetoric of cultivation and civilization that can be detected in a set of developments that preceded colonial intervention. Following one of his military expeditions into "Indian country" in 1856, Governor James Douglas reported that Native peoples revered "the power and genius of civilisation" – the civilizing mission of British colonialism, which, increasingly through the colonial period, linked sovereign tactics of rule and disciplinary strategies of cultural transformation. If Native peoples embraced aspects of this colonial mission – accepting missionaries and Indian agents, becoming wage labourers in a White economy, and acknowledging the rule of law – then it was due to conditions of colonial upheaval rather than to some general reverence for White ways. Their territories had been redefined by Western powers, their lands were being resettled, the coast was being patrolled by British gunboats, resources were beginning to be harvested on an industrial basis, and Native peoples were dying from Western diseases. Native groups looked to missionaries and Indian agents to reason with the colonial government over land, but Native-White conflict also ensued and there were power struggles between Native groups over territory and trade with Whites.

How did Vancouver Island become a place of antagonism where cultural divisions were written into the cultural apparatus of colonialism, entrenched in a land system, and remain difficult to bridge? Scholars of early British Columbia have rightly argued that the colonial resettlement of land was the chief turning point in Native-White relations, but in my view they have not fully explored how and why the transition from trade to colonialism – from "contact to conflict" – came about. My research on Vancouver Island covers the colonial as well as the pre-colonial period, and I originally planned to write a study of both periods. But I became absorbed with the late eighteenth century, partly because I saw there the formation of imperial knowledges about the Northwest Coast, and strategies of representation mediating face-to-face processes of contact, that played a more crucial role in the configuration of imperial attitudes, constructions of the past, and understandings of the present than other scholars have acknowledged. I also saw a convoluted realm of Native-White and Native-Native interaction that is worthy of examination in its own right.

The cartographic and geopolitical processes of inscription I have charted were modes of appropriation that prepared the ground for colonists. They constituted what Brian Harley has called an "anticipatory geography" of colonialism.[2] Pre-colonial and colonial Vancouver Island, and the nineteenth and twentieth centuries, are connected by a discourse of sovereignty. I have argued that the shift from contact to conflict was circumscribed by the recontextualization of the Northwest Coast as an imperial domain and the redefinition of Native territory as Crown land. This shift in the status of land remains a principal source of Native-White agitation.

These processes of imperial fashioning, and their longer-term implications for Native peoples, were not peculiar to the Northwest Coast, of course. As Edward Said formulates the geographical relationship between imperial practices and colonial rule: "For the native the history of colonial servitude is inaugurated by loss of the locality to the outsider; its geographical identity must thereafter be searched for and somehow restored ... If there is anything that radically distinguishes the imagination of anti-imperialism, it is the primacy of the geographical element."[3] Native struggle against the course and legacies of colonialism is not mediated solely by the physical experience and memory of colonization. Native struggles in British Columbia cannot be fully appreciated unless this late eighteenth-century era of European imperial aggrandizement is explored. Many non-Native British Columbians believe that the province rightly belongs to the Crown by virtue of international treaties, imperial proclamations, and colonial land laws – that their right to private property is guaranteed by a colonial apparatus that was inflected by a body of assumptions about territory. Native peoples, on the other hand, have tried to impress on non-Natives that their cultures cannot be rejuvenated unless their lands are restored; that while they have been stripped of territory, they have never lost their links with the land. Recent court battles and treaty negotiations over Native rights and title to land show that Native groups are not simply engaged in a postcolonial struggle against economic deprivation, social oppression, and political marginalization. More fully, their struggle is an anti-imperialist struggle against a set of geographical impressions about land and legal formulae about property that were introduced by Western politicians before formal colonialism began and that, over the last 150 years, have been used to beat down Native demands for redress for the loss of their territories. Native peoples are struggling against regimes of truth as well as an entrenched apparatus of power.

While the loss of locality was an intrinsic feature of Western imperialism, anticipatory geographies of colonialism varied over space and through time. Vancouver Island had a specific place in the British Empire. The colony stemmed from the activities of explorers and traders, and it reflected Britain's imperial philosophy of commerce. The details of Western exploration and trade on the coast were organized into useful patterns of knowledge that allowed the British to make plans for the region. The timing and spacing of Western engagement with the coast became folded into Western projects that slowly fixed Vancouver Island as an arena of imperial interest and space of colonial intervention. In turn, colonial Vancouver Island became a labyrinth of hopes and memories: a place of colonial romance and a site of imperial nostalgia. It was perceived as a shell awaiting development – a waste land applicable to systematic colonization – and it juxtaposed American and British imperial philosophies (annexation versus free trade; continental nation-building versus global imperial affiliation).

I gleaned these themes of imperial appropriation from the archives and approached them with contemporary issues in mind. But I was also sensitized to these links between knowledge and power, truth and history, and land and identity by theorists of colonialism who have persuasively argued that metropolitan-colonial relationships were produced and sustained by Western "imaginative geographies" of other lands and peoples. Such geographies were both vague and detailed. They revolved around general cultural assumptions and fantasies about the non-Western world and more exact bodies of knowledge that stemmed from a close engagement with distant peoples and places. This mixture of fantasy and detail was organized in Eurocentric grids of cultural power. As Gayatri Chakravorty Spivak argues, cultural apparatuses of imperialism disciplined the world in epistemological terms, overhauling, ruling out, burying, or denigrating other ways of knowing, and thus sanctioning ignorance.[4]

The imperial fashioning of Vancouver Island involved a mixture of discipline and sanctioned ignorance, and it combined metropolitan forces and local details. Native space was reproduced as an absolute space of British sovereignty. Considerable work went into the imperial rationalization of knowledges that had been produced in other situations and for other reasons. The Northwest Coast would not have been made amenable to empire without the work of politicians and diplomats. They packaged the region as an imperial domain, using the facts and exigencies of Native-Western interaction. And if the colonization of Vancouver Island was fuelled by the mythology of empty land, then it was partly because of Vancouver's cartography. The sovereign-Cartesian framework of empire that a range of Western actors fashioned between 1790 and the 1840s induced visions of colonial opportunity and legitimate possession that were connected to Eurocentric constellations of knowledge and power – to constellations that absolutized, exhibited, and schematized space and time. Said and Timothy Mitchell have explored how the West imagined and dealt with the world in meta-cultural and geographical terms, dividing it into oppositional structures of West and rest, Occident and Orient.[5] The plans, protocols, schemes, and compartments of empire, as well as broader fetishistic orders of self and other, were fabricated by scholars, travellers, and metropolitan institutions and presented to the public in books, at museums, and at world exhibitions. Vancouver Island had a specific marginality in this imperial technology of vision and representation. It was neither a prize colonial possession like India nor a keenly debated settler colony like New Zealand. It cohered in the British imperial imagination initially as a cartographic space, and the Colonial Office dealt with it through a scheme of systematic colonization. Emigrants and politicians had a rarefied understanding of the northwest coast, and the slimness of their understanding was a constitutive feature of colonialism in this part of the world.

Colonial Vancouver Island was an expedient and contradictory space. Britain had held the Northwest Coast at bay as a commercial preserve and had colonized part of it in response to the American occupation of the region south of the Columbia River. The Hudson's Bay Company acknowledged that philosophies of commerce and philosophies of settlement did not sit together very well, and, in relatively short order, the latter became more forceful than the former. With British sovereignty assumed and Native peoples hardly within the realm of general British awareness, colonists had few qualms about occupying the island; thus the protection of their life and property, rather than the extension of trade, quickly became the centrepiece of colonial power. The Hudson's Bay Company was never quite able to administer the region in its own commercial terms.

I aimed foremost to document the development of these processes of imperial appropriation, but I have also sought to question their make-up and their place in the present. The work of Said, Foucault, and others theorists who insist that knowledge and power are constructed rather than immutable – that knowledge produces reality and truth through modes of inclusion and exclusion and that power produces rather than represses identities – prompted me to consider the arbitrariness of sovereign claims to land. There are methodological and substantive dimensions to this side of *Islands of Truth*. When I tracked James Cook's and George Vancouver's place in the non-Native British Columbian imagination, I began to see how representations of the past have served local cultural identity and power. The moments of local reinscription I focused on – especially the unveiling ceremony at Nootka Sound in 1924 – suggest that for all their assumptions about land and their stereotypes of Native peoples, non-Native British Columbians have found neither a legal philosophy of sovereignty nor the British cultural backdrop of empire entirely satisfactory sources of local identity. Local scholars, especially, have felt the need to shroud Britain's occupation of the land in the words and deeds of "founding" figures. Such is the case, of course, with colonial societies in other parts of Britain's former settler empire. Figures like Cook and Vancouver continue to fascinate the non-Native public. But they infuriate Native groups, who see the past narrated around the arrival of Whites and encounter judges who treat the texts of dead White explorers as superior guides to the past than their own living memories.

The literature on colonialism sensitizes us to the ways in which practices of representation and narratives of identity and possession are simultaneously media of cultural power, anxiety, protest, and negotiation. Much has been written recently about the ambivalences of colonial discourse and the hybridities of colonial rule. Prominent postcolonial theorists such as Homi Bhabha and Gyan Prakash have portrayed nineteenth-century colonialism – and, more specifically, British colonialism in India – as intrinsically contradictory and disjunctive. They show that colonial categories were not cut from one cloth for all time; they were continually retailored. These theorists are responding, in part, to Said's seemingly overbearing formulation of imperialism as a systematic will to overseas domination and, particularly, to his argument that manifest domains of colonial power were drawn quite smoothly from latent attitudes of dominance through the circulation – or, as Said has it, the repeated citation – of reality-constituting knowledges and representations. Bhabha and Prakash do not question the representational violence of colonialism; rather, they see it as anxiety-ridden.[6]

While these arguments about anxiety are an important corrective to Manichaean readings of colonialism, they are often worked through tightly epistemological corridors of inquiry and are not very carefully contextualized or historicized. I see little anxiety in the modulation of Western imperial knowledge into British colonial power on Vancouver Island. If nineteenth-century colonial discourses on British India were anxiety-ridden, as Bhabha has argued, it was partly because India was not constructed as an imperial space from afar before the British occupied the region. British knowledge and power were elaborated together, in ongoing interrelation, by East India Company personnel and then by British Crown officials in a space where the British were vastly outnumbered by Indians and encountered sophisticated Indian societies and polities. In British Columbia, on the other hand, where Natives were not outnumbered by non-Natives until the 1890s, early colonists imagined that the land was unoccupied and so the colonial government did not seek to share power with Native leaders. Native people were effectively marginalized before colonists arrived; if colonists felt threatened by them, then this did not rock their confidence in the legitimacy of colonialism.

Yet the alluring simplifications of Vancouver's cartography and assumptions of sovereignty only licensed British colonialism. They furnished a powerful yet slim and volatile context within which settlers, merchants, colonial officials, and missionaries dealt with Native peoples. Such volatility can be perceived in early twentieth-century appreciations of Cook and Vancouver. Local scholars deemed it important to authenticate Vancouver's circumnavigation of the island and to mark Cook's discovery of Nootka Sound, making it a local fount of history. Colonies, and the colonial discourses mediating them, do not have a coherent or timeless make-up. We can debate the extent to which British Columbia as a whole was worked up as a space of White identity in response to Native agitation over land questions. In the early twentieth century Asian immigrants probably posed a greater threat to Whiteness than did Native peoples. Yet scholars such as Howay and Sage were trying to foster White roots in the land. At Nootka Sound, which was a Native place before it was a marker of White history, it is the hierarchization of Native and White fortunes that comes to the fore.

One of the undercurrents of this book is that, although the critical literature on colonialism is a crucial theoretical resource for studying Vancouver Island, it should be drawn on selectively, in relation to specific archival arrangements and local issues. In Part 1, for instance, in discussing Cook I tried to dissolve historical truth into a plethora of perspectives and interested positions that revolve around issues of cultural power and anxiety, but I did not treat this as a licence to suspend judgement on the past altogether, to focus entirely on the politics of representation, or to treat Vancouver Island as a local example of a general theoretical problematic. When I worked through Cook's sojourn at Nootka Sound and discovered a diverse field of interaction and representation, a judge's handling of historical evidence came to mind and led me towards a wider methodological discussion of how British Columbians have narrated their relationship with the land. I was concerned with knowledge claims that became embedded in both a local and a European archive. But analyses of the texts of contact should not lead solely into these methodological domains, and the emergence of British sovereignty was not the only vector of change between the 1780s and 1850s.

Native life and aspirations changed during this period. Native populations were thinned by European diseases and Native geographies were altered by commercial contact. Traders focused on places such as Nootka Sound and Clayoquot Sound and then abandoned them when profits dried up. Native centres and peripheries shifted as sea otter populations dwindled, Natives and traders came into contact and conflict, and commercial capital moved around the coast. Native peoples became more familiar with Westerners and probably came into more frequent and geographically extensive contact with each other. But Native-Western relations were stormy, and the effects of the trade on Native peoples were not egalitarian. Wealth flowed into selective Native areas and hands, making some Native groups and chiefs powerful and others vulnerable to colonization. Along the west coast of Vancouver Island, Native social hierarchies of power probably intensified as Native chiefs drew on Western goods as sources of prestige.

I found it more difficult to interpret Native aspects of this encounter than to work out Western modes of representation and power. In Part 2, I work through the filters of a refractory historical and ethnographic record and delve into a past that was no doubt lived in more ways than I have been able to invoke. Yet this does not mean that interpretation of the Native past is hopelessly compromised. We all write from particular positions of privilege, and I have discussed Vancouver Island in ways that Native peoples would not; but, given what I have argued about the courts and the power of distancing, I think it is important to at least open up different sides of the past from different cultural and geographical positions.

There are analytical and rhetorical connections between my treatment of interaction and imperialism. My points about commercial interaction and Native change put my discussion of Cook, Vancouver, and geopolitics in a particular light. I try to show how the imperial construction of Vancouver Island *worked over* – reinscribed and partially buried – Native agendas, knowledges, and expectations. American, British, and Spanish constructions of Vancouver Island and the Oregon Territory manufactured a context within which colonial agendas could be elaborated. We can draw out the constructedness and arbitrariness of this imperial context by showing how it overrode intricate Native constructions of these regions. This is especially significant in the case of Vancouver. While his cartography influenced colonial sensibilities, the landscape he captured and that colonists discovered had been shaped by Native and Native-Western projects of engagement. This book has focused on the Nuu-chah-nulth contact zone, and I do not want to pretend that my generalizations about Native change can be extended to other parts of the coast and, especially, to the interior. Moreover, the first colonists on Vancouver Island came into contact with Coast Salish people and Native peoples from other parts of the coast and interior who travelled to Victoria to trade. Central and northern Nuu-chah-nulth groups were much less affected by the arrival of settlers. In the long run, however, the resettlement of British Columbia was disjunctive for all Native groups, and colonists occupied Native territories that had been repositioned from afar with details of inter-action that came from the west coast of Vancouver Island.

If *Islands of Truth* has wider implications for the analysis of colonialism, then I should think that they fall into two categories. First, one of the main ideas in this book is that distance is both an enabling and a constraining variable in power/knowledge relationships at both an imaginative and material level. Rec-ognition that different forms of power worked on and around regions like Van-couver Island, and operated at a variety of scales – "from the great strategies of geo-politics to the little tactics of the habitat," to borrow Foucault's vivid image of what a history of space and power might include – made me think harder about what constitutes colonialism and its ongoing relations with the present. Other scholars of the region have said relatively little about how imperial atti-tudes and colonial categories emerged through processes of representation and distancing. So, second, I have been writing Vancouver Island into the interna-tional literature on colonialism. I have suggested that scholarship on early Brit-ish Columbia has suffered from a lack of theoretical inquisitiveness, especially about the geographical conditioning of knowledge and power. Neither the ar-chives nor longer-term questions of land and colonialism can be explored fully without these ideas about discourse and power. I have tried to write a postcolonial geography that acknowledges both the globalization of Western interest and in-fluence in the world (the increasing interconnectedness of "West and rest" through common processes of interaction and representation, power, and change) and the geographically and historically diverse emergence of colonial relations and performance of cultural practices. I make such connections, however, at a time when the literature on colonialism shows signs (1) of losing sight of the links between the representational and geographical violence of imperialism and (2) of making too much theoretical mileage out of colonial complexes in specific parts of the world. Theoretical work on colonialism will become vapid and circular if it is not married to empirical investigation and an awareness of the geographical diversity of European overseas expansion.

To conclude, Vancouver Island emerged as colonial space through processes of effacement *and* engagement, and my account of the region mixes archival exposition and methodological reflexiveness. How one blends these styles of analysis depends on what sort of place one relates to. I relate to a place that has been largely taken over by Whites and cannot be given back to Native peoples in full. And I recognize that the notions of Native loss and imperial power that feather my narrative are uncomfortable bedfellows. Aboriginality cuts across British Columbia in uneasy ways. This may not be the moment to offer master narratives of Native continuity or descent, White power and Native resistance, and/or of historical winners and losers. The theoretical climate and empirical grounds for this style of analysis are fast disappearing. We now entertain diversity and difference, and the archive of Native-Western engagement seems more complex than it did just a few decades ago, when questions of epistemological violence were less prominent and scholarship had less interdisciplinary momentum. Master narratives remain politically appealing, however, and may be strategically salient. Native peoples need to stress their continuity with the land on moral and political grounds because the imperial forces that encroached on them framed the making of immigrants homes. Many non-Native British Columbians may not want to entertain the idea that their place is based on a discourse of sovereignty that ranks rights to land in terms of civilization and cultivation. Immigrants have worked hard to make themselves at home in British Columbia and do not feel anxious about their place on the land. The contemporary language of compromise that tries to bridge these discrepant Native and White perspectives frequently breaks down into a rhetoric of blame and cultural capitulation.

Academic studies of the past cannot solve contemporary cultural problems, but I hope that this book raises awareness of where some of them came from and of the dilemmas involved in thinking about them. Native peoples have been locked into a legal calculus of power that glues them to place in primordial ways, but I want neither to suggest that Native peoples do not have deep attachments to land nor simply conclude that they were colonized first of all, or decisively, from a distance; rather, I wonder whether processes of imperial appropriation and Native aggrandizement would be seen in more open-ended ways if the courts did not fix "Indianness" in culturally divisive ways and if scholarly debates about Native agency and White domination did not rely so heavily on the notion that only Whites were colonizers. I have sketched Native practices of dominance and imposition, as best I can see them, but I do not want to imply that Native colonialisms were like Western ones; rather, I think that the roots and tenor of domination should be investigated from both Native and White positions and at a variety of scales. In a more methodological vein, I have suggested that regions like Vancouver Island should be studied with a range of ideas and materials, and they should be discussed in ways that simultaneously evaluate the past and unsettle its implications for the present.

Notes

Introduction

1 There are parallels between my argument and Nicholas Thomas's argument that colonial projects were simultaneously partial and transformative. See his *Colonialism's culture: Anthropology, travel and government* (Princeton, NJ: Princeton University Press, 1994), especially 105-106.

2 For good surveys of some of the main ideas in this literature, see Frederick Cooper and Laura Stoler, eds., *Tensions of empire: Colonial cultures in a bourgeois world* (Berkeley: University of California Press, 1997); Nicholas B. Dirks, ed., *Colonialism and culture* (Ann Arbor: University of Michigan Press, 1992). I work most explicitly with the literature on the Pacific.

3 Michel Foucault, "Truth and power," in his *Power/Knowledge: Selected interviews and other writings, 1972-1977,* ed. Colin Gordon, trans. Colin Gordon et al. (New York: Pantheon, 1980), 109-33 (quotation is from 131); Edward W. Said, *Culture and imperialism* (New York: Knopf, 1993), xiii.

4 Said has worked on the Middle East, issues of Orientalism, the connections between imperialism and European culture, and the geographical and representational violence of colonialism. Bhabha's work ranges between British India, the ambivalences of imperial authority and colonial rule, and the diasporic make-up of the colonial and postcolonial world. For deft overviews of their ideas, and recent colonial and postcolonial studies more generally, see Robert Young, *White mythologies: Writing history and the West* (London: Routledge, 1990); Ania Loomba, *Colonialism/Postcolonialism* (London: Routledge, 1998); and Leela Gandhi, *Postcolonial theory: A critical introduction* (Edinburgh: Edinburgh University Press, 1998).

5 The quotation is from Homi K. Bhabha, *The location of culture* (London: Routledge, 1994), 20-21. See also Robert J.C. Young, *Colonial desire: Hybridity in theory, culture and race* (London: Routledge, 1995), 160, who notes that Said's work on Orientalism has encouraged "a certain lack of historical specificity" in colonial and postcolonial studies, for "if Orientalist discourse is a form of Western fantasy that can say nothing about actuality [as many read Said], while at the same time its determining cultural pressure means that those in the West cannot but use it, then any obligation to address the reality of the historical conditions of colonialism can be safely discarded."

6 Thomas, *Colonialism's culture,* 195.

7 The point has been made emphatically by postcolonial theorists from India. See, especially, Dipesh Chakrabarty, "Postcoloniality and the artifice of history: Who speaks for 'Indian' past?," *Representations* 37 (1992): 1-27.

8 Foucault, *Power/Knowledge,* 114

9 See, for example, F.W. Howay, *British Columbia: The making of a province* (Toronto: Ryerson, 1928); John S. Galbraith, *The Hudson's Bay Company as an imperial factor, 1821-1869* (Toronto: University of Toronto Press, 1957); Margaret Ormsby, *British Columbia* (Toronto: Macmillan, 1958).

10 Fisher has defended his position in a number of places. See his preface to the second edition of *Contact and conflict* (Vancouver: UBC Press, 1992); and Robin Fisher, "Contact and trade, 1774-1849," in *The Pacific province: A history of British Columbia*, ed. Hugh J.M. Johnston (Vancouver: Douglas and McIntyre, 1996). See also Jean Barman, *The west beyond the west: A history of British Columbia* (Toronto: University of Toronto Press, 1991).

11 See Robert Thomas Boyd, "The introduction of infectious diseases among the Indians of the North west coast, 1774-1784" (PhD diss., University of Washington, 1985); and Cole Harris, *The resettlement of British Columbia: Essays on colonialism and geographical change* (Vancouver: UBC Press, 1996), chap. 1.

12 For an overview of current research on early contact processes, see Cole Harris, "Social power and cultural change in pre-colonial British Columbia," *BC Studies* 115-16 (1997-98): 45-82.

13 See the special issue of *BC Studies* 95 (1992) entitled "Anthropology and history in the courts." The quotation is from Robin Fisher's essay in this issue: "Judging history: Reflections on the reasons for judgment in Delgamuukw v. B.C.," 43-54.

14 While the archival record and academic history have carried the greatest weight in the courts, judges have treated many documents at face value and have bypassed academic debates about historical methods. Judges have been less persuaded by the ethnographic record and expert witnesses from the discipline of anthropology. The most complex and astounding judgement on Native title to land is *Delgamuukw et al. v. The Queen*, Reasons for Judgement of the Honourable Chief Justice Allan McEachern, 8 March 1991. B.C.S.C., Smithers Registry No. 0843, to which I return at the end of Chapter .

15 Arjun Appadurai, *Modernity at large: Cultural dimensions of globalization* (Minneapolis: University of Minnesota Press, 1996), 3.

Part 1: Introduction

1 I quote and paraphrase from W.N. Sage, "Unveiling of memorial tablet at Nootka Sound," *Second Annual Report and Proceedings of the British Columbia Historical Association*, 1924, 17-22; Sage, "Trip to Nootka Sound," August 1924, Walter Noble Sage Papers, box 31, file 6, UBCL-SC; Charles Moser, "Thirty years a missionary on the west coast of Vancouver Island," 117-19, BCARS Add. MSS. 2172; correspondence relating to Nootka Sound, F.W. Howay Papers, box 33, file 6, UBCL-SC.

Kipling wrote his *Recessional* for Queen Victoria's Diamond Jubilee in 1897. It was sung at the end of church services and was seen as a celebration of Empire. The first stanza reads:

God of our fathers, known of old,
Lord of our far-flung battle-line,
Beneath whose awful Hand we hold
Dominion over palm and pine –
Lord God of Hosts, be with us yet,
Lest we forget, lest we forget!

But Kipling also wrote it to voice concern over the abuse of power in the Empire. He saw "Dominion over palm and pine" as incompatible with "An humble and contrite heart" – the fourth line of the second stanza. See Sandra Kemp, *Kipling's hidden narratives* (Oxford: Blackwell, 1988), 82. For the full text, see *Rudyard Kipling's verse: Definitive edition* (London: Hodder and Stoughton, 1940), 328-29.

2 Howay to Ditchburn, 18 November 1923, Howay Papers, box 8, folder 2.

3 I put Nootka Sound in scare quotes this once to point out that it is not a Native place name and to highlight that processes of naming and mapping were integral to the way Europeans appropriated Native land. On this point, see, especially, J. Brian Harley, "Rereading the maps of the Columbian encounter," *Annals of the Association of American Geographers* 83, 2 (1992): 522-42. The Native groups of the west coast of Vancouver Island took Nuu-chah-nulth as their collective name in 1978. Before that Europeans called them "Nootkans." The Native groups of this region did not identify themselves collectively in 1778.

   Cook first named Nootka Sound "King George's Sound" but changed the name later, thinking that "Nootka" was the indigenous name for this area. The Spanish naturalist José Mariano Moziño, who visited the sound in 1792, thought that Nootka was derived from *Nut-chi*, or mountain, and noted: "Cook's men, asking the [Natives] by signs what the port was called, made for them a sign with their hand, forming a circle and then dissolving it, to which the Natives responded Nutka, which means to give away." See José Mariano Moziño, *Noticias de Nutka: An account of Nootka Sound in 1792*, trans. Iris H. Wilson Engstrand (Seattle and London: University of Washington Press/Douglas and McIntyre, 1980; second ed. 1991), 66. There have been other interpretations of Cook's mistake.

Chapter 1: Captain Cook, the Enlightenment, and Symbolic Violence

1 Glyndwr Williams, "Buccaneers, castaways, and satirists: The South Seas in the English consciousness before 1750," *Eighteenth-Century Life* (n.s.) 18, 3 (1994): 114-28 (quotation is from 114).

2 For an introduction to European exploration in the Pacific, see J.C. Beaglehole, *The exploration of the Pacific* (London: Black, 1934). For an accessible overview of Cook's voyages, see Lynne Withey, *Voyages of discovery: Captain Cook and the exploration of the Pacific* (New York: Morrow, 1987).

3 See Derek Howse, "The principal scientific instruments taken on Captain Cook's voyages," *Mariner's Mirror* 65, 2 (1979): 119-35; R.A. Skelton, "Captain James Cook as a hydrographer," *Mariner's Mirror* 40 (1954): 92-119; Sir James Watt, "Medical aspects and consequences of Cook's voyages," in *Captain James Cook and his times*, ed. Robin Fisher and Hugh Johnston (Seattle: University of Washington Press, 1979), 129-57; and Christopher Lawrence, "Disciplining disease: scurvy, the navy, and imperial expansion, 1750-1825," in *Visions of empire: Voyages, botany, and representations of nature*, ed. David Philip Miller and Peter Hanns Reill (Cambridge: Cambridge University Press, 1996), 80-106.

4 For different approaches to this shift, compare Mary Louise Pratt, *Imperial eyes: Travel writing and transculturation* (London: Routledge, 1993); Edward Said, *Orientalism* (New York: Vintage, 1979); and Barbara Maria Stafford, *Voyage into substance: Art, science, and the illustrated travel account, 1760-1840* (London: MIT Press, 1984).

5 See Charles L. Batten Jr., *Pleasurable instruction: Form and convention in eighteenth-century travel literature* (Berkeley: University of California Press, 1978), chap. 1. In 1772, J.R. Forster, who sailed on Cook's second voyage, wrote in his translator's preface to Bougainville's voyage: "Circumnavigations of the globe have been of late the universal topics of all companies." See Lewis de Bougainville, *A voyage round the world. Performed by order of his most Catholic majesty, in the years 1766, 1767, 1768, and 1769* (London: J. Nourse and T. Davies, 1772), v. Dr. John Hawkesworth's account of the voyages of Byron, Wallis, Carteret, and Cook was published the following year.

   Public enthusiasm was neither universal nor unqualified, however. The essayist Horace Walpole wrote to Lady Ossory: "Capt. Cooke's [third] voyage I have neither read nor intend to read. I have seen the prints – a parcel of ugly faces with blubber lips and flat noses, dressed as unbecomingly as if both sexes were ladies of the first fashion; and rows of savages with backgrounds of palm-trees ... nor do I desire to know how unpolished the north or south poles have remained ever since Adam and Eve were just such mortals." See W.S. Lewis, ed., *The Yale edition of*

Horace Walpole's correspondence, vol. 33 (New Haven: Yale University Press, 1965), 436. A fan of the Gothic, Walpole perhaps objected to the empirical-ethnographic strain in the work of Cook's artist, John Webber. His remarks were also underwritten by a complex set of ideas about civility and masculinity.

6 The official account of Cook's third voyage, comprising three quarto volumes of text and a folio volume of engravings, was priced at 4 1/2 guineas and sold out in three days. See London, *Monthly Review* 70 (1784): 460-74.

7 The impact of knowledge about the non-European world on late eighteenth-century European philosophy is traced in detail in Antonello Gerbi, *The dispute of the New World: The history of a polemic, 1750-1900,* trans. Jeremy Moyle (Pittsburgh: University of Pittsburgh Press, 1973). The knowledge generated by Cook's voyages contributed to the emergence of new "sciences of living," Gerbi argues. Kant and Hegel became interested in the genesis and variation of species in time rather than in their distribution over the face of the earth.

8 See Rudigger Joppien, "The artistic bequest of Captain Cook's voyages – popular imagery in European costume books of the late eighteenth and early nineteenth centuries," in *Captain James Cook and his times,* ed. Fisher and Johnston, 187-210; and Adrienne L. Kaeppler, ed., *Cook voyage artifacts in Leningrad, Berne, and Florence museums* (Honolulu: Bishop Museum Press, 1978).

9 Bernard Smith offers a stimulating account of "Cook's posthumous reputation" in Fisher and Johnston, *Captain James Cook and his times,* 159-86.

10 The tenor of this "code" remained unchanged over Cook's three voyages.

11 "Secret instructions for Capt James Cook," in J.C. Beaglehole, ed., *The journals of Captain Cook on his voyages of discovery,* vol. 3: *The voyage of the* Resolution *and* Discovery, *1776-1780,* 2 parts (Cambridge: Hakluyt Society, extra series xxxvi, 1967), ccxx-ccxxiv (quotation is from ccxxiii). These instructions were also printed in the official account of Cook's third voyage: James Cook and James King, *A voyage to the Pacific Ocean ... performed under the direction of captains Cook, Clerke, and Gore, in his majesty's ships the* Resolution *and the* Discovery. *In the years 1776, 1777, 1778, 1779, and 1780,* 3 vols. and atlas (London: G. Nichol and T. Cadell, 1784), I, xxxi-xxxv.

12 "*Hints* offered to the consideration of Captain Cooke, Mr Bankes, Doctor Solander, and the other gentlemen who go upon the expedition on board the *Endeavour,*" in *The journals of Captain James Cook on his voyages of discovery,* vol. 1: *The voyage of the* Endeavour, *1768-1771,* ed. J.C. Beaglehole (Cambridge: Hakluyt Society, extra series xxxiv, 1955), 514-19. In the second half of the eighteenth century most British and French explorers carried similar instructions.

13 Cook and King, *Voyage to the Pacific Ocean,* I, lxxvi.

14 Thomas Warton, preface to his *History of English Poetry* (1774), quoted by Douglas ibid., I, lxix-lxx.

15 John Callender, *Terra australis cognita: Or, voyages to the terra australis, or southern hemisphere,* 3 vols. (London: A. Donaldson, 1766-68), III, book v, 736. This was a virtual copy of the French geographer Charles de Brosses's *Histoire des navigations aux terres australes* (Paris: Durand, 1756), though Callender does not mention de Brosses by name and adapted de Brosses's argument to make a case for the utility of English rather than French exploration in the Pacific. See John Dunmore, *French explorers in the Pacific,* vol. 1: *The eighteenth century* (Oxford: Clarendon, 1965), 49-52.

    With the results of Cook's first voyage in mind, Thomas Warton claimed that Europeans could now look back on their past with a heightened sense of their own importance in world history. Cook offered further proof of the steps Europeans had taken from "rudeness to elegance." Warton concluded that Cook allowed Europeans "to set a just estimation on [their] ... own acquisitions."

16 See Ronald L. Meek, *Social science and the ignoble savage* (Cambridge: Cambridge University Press, 1976); and Johannes Fabian, *Time and the other: How anthropology makes its object* (New York: Columbia University Press, 1983).

17 Beaglehole, *Journals,* I, 514.
18 See Jean Franco, "The noble savage," in *Literature and western civilization: The modern world,* vol. 1, ed. David Daiches and Anthony Thorlby (London: Aldus, 1975), 565-93. On "enlightened opinion" about non-European peoples in eighteenth-century Britain, see Paul Langford, *A polite and commercial people: England 1727-1783* (Oxford: Oxford University Press, 1992), 505-18. On the humanitarian underpinnings of Cook's instructions, see Urs Bitterli, *Cultures in conflict: Encounters between European and non-European cultures, 1492-1800,* trans. Ritchie Roberston (Cambridge: Polity, 1989), 165-69.
19 Callender, *Terra australis cognita,* I, book 1, 11.
20 Stafford, *Voyage into substance,* 32-33, 25.
21 Quoted in ibid., 20. In the 1920s, Joseph Conrad termed this new beginning "geography militant." Cook's voyages, he claimed, were untainted by "the idea of lucre ... His aims needed no disguise. They were scientific." See Joseph Conrad, "Geography and some explorers," in his *Last essays* (New York: Doubleday, Page, 1926), 1-21 (quotation is from 10).
22 Vincent T. Harlow, *The founding of the second British Empire, 1763-1793,* vol. 1: *Discovery and revolution* (London: Longmans, 1953). Callender and de Brosses shared the sentiment that "EXPERIENCE has taught us, that a solid and well-regulated commerce should form our principal object in those distant climes, and not the conquest of large kingdoms beyond the Line." Callender, *Terra australis cognita,* I, book 1, 12.
    The quotations are from Smith, "Cook's posthumous reputation," 179. Adam Smith's *The wealth of nations* was published in 1776 – the year Cook embarked on his third voyage. In his book *New lands, new men: America and the second great age of discovery* (New York: Viking Penguin, 1986), 44, William Goetzmann suggests that the purpose of Cook's second voyage (at least) was to stretch the British Empire to the Pacific, with science in the service of empire, but he produces little evidence to support his view. For a more thorough treatment of these issues, see David Mackay, *In the wake of Cook: Exploration, science, and empire, 1780-1801* (London: Croom Helm, 1985).
23 Recent historians have tended to deduce imperial motives from the *results* of Cook's travels. Bernard Smith's work is the most difficult to fathom in this respect. In "Cook's posthumous reputation" he argues that the image of Cook as Adam Smith's "global agent" was constructed posthumously. In a more recent essay focusing on Cook's third voyage, though, he suggests that playing the role of "Adam Smith's god" became part of Cook's *self*-image. See Bernard Smith, "Portraying Pacific people," in his *Imagining the Pacific: In the wake of the Cook voyages* (New Haven: Yale University Press, 1992), 209.
24 See Glyndwr Williams, "Seamen and philosophers in the south seas in the age of Captain Cook," *Mariner's Mirror* 65, 1 (1979): 3-22.
25 Beaglehole, *Journals,* III, ccxxiii. The earl of Morton argued that Native peoples "are the natural, and in the strictest sense of the word, the legal possessors of the several Regions they inhabit" and that "no European Nation has a right to occupy any part of their country, or settle among them without their voluntary consent." See Beaglehole, *Journals,* I, 514.
26 Ronald Hyam, "Imperial interests at the Peace of Paris (1763)," in *Reappraisals in British imperial history,* ed. Ronald Hyam and Ged Martin (London: Macmillan, 1975), 21-43 (quotation is from 38).
27 Linda Colley, *Britons: Forging the nation, 1707-1837* (New Haven: Yale University Press, 1992), 103.
28 Ibid., 105. See also T.O. Lloyd, *The British Empire, 1558-1983* (Oxford: Oxford University Press, 1984), 83-97.
29 On Dalrymple's "lifelong commitment to British commercial expansion," see Howard T. Fry, "Alexander Dalrymple and Captain Cook: The creative interplay of two careers," in Fisher and Johnston, *Captain James Cook and his times,* 41-57 (quotation is from 41).
30 Alexander Dalrymple, *An historical collection of the several voyages to the south Pacific Ocean,* 2 vols. (London: J. Nourse, 1770-71), I, xxi-xxx (quotation is from xxx [emphasis in original]).

31 Daniel A. Baugh, "Seapower and science: The motives for Pacific exploration," in *Background to discovery: Pacific exploration from Dampier to Cook*, ed. Derek Howse (Berkeley: University of California Press, 1990), 1-55 (quotation is from 34).

32 See Mackay, *In the wake of Cook*.

33 Charlotte Barrett, ed., *Diary and letters of Madame D'Arblay*, vol. 1, *1778-June 1781* (London: Macmillan, 1904), 318. Burney's father had recommended Dr. John Hawkesworth to Lord Sandwich as a possible editor of Cook's first voyage. James Burney, Frances's brother, sailed on Cook's second and third voyages.

34 J.C. Beaglehole, *The life of Captain James Cook* (Stanford: Stanford University Press, 1974). Or, as he put it in an earlier essay, "the humanity that is kindness, understanding, tolerance, wisdom in the treatment of men, a quality practised naturally as well as planned for, is what gave Cook's voyages their success, as much as the soundness of his seamanship and the brilliance of his navigation." See J.C. Beaglehole, "On the character of Captain James Cook," *Geographical Journal* 122, part 4 (1956): 417-29 (quotation is from 425).

35 Beaglehole, *The life*, 698 and 702.

36 J.C. Beaglehole, *Cook the writer* (Sydney: Sydney University Press, 1970), 20.

37 See Smith, "Cook's posthumous reputation," and see the review in the *Gentleman's Magazine* 54, part 2 (1784): 35, which tallies with Beaglehole's sentiments. Some of the first posthumous treatments of Cook portrayed him as a *national* hero and used the success of his voyages for propaganda purposes. See, for example, *The annual register; or a view of the history, politics, and literature, for the years 1784 and 1785* (London: J. Dodsley, 1787), 150. Beaglehole worked with a more cosmopolitan intellectual genealogy, which started with Fanny Burney, G. Forster's *Cook der Entdecker* (1787), and Pierre Lemontey's *Elogé de Jacques Cook* (1789), and which viewed Cook as a European culture hero serving worldly rather than national interests.

38 Smith, "Cook's posthumous reputation," 164. On the parallels between Forster's essay and Beaglehole's views, see Michael E. Hoare, "Two centuries of perception: George Forster to Beaglehole," in Fisher and Johnston, *Captain James Cook and his times*, 211-28.

39 This thesis is associated most directly with Alan Moorehead's *The fatal impact: An account of the invasion of the South Pacific, 1767-1840* (New York: Harper and Row, 1966), though I do not think that his argument can be reduced to the caricature of the title.

40 Or in the words of one of Beaglehole's intellectual allies, "Cook was able to bring back a priceless record of a way of life that the other Europeans were to destroy." See R.A. Skelton, *Captain James Cook: After two hundred years* (London: The Hakluyt Society, 1969), 30.

41 Dorinda Outram, *The Enlightenment* (Cambridge: Cambridge University Press, 1995), chap. 5.

42 See Anthony Pagden, *European encounters with the New World: From Renaissance to romanticism* (New Haven: Yale University Press, 1993), 142, who sees Montesquieu and Voltaire as part of "a genre in which the 'savage,' natural-man and child-of-nature reverses the traditional order of travel. Now it is not we, the perennially itinerant European, who visit him, but he who visits us. In Europe, confronted by the self-evident folly of European customs, this 'savage' finds himself, as do Montesquieu's Persians ... 'in another universe.' Remote, yet like all good fictions pervasively real, the savage is made to speak from the position of a culture which could never have been his, a culture which has been fabricated by the simple procedure of stripping away whatever the author most disliked about his own."

43 And Diderot, like many other writers, focused on Europe's encounter with Tahiti: "The life of savages is so simple, and our societies are such complicated machines! The Tahitian is close to the origin of the world, while the European is closer to its old age ... They understand nothing about our manners or our laws, and they are bound to see in them nothing but shackles disguised in a hundred different ways. Those shackles could only provoke the indignation and scorn of creatures in whom the most profound feeling is a love of liberty." Diderot worked with the images of Philippe Commerson, Bougainville's supernumary, who was even more enthusiastic about Tahiti, writing to a friend during his trip back to France: "If happiness consists in an abundance of all things necessary to life, in living in a superb land with the finest climate, in enjoying the best of health, in breathing the purest and most salubrious air, in leading a simple,

soft, quiet life, free from all passions, even from jealousy, although surrounded by women, if these women can themselves even disperse happiness, then I say that there is not in the world a happier nation than the Tahitian one." Quoted in Outram, *The Enlightenment*, 67. On Commerson, see John Dunmore, *French explorers in the Pacific*, I, 110-11.

44 Artists and engravers depicted the peoples of the Pacific with Greek and Roman physiques and garb. By the end of the eighteenth century, Outram continues, "the exotic was both profoundly other, and yet intimately linked to European origins." The association of utopia with island life had a much longer genealogy in European thought, of course, but what appealed to thinkers such as Diderot was the idea that there might be spaces in the world where people actually lived according to Enlightenment principles of goodness and purity. See Outram, *The Enlightenment*, chap. 5; and Krishan Kumar, *Utopia and anti-utopia in modern times* (Oxford: Blackwell, 1991); and Frank Manuel and Fritzie Manuel, *Utopian thought in the western world* (Cambridge, MA: Harvard University Press, 1979).

45 Henri Baudet, *Paradise on earth: Some thoughts on European images of non-European man* (New Haven: Yale University Press 1965), 55.

46 Bernard Smith, *European vision and the south Pacific 1768-1850: A study in the history of art and ideas* (Oxford: Clarendon, 1960), 2-4; and Smith, *Imagining the Pacific*.

47 Greg Dening, *Performances* (Chicago: University of Chicago Press, 1996), 109.

48 Pratt, *Imperial eyes*. See also Peter France, *Rhetoric and truth in France: Descartes to Diderot* (Oxford: Oxford University Press, 1972), 73, who notes that Paris's main institutions of learning were meeting places "between the man of learning and the world."

49 Pratt, *Imperial eyes*, 24-36.

50 Her point can be made more modestly, however. "By putting remote parts of the world within reach," Mackay argues, "Cook [and other explorers] ... facilitated the sort of imperial economic unity which these scientists almost by instinct envisaged." See Mackay, *In the wake of Cook*, 194. See also Miller and Reill, *Visions of empire*, introduction.

51 Pratt, *Imperial eyes*, 23.

52 This emphasis forms the backbone of Edward Said's *Orientalism* (New York: Vintage, 1979), 5: "as much as the West itself, the Orient is an idea that has a history and a tradition of thought. These two geographical entities thus support and to a extent reflect each other."

53 Paul Carter, "Violent passages: Pacific histories," *Journal of Historical Geography* 20, 1 (1994): 81-86 (quotation is from 85).

54 This criticism is emphasized in Stuart Schwartz, ed., *Implicit understandings: European encounters* (Cambridge: Cambridge University Press, 1994).

55 Gananath Obeyesekere, *The apotheosis of Captain Cook: European mythmaking in the Pacific* (Princeton, NJ: Princeton University Press, 1992). See, especially, Marshall Sahlins, "The apotheosis of Captain Cook," in *Between belief and transgression: Structuralist essays in religion, history and myth*, ed. Michael Izard and Pierre Smith (Chicago: University of Chicago Press, 1982); Sahlins, "Captain Cook at Hawaii," *Journal of Polynesian History*, 98 (1989): 371-425. Beaglehole and Smith also believe that Cook was apotheosized by the Hawaiians and have done much to perpetuate the story, though they have different concerns than Sahlins.

56 Obeyesekere, *Apotheosis of Captain Cook*, 14-15. James Boswell met Cook in April 1776 and described him to Dr. Johnson as "a grave steady man." "My metaphor" for him, Boswell recalled in his journal, "was that he had a balance in his mind for truth as nice as scales for weighing a guinea." See Boswell, *The journals of James Boswell, 1760-1795*, selected by John Wain (London: Heinemann, 1991), 296.

The fact that Cook lost his balance, so to speak, on his third voyage and became irrational and violent did not escape other members of British high society, however. Edmund Burke, who was acquainted with some of Cook's officers, noted that James King "loved and honourd Captn Cooke, and never spoke of him but with respect and regret. But he lamented the Roughness of his manners and the violence of his Temper." See J. Marshall and John A. Woods, eds., *The correspondence of Edmund Burke*, vol. 7, *January 1792-August 1794* (Cambridge: Cambridge University Press, 1968), app. 1, "Edmund Burke's character of his son and brother," 589.

57 Obeyesekere argues that Cook had a dual persona, one half of which he calls the "'Prospero' syndrome ... that of the redoubtable person coming from Europe to a savage land, a harbinger of civilization who remains immune to savage ways, maintaining his integrity and identity"; the other half of which he calls the "'Kurtz' syndrome ... the civilizer who loses his identity and goes native and becomes the very savage he despises." He claims that the latter won out over the former on Cook's third voyage. See Obeyesekere, *Apotheosis of Captain Cook*, 11-12.

58 Deborah Bird Rose, "Worshipping Captain Cook," *Social Analysis* 34 (1993): 43-49 (quotation is from 47). Rose's comments are sparked, in part, by her work with Aboriginal peoples in northern Australia, who view Cook as the "quintessential immoral European." For them, Cook stands for a history of destruction and dispossession rather than "listening and talking." By not letting Cook die – in continuing to treat him as a culture hero – White Australians are reproducing structures of White domination. Rose argues that the Hawaiians Cook encountered, like the Aboriginal peoples with whom she works, sought a "balanced intersubjectivity, effectively seeking to bridge the distance between the two groups by bringing others into their own sociality." They expected Cook to reciprocate, but the "attribution of primitive credulity to Hawaiians and innovative superiority to Europeans" ensured that cultural difference and distance was bridged on European terms. See Ibid., 46-47; and Deborah Bird Rose, *Dingo makes us human: Life and land in an Aboriginal Australian culture* (Cambridge: Cambridge University Press, 1992), 186-202.

59 Rose, "Worshipping Captain Cook," 48.

60 Obeyesekere, *Apotheosis of Captain Cook*, 21. This is hardly a novel maneouvre more generally, of course; Weber's ideas permeate many disciplines. But Obeyeskere is one of the first scholars to raise such issues in relation to Cook's voyages.

61 Marshall Sahlins, *How "natives" think: About Captain Cook, for example* (Chicago: University of Chicago Press, 1995).

62 Ibid., 197.

63 See, especially, James Clifford and George Marcus, eds., *Writing culture: The poetics and politics of ethnography* (Berkeley: University of California Press, 1986).

64 Carter, "Violent passages," 85-86.

65 Ibid. Carter does not elaborate such claims, but they have been made by a number of historians and anthropologists. See, especially, Greg Dening, "Sharks that walk on the land," in his *Mr Bligh's bad language: Passion, power and theatre on the Bounty* (Cambridge: Cambridge University Press, Canto Edition, 1994), 159-73.

66 Paul Carter, *The road to Botany Bay: An essay in spatial history* (London: Faber and Faber, 1987), xiii-xxv, 1-33 (quotations are from xxiii, 34, and 28).

67 Indeed, Derek Gregory argues that spatial history cannot recover Aboriginal perspectives because it "fixes its gaze so firmly on the West that it can only catch glimpses of other human beings through a glass, darkly." Carter acknowledges this problem, yet insists that by recovering "the intentional nature" of explorers' appreciation of the world, we "might evoke their historical experience without appropriating it to white ends." Gregory's point is that such an *intense* focus on the intentionality of the White (and usually male) explorer "effaces the inscriptions of power in the jostling, colliding construction of ... different spatialities." See Gregory, *Geographical imaginations*, 179-80; Carter, *Road to Botany Bay*, 350.

68 Carter, *Road to Botany Bay*, xxiii.

69 Australian Aboriginal groups do not share Carter's views. As one Aboriginal leader put it to Bird Rose: "A thousand million years ago / Before I was born / Captain Cook sailed out from big England / And started shooting all my people." Cook never visited Australia's Northern Territory where these narratives were recorded, but Rose insists that they are not myths. "Nit-pickers will quibble about the date and the locality. Tommy Vincent, Hobbles, and all the other men and women whose lives have been so radically transformed by invasion say that from Captain Cook all else follows." See Rose, "Worshipping Captain Cook," 44

70 Beaglehole, *Journals*, III, vii.

Chapter 2: Successful Intercourse Was Had with the Natives?

1 Cook and King, *Voyage to the Pacific Ocean*, II, 265-66.
2 Ibid., 265.
3 Stafford, *Voyage into substance*, 400. Stafford focuses mainly on representations of nature, but similar principles were obviously at work in European representations of people.
4 Ibid., 28.
5 Ibid., 408.
6 Ibid., 421.
7 This passage was also written in the past tense. This did not necessarily imply that observation was rooted in the surveying, perspectival mode of vision and narration that is often associated with retrospection. Many explorers wrote in the first person and used the present tense to emphasize that they had relied on their senses and had not leaned on the crutch of memory. But in effect, all explorers such as Cook had to do to denote first-hand contact and objectivity was to convince their readers that their senses had been fixed on the objects under inspection long enough for them to have made an impression on the mind and be put down on paper. Narrating in the first person could imply that the explorer had not looked long or hard enough; that observation had been conditioned by subjective whim.
8 John Hawkesworth also took many liberties with Cook's descriptions. Cook was mortified by the inaccuracies and distortions in Hawkesworth's account of his first voyage, kept a closer eye on the editing of his journal of his second voyage, and planned to edit the official account of his last voyage himself. See Withey, *Voyages of discovery*.
9 Beaglehole, *Journals*, III, 295.
10 I.S. MacLaren, "Exploration/travel literature and the evolution of the author," *International Journal of Canadian Studies* 5 (1992): 39-68, especially 41-58. For a fuller, if slightly different, treatment of the editing of Cook's journals, see Helen Wallis, "Publication of Cook's journals: Some new sources and assessments," *Pacific Studies* 1, 2 (1978): 163-94.
11 Cook and King, *Voyage to the Pacific Ocean*, I, lxxvii (emphasis in original).
12 Douglas drew extensively on the journal of William Anderson, surgeon and naturalist on the *Resolution*. Unfortunately, Anderson's journal is lost. This mode of comparison culminated in "modern" European discourses of causation. In the late eighteenth century this discourse was shaped by figures such as the Forsters, who sailed on Cook's second voyage. Cook compared the dispositions of indigenous societies in a more rudimentary fashion. When he inscribed "the new," he generally fell back on his recollections and journal rather than on natural history manuals and geography books. Perhaps he did not like "taking on trust," as Beaglehole suggested.
13 Carter, *Road to Botany Bay*, 27.
14 Beaglehole, *Journals*, III, 294-95.
15 A short account of these Spanish expeditions of 1774 and 1775 was published in London in 1776, just before Cook departed on his third voyage, as an appendix to a pamphlet concerning the Northwest Passage. See Warren L. Cook, *Flood tide of empire: Spain and the North west coast, 1543-1819* (New Haven: Yale University Press, 1973), 85.
16 Beaglehole, *Journals*, III, 321-22.
17 Cook and King, *Voyage to the Pacific Ocean*, II, 330-31.
18 Herbert Beals has ascertained that the *Santiago*, piloted by Juan Perez, anchored about ten miles from the entrance to Nootka Sound on 7 August 1774 and stayed in the vicinity for two days. Perez's "diario" states that as his ship got close to land, "canoes began coming out from the land ... but without wanting to come near regardless of how much they were called." See Herbert Beals, *Juan Perez on the northwest coast: Six documents of his expedition in 1774* (Portland: Oregon Historical Society Press, 1989), 88.
   When a launch was lowered into the water to look for an anchorage, the Native canoes around the ship fled, though they soon returned "giving us their advice." As the *Santiago* started to drift south in the wind, more canoes "came within speaking distance" and started trading furs for shells. The accounts of two Roman Catholic priests accompanying Perez give a different view.

One of the priests wrote that Native canoes approached the ship "making gestures that we should go away," though "after some time, we having made signs to them that they should draw near without fear, they did so ... but they could not have been very satisfied with our signs, and went back to land." The other priest gave virtually the same story. See "The Diary of Fray Tomàs de la Peña kept during the voyage of the *Santiago*," document 18 in Donald Cutter, ed., *The California coast: A bilingual edition of documents from the Sutro Collection* trans. and ed. George B. Griffin (Norman: University of Oklahoma Press, 1969 [orig. pub. 1891]), 179. Document 19 is the diary of the other priest, Fray Juan Crespi.

19 Ingraham to Martinez (1789), Mexico City, Archivo General de la Nacion, Ramo, Historia, 65, in the Freeman Tovell Collection, BCARS Add. MSS. 2826. Ingraham was reporting to the Spanish naval commander at Nootka Sound and noted that Native testimony fitted in "every particular" with the description of the *Santiago* he had been given. The Spanish took this as further evidence that they had contacted the Natives of Nootka Sound before Cook. Martínez, who had been with Perez in 1774, took this imperial propaganda one step further by claiming that two Spanish silver spoons that Cook traded from the Natives of the sound had been stolen from him. See Don Esteban José Martínez, "Diary of the voyage ... in the present Year 1789," 81, trans. William L Schurtz, UBCL-SC. The image of fear related by Ingraham was not strictly part of this imperial pitch, however, and might be taken in its own right.

In his collection of Spanish voyages to the Northwest Coast, compiled in 1802, the Spanish naval historian Martin Navarrete argued that the Native account recorded by Ingraham fit better with documents relating to the voyage of Bruno de Hezeta, who was on the Northwest Coast in 1775, than with Perez's voyage. Navarrete thought that by 40 months the Natives meant 40 moons – or 38 months before Cook – which would have placed Hezeta at Nootka Sound. He noted that there was only one officer on Perez's ship with a decorated uniform, whereas in 1775 Hezeta's officers were dressed in "full uniform" to take possession. Furthermore, Navarrete claimed that the two spoons could not have been stolen from Martínez because the Natives did not board the *Santiago*; he suggested that "it was ... Quadra [in 1775] who suffered the loss of the spoons, which the servants said probably had slid down the scupper hole." See Martin F. Navarrete, "Viajes en las costa al norte de las Californias, 1774-1790" (1802), 773-775, trans. George Davidson, Bancroft Library, Berkeley, P-B 26. From Herbert Beals's cautious reconstruction of this 1775 voyage, it seems likely that Hezeta was in the vicinity of Nootka Sound on 11 and 12 June. See Herbert K. Beals, ed., *For honor and country: The diary of Bruno de Hezeta* (Portland OR: Oregon Historical Society, 1985), 81-83. As far as is known, these were the only two European ships that were in the vicinity of Nootka Sound before Cook arrived.

20 Moziño, *Noticias de Nutka*, 66.

21 This account is in Brabant's Miscellaneous papers in BCARS and is printed verbatim in the *B.C. Orphans' Friend* (1913), 81. Peter Webster related a similar story to anthropologists in the 1970s: "I do know [the Spanish ship] was seen south-east side of Estevan Point. This Hesquiat seen something strange out in the open Pacific." When they went to see, "The blocks look[ed] like skulls ... of a dead human .... And this is what they thought it was, dead people that was aboard that ship." See Barbara S. Efrat and W.J. Langlois, eds., "The contact period as recorded by Indian oral tradition," in "nu.tka.: Captain Cook and the Spanish explorers on the coast," *Sound Heritage* 7, 1 (1978): 54-62 (quotation is from 59-60).

22 F.W. Howay and E.O.S. Scholefield, *British Columbia: From the earliest times to the present*, 4 vols. (Vancouver: Clarke, 1914), I, 81-83. According to a Native account heard by Brabant, Cook entered the sound at night or in fog, and his ships were not discovered until they had reached their anchorage on Bligh Island. See Brabant to Walbran, 19 July 1905, Roman Catholic Church, Diocese of Victoria. Papers, 1842-1912, BCARS Add. MSS. 2742.

23 These three account are in Efrat and Langlois, "Contact period," 54-58.

24 These and other Native accounts figured prominently in Native protest over the Cook bicentenary. The West Coast District Council of Chiefs criticized the provincial government for giving the public "a distorted view of Cook's visit" and boycotted its plans to send tourists to the sound.

See "Cook's angry legacy," *Daily Colonist*, 17 January 1978. According to a Native account reported in the *Victoria Times* (8 March 1978), Mowachaht people discovered Cook and his crew flailing around in the fog and in poor health. They rescued him, tended to his sick, and helped to repair his ships. He was asked to leave the sound by Chief Maquinna because his crew were disrespectful to Native women and stole food. The Nootka word for White men, which was derived from this experience with Cook, translates as "people lost at sea."

25 Tate Family Papers, box 1, file 6, BCARS Add. MSS. 303. It should be noted that missionary enthusiasm for recording events of early contact was tied to a politics of conversion. Stories about first contact were used to mark the spiritual gulf between (Native) heathenism and (White) civilization that was to be closed by the missionary. Nevertheless, it seems that this account was proffered by a Native person rather than solicited by Tate. See Tate's amended reminiscence of this account in J.S. Matthews, ed., *Early Vancouver: Narratives of pioneers of Vancouver B.C.*, 2 vols. (Vancouver: Matthews, 1933), II, 130-31.

26 Smithsonian Institution, National Anthropological Archives, MS. No. 4516, Philip Drucker, vol. 2, "The northwest coast: Nootka tribes," Part 23, "Nootka field notebooks, Nos. 11-15," noteboook 12, 19-24, photocopy, BCARS Add. MSS. 870.

27 These accounts are not radically different from other Native accounts of first contact with Whites on other parts of the coast. See Susan Marsden, "Controlling the flow of furs: North-coast nations and the maritime fur trade," paper presented at the BC Studies Conference, 1990.

28 It is exactly these dimensions that Carter's "spatial history" ignores or, in Gregory's view, cannot recover. While Cook tried to detach himself from what was going on around him, we sense in these Native texts that objects from the "outside" were being used by Native interpreters to regulate a world "inside." For a fascinating discussion of symbolic constructions of geographical space, see Mary W. Helms, *Ulysses' sail: An ethnographic odyssey of power, knowledge, and geographical distance* (Princeton: Princeton University Press, 1988).

Drucker did not discuss Muchalat Peter's account in his published ethnography of the Nootka, and his chapter on "religious life" leaves us with few pointers for thinking about these texts. He does discuss the role of the shaman in the interpretation of esoteric knowledge, however, and suggests that the sea harboured fewer perils than the land. See Philip Drucker, *The northern and central Nootkan tribes*, Smithsonian Institution of American Ethnology Bulletin 144 (Washington, DC: US Government Printing Office, 1951), 151-218.

29 Beaglehole, *Journals*, III, 1,088-89.

30 Ibid., 1,393-94.

31 Ibid., 308; also observed in John Rickman, "Log," n.d. PRO ADM 51/4529[46], fol. 217.

32 Beaglehole, *Journals*, III, 304.

33 Edward Riou, "A log of the proceedings of his majesty's ship *Discovery*," Book 2nd, 20 April 1778, PRO ADM 51/4529[42], fol. 78v.

34 Beaglehole, *Journals*, III, 1,350. Thomas Edgar also recorded this event in "A journal of a voyage undertaken to the south seas by his majesty's ships Resolution and Discovery," 4 April 1778, fols. 91-91v, BM Add. MS. 37,528, a partial copy of which was deposited in the provincial library in Victoria, British Columbia, but not until after Drucker had interviewed Muchalat Peter. See Thomas Edgar, "Incomplete journal," 7 March-6 June 1778, BCARS A/A/20/D63E. Some "facts" from the European record may have been smuggled into Native oral histories over the years. It seems unlikely that this event was, however. Beaglehole is the first scholar that I know of who cites either Williamson's or Edgar's observation.

35 These Native accounts relate to Cook rather than to subsequent voyagers, though a few of the cultural emphases in them may point to a more composite set of Native understandings of non-Native strangers synthesized from the first ten or so years of contact. After 1778, however, Nootka Sound was not visited again by Europeans until August 1785, when the brig *Sea Otter* under James Hanna arrived to trade sea otter furs. A few days after Hanna arrived, a Native group in the sound attacked his vessel and was "repulsed [by Hanna] with considerable slaughter." Surely,

the Native accounts that I have presented would have related this slaughter if they were chronicling Hanna's stay; Hanna's actions are recounted in other Native accounts. After 1785, when British and American trading vessels came to Nootka Sound in increasing numbers, the Native peoples of the sound grew increasingly accustomed to non-Natives and knew some vessel captains by name. The quotation about Hanna's voyage is from an English newspaper: London, *World*, 6 October 1788, reprinted in *White Knight chapbooks: North west coast series*, no.4 (San Francisco: White Knight, 1941).

36 In 1778, over fifteen Native groups lived at Nootka Sound, each of which hailed from particular villages and owned specific territories. A number of groups on the west side of the sound were at this time probably allied in a political and economic confederacy. Most of the groups on the east side of the sound were autonomous. See Yvonne Marshall, "A political history of the Nuu-chah-nulth: A case study of the Mowachaht and Muchalaht tribes" (PhD diss., Department of Archaeology, Simon Fraser University, 1993); and Chapter 6.

37 I borrow this phrase, and my title for this chapter, from Tom Dutton's exemplary essay, "'Successful intercourse was had with the natives': Aspects of European contact methods in the Pacific," in *A world of language: Papers presented to Professor S.A. Wurm on his 65th birthday*, ed., Donald C. Laycock and Werner Winter (Pacific Linguistics, C-100, 1987), 153-71.

38 Charles Clerke, "Log and proceedings, 10 February 1776-12 February 1779," 29 March 1778, PRO ADM 55/22, fol. 151.

39 John Law, "On methods of long-distance control: Vessels, navigation and the Portuguese route to India," in *Power, action and belief: A new sociology of knowledge?* ed., John Law (London, Boston and Henley: Routledge and Kegan Paul, 1986), 234-63; and Dening, *Mr. Bligh's bad language*, 113-56.

40 Law, "On methods of long-distance control," 235, 245.

41 This process of amanuensis is most obvious in the case of Williamson and Edgar, but similar expressions, sentences, and paragraphs can be tracked across a number of the journals.

42 F.W. Howay, ed., *Zimmermann's Captain Cook: An account of the third voyage of Captain Cook around the world, 1776-1780* (Toronto: Ryerson, 1930 [orig. German 1781]), 21-22.

43 I have not tried to contextualize these Native texts here (I look at Native agendas in Part 2). I draw on them here to augment the notion that there was a cacophony of voices and perspectives at Nootka Sound in 1778. I will now explore the diversity of statements in the journals of Cook and his officers in more detail.

Chapter 3: Captain Cook and the Spaces of Contact at Nootka Sound

1 Beaglehole, *Journals*, III, 296. Now called "Resolution Cove," on the southern tip of "Clerke Peninsula" on "Bligh Island" in the middle of Nootka Sound.

2 Ibid.

3 Ibid., 1,395. Lieutenant James Burney thought that the ship should have anchored in the cove near the village discovered by King, and he states that Cook did not find his snug cove until the evening. James Burney, "Journal of a voyage in the Discovery," 30 March 1778, PRO ADM 51/4528/45, fol. 224v.

4 Smith, *Imagining the Pacific*, 198-210, especially 202-205. Smith works within the fatal impact thesis: "What Adam Smith's free market economy offered the South Seas was not really the difference between civilisation and savagery but the difference between exploitation and extermination" (209). I do not agree with Smith on this, but his comments about Cook's art program are still useful.

5 Ibid., 206 and 198.

6 Rudiger Joppien and Bernard Smith, *The art of Captain Cook's voyages*, vol. 3: *The voyage of the Resolution and Discovery, 1776-1780*, 2 parts (Melbourne: Oxford University Press, 1987), I, 80-81, II, 433.

7 It is not known exactly when Webber made this sketch, but Joppien and Smith suggest around 6 April. The observation tents on shore were erected on 31 March, by which time the Natives

were boarding the ships. We should perhaps think about this photographic metaphor in relation to Smith's thesis that Cook was "Adam Smith's god," spreading market relations. For as Jonathan Crary argues, "Photography and money become homologous forms of social power in the nineteenth century. They are equally totalizing systems for binding and unifying all subjects within a single global network of valuation and desire." Smith's and Joppien's use of the metaphor is perhaps more innocent than this, but Smith nevertheless sees Cook as one of the instigators of this global network. See Jonathan Crary, *Techniques of the observer: On vision and modernity in the nineteenth century* (Cambridge USA and London UK: MIT Press, 1990), 13.

8   Beaglehole, *Journals*, III, 297.
9   Ibid., 297-98, 1,395. Other officers noted the same.
10   Ibid., 1,090.
11   He noted that "our first friends ... seemed determined to ingross us intirely to themselves." Ibid., 299.
12   Burney, "Journal," 4 April 1778, fol. 227.
13   Beaglehole, *Journals*, III, 1,397.
14   Christine Holmes, ed., *Captain Cook's final voyage: The journal of midshipman George Gilbert* (Horsham: Caliban, 1982), 70.
15   Beaglehole, *Journals*, III, 1,092-93.
16   Ibid., 1,093.
17   Clerke, "Log and proceedings," 4 April 1778, fol. 152.
18   Riou, "Log," April 1778, fol. 77. Cook noted as much later in his stay: "the very wood and water we took on board they at first wanted us to pay for, and we had certainly done it [sic], had I been upon the spot when the demands were made; but as I never happened to be there the workmen took but little notice of their importunities." Beaglehole, *Journals*, III, 306.
19   Beaglehole, *Journals*, III, 1,094. This could be the same incident that Burney reported on 1 April: "Journal," fol. 226v.
20   William Bayly, "Journals and a log kept on Capt. Cook's second and third voyages around the world," 2nd. journal, 4 April 1778, fol. 92., Alexander Turnbull Library, National Library of New Zealand.
21   Nathaniel Portlock, "Log, November 1 1777-May 21 1778," 4 April 1778, PRO ADM 51/4531 [68], fol. 293v.
22   See Beaglehole, *Journals*, III, 1,094 and 1,398.
23   Riou, "Log," 5 April 1778, fols. 77v-78; Edgar, "Log," 5 April 1778, fol. 150.
24   In his entry for 4 April, Cook states that he witnessed Native territorial rivalries "on other occasions," suggesting that his version of this event was polished much later in his stay.
25   John Webber, "A view in ship cove," BM Add. MS. 17,277.
26   Beaglehole, *Journals*, III, 299.
27   See Riou, "Log," April 1778, fol. 77v-78, who noted that "in their harangues ... [these competing groups] frequently held up a large Tin Kettle, a Commodity they are exceedingly fond of."
28   Beaglehole, *Journals*, III, 306.
29   Ibid., 315.
30   Portlock was convinced that it was simply the sight of the ships that had scared the strangers away. See Portlock, "Log," 4 April 1778, fol. 294.
31   Beaglehole, *Journals*, III, 1,093 and 1,100.
32   Portlock, "Log," 4 April 1778, fol. 293v.
33   Burney, "Journal," 4 April 1778, fol. 227.
34   Riou, "Log," 4 April 1778, fol. 80v. Clerke also noted that they "did not think [it] proper to knock one another on the head." See Clerke, "Log and proceedings," 4 April 1778, fol. 152.
35   James Trevenan, "Notes regarding the death of Captain Cook," 3, BCARS A/A/40/C77T/A2.
36   William Bayly, "A log and journal kept on board his majesty's sloop Discovery," PRO ADM 55/20, fol. 115.
37   Beaglehole, *Journals*, III, 1,400-401.
38   Ibid., 1326-1327.

39 Burney, "Journal," 8 April 1778, fols. 227v-228.
40 This distinction is most marked in the journals of Cook, Bayly, and King. Beaglehole height-
    ened the scientific pretense of Cook's "manners-and-customs" descriptions by inserting sub-
    headings and annotating his remarks using botanical and zoological systems of classification.
    The distinction is less obvious in the journals of most of Cook's officers. Logs of daily events
    often blur into more general descriptions of "manners and customs."
41 In his discussion of Cook, Paul Carter makes a trenchant distinction between botany and geog-
    raphy. The former was part of the Enlightenment project of universal knowledge – the reduc-
    tion of diversity to "a uniform and universally valid taxonomy." He associates geography with
    Hume's critique of rationalism and Cook's open-ended way of exploring. What informs repre-
    sentational practices at Nootka Sound is a tension, not a division, between reason and experi-
    ence – between these universalizing and particularizing currents of Enlightenment thought. See
    Carter, *Road to Botany Bay*, 18.
42 The logs and journals of Cook's officers vary enormously in length and insight. Some logs focus
    almost entirely on the shipboard activities of Cook's crews and scarcely mention Native people.
    See, for example, Anon., "A log of the proceedings of the Discovery, 29 November-28 December
    1778," 2nd. journal, PRO ADM 51/4530. Cook's senior officers, and some of his aspiring junior
    officers, were the keenest observers.
43 This quotation is from Terry Eagleton, *The ideology of the aesthetic* (Oxford: Basil Blackwell,
    1990), 32.
44 Ibid., 32-33 and passim. Eagleton *does* think of this prototypical public sphere as masculine.
45 Ibid., 34.
46 Ibid.
47 John Barrell, *English literature in history, 1730-80: An equal, wide view* (New York: St. Martin's,
    1983), 108.
48 Ibid., 109.
49 Boswell, *Journals of James Boswell*, 306-307.
50 At Nootka Sound, Cook stated: "Of the Government and Riligion [sic] of these people, it can-
    not be supposed we could learn much." Beaglehole, *Journals*, III, 322.
51 Bayly, "Journals," 2nd., n.d., fol. 102. And, as I argued above, Cook's officers leaned on each
    other for information.
52 Pratt, *Imerial eyes*, 1-37.
53 See Lisa Lowe, *Critical terrains: French and British orientalisms* (Ithaca: Cornell University Press,
    1992). Anglo-European cultural antagonism can be detected in Douglas's remarks on the
    Nootkans' complexion. Cook noted that their colour was not "alltogether natural" because the
    men and women painted their faces and were covered with dirt and grease; but when washed,
    Bayly remarked, they were "as fair as any European." Douglas embellished this by stating that
    "the whiteness of the skin appeared almost to equal that of Europeans; though rather of that
    pale effete cast which distinguishes those of our Southern nations." He tried to diffuse the im-
    pression he may have got from Cook's journal that "the Nootkans" did not look on their visitors
    as superior by claiming that these people resembled effete Europeans rather than robust Eng-
    lishmen. This was a common trope in British writing and art at this time. Colley shows that the
    British represented Roman Catholic Europeans as "impoverished, downtrodden, credulous, and
    even somehow unmanly." See Beaglehole, *Journals*, III, 311; Bayly, "Log," n.d, fol. 115; Cook and
    King, *Voyage to the Pacific Ocean*, II, 303; Colley, *Britons*, 35-36.
54 Adam Smith tackled this moral conundrum in *The wealth of nations*, as I will note in Part II.
    Pratt does not discuss Cook's voyages. Cook may have constructed "pacific people" and charted
    commercial possibilities, but he did not assume the neutrality of the ground everywhere he
    went. And I am not sure that scientific exploration can be modelled either on the project of
    natural history or on Foucault's arguments about classification, which Pratt works with. The
    project of natural history, as Foucault represented it, did not produce the world *to* or *for* the
    bourgeois subject in any direct sense. Foucault described this project as "a fundamental ar-

rangement of knowledge, which orders the knowledge of beings so as to make it possible to represent them in a system of names" – as one facet of a broader classical episteme. In any case, on Foucault's account, the bourgeois subject, as Pratt understands him, was not "born" until the nineteenth century. It should also be noted that Foucault's discussion of the classical episteme is Eurocentric and, as Edward Said has suggested, should not be invoked as the only discursive order (or ontological mechanism) of European engagement with the wider world in the eighteenth century. See Michel Foucault, *The order of things: An archaeology of the human sciences* (New York: Random, 1970 [orig. pub. 1966]), 157-160; Said, *Orientalism*, chap. 2.

55 Trevenan noted that the short "excursions" Cook led into Nootka Sound offered a welcome relief from the discipline of ship life, and he added: "Captain Cook also on these occasions would sometimes relax from his almost constant severity of disposition and condescended now and then to converse familiarly with us." See Christopher Lloyd and R.C. Anderson, eds., *A memoir of James Trevenan* (London: Navy Records Society, 1959), 20.

56 For an argument along these lines, see Jonathan Lamb, "Minute particulars and the representation of South Pacific discovery," *Eighteenth-Century Studies* 28, 3 (1995): 281-94. See also Deborah Poole, *Vision, race and modernity: A visual economy of the Andean image world* (Princeton: Princeton University Press, 1997), who argues that eighteenth-century French and Spanish descriptions of the Incas "reveal an embodied discourse of encounter and sensory perception ... [wherein] the body (or nervous system) rather than the eye alone ... provided the sensory contact between the self and the world, the self and the other" (37-38). If we are to seek a collective European discourse of encounter during the eighteenth century, then I suspect that issues of embodiment need to be taken seriously. Pratt, of course, focuses on the second half of the eighteenth century.

57 Beaglehole, *Journals*, III, 1,406-407.

58 Eagleton, *Ideology of the aesthetic*, 70 (his emphasis).

59 Ibid., 70-71.

60 Ibid., 72

61 Harriet Guest, "Curiously masked: Tattooing, masculinity, and nationality in eighteenth-century perceptions of the south Pacific," in *Painting and the politics of culture: New essays on British art, 1700-1850*, ed. John Barrell (Oxford and New York: Oxford University Press, 1992), 101-34 (quotation is from 105). Samuel Johnson remarked that "everything abstract – [Native] politicks, morals, and religion" in European accounts of the Pacific was "darkly guessed," and he was ambivalent about whether one could come to any definitive understanding of the non-European world with one's senses. But James Boswell, inspired by Cook's voyages, still admitted that he was "carried away with the general grand and indistinct notion of A VOYAGE ROUND THE WORLD." Johnson, quoted in Chester Chapin, "Samuel Johnson, anthropologist," *Eighteenth-Century Life*, 19 (November 1995): 22-37. Boswell, in *Boswell's life of Johnson*, vol. 3: *1776-1780*, ed. George Birkbeck Hill and L.F. Powell (Oxford: Clarendon, 1971), 7. The irony in Johnson's remark is that he had shown interest in going on Cook's second voyage but could not do so because of his short-sightedness! Instead, he and Boswell went on a tour of the Hebrides, which Pat Rogers interprets "as a prolonged replay of Cook's first voyage." Johnson set out "to conduct a limited expedition along the lines of Sir Joseph Banks." See Pat Rogers, "The noblest savage of them all: Johnson, Omai, and other primitives," in *The age of Johnson: A scholarly annual*, vol. 5, ed. Paul J. Korshin (New York: AMS Press, 1992), 281-302 (quotations are from 282 and 288).

62 Thomas, *Entangled objects*, 130 and 127. For a more thorough discussion of the complexity and ambuity of "curiosity" in seventeenth- and eighteenth-century European thought, see Lorraine Daston, "Curiosity in the early modern period," *World and Image* 11, no.4 (1995): 391-404.

63 Ibid., 127-29.

64 At Nootka Sound, many of the objects brought for trade by the Natives were called "curiosities," and Cook noted that "such was the passion for these things among our people that they always came to a good Market whether they were of any value or no[t]." Beaglehole, *Journals*, III, 302.

65 Edgar, "Journal," n.d., fol. 95.
66 Riou, "Log," 30 March 1778, fol. 76.
67 Beaglehole, *Journals*, III, 1,088.
68 Ibid., 1,091.
69 King, for instance, noted that the "Nootkans" would not part with their knives. Ibid., 1,396.
70 Thomas, *Entangled objects*, 137.
71 Ibid., 139.
72 See Outram, *The Enlightenment*; and Thomas, *Colonialism's culture*, 101-103.
73 For a good overview of the place of cannibalism in colonial discourse, and the theoretical issues it raises, see the debate between Peter Hulme and Myra Jehlen in *Critical Inquiry* 20, 1 (Autumn 1993): 179-91. On the way cannibalism was defined in Cook's voyages, see Gananath Obeyesekere, "'British Cannibals': Contemplation of an event in the death and resurrection of James Cook, explorer," *Critical Inquiry* 18, 4 (1992): 630-54.
    At Nootka Sound, Cook and his officers were offered human hands and skulls for sale, and they debated whether the Nootkans were cannibals. Williamson summarizes the course of their enquiries: "A notion for some time prevailed amongst us that these people were cannibals, from their several times bringing Skulls & hands to sell, which had much the appearance of having been roasted or boiled ... but a convincing proof I had this morning of the fallacy of our notions, made it evident we did not understand each other; a Man having come to me at my Landing, with some hands, I bought one of them, and then desired him to eat it, which he refused to do. I then offered him some Iron & Brass ... if he would eat part of it, but all those offers he treated with great contempt, & departed in a rage; yet many Gents in the two Ships remain prepossess'd in their first notion." See John Williamson, "Log of the proceedings of the Reslolution," 25 April 1778, PRO ADM 55/117, fol. 100. And see Beaglehole, *Journals*, III, 297. Recalling the Native account recorded by Tate, it is possible that these Nootkans thought that Cook's crew were cannibals, which is why they supplied them with human flesh.
74 Thomas, *Entangled objects*, 151-84.
75 Beaglehole, *Journals*, III, 1,323.
76 Ibid., 296-297. Douglas retained both of Cook's phrases. Cook and King, *Voyage to the Pacific Ocean*, II, 270-71.
77 Beaglehole, *Journals*, III, 312.
78 Ibid., 303.
79 Ibid., 301.
80 Bayly, "Journals," 2nd, n.d., fol. 111.
81 Riou, "Log," n.d., fol. 80v.
82 See Beaglehole, *The life*; and Dutton, "'Successful intercourse was had with the natives,'" for discussions of this issue.
83 See Dening, *Mr. Bligh's bad language*, for a rigorous discussion of Bligh's policies, which he picked up from Cook.
84 Beaglehole, *Journals*, III, 1408.
85 Riou, "Log," 1 April 1778, fol. 77.
86 Trevenan, *Memoir*, 20.
87 Beaglehole, *Journals*, III, 1,407.
88 Dening, *Islands and beaches*, 18.
89 Margaret Hunt, "Racism, imperialism, and the traveller's gaze in eighteenth-century England," *Journal of British Studies* 32 (October 1993): 333-57. And see E.P. Thompson, *Customs in common: Studies in traditional popular culture* (New York: New Press, 1993), chaps. 3-5.
90 Samwell reported on such matters in detail. See Beaglehole, *Journals*, III, 1,095.
91 Bridget Orr, "'Southern passions mix with northern art': Miscegenation and the *Endeavour* voyage," *Eighteenth-Century Life* (n.s.) 18, 3 (1994): 212-31 (quotations are from 225-26).
92 Burney, "Journal," 4 April 1778, fol. 227.
93 Williamson, "Log," 25 April 1778, fol. 100. Edgar wrote the same. And see Bayly, "Journals," 2nd, n.d., fol. 95.

94 Bayly, "Journals," 2nd., n.d. and 3 April 1778, fols. 115, 91, and 116.
95 Beaglehole, *Journals*, III, 1095.
96 Riou, "Log," n.d., fol. 80v.
97 Gregory, *Geographical imaginations*, 131.
98 Alan Bewell, "Constructed places, constructed peoples: Charting the improvement of the female body in the Pacific," *Eighteenth-Century life* (n.s.) 18, 3 (1994): 37-54 (quotation is from 52).
99 Ibid.
100 Smith, *Imagining the Pacific*, 210.
101 See Clerke, "Log and proceedings," 29 March 1778, fol. 151.
102 Bewell, "Constructed places, constructed people," 38.
103 For a different – and perceptive – set of observations about gender and sexuality at Nootka Sound, see Noel Elizabeth Currie, "Captain Cook at Nootka Sound and some questions of colonial discourse" (PhD diss., Department of English, University of British Columbia, 1994).
104 MacLaren, "Exploration/travel literature," 46-56.
105 Beaglehole, *Journals*, III, 306.
106 Cook and King, *Voyage to the Pacific Ocean*, II, 283-84.
107 MacLaren, "Exploration/travel literature," 48.
108 Ibid., 48-49
109 Beaglehole, *Journals*, III, 306.
110 Carter, *Road to Botany Bay*, xxiv.

Chapter 4: Cook Books

1 Bancroft simply noted that Cook gave "an extended and accurate description" of Nootka Sound. See H.H. Bancroft, *History of the northwest coast*, vol. 1: *1543-1800* (San Francisco: A.L. Bancroft, 1884), 171; Alexander Begg C.C., *History of British Columbia: From its earliest discovery to the present time* (Toronto: William Briggs, 1894), 19-20. In his *History of British Columbia, 1792-1887* (1887), Bancroft discussed the life and character of Northwest Coast Native peoples in a chapter on the natural environment. In a handwritten "plan" for this *History*, he noted that he would start with the American, British, and Canadian land-based fur trade companies on the coast in the early 1800s. He came to Victoria in the 1880s to gather information from many old fur traders and colonial officials (and retrieved the private papers of Sir James Douglas), leaving with over 4,000 manuscript pages. See Hubert Howe Bancroft, "Miscellaneous Papers," BCARS E/C/B22.3.
2 The explorations of Alexander Mackenzie and Simon Fraser; George Vancouver's circumnavigation of Vancouver Island (1792); Britain's tussle with Spain over Nootka Sound (1790); the creation of the colonies of Vancouver Island (1849) and British Columbia (1858); the gold rush of 1858; and British Columbia's Confederation with Canada (1871).
3 Allan Smith, "The writing of British Columbia history," *BC Studies* 45 (1980): 73-102 (quotations are from 74-75).
4 *Daily Colonist*, 15 August 1924.
5 F.W. Howay, "Two memorable landmarks of British Columbia," *The historic landmarks of Canada, annual report* (1921), 28-30 (quotation is from 29).
6 *Calgary Albertan*, 13 May 1926, clipping in Howay Papers, box 18, folder 2.
7 Walter N. Sage, "Towards new horizons in Canadian history," *Pacific Historical Review* 7, 1 (1939): 47-57 (quotation is from 51-52).
8 Terry Goldie, *Fear and temptation: The image of the indigene in Canadian, Australian, and New Zealand literatures* (Montreal: McGill-Queen's University Press, 1989), 13.
9 Ibid.
10 Ibid., and passim.
11 Howay and Scholefield, *British Columbia*, I, 92.
12 The only work I know of that deals with Nootka Sound during this period, Marshall's "Political history of the Nuu-chah-nulth," is silent on this matter.

Ironically, in the 1950s Sage chastised British Columbia's early historians for neglecting the history of Native peoples. See W.N. Sage, "Some early historians of British Columbia," *British Columbia Historical Quarterly* (hereafter *BCHQ*) 21, 1 (1958): 1-14.

13 *Daily Colonist*, 13 August 1924. See R.E. Gosnell, *The year book of British Columbia and manual of provincial information* (Victoria, 1903), 18: "The village [Yuquot] is the same, the houses are the same, and the people are the same [as 107 years ago] ... the latter still wrapped in blankets and still governed by a descendent of old King Maquinna."

14 See R.M. Galois, "The Indian Rights Association, Native protest activity and the 'land question' in British Columbia, 1903-1916," *Native Studies Review* 8, 2 (1992): 1-34; Douglas Cole and Ira Chaikin, "'A worse than useless custom': The potlatch law and Indian Resistance," *Western Legal History* 5, 2 (1992): 187-216; Paul Tennant, *Aboriginal people and politics: The Indian land question in British Columbia, 1849-1989* (Vancouver: UBC Press, 1990), chaps. 7 and 8.

15 Sproat to Schoefield, [1908?], G.M. Sproat Papers, file 6, BCARS Add. MSS. 257; Scholefield to Howay, 2 August 1911, Howay Papers, box 6, folder 7.

16 Sproat to Minister of the Interior, "Memorandum on Indian Affairs," February 1876, Sproat Papers, file 15.

17 Said, *Culture and imperialism*.

18 Michel Foucault, "Nietzsche, genealogy, history," in his *Language, counter-memory, practice: Selected essays and interviews*, ed. D. Bouchard (Ithaca, NY: Cornell University Press, 1977), 139-64 (quotation is from 153-54).

19 Carter, *Road to Botany Bay*, xx.

20 The details in this paragraph are recorded in Sage, "Trip to Nootka Sound," August 1924, Sage Papers, box 31, file 6.

21 Michel Foucault, "What is an author," in *Language, counter-memory, practice*, 113-38 (quotation is from 134).

22 Howay to Hankin, 4 September 1923, Howay Papers, box 8, folder 2.

23 F.W. Howay, *British Columbia: The making of a province* (Toronto: Ryerson, 1928), 1.

24 F.W. Howay, "The earliest pages of the history of British Columbia," *First Annual Report of the British Columbia Historical Association*, 1923, 12-22 (quotation is from 17).

25 Howay to Newcombe, 29 August 1924, Newcombe Family Papers, vol. 4, file 82, BCARS Add. MSS. 1077.

26 Howay, "Historical research," 17.

27 Stephen Greenblatt, *Marvellous possessions: The wonder of the New World* (Chicago: University of Chicago Press, 1991), 122.

28 F.W. Howay, "The fur trade in northwestern development," in *The Pacific Ocean in history*, ed. H. Morse Stevens and Herbert E. Bolton (New York: Macmillan, 1917), 276-86 (quotation is from 276).

29 Ibid., 286.

30 Howay, *British Columbia*, 8.

31 Gilbert Malcolm Sproat, *The Nootka: Scenes and studies of savage life* [1868], ed. Charles Lillard (Victoria: Sono Nis, 1987), 183.

32 H.H. Bancroft, *The works of Hubery Howe Bancroft*, vol. 32: *History of British Columbia 1792-1887* (San Francisco: History Company, 1887), 46.

33 This quotation is from the inscription on an obelisk laid in Cook's honour in Easby in 1827, which illustrates *Souvenir of the Bi-centenary celebrations arranged in the Cleveland district* (Middlesborough: Sanbride, 1928).

34 His personal library now forms the core of the Special Collections Division of the University of British Columbia Library.

35 He appealed to the public through the press. See, for expample, *Kamloops Centinel*, March 1894.

36 Helmcken to Gosnell, 29 November 1911, J.S. Helmcken Papers, vol. 2, file 41, BCARS Add. MSS. 505.

37 Gosnell to Howay, 20 October 1923, Howay Papers, box 3, folder 15.

38 See Sage, "Some early historians of British Columbia," 10-13.

39 Terry Eastwood, "R.E. Gosnell, E.O.S. Scholefield and the founding of the provincial archives of British Columbia, 1894-1919," *BC Studies* 54 (1982): 38-62 (quotation is from 61-62).

40 Thomas Richards, "Archive and utopia," *Representations* 37 (1992): 104-35 (quotation is from 107).

41 Howay, "Historical research in British Columbia," 9, Howay Papers, box 5, folder 15. In 1924, John Hosie, the provincial librarian, informed Howay that "no effort has ever been made to find out whether the logs deposited by Capt Cook are still to be had." The only log Hosie had was Samwell's, in French. Howay to Hosie, 11 September 1926; Hosie to Howay, 16 September 1926, Howay Papers, box 8, folder 8, and box 46 – addendum no. 8.

42 Sage, "Some early historians of British Columbia," 11-13.

43 Scholefield to Howay, 5 October 1911, Howay Papers, box 6, folder 8.

44 Bhabha, *The location of culture*, 246 (his emphasis).

45 *Victoria Times*, 8 February and 2 March 1978.

46 Ibid., 9 March 1978.

47 Ibid.

48 *Daily Colonist*, 22 February 1978.

49 Ibid., 28 January 1978.

50 Ibid., 11 May 1978.

51 Ibid., 17 January 1978.

52 Fisher and Johnston, *Captain James Cook and his times*, 4.

53 Ibid., 84.

54 Fisher, *Contact and conflict*, 74-75.

55 *Vancouver Sun*, 13 August 1993.

56 These quotations are from *Delgamuukw et al. v. The Queen*, "Reasons for judgement," 49, 17-20, 48-50, and 13.

Chapter 5: Histories, Genealogies, and Spaces of the Other

1 The quotation is from Howay, "Historical research," 17.

2 Appadurai, *Modernity at large*, 74.

3 Dening, *Performances*, 109-10; Walter Benjamin, *Illuminations* (New York: Schocken, 1969).

4 Foucault, "Nietzsche, genealogy, history," 142.

Part 2: Introduction

1 Burney, "Journal," 25 April [sic] 1778, fol. 230.

2 Rickman, "Log," n.d., fol. 217; Bayly, "Journals and a log," 2, fol. 127.

3 Beaglehole, *Journals*, 307-308.

4 James Hanna, "Brig Sea Otter from Macao towards America through the Pacific Ocean," 9 August 1785, BCARS A/A/20.5 Se1H. This, probably a fair copy of a log kept by Hanna, stops when the *Sea Otter* reaches Nootka Sound. For details and background on Hanna's two trading voyages see W. Kaye Lamb and Tomas Bartroli, "James Hanna and John Henry Cox: The first maritime fur trader and his sponsor," *BC Studies* 84 (Winter 1989-90): 3-36.

5 London, *Daily Universal Register*, 21 August 1787, reprinted in Bob Galois, "The voyage of James Hanna to the northwest coast: Two documents," *BC Studies* 103 (Fall 1994): 83-88, at 86.

6 London, *World*, 6 October 1788, reprinted in *White knight chapbooks: Pacific northwest series*, no.4 (San Francisco: White Knight, 1941), n.p.; Lamb and Bartoli, "James Hanna and John Henry Cox," 7-8.

7 Robin Fisher and J.M. Bumstead, eds., *An account of a voyage to the northwest coast of America in 1785 and 1786 by Alexander Walker* (Vancouver/Seattle: Douglas and McIntyre/University of Washington Press, 1982), 199-200. Hereafter cited as Walker.

8 In the official account of Cook's voyage Douglas pumped up this event into an encounter between unequals, with Cook bestowing presents on the chief.

9 See Lamb and Bartoli, "James Hanna and John Henry Cox," for details. The London newspapers were obviously interested in Hanna's voyage, as it was the first British trading expedition to the coast.

10 Some of the earliest British traders on the coast claimed that trade and exploration were joint aims, mainly to attract investors and public attention and to court state patronage. Nevertheless, John Meares, one such trader, noted that, on balance, he had conducted "Voyages of COMMERCE, and not of DISCOVERY." John Meares, *Voyages made in the years 1788 and 1789, from China to the north west coast of America* ... (London: Logographic Press, 1790), v-vi.

11 "Robert's Haswell's log of the first voyage of the 'Columbia,'" in *Voyages of the "Columbia" to the Northwest Coast, 1787-1790 and 1790-1793*, ed., Frederic W. Howay (Portland: Oregon Historical Society and the Massachusetts Historical Society, 1990 [orig. pub. 1941]), 29.

12 Marshall Sahlins, "Goodbye to *tristes tropes*: Ethnography in the context of modern world history," *Journal of Modern World History* 65 (1993): 1-25 (quotation is from 2).

Chapter 6: The Conflictual Economy of Truth of the Maritime Fur Trade

1 William Bligh, *A voyage to the South Seas ... in his majesty's ship the Bounty* (London: G. Nicol, 1792), 7.

2 Harlow, *The founding of the second British Empire*. The most important critiques of Harlow's thesis are: Peter J. Marshall, "The first and second British Empires: A question of demarcation," *History* 49 (1964): 13-23; and D.L. Mackay, "Direction and purpose in British imperial policy, 1783-1801," *Historical Journal* 17, 3 (1974): 487-501.

3 See H.V. Bowen, "British conceptions of global empire, 1756-83," *Journal of Imperial and Commonwealth History* 26, 3 (1998): 1-27.

4 See Alan Frost, "Nootka Sound and the beginnings of Britain's imperialism of free trade," in *From maps to metaphors: The Pacific world of George of Vancouver*, ed. Robin Fisher and Hugh Johnston (Vancouver: UBC Press, 1993), 104-26; Mackay, *In the wake of Cook*; Margaret Steven, *Trade, tactics and territory: Britain in the Pacific, 1783-1823* (Victoria: Melbourne University Press, 1983); and Glyndwr Williams, "The Pacific: Exploration and exploitation," in *The Oxford History of the British Empire*, vol. 2: *The eighteenth century*, ed. P.J. Marshall (Oxford: Oxford University Press, 1998), 552-75. See also below, Part 3.

5 Mackay, *In the wake of Cook*, 192.

6 See Robin Blackburn, *The making of New World slavery: From the baroque to the modern, 1492-1800* (London: Verso, 1997).

7 C.A. Bayly, *Imperial meridian: The British Empire and the world, 1780-1830* (London: Longman, 1989), 252.

8 Ibid., 2, and see his "The first age of global imperialism," *Journal of Imperial and Commonwealth History* 26, 3 (1998): 28-47.

9 Kathleen Wilson, "The good, the bad, and the impotent: Imperialism and the politics of identity in Georgian England," in *The consumption of culture, 1600-1800*, ed. Ann Bermingham and John Brewer (London: Routledge, 1995), 237-62 (quotation is from 254). And see Colley, *Britons*, 132-94.

10 Malachy Postlethwayt, *The universal dictionary of trade and commerce* ... 5 vols. (London: 1771), II, 10.

11 Cook and King, *Voyage to the Pacific Ocean*, III, 437-40. King jotted a plan for prosecuting a fur trade between Canton and the Northwest Coast. Cook himself noted that a lucrative trade in sea otter skins might be developed, though he doubted that Britain would profit by it greatly unless a Northwest Passage was discovered. See ibid., III, 401-402. On the various British scenarios entertained for establishing a sea otter trade from London and India, see B.M. Gough, "India-based expeditions of trade and discovery in the north Pacific in the late eighteenth century," *Geographical Journal* 155, 2 (1989): 215-23.

12 See John Ledyard, *A journal of Captain Cook's last voyage to the Pacific Ocean ... in the years 1776, 1777, 1778, and 1779* (Chicago: Quadrangle, 1963 [orig. pub. 1783]), 70: "Skins which did not cost the purchaser sixpence sterling sold in China for 100 dollars."

13 The most recent and detailed – if largely descriptive – account of the trade is James R. Gibson's *Otter skins, Boston ships, and China goods: The maritime fur trade of the northwest coast, 1785-1841* (Montreal: McGill-Queen's University Press, 1992), table 1, 299-310, provides the definitive list of the number of trading vessels on the coast between 1785 and 1841.

14 The licensing powers of the EEIC were reduced in 1793 and 1802, but it was not until 1833 that traders could sail from Canton to the North Pacific without a licence from the company.

15 See Fernand Braudel, *Civilization and capitalism 15th-18th century,* vol. 3: *The perspective of the world,* trans. Sian Reynolds (New York: Perennial Library Edition, 1986 [orig. pub. 1979]), 523 and passim.

16 These arrangements can be tracked in Great Britain – India Office. Factory Records (China), volumes 86-94, BCARS GR 333. Some British traders complained about them quite bitterly (see, for example, vol. 89, 104, and vol. 94, 61). The company confirmed its position in 1791, declaring (1) that maritime fur trade vessels were not allowed to import any European goods into Canton and could only sell their furs at Canton; (2) that at Canton these vessels should be subject to the orders of the supercargoes of the company; (3) that on their return to Britain they were not to freight Asian goods, except those on the account of the company; and (4) that the company would receive from these vessels any bullion money in exchange for bills of exchange to be drawn on the company treasury in London. See "Opinion of the select committee appointed by the court of directors of the East India Company," 10 March 1791, PRO BT 6/227.

Braudel described the English and Dutch Indies companies as states both within and beyond European states. Company officials "did battle with their shareholders, creating a form of capitalism at odds with traditional [British and southeast Asian] trading practices," but they had "to keep an eye ... on several foreign markets and relate these to the possibilities and advantages of their national market." These companies established trading posts and factories at main crossroads of indigenous trade such as Batavia, Bombay, Macao, Madras, and Surat, and they tied regional economies to a global network of economic flows. See Braudel, *Capitalism and civilization,* III, 494-95.

In the 1760s and 1770s the EEIC looked for more bases in southeast Asia in order to consolidate its China trade, to reduce its trade deficit with Asia, and to subsidize the cost of British rule in India. During the eighteenth century independent traders played an increasingly important role in this mercantilist world economy. By the 1770s, nearly three-quarters of the British and Indian goods exported to China were being delivered by private or "country" traders licensed by the EEIC. See P.J. Marshall, *East India fortunes: The British in Bengal in the eighteenth century* (Oxford: Clarendon, 1976).

17 See Mary Malloy, "'Boston men' on the northwest coast: Commerce, collecting, and cultural perceptions in the American maritime fur trade, 1788-1844' (PhD diss. Brown University, 1994), 80-82. The sea otter trade became part of a much broader American commercial interest in Asia. See Herman E. Kross and Charles Gilbert, *American business history* (Englewood Cliffs, NJ: Prentice-Hall, 1972). The sea otter trade never constituted more than 10 perdent of the United States's foreign commerce, however. See Gibson, *Otter skins, Boston ships, and China goods,* 292 ff.

18 Since this last leg of the sea otter trade was often the most lucrative, American traders initially had an advantage over the British. After 1793, however, many British traders based themselves in China in order to sidestep the company's control over British imports from China. And by the 1790s, traders were wintering on the Northwest Coast or on the Hawaiian Islands in order to reduce the number of months they spent at sea, to spare wear and tear on their vessels, and to be the first in the commercial fray the following season.

For a sense of American commercial optimism during this period, and the implications of American trade for the British, see "Letters of Phineas Bond, British Consul at Philadelphia, to the Forein Office of Great Britain, 1787, 1788, 1789," *Annual Report of the American Historical Association for the Year 1896,* 2 vols., I, 513-659.

19 See Gibson, *Otter skins, Boston ships, and China goods,* chaps. 6 and 8.

20 For example, a British plan for establishing a sea otter trade, discussed by the EEIC's court of directors in 1785, stated that trade vessels should "be laden entirely with such produce and manufactory of this country that will tempt the natives on the islands and the coast of America to barter for their produce which chiefly consists of furs." "Additional proposals relative to the establishing a trade between the north west coast of America and the coast of Asia ... ," in *British colonial developments 1774-1834: Select documents*, ed. Vincent Harlow and Frederick Madden (Oxford: Clarendon, 1953), 23.

21 Argonaut [John Cadman Etches], *An authentic statement of the facts relative to Nootka Sound ... in an address to the King* (London: Debrett, 1790), 17-18.

22 Thomas, *Entangled objects*, 84-85.

23 Ibid., 84.

24 Eve Kornfeld, "Encountering 'the Other': American intellectuals and Indians in the 1790s," *William and Mary Quarterly* (3rd. ser.) 52, 2 (1995): 287-314 (quotation is from 290-91).

25 Mary Malloy, "The northwest coast voyage in American literature" (1992), UBCL-SC. Malloy discusses Cooper's novel *Afloat and Ashore* (1844), which centres on the trading adventures of Miles Wallingford between the Northwest Coast and China in the brig *Crisis*, and she notes that Herman Melville's *Typee* (1846) draws on the texts of a number of British explorers.

26 "John Hoskins' narrative of the second voyage of the 'Columbia,'" in Howay, *Voyages of the "Columbia*," 262.

27 Among the first traders on the coast: James Colnett, George Dixon, and Nathaniel Portlock had sailed with Cook. The American trader William Sturgis, who was on the coast in the 1790s, became a promient Boston merchant and financier of the sea otter trade. R. David Coolidge came to the coast as first-mate of the *Washington* in 1788 before commanding the trading schooner *Grace* in the early 1790s. Joseph Ingraham and John Boit, who apprenticed on the coast as mates on the *Columbia*, returned in the 1790s in command of trading expeditions. An American trader noted that Captain John Kendrick – the first American trader on the coast – "taught many of his countrymen the way to wealth, and the method of navigating distant seas with ease and safety." See Amasa Delano, *A narrative of voyages and travels ... comprising three voyages round the world ...* (Boston: E.G. House, 1817), 400.

28 "John Hoskins' narrative of the second voyage of the 'Columbia,'" in Howay, *Voyages of the "Columbia*," 232.

29 Marcus Rediker, *Between the devil and the deep blue sea: Merchant seamen, pirates, and the Anglo-American maritime world, 1700-1750* (Cambridge: Cambridge University Press, 1989), 64-67, 158-59.

30 Howay, "The earliest pages of the history of British Columbia," 22.

31 Horatio Appleton Lamb, "Notes on trade with the northwest coast, 1790-1810," photostat from the Houghton Library, Harvard University, UBCL-SC.

32 Dorr to J. and T. Perkins, 23 October 1802, in Howard Corning, ed., "Letters of Sullivan Dorr," *Proceedings of the Massachusetts Historical Society*, vol. 67 (October 1941-May 1944), 178-364 (quotation is from 333).

33 In 1817, for instance, Bryant and Sturgis suggested to Captain Clark of the *Borneo* that he "divide skins, rather than enhance their value by attempting to outbid each other." See "Extracts from the Bryant and Sturgis Letters," photostat from the Baker Library, Harvard University, UBCL-SC.

34 Such expressions pervade the journals and letters of late eighteenth-century traders and explorers, and they became fixed in the European imaginary. See, for example, Menzies to Banks, 4 April 1790, in Richard H. Dillon, "Archibald Menzies' trophies," *BCHQ* 15, 3 and 4 (July-October 1951), 151-59, at 155. Menzies, who had traded on the Northwest Coast in 1787-88, listed trade articles that he thought would appeal to "the fickle disposition of the Natives."
    Scholars have perpetuated such views. I turn to historiographical matters below, but as a taste of how early twentieth-century historians viewed Native participation in the trade, this is F.W. Howay in his "Outline sketch of the maritime fur trade," *Canadian Historical Association*,

Annual Report, 1932, 5-14, at 8: "When the Indian had been supplied with these [trade staples, such as iron bars, copper sheets, and cloth] the trader's resourcefulness was taxed to offer something that caught his changeful fancy. Whimsical always, his whimsicality increased with competition."

35 In anthropology see, particularly, Thomas, *Entangled objects*. With regard to European-Native contact in North America see Richard White, *The middle ground: Indians, empires, and republics in the Great Lakes region, 1650-1815* (Cambridge: Cambridge University Press, 1991).

36 Sahlins, "Goodbye to *tristes tropes*," 11.

37 See Susan Marsden and Robert Galois, "The Tsimshian, the Hudson's Bay Company, and the geopolitics of the northwest coast fur trade, 1787-1840," *Canadian Geographer* 39, 2 (1995): 169-83, on the partnerships forged between traders and the Coast Tsimshian.

38 S.W. Jackman, ed., *The journal of William Sturgis* (Victoria: Sono Nis, 1978), 121. "The laws of supply and demand were frequently disregarded," Sturgis noted elsewhere. See William Sturgis, "The northwest fur trade," ed. Elliot C. Cowdin, *Hunt's Merchant's Magazine* 14, 6 (1846): 532-39 (quotation is from 537).

39 For an elaboration of this theme in other parts of the world, see Arjun Appadurai, ed., *The social life of things: Commodities in cultural perspective* (Cambridge: Cambridge University Press, 1986).

40 Karl Marx, *Capital: A critique of political economy*, vol. 1, trans. Ben Fowkes (Harmondsworth, UK: Penguin, 1976), 163.

41 George Vancouver, "Papers relating to the voyage of the Discovery and Chatham, 1790-1795," fol. 13v BM Add. MS. 17,552.

42 Ingraham, log, 1791, quoted in Malloy, "'Bosten men,'" 81-82.

43 C.P. Claret Fleurieu, *A voyage round the world performed during the years 1790, 1791, and 1792, by Étienne Marchand*, 2 vols. (London: Longman and Rees, Cadell and Davies, 1801), I, 352. Marchand was on the coast in 1791 in the French trading vessel *Solide*. This text, edited by Fleurieu, stemmed from either Marchand's journal or the log of his second-officer. See Dunmore, *French explorers in the Pacific*, I, 345, note 1.

44 William Beresford, *A voyage round the world ... performed in 1785, 1786, 1787, and 1788, in the King George and Queen Charlotte, Captains Portlock and Dixon* (London: Geo. Goulding, 1789), 236.

45 See Gibson, *Otter skins, Boston ships, and China goods*, chap. 8.

46 Some of the first merchants in the business thought about establishing trading factories in areas where furs seemed plentiful and the Natives seemed friendly. One early British trader claimed in the introduction to his account of the business that the "inestimable value of their furs will ever make it a desirable trade, and wherever it is established upon a proper foundation, and a settlement made, it will become a very valuable and lucrative branch of commerce." See Captain Nathaniel Portlock, *A voyage round the world; but more particularly to the north-west coast of America: Performed in 1785, 1786, 1787, and 1788 ...* (London: John Stockdale and George Goulding, 1789), 7. But such plans were "liable to serious objections," as the French explorer J.F.G. De La Pérouse explained, because of the cost involved in maintaining overseas posts and since furs could "so easily be procured along the whole coast." See L.A. Milet-Mureau, ed., *A voyage round the world, performed in the years 1785, 1786, 1787, and 1788, by the Boussole and Astrolabe, under the command of J.F.G. De La Pérouse*, 2 vols. (London: G.G. Robinson and J. Robinson, 1799), II, 433.

47 Banks to Grenville, 20 February 1791, PRO HO 42/18 [33], fol. 168. See East India Company memo, n.d. (1791?), PRO BT 6/227, for Dalrymple's views of maritime fur traders' surveying abilities. Banks and Dalrymple were the veritable custodians of geographical knowledge about the Northwest Coast during this period.

48 One British trader reported to the British government that rivers and inlets were explored most successfully in boats and sailing vessels under 100 tons. Untitled report on the discoveries of Charles Duncan, n.d. (1790?), PRO HO 42/13[57]. Some of the first traders sailed in 100-200 ton snows, but found them difficult to manoeuvre in estuaries and inlets.

49 Mark D. Kaplanoff, ed., *Joseph Ingraham's journal of the brigantine HOPE on a voyage to the northwest coast of America, 1790-1792* (Barre, MA: Imprint Society, 1971), 146-47.

50 Ibid., 147.

51 Jackman, *Journal of William Sturgis,* 88.

52 Walker, *Account of a voyage,* 56.

53 See, for example, F.W. Howay, ed., "Four letters from Richard Cadman Etches to Sir Joseph Banks, 1788-92," *BCHQ* 3 (1942): 125-39, regarding the activities of Portlock and Dixon.

54 See, especially, Foucault, *Power/knowledge.*

55 James Strange (with the *Captain Cook* and *Experiment*) met William Tipping (commander of the *Sea Otter*) in Prince William Sound in 1786, noting that they "could not fail to View each other with a very Jealous Eye." After this exchange, Tipping abandoned his plan to sail south, believing that Strange had exhausted the Natives' supply of furs. See James Strange, *James Strange's journal and narrative of the commercial expedition from Bombay to the north-west coast of America* (Madras: Government Press, 1929), 37-38.

56 See F.W. Howay, "Indian attacks upon maritime traders of the north-west coast, 1785-1805," *Canadian Historical Review* 6, 4 (1925): 287-309.

57 George Dixon, "Remarks on the voyages of John Meares, Esq" (1790), reprinted in *The Dixon-Meares controversy,* ed. F.W. Howay, (Toronto: Ryerson, 1929) (quotation is from 27).

58 "Robert Haswell's log of the first voyage of the 'Columbia,'" in Howay, *Voyages of the "Columbia,"* 49.

59 Thomas Manby, "Manuscript journal of the voyage of H.M.S. *Discovery* and *Chatham,* Dec 10 1790-June 22 1793," 28 April 1792, photostat from the Roberston Coe Collection, Yale University, W. Kaye Lamb Collection, 1-3, UBCL-SC.

60 Captain John Myers, *The life, voyages and travels of Capt. John Myers, detailing his adventures during four voyages round the world ...* (London: Longman, Hurst, Rees, 1817), vi. Myers came to the Northwest Coast in 1795 in the vessel *Jane.*

61 "Orders given to Captain John Kendrick of the ship Columbia ... 1787," in Howay, *Voyages of the 'Columbia',* 111.

62 "Argonaut's sailing orders," in *The journal of captain James Colnett aboard the 'Argonaut' ...,* ed. F.W. Howay (Toronto: Champlain Society, 1940), 20.

63 John Kendrick, trans., *The voyage of the Sutil and Mexicana 1792: The last Spanish exploration of the northwest coast of America* (Spokane, WA: Clark, 1991), 87. Kendrick is not entirely sure about who edited this journal, but he is confident that Galiano wrote most of it.

64 A large crowd gathered in Boston to welcome home the *Columbia,* the first American vessel to circumnavigate the globe. Hamilton Andrews Hill, "The trade, commerce, and navigation of Boston, 1780-1880," in *The memorial history of Boston ... 1630-1880,* 4 vols., ed. Justin Windsor (Boston: James R. Osgood, 1881), IV, part I, 195-234, at 208.

65 Samuel Hill, "Autobiography," fol. 14, photostat from New York Public Library, UBCL-SC. The Spanish and the British cast each other in a bad light for their own imperial ends, adding another dimension to the nature of representation in the maritime fur trade.

66 These instructions to avoid violence and generate friendship were perhaps a concession to the wave of humanitarianism in Europe and America that marked Cook's voyage. Merchants in Boston and London may have included such clauses in order to court the approval of their peers.

67 Michael Roe, ed., *The journal and letters of Captain Charles Bishop on the north-west coast of America, in the Pacific and in New South Wales, 1794-1799* (Cambridge: Hakluyt Society, 1967), 65.

68 Bernard Magee, "Log of the Jefferson," 8 October 1793, photostat from the Massachusetts Historical Society, UBCL-SC.

69 William Shaler, "Journal of a voyage between China and the north-western coast of America, made in 1804," *American Register* 3, pt. 1 (1808): 137-75 (quotation of from 140).

70 Sturgis, quoted in William D. Phelps, "Solid men of Boston" [c. 1870], 4, typescript from the Bancroft Library, Berkeley, BCARS A/A/30/So4.

71 Samuel Eliot Morrison, *The maritime history of Massachusetts, 1783-1869* (Boston: Houghton Mifflin, 1921), 55-56.

72 Howay, *Journal of Captain James Colnett*, 90-191.

73 Ibid.

74 H.W.S. Cleveland, *Voyages of a northwest navigator ... compiled from the journals and letters of the late Richard J. Cleveland* (New York: Harper and Brothers, 1886), 50-51.

75 "Hoskins' narrative of the second voyage of the 'Columbia,'" in Howay, *Voyages of the "Columbia,"* 272.

76 W. Kaye Lamb, ed., *The voyage of George Vancouver 1791-1795*, 4 vols. (London: The Hakluyt Society, 1984), III, 1,016.

77 George Goodman Hewett, "Notes in Vancouver's voyages," on volume III, 72, line 12, BCARS A/A/20/V28H.

78 Francois Péron, *Mémoires du captaine Péron, sur ses voyages*, 2 vols. (Paris: Bissot-Thrivars, 1824), II, 24. I am indebted to Lynn Stewart for this translation.

79 Sturgis, "Ms. of 3 lectures," lecture 2, 26; Idem., "The northwest fur trade, and the Indians of the Oregon Country, 1788-1830," ed. S.E. Morrison, *Old Southern Leaflets*, no. 219 (n.d), 16.

80 Samuel Patterson used this last expression to describe Chief Maquinna of Nootka Sound in his *Narrative of the adventures and sufferings of Samuel Patterson ... 1825 edition* (Fairfield, WA: Ye Galleon, 1967), 56.

81 Bern Anderson, ed., "The Vancouver expedition: Peter Puget's journal of the examination of Puget Sound May 7-June 11, 1792," Pacific Northwest Quarterly 30, 2 (1939): 177-217 (quotation is from 181).

82 Gibson, *Otter skins, Boston ships, and China goods*, 50.

83 Sturgis, "Northwest fur trade, and the Indians of the Oregon country," 17. Ebenezer Johnson made a similar comparison between the Natives of the Northwest Coast and those of New England in his *A short account of a northwest voyage, performed in the years 1796, 1797 & 1798* (Massachusetts: Printed for the author, 1798), 11.

84 Although traders such as Meares and Dixon obviously did, as I noted above.

85 C.F. Newcombe, ed., *Menzies' journal of Vancouver's voyage April to October, 1792* (Victoria: Archives of British Columbia Memoir no. 4, 1923), 17.

86 Menzies to Banks, 1 January 1793, Dawson Turner copies of the correspondence of Sir Joseph Banks, vol. 8, 146, British Museum (Natural History). I am grateful to the British Museum for permission to quote from this source.

87 Bhabha, *The location of culture*, 72.

88 Ibid., 75 and 67.

89 Ibid., 82 (his emphasis).

90 Dorr to Dorr, 16 August 1801, Ebenezer Dorr Papers, BCARS Add. MSS. 828. Richard Cleveland informed his American readers that "The Indians are sufficiently cunning to derive all possible advantage from competition" between traders. Richard J. Cleveland, *A narrative of voyages and commercial enterprises ...*, 2 vols. (Cambridge, MA: John Owen, 1842), I, 74-75.

91 Meares, *Voyages*, 141-42.

92 Walker, *Account of a voyage*, 188.

93 Benita Parry, "Signs of our times: Discussion of Homi Bhabha's *The location of culture*," Third Text 28-29 (1994): 5-24 (quotation is from 9).

94 Malloy, "'Boston men,'" 14.

95 Michael Taussig, *Shamanism, colonialism, and the wild man: A study in terror and healing* (Chicago and London: University of Chicago Press, 1987). The Putumayo Indians were starved, tortured, shot, burned, beheaded, and flogged to death. Rubber traders also raided and burned Indian villages and developed a debt-peonage system to extort rubber. Britain sent an envoy to investigate after a series of articles appeared in a London magazine in 1909 exposing these details and the fact that the rubber company responsible for the atrocities was a British-Peruvian consortium.

96 Ibid., 3-138 (quotations are from 100, 75, and 109).

97 Ibid., 75.

98 Ibid., 133.

99 Sara Suleri, who also appeals to Taussig's work, has made a similar, extentuated point about the imaginative geographies of British colonialism in India. "The Indian subcontinent is not merely a geographic space upon which colonial rapacities have been enacted, but is furthermore that imaginative construction through which rapaciousness can worship its own misdeeds, thus making the subcontinent a tropological repository from which colonial and postcolonial imaginations have drawn – and continue to draw – their most basic figures for the anxiety of empire." See Sara Suleri, *The rhetoric of English India* (Chicago: University of Chicago Press, 1992), 4-5.

100 "John Hoskins' narrative of the second voyage of the 'Columbia,'" in Howay, *Voyages of the "Columbia,"* 192.

101 Ibid., 193.

102 Jackman, *Journal of William Sturgis*, 48.

103 Roe, *Journal and letters of Captain Charles Bishop*, 101. See also John Nicol, *The life and adventures of John Nicol, mariner* (London: T. Caddell, 1822), 89, who referred to the Northwest Coast as "a hostile region."

104 Silas Holbrook, *Sketches, by a traveller* (Boston: Carter and Hendee, 1830), 10. These sketches appeared first in the *New England Galaxy* and the *Boston Courier*.

105 Walker, *Account of a voyage*, 123

106 Ibid., 37.

107 Quoted in Malloy, "'Boston men,'" 105-106.

108 For a vivid portrayal of shipboard life and an attempted mutiny, see Ebenezer Dorr and Sons, "Ship Hancock, Log Book" [1798-1800], UBCL-SC.

109 Said, *Orientalism*, 54.

110 Ibid.

111 Quoted in Malloy, "'Boston men,'" 103-104.

112 Susan Buck-Morss, "Envisioning capital: Political economy on display," *Critical Inquiry* 21, 2 (1995): 434-65.

113 Smith was trying to overcome a moral conundrum: that the division of labour enhanced productivity and equality but was premised, to some extent, on inequalities of talent and wealth.

114 Jackman, *Journal of William Sturgis*, 121.

115 Myers, *Life, voyages, and travels*, 61-62.

116 Patrick Brantlinger, *Fictions of the state: Culture and credit in Britain, 1694-1994* (Ithaca: Cornell University Press, 1996).

117 Meares, *Voyages*, lxix. The Spanish explorer Don Alejandro Malaspina, who visited Nootka Sound in 1791, made the same point: "The coast of Northwest America offers nothing to European commerce other than a great number of fine pelts ... which, purchased at little cost from peoples who appreciate neither commodities nor luxuries, attain a greater value in the market of Canton." See Malaspina, "Politico-scientific voyage round the world ... from 1789-1794," 3 books, trans. Carl Robinson, II, 240, UBCL-SC.

118 This was not the only tack that traders took to recuperate difference and distance. They also focused on social habits, claiming that Native peoples were uncivilized because they were dirty, or half-naked, or allowed their furs to become riddled with lice, or did not eat with metal knives and forks. See, for example, Strange, *Journal*, 20. Traders also looked for signs of cannibalism – a form of enquiry which pervades the annals of European exploration and trade and was a leitmotif of colonial discourse between the sixteenth and eighteenth centuries. See Peter Hulme, *Colonial encounters: Europe and the native Caribbean, 1492-1797* (London: Metheun, 1986). Scholars of early British Columbia have also been animated by the subject of cannibalism. For a recent assessment, see Joyce A. Wike, "A re-evaluation of northwest coast cannibalism," in *The Tsimshian and their neighbors of the north Pacific coast*, ed. Jay Miller and Carol M. Eastman (Seattle: University of Washington Press, 1984), 239-54. As I will register below, the

spectre of cannibalism contributed to maritime fur traders' fears, but I do not treat the issue here because I do not think it was the distinguishing feature of this economy of truth.

119 Sturgis, "The northwest fur trade," 534.

120 F.W. Howay, "A ballad of the northwest fur trade," *New England Quarterly* 1 (1928): 71-79 (quotation is from 73).

121 Quoted in Kornfeld, "Encountering 'the other,'" 292.

122 Fleurieu, *Voyage round the world*, I, 450 and 479-80.

123 Fleurieu discussed the maritime fur trade, and outlined Marchand's travels, before the French National Institute of Arts and Sciences.

124 John Jewitt, *A journal kept at Nootka Sound* (Boston: Printed for the author, 1807), 13. A Native informant told the ethnologist and collector C.F. Newcombe the same thing in the early twentieth century, stating that sixty people had been killed by Hanna. See Newcombe Family Papers, vol. 16, file 16.

Chapter 7: Native Power and Commercial Contact at Nootka Sound

1 John Hoskins, "Memorandum on the fur trade at Nootka Sound," in Howay, *Voyages of the "Columbia,"* 485-86.

2 Cook and King, *Voyage to the Pacific Ocean*, II, 266.

3 On the meaning and significance of copper in Northwest Coast Native trade, see Carol F. Jopling, "The coppers of the northwest coast Indians: Their origin, development, and possible antecedents," *Transactions of the American Philosophical Society* 79, pt. 1 (1989): 1-164.

4 Hoskins and Gray to Barrell, 12 July 1792, in Howay, *Voyages of the "Columbia,"* 472. These were the commodities in hottest demand, but traders worked the coast with a medley of goods. In 1795, Charles Bishop of the *Ruby* listed nearly fifty different goods that he had traded for furs. See Roe, *Journal and letters of Captain Charles Bishop*, 162-63. Vancouver left England with well over 200 different trade items. See Alexander Davidson, "Invoice of sundry artices of merchandise ... on board his majesty's ship Discovery," 15 January 1791, PRO ADM 1/4156.

5 Edmond S. Meany, ed., *A new Vancouver journal on the discovery of Puget Sound* (Seattle, WA: n.p., 1915), 38. Meany thought that this journal was written by Edward Bell, clerk of the *Chatham*.

6 The vessel *La Flavie* stayed at Nootka Sound for a few days and then sailed directly to the Queen Charlotte Islands, where the Spanish explorer Jacinto Caamaño saw it on 29 June. See Henry R. Wagner and W.A. Newcombe, eds., "The journal of Don Jacinto Caamaño," *BCHQ* 2 (1938): 189-222, 265-301, at 200 and 207. The basin was spotted at "Cheslakees" by Archibald Menzies. See Newcombe, *Menzies journal*, 89.

7 Manby, "Manuscript journal," fol. 46v.

8 This formulation is also expressed in R. Brian Ferguson and Neil L. Whitehead, *War in the tribal zone: Expanding states and indigenous warfare* (Santa Fe, NM: School of American Research Press, 1992), 6.

9 Captain John D'Wolf, *A voyage to the north Pacific Ocean ...* (Cambridge: Welch, Bigelow, 1806), 18; the harbour of Newitty is described in Anon., "Directions for entering the principal harbours on the north west coast of America by different commanders," BCARS A/B/20.5/C76. By the early 1810s, however, there were signs that the supply of furs at Newitty was drying up. See "Ship Atahualpa of Boston," log, 16 July-13 August 1812, Bancroft Library, Berkeley, P-K 211.

In 1817, a French trader was told by a chief of Nootka Sound that, since the Spanish had vacated Yuquot in 1795 and British and American traders had moved north, only three or so vessels had visited the sound. See M. Camille de Roquefeuil, *A voyage round the world, between the years 1816-1819* (London: Sir Richard Phillips and Co., 1823), 31.

10 Philip Drucker, *The northern and central Nootkan tribes*, Smithsonian Institution, Bureau of American Ethnology, Bulletin 144 (Washington, DC: US Government Printing Office, 1951), 220. More recently, Susan Kenyon has argued that "the Nootkan local group was conceived as an idealized family, expanded over time, which owned a distinctive territory and shared

common ceremonial and ritual property." See Susan M. Kenyon, "The Kyuquot way: A study of a west coast (Nootkan) community," *National Museums of Canada, Canadian Ethnology Services Paper*, no. 61 (1980), 84.

There has been both continuity and change among Nuu-chah-nulth groups over the last few thousand years. I will discuss Native social practices in the past tense and hope that I am not being disrespectful to Nuu-chah-nulth peoples, who still identify themselves in terms of local groups and tribes, and hereditary villages and territories. I certainly do not want to imply that pre-contact Native societies were radically, easily, or quickly disrupted by contact with non-Natives. Nonetheless, while some of the most basic concepts of Nuu-chah-nulth social organization may have remained intact over the last 200 to 300 years, details and patterns of Native group composition have changed.

11 See Susan Golla, "He has a name: History and social structure among the Indians of western Vancouver Island" (PhD diss., Columbia University, 1987), 86, 99-111.

12 See Edward Sapir, "The social organisation of the west coast tribes," (orig. pub. 1915), in *Selected writings of Edward Sapir in language, culture and personality*, ed. David G. Mandelbaum (Berkeley: University of California Press, 1985 [orig. pub. 1949]), 468-87.

13 Drucker, *Northern and central Nootkan tribes*, 247. See also Alice H. Ernst, *The wolf ritual of the northwest coast* (Eugene: University of Oregon Press, 1952).

14 See William J. Folan and John T. Dewhirst, "Yuquot: Where the wind blows from all directions," *Archaeology* 23, 4 (1970): 276-86. Yuquot was excavated by Parks Canada in 1966. On Nuu-chah-nulth groups more generally, see Eugene Arima and John Dewhirst, "Nootkans of Vancouver Island," in *Handbook of North American Indians*, vol. 7: *Northwest coast* (vol. ed. Wayne Suttles), ed. William C. Sturevant (Washington: Smithsonian Institution, 1990), 391-411.

15 See, especially, William Joseph Folan, "The community, settlement and subsistence patterns of the Nootka Sound area: A diachronic model" (PhD diss., Southern Illinois University, Carbondale, 1972), 175-192.

16 Mozño, *Noticias de Nutka*, 24-25, 42 (emphasis in original). On the genealogy of these terms, see Marshall, "Political history of the Nuu-chah-nulth," 207-208.

17 Other observers tried to piece together this social system. Juan Francisco de la Bodega y Quadra, the Spanish commander at Nootka Sound in 1792, concurred with Mozño and emphasized that commoners and slaves lived under the same material conditions. See "Voyage to the n.w. coast of North America by Don Juan Francisco de la Bodega y Quadra ... 1792," 51-52, trans. V.D. Webb, typescript of photostat in the Huntingdon Library, UBCL-SC. Roquefeuil, on the other hand, judged (correctly, according to some ethnographers) that commoners were part of the kinship system, but slaves ("Mitschimis") were not. See Roquefeuil, *Voyage round the world*, 100.

It is difficult to know how rigid were the boundaries between these "classes." Drucker claimed that there was "an unbroken series of graduated statuses" among the non-slave population. See Philip Drucker, "Rank, wealth, and kinship in northwest coast society" (orig. pub. 1939), in *Indians of the northwest coast*, ed. Tom McFeat (Seattle: University of Washington Press, 1967), 134-46 (quotation is from 134). See also Drucker, *Northern and central Nootkan tribes*, 243-44.

18 Drucker drew a distinction between "economic privileges," which were associated with "shelter, food, and wealth, the ownership of habitations, domains for fishing and hunting, salvage rights, and all the special expressions of such rights," and "ceremonial privileges," which included "the right to give certain rituals or to perform a certain act in them, the ownership of dances and songs, and the ritual names that went with each privilege of any sort." See Drucker, *Northern and central Nootkan tribes*, 247-48.

19 Philip L. Newman, "An intergroup collectivity among the Nootka" (MA thesis, University of Washington, 1957), 29-36.

20 Drucker, *Northern and central Nootkan tribes*, 273.

21 See Philip Drucker, "Ecology and political organization on the northwest coast of America," in *The development of political organization in native North America*, ed. Elizabeth Tooker (Washington, DC: American Ethnological Society, 1983), 86-96.

22 Wayne Suttles, "Variation in habitat and culture on the northwest coast," orig. pub. 1960, in his *Coast Salish essays* (Seattle/Vancouver: University of Washington Press/Talon, 1987), 26-44 (quotation is from 41).
23 See, especially, Drucker, *Northern and central Nootkan tribes*, 15-61, 243-273, and passim.
24 Ibid., 478, 274; Edward Sapir, "Sayach'apis, a Nootkan trader," in *American indian life: By several of its students*, ed. Elise Clews Parsons (New York: B.W. Huebsch, 1922), 297-323.
25 See Newman, "Intergroup collectivity," 10.
26 Drucker, *Northern and central Nootkan tribes*, 141; Newman, "Intergroup collectivity," 11.
27 Drucker, *Northern and central Nootkan tribes*, 279.
28 Ibid. Or as one of his informants put it: "After a man had stayed with one chief for a while, fishing and working for him, he would decide he had helped that chief enough, and would move to the house of another chief to whom he was related."
29 This tendency was documented by Edward Sapir and Morris Swadesh, who worked with Nuu-chah-nulth groups in the region of Clayoquot Sound, Barkley Sound, and Alberni Inlet. See their *Native accounts of Nootka ethnography* (New York: AMS Press, 1978 [orig. pub. 1955]), 111, 315, and 346.
30 Drucker, *Northern and central Nootkan tribes*, 454.
31 Ibid., 220-21.
32 Ibid., 221.
33 Edward Sapir, "Sayach'apis,' a Nootkan trader," 308. See also Sapir and Swadesh, *Native accounts of Nootka ethnography*, 43-45.
34 See Drucker, *Northern and central Nootkan tribes*, 342-43. He judged that in times of war, women tended to favour their blood kin rather than their husbands or in-laws, and "thus it was that plans were often betrayed, and information was given to attackers."
35 Thomas, *Entangled objects*, 36.
36 White, *The middle ground*, xiv.
37 Drucker was in the field in the 1930s and noted that he could not date much of his data. Sapir, who worked with Nuu-chah-nulth groups in the 1910s, wrote to a colleague that because of "the strong development of family property rights" among these groups, "to get a really adequate idea of their customs one must get separate accounts of almost every custom and separate versions of family legends and songs from several families. In other words an almost endless field of work is opened up." Yet Sapir (with characteristic insight) suggested that any "adequate" or holistic interpretation of Nuu-chah-nulth social life should take as its centrepiece the pervasiveness and sophistication of these kin relations in "Nootkan" memory and the social order and dynamism they created. See Drucker, *Northern and central Nootkan tribes*, 3; the quotation is from Sapir to Newcombe, 25 November 1910, Newcombe Family Papers, vol. 5, file 126.
38 These local politics are not immediately identifiable in Sapir's published work on the Nootka, but they shine through his correspondence with his field informants and with provincial and federal officials. Richard Inglis kindly loaned me copies of Sapir's correspondence and his field notebooks, which are housed in the anthropology division of the Royal British Columbia Museum.
39 Drucker's arguments about the importance of property in Nuu-chah-nulth societies reflected, in part, the ideas of Alfred Kroeber, his teacher and mentor. See A.L. Kroeber, "American culture and the northwest coast," *American Anthropologist* (n.s.) 25 (1923): 1-20, especially 9.
40 Walker, *Account of a voyage*, 48.
41 Galiano, for instance, noted that a close friendship prevailed between the Spanish and the Indians. "Moved by the gifts and good treatment of the commandant [Quadra], Maquinna had come to live very close to the ships. He ate nearly every day from the table of the commandant ... He used a knife and fork like the most polite European, letting the servants wait on him, and himself contributing to the good humour of the society." See Kendrick, *Voyage of the Sutil and Mexicana*, 73.
42 Kaplanoff, *Joseph Ingraham's journal*, 222.
43 Malaspina, "Politico-scientific voyage," II, 225.

44 They also used such images to suggest to the world that the Spanish were not imperial bullies. Spanish officials in New Spain and Madrid were secretive about their imperial plans for the Northwest Coast, however; the journals of Spanish explorers were locked in government vaults, or buried in archives, for many years.

45 Malaspina, "Politico-scientific voyage," I, 285.

46 Newcombe Family Papers, vol. 43, folder 47; Quimper to Quadra, 3 December 1790, in Mary Elizabeth Daylton, trans., "Official documents relating to Spanish and Mexican voyages of navigation, exploration, and discovery, made in North America in the 18th century," 135, BCARS A/A/10/M57t.

47 Spain – Colonial Office, "Letters of Pedro Alberni, Commander Quadra, Gigedo and other Spanish officials concerning the Spanish occupation of the northwest coast of America," 1-52, trans. Jose Rodriguez, BCARS A/A/10.1/Sp1A. On Spain's military establishment at Nootka Sound, see Joseph Sanchez, "Pedro de Alberni and the Spanish claim to Nootka: The Catalonian Volunteers on the northwest coast," *Pacific Northwest Quarterly* (April 1980), 72-77. Native people asked continually about when the Spanish would leave the village. See "Extract of the navigation made by the pilot Don Juan Pantoja y Arriago ...," in Henry R. Wagner, *Spanish explorations in the Straits of Juan de Fuca* (Santa Ana, CA: Fine Arts Press, 1933), 162.

48 After a severe winter in 1793-94, a Spanish official was obliged to cook kidney beans for Maquinna each day to offset starvation. See Ramón Saavedra, "Report on Nootka Sound," 1793-1794, Daylton, "Official documents," 291.

49 Moziño, *Noticias de Nutka*, 79-84; Saavedra to Quadra, 27 August 1791, Daylton, "Official documents," 213. For Native reminiscences of the Spanish, see Peter S. Webster, *As far as I know: Reminiscences of an Ahousat elder* (Campbell River: Campbell River Museum and Archives, 1983). On these strained Spanish-Native relations, see Richard Inglis, "The Spanish on the north Pacific coast – an alternative view from Nootka Sound," in *Spain and the north Pacific coast: Essays in recognition of the bicentennial of the Malaspina expedition, 1791-1792*, ed. Robin Inglis (Vancouver: Vancouver Maritime Museum Society, 1992), 133-36; and Christon I. Archer, "Seduction before sovereignty: Spanish efforts to manipulate the natives in their claims to the northwest coast," in *From maps to metaphors: The Pacific world of George Vancouver*, ed. Robin Fisher and Hugh Johnston (Vancouver: UBC Press, 1993), 127-59.

50 James Colnett, "The journal of James Colnett aboard the Prince of Wales & sloop Princess Royal from 16. Oct. 1786 to 7. Nov. 1788," 2 vols., I, 52, typescript of the original in the British Museum, UBCL-SC.

51 "Haswell's log of the first voyage of the 'Columbia,'" in Howay, *Voyages of the "Columbia,"* 53.

52 Saavedra to Quadra, 27 August 1791, Daylton, "Official Documents," 220.

53 In September 1818, Roquefeuil was told by a Native chief of the sound that an American vessel had just departed, having seized Maquinna and his son and demanded a large ransom of furs. See Roquefeuil, *Voyage round the world*, 93. Galiano noted that Maquinna "complained a great deal about the treatment [of his people] by foreign ships which trafficked along the coast, because of several outrages which he said his people had received." Kendrick, *Voyage of the Sutil and Mexicana*, 73. For Mowachaht accounts of the way traders abused Native people, see Edward Curtis, *The North American Indian*, vol. 11: *The Nootka; the Haida*, ed. Frederick Webb Hodge (Norwood, MA: Plimpton, 1916), 7-9; Newcombe Family Papers, vol. 36, folder 16, and vol. 43, folder 38.

54 Brabant to Walbran, 19 July 1905, Diocese of Victoria, Papers.

55 John R. Jewitt, *The adventures and sufferings of John R. Jewitt, captive among the Nootka, 1803-1805*, Edinburgh, 1824 edition, ed. Derek G. Smith (Toronto: McCelland and Stewart, 1974), 80.

56 Strange, *Journal*, 28.

57 Meares, *Voyages*, 142.

58 See Harlow and Madden, *British colonial developments*, 21-32.

59 Ibid., 270-71.

60 Walker, *Account of a voyage*, 60-61.

61 Ibid., 61.

62 As such they noticed some of the geopolitical relations described by Cook. Meares and Walker had copies of Cook's *Voyage to the Pacific Ocean* in their cabins. Meares claimed that the official account of Cook's third voyage was "universally read and known" by the first traders. See Meares, *Voyages*, xliii. Walker referred to Cook frequently in his journal. But Meares's and Walker's remarks about socio-political relations at Nootka Sound have a different texture than Cook's. Cook and his officers struggled to distinguish between chiefs and Native people of lower status. Cook wrote little about chiefs at Nootka Sound and simply ventured that their authority did not extend much further than over their families. See Beaglehole, *Journals*, III, 317 and 322; Cook and King, *Voyage to the Pacific*, II, 333; and see above, Part I.

63 See Jewitt, *Adventures and sufferings*, 68-70.

64 Walker, *Account of a voyage*, 40; Colnett, "Journal," I, 47, 53-54.

65 See Walker, *Account of a voyage*, 43-59.

66 See Meares, *Voyages*, 112-14.

67 See Meares's testimony to British government officials during the Nootka Sound crisis: Great Britain, Privy Council, Register, 8 February 1791, PRO PC 2/135, 442-43.

68 Colnett, "Journal," I, 47; Meares, *Voyages*, 114, 122-23; Ingraham to Martínez (1789), Freeman Tovell Collection; Archer, "Seduction before sovereignty," 151.

69 See Jewitt, *Adventures and sufferings*, 39 and passim.

70 Walker, *Account of a voyage*, 67. Strange tried to make amends for his mistake by offering Maquinna a present of copper, iron tools, and copper ear rings for his wife.

71 Walker, *Account of a voyage*, 68-69.

72 "Testimony of John Meares," PRO PC 2/135, 442. These statements by Meares and Walker were independent observations. Meares did not have access to Walker's journal.

73 Meares, *Voyages*, 255.

74 Meares thought that Maquinna had appointed Callicum to be "our guardian and protector." See Meares, *Voyages*, 114

75 See Walker, *Account of a voyage*, 51 and 59; Meares, *Voyages*, 133.

76 Meares, *Voyages*, 119-20.

77 Walker, *Account of a voyage*, 108-109, 58.

78 See Colnett, "Journal," I, 48-64.

79 Meares claimed that the only metal tools these Native people valued were saws and chizzels. See Meares, *Voyages*, 262.

80 See, for example, Strange, *Journal*, 26; Walker, *Account of a voyage*, 40 and passim; Colnett, "Journal," I, 53, 63-64.

81 Strange, *Journal*, 22.

82 Walker, *Account of a voyage*, 40.

83 Roquefeuil, *Voyage round the world*, 33.

84 Walker, *Account of a voyage*, 70

85 Ibid.

86 Ibid., 71.

87 Strange, *Journal*, 24.

88 Meares, *Voyages*, 265; Colnett, "Journal," I, 63.

89 I agree with Obeyesekere that "statements about cannibalism reveal more about the relations between Europeans and Savages during early and late contact than, as ethnographic statements, about the nature of Savage anthropophagy." See Obeyesekere, "'British cannibals,'" 631.

90 See "Log of Jacinto Caamaño," 1790, Daylton, "Official documents," 158.

91 Péron, *Mémoires*, II, 2.

92 The fact that it was mostly slave women who were prostituted was emphasized in some of the unofficial accounts of Cook's third voyage, written by crewmen. See, for example, W. Ellis, *An authentic account of a voyage performed by Captain Cook and Captain Clerke ...* 2 vols. (London: Robinson, Sewell, and Debrett, 1782), I, 216. It was also noted by the Spanish and by Jewitt. See "Log of Jacinto Caamaño," 1790, Daylton, "Official documents," 157; Jewitt, *Adventures and sufferings*, 65. See also Drucker, *Northern and central Nootkan tribes*, 309.

93   Nevertheless, Moziño noted that the Natives of Nootka Sound were afflicted by venereal disease. See Moziño, *Noticias de Nutka*, 43-44.
94   Walker, *Account of a voyage*, 87.
95   Meares, *Voyages*, 115.
96   Strange, *Journal*, 23.
97   Walker, *Account of a voyage*, 56-57.
98   Ibid.; and see Colnett, "Journal," I, 64.
99   Walker, *Account of a voyage*, 43
100 Argonaut [John Cadman Etches], *A continuation of an authentic statement of the facts relative to Nootka Sound ...* (London: T. Beckett, 1790), 9-10.
101 Quadra to Revillgigedo, 24 October 1792, Daylton, "Official documents," 225.
102 Bob Galois, personal communication. Galois is preparing Colnett's journal for publication.
103 Kendrick, *Voyage of the Sutil and Mexicana*, 76.
104 Marshall, "Political history of the Nuu-chah-nulth," 222.
105 Walker, *Account of a voyage*, 179-80.
106 Donald C. Cutter, *Malaspina and Galiano: Spanish voyages to the northwest coast, 1791 and 1792* (Seattle/Vancouver and Toronto: University of Washington Press/Douglas and McIntyre, 1991), 101.
107 Kendrick, *Voyage of the Sutil and Mexicana*, 79.
108 Martínez, for instance, noted that some Natives from Hesquiat Harbour came to Yuquot to steal some iron pipes from the Spanish settlement. Martínez to Quadra, December 1790, Daylton, "Official documents," 135.
109 Drucker, *Northern and central Nootkan tribes*, 313. Colnett described some of the people of the sound as "free booters." See Colnett, "Journal," I, 68.
110 Walker, *Account of a voyage*, 41.
111 *Columbia Centinel*, 20 May 1807. See F.W. Howay, "An early account of the loss of the Boston in 1803," *Washington Historical Quarterly* 17, 4 (October 1926): 280-88, for this and other contemporary accounts.
112 This point has been emphasized by Richard Inglis in his foreword to a new edition of Jewitt's text. See Alice W. Shurcliff and Sarah Shurcliff Ingelfinger, *Captive of the Nootka Indians: The northwest coast adventure of John R. Jewitt, 1802-1806* (Boston: Back Bay, 1993), xi-xvi.
113 Maquinna asked Jewitt whether "I would be his slave during my life – if I would fight for him in his battles, if I would repair his muskets and make daggers and knives for him." See Jewitt, *Adventures and sufferings*, 29. The same can be said about Mackay. Strange noted that Maquinna wanted Mackay to stay because he was a doctor and had cured a skin complaint afflicting one of Maquinna's children. See Strange, *Journal*, 22. Walker noted that Mackay was paraded in front of guests and that his musket was the centrepiece of attention. See Walker, *Account of a voyage*, 180.
114 Jewitt, *Adventures and sufferings*, 37.
115 Ibid., 39.
116 Meares, *Voyages*, 109.
117 Walker, *Account of a voyage*, 62; Marshall, "Political history of the Nuu-chah-nulth," 213. Galliano noted that Maquinna had four wives. See Kendrick, *Voyage of the Sutil and Mexicana*, 76.
118 Howay, *Voyages of the "Columbia,"* 82, 100, 163, 265, 278. Bell named this chief "Clequawkini." See Meany, *New Vancouver journal*, 22.
119 Kendrick, *Voyage of the Sutil and Mexicana*, 80.
120 Saavedra, "Report on Nootka Sound," 1793-1794, Daylton, "Official documents," 291.
121 See "Plano de los Canales interiores del Puerto de Nutzca examinado en los años de 90 y 91 por Dn. Francisco Eliza y Dn. Alexandro Malaspina," 1793, plate 23, in *The American west coast and Alaska: Original drawings and maps from the expedition to Nootka Sound of Juan Francisco de la Bodega y Quadra, 1792* (New York: Krauss, Catalogue 144, 1976).
122 See Tomàs Bartroli, "The Malaspina expedition at Nootka," in Inglis, *Spain and the north Pacific coast*, 85-99.

123 Saavedra, "Report on Nootka Sound," 1793-1794, Daylton, "Official documents," 292.
124 Jewitt, *Adventures and sufferings*, 67.
125 Kendrick, *Voyage of the Sutil and Mexicana*, 74.
126 Moziño, *Noticias de Nutka*, 31; Henry R. Wagner, trans. and ed., "Journal of Tomás de Suria of his voyage with Malaspina to the northwest coast of America in 1791," *Pacific Historical Review* 5 (1936): 234-76, especially 273-76; Malaspina, "Politico-scientific voyage," II, 217; Cutter, *Malaspina and Galiano*, 81. Vancouver called this chief "Clewpenaloo." See Lamb, *Voyage of George Vancouver*, III, 916.
127 Saavedra, "Report on Nootka Sound," 1793-1794, Daylton, "Official documents," 292.
128 Cutter, *Malaspina and Galiano*, 97, 103, 88, 104; Saavedra, "Report on Nootka Sound," 1793-1794, Daylton, "Official documents," 297.
129 Some of these chiefly connections among the Mowachaht can also be traced in Jean Braithwaite, "Genealogical and selected biographical data on the Mowachaht," unpublished typescript, Parks Canada. I thank Richard Inglis for bringing this reference to my attention.
130 Marshall, "Political history of the Nuu-chah-nulth," 163-241.
131 Drucker called these Muchalaht groups a confederacy because they shared the summer village of Lupatcsis, but he did not ascertain when or how this alliance was established. See Drucker, *Northern and central Nootkan tribes*, 227-37.
132 See Curtis, *North American Indian*, 9, 182-86; Drucker, *Northern and central Nootkan tribes*, 228-31 and passim; Folan, "Community, settlement and subsistence patterns of the Nootka Sound area"; John Dewhirst, "Mowachaht ownership and use of the Salmon resources of the Leiner River and upper Tahsis Inlet, Nootka Sound, British Columbia," unpublished report prepared by Archeo Tech Associates, Victoria, 1990.
133 Marshall, "Political history of the Nuu-chah-nulth," chaps. 5 and 6.
134 Ibid., 203.
135 Before the formation of the Yuquot-Thasis confederacy there were probably five areas of political cooperation: the upper part of Tahsis, the upper part of Tlupana Inlet, Muchalat Inlet, the central part of the sound south to Hesquiat Peninsula, and the outside coast of Nootka Island. The inlets tended to be occupied by single lineage local groups; arrangements on the outside coast were more complicated. See Drucker, *Northern and central Nootkan tribes*, 248-51; Marshall, "Political history of the Nuu-chah-nulth," 192-97.
136 Walker, *Account of a voyage*, 106.
137 Strange, *Journal*, 18. In 1787, Colnett traded around the mouth of Muchalat Inlet. When the supercargo of the *Prince of Wales* explored the sound, he discovered that there were a number of groups wanting to trade. Native people from the east side of the sound insisted that Colnett change his anchorage before they commenced trading, as they "dared not offend the Chief whose district we lay in." See Colnett, "Journal," I, 57.
138 Ingraham to Martínez (1789), Freeman Tovell Collection.
139 Ibid.
140 In 1785, Hanna exchanged names with Cleaksinah, a Kelsemaht chief, who promised to hold furs for him if he returned the following year. See Lamb and Bartroli, "James Hanna and John Henry Cox," 12-13.
141 Alexander Dalrymple, *Plan for promoting the fur-trade* ... (London: George Bigg, 1789), 32.
142 Quadra to Revillagigedo, 24 October 1792, Daylton, "Official documents," 226.
143 Kaplanoff, *Joseph Ingraham's journal*, 233.
144 Meany, *New Vancouver journal*, 31.
145 Walker, *Account of a voyage*, 66 and 202.
146 Quadra, "Voyage to the n.w. coast," 44.
147 Marshall, "Political history of the Nuu-chah-nulth," 230.
148 Kendrick, *Voyage of the Sutil and Mexicana*, 80.
149 Ibid.
150 Ibid.
151 Wagner, "Journal of Tomás de Suria," 274.

152 Quadra, "Voyage to the n.w. coast," 47.
153 Lamb, *Voyage of George Vancouver*, II, 671-72
154 Newcombe, *Menzies journal*, 120 and 115. And as Marshall has pointed out, there is no evidence that any of the chiefs ranked in the Yuquot-Tahsis confederacy challenged the seating arrangements at such feasts, implying that they acknowledged Maquinna as the highest ranking chief. See Yvonne Marshall, "Dangerous liaisons: Maquinna, Quadra, and Vancouver in Nootka Sound, 1790-5," in Fisher and Johnston, *From maps to metaphors*, 160-75.
155 After the Spanish left, the British felt indebted to him for passing on important letters about the restitution of Nootka Sound. See William Robert Broughton, *A voyage of discovery to the north Pacific Ocean ... performed in his majesty's sloop Providence, and her tender, in the years 1795, 1796, 1797, 1798* (London: T. Caddell and W. Davies, 1804), 30; Roe, *Journals and letters of Captain Charles Bishop*, 95.
156 Archer, "Seduction before sovereignty," 155.
157 Walker, *Account of a voyage*, 54-55.
158 Jewitt, *Adventures and sufferings*, 36 and passim.
159 Martínez, "Diary," 213.
160 Jewitt, *Journal*; Idem., *Adventures and sufferings*, 36-37 and passim.
161 Wagner, "Journal of Tomás de Suria," 273.
162 Drucker, *Northern and central Nootkan tribes*, 333-36.
163 About one-third of these 107 vessels were one-time visitors; the majority of vessels that traded at Nootka Sound visited in two or more separate seasons. See Gibson, *Otter skins, Boston ships, and China goods*, table 1, 299-310. My figures for vessels at Nootka Sound between the years 1789 and 1793 are derived from the American, British, and Spanish sources cited above. In addition, there were six vessels at Nootka Sound in September 1794. See Thomas Manby, "Log of the proceedings of his majesty's armed tender Chatham, 27 September 1792-8 October 1794," PRO ADM 51/2251, fols. 127-127v, photostat in W. Kaye Lamb Collection, 4-3; and Archibald Menzies, "Journal," February to September 1794, fol. 184, photostat from the National Library of Australia, W. Kaye Lamb Collection, 11-8. I know of four vessels that visited in 1795: see Edmund Hayes, ed., *Log of the Union: John Boit's remarkable voyage to the northwest coast and around the world, 1794-1796* (Portland: Oregon Historical Society and Massachusetts Historical Society, 1981), 59; and Roe, *Journal and letters of Captain Charles Bishop*, 94.
164 Marshall, "Dangerous liaisons," 163.
165 Fidalgo reported on this event to Quadra. See Daylton, "Official documents," 87-88.
166 Marshall, "Dangerous liaisons," 170.
167 Ibid., 175.
168 And if lifted out of the context of late eighteenth-century Nuu-chah-nulth socio-political practices, projected unequivocally into the future, or treated too didactically, such reasoning can also entail Eurocentrism in reverse – a denial or retreat from the issue of cultural difference, the imputation that Native chiefs operated like modern, liberal Europeans, and the implication that Native leaders cherished the same tenets of European ideology that were instrumental in their dispossession and marginalization. Maquinna may have been a peaceful, consensus-oriented diplomat, but this does not change the fact that British colonial officials viewed Native peoples as warlike and irrational and that European powers used a liberalist rhetoric of reason and order to legitimise their colonial projects. Should we discuss European-Native contact processes on this European discursive terrain of diplomacy, consensus, and rationality? I am not sure, but arguments sometimes escape their authors, and Marshall might have acknowledged the cultural-historical provenance of the terminology she uses. Also see my review of the Obeyesekere-Sahlins debate in Chapter .
169 Moziño, *Noticias de Nutka*, 63.
170 Ibid., 31.
171 Roquefeuil, *Voyage around the world*, 103.
172 Strange, *Journal*, 27.

173 Walker, *Account of a voyage*, 114.
174 Meares, *Voyages*, 196.
175 Ibid., 208-209.
176 "Haswell's log of the first voyage of the 'Columbia,'" in Howay, *Voyages of the "Columbia*," 55.
177 Ramón Saavedra to Bodega y Quadra, 27 August 1791, Daylton, "Official documents," 224.
178 "Haswell's log of the first voyage of the 'Columbia,'" in Howay, *Voyages of the "Columbia*," 62. This point about firearms is elaborated by Robin Fisher in "Arms and men on the northwest coast, 1774-1825," *BC Studies* 29 (1976): 3-18.
179 Saavedra, "Report on Nootka Sound," 1793-1794, Daylton, "Official documents," 301.
180 "Log of Jacinto Caamaño," 1790, Daylton, "Official documents," 161.
181 Folan, "Community, settlement and subsistence patterns of the Nootka Sound area," 42-43.
182 Walker, *Account of a voyage*, 54.
183 Jewitt, *Adventures and sufferings*, 59 and 68.
184 Robert M. Galois, *Kwakwaka'wakw settlements, 1775-1920: A geographical analysis and gazetteer* (Vancouver/Seattle: UBC Press/University of Washington Press, 1994), 237-44.
185 Ibid. The Hahamatsees are listed as a Lewkiltok tribe in some the first Hudson's Bay Company censuses of the Native population of the Northwest Coast taken between 1835 and 1841. See ibid., Appendix 1, for details.
186 Ibid., 347-80. On this point, Galois relies mainly on Franz Boas, "The Indians of British Columbia: Lku'ugen, Nootka, Kwakiutl, Shushwap. Sixth report on the north-western tribes of Canada, 1890," *British Association for the Advancement of Science, Report 1890*, 553-715, especially 608.
187 Franz Boas, *Kwakiutl ethnography*, ed. Helen Codere (Chicago: University of Chicago Press, 1966), 117-18.
188 Malaspina, 1791, quoted in Cutter, *Malaspina and Galiano*, 102.
189 Ibid.
190 On the Ninelkaynuk, see Galois, *Kwakwaka'wakw settlements*, 319-20. Galois relies mainly on Wilson Duff's field notes. Archer Martin, a British Columbia lawyer, believed that there was a large inland tribe living between the Nimpkish River and Nootka Sound that was wiped out by warfare or disease around the time of contact, though he did not name the group. See Martin, "The inland tribes of Vancouver Island," BCARS F/1/M36. He got his information in 1903 from George Blenkinsop, a Hudson's Bay Company trader and, later, an Indian agent.
191 Drucker, *Northern and central Nootkan tribes*, 332-33; Sapir and Swadesh, *Native accounts of Nootka ethnography*, part 8; E.Y. Arima, *The west coast people: The Nootka of Vancouver Island and Cape Flattery* (Victoria: British Columbia Provincial Museum, Special Publications, no. 6, 1983), 105 and passim.
192 See, especially, Morris Swadesh, "Motivations in Nootkan warfare," *Southwestern Journal of Anthropology* 4, 1 (Spring 1948): 76-93. Brian Ferguson has argued that control over critical resources was the predominant motivation for war among Nuu-chah-nulth groups. See R. Brian Ferguson, "A reexamination of the causes of northwest coast warfare," in Ferguson, ed., *Warfare, culture, and environment* (London: Academic Press, 1984), 267-328.
193 Cutter, *Malaspina and Galiano*, 103.
194 Meares, *Voyages*, 229.
195 Ibid., 228-29.
196 Ibid., 228.
197 Walker, *Account of a voyage*, 59. When Colnett reached the sound the following year, the Natives told him that they had sold all their furs to Charles Barkley, another British trader. See Colnett, "Journal," I, 46-48. See also Meares, *Voyages*, 120; Wagner, "Journal of Tomás Suria," 273.
198 Meares, *Voyages*, 120-21. Martínez noted: "All these natives trade among themselves from one village to another ... It is known that although the Nootka Indians have received so much copper and iron from the different ships ... scarcely a piece of either can be seen among them now." See Martínez, "Diary," 200.

278 Notes to pages 125-27

199 John Dewhirst, "Nootka Sound: A 4,000 year perspective," in Barbara S. Efrat and W.J. Langlois, eds., "Nu.tka.: The history and survival of Nootkan culture," *Sound Heritage* 7, 2 (1978): 1-29; Marshall, "Political history of the Nuu-chah-nulth," chap. 5. Meares noted that "it was seldom that we could persuade them to make use of our utensils in preference to their own." See Meares, *Voyages*, 262.

200 There were scarcely any sea otters at Nootka Sound by the early 1790s. See "Log of Jacinto Caamaño," 1790, Daylton, "Official documents," 159; Moziño, *Noticias de Nutka*, 48; Kendrick, *Voyage of the Sutil and Mexicana*, 200-201.

201 See, especially, Quadra to Revillagigedo, 22 June 1792, Daylton, "Official documents," 235.

202 Malaspina, "Politico-scientific voyage," II, 228-29. It should be noted, however, that we know very little about the distribution of the sea otter and whether or not they lived in large numbers in inland lakes such as Woss Lake.

203 "Log of Jacinto Caamaño," 1790, Daylton, "Official documents," 159.

204 See Jopling, "Coppers of the northwest coast Indians," 127-32; Helen Codere, *Fighting with property: A study of the Kwakiutl potlatching and warfare, 1792-1930* (Washington: American Ethnological Society, Monograph 18, 1950).

205 Lamb, *Voyage of George Vancouver*, II, 625-27. Vancouver stated that the village consisted of thirty-four houses, and he found two or three muskets in each house.

206 Newcombe, *Menzies journal*, 88.

207 Kendrick, *Voyage of the Sutil and Mexicana*, 184-85. For a summary of Vancouver's and Galiano's activities in this region, see Galois, *Kwakwaka'wakw settlements*, Appendix 2.
Interestingly, Chief Cheslakees informed Vancouver that Maquinna "seldom visited" his village; nor is it documented that Cheslakees ever visited Nootka Sound. This raises the possibility that Natzape acted as a middleman between the Nimpkish and Nootka Sound groups. Natzape could have had connections with the Ninelkaynuk tribe, which lived around Woss Lake and whose members were probably bilingual. Wilson Duff notes that this group joined the Nimpkish "after the traders came." Wilson Duff Papers, file 122, microfilm in possession of the Department of Geography, UBC.

208 Moziño, *Noticias de Nutka*, 65. Hoskins noted that the Nootka Sound groups traded furs from the Nimpkish "for a trifling consideration in comparison to what they are afterwards sold to foreigners" at Nootka Sound. See "Hoskins' narrative of the second voyage of the 'Columbia,'" in Howay, *Voyages of the "Columbia,"* 265.

209 "Log of Jacinto Caamaño," 1790, Daylton, "Official documents," 159-60.

210 Jewitt, *Adventures and sufferings*, 68. The sea otter population around Queen Charlotte Sound was starting to decline, and traders were venturing more frequently to the vicinity of Nimpkish River.

211 On these economic changes, see Marshall, "Political history of the Nuu-chah-nulth," chap. 8.

212 See Drucker, *Northern and central Nootkan tribes*, 231. Mowachaht is derived from "Mowatca" – Tlupananul's village. See George Hunt, "Nootka tales," in "Tsimshian mythology," *Thirty-first annual report of the Bureau of American Ethnology, 1909-1910* (Washington, DC: Government Printing Office, 1916), 883-935, at 903; Folan, "Community, settlement and subsistence patterns of the Nootka Sound area," 72.

213 Augustus Brabant, "The death of Shewith the Mowachat (Nootka) chief," [1903], Diocese of Victoria, Papers.

214 Jewitt, *Adventures and sufferings*, 99.

215 Newcombe Family Papers, vol. 36, fol. 16.

216 John Dewhirst, "The Yuquot project vol. 1: The indigenous archaeology of Yuquot, a Nootkan outside village," *History and Archaeology* 39 (1980): especially 15, 346, 336.

217 Richard I. Inglis and James C. Haggarty, "Cook to Jewitt: Three decades of change in Nootka Sound," in *Le castor fait tout: Selected papers of the fifth North American fur trade conference, 1985*, ed. B. Trigger, T. Morantz and L. Dechène (Lake St. Louis Historical Society, 1987), 193-222.

218 And with these studies has come methodological debate among archaeologists about how to characterize continuity and change among Native groups. For a summary of different approaches to Northwest Coast archaeology, see Marshall, "Political history of the Nuu-chah-nulth," chaps. 1 and 2.

219 See Beaglehole, *Journals*, III, 303, 311, 1097, 1396, 1404; Strange, *Journal*, 37; Meares, *Voyages*, 201-202, 344; Howay, *Voyages of the "Columbia,"* 48, 55, and 83.

220 In September 1791, Maquinna purportedly told Malaspina: "I have not paid more visits [to Yuquot] because it is the season for laying fish to dry in the open. Since your people have been occupying this Cove I have been obliged to dwell permanently at Tahsis, where I try in summertime to make sufficient provision of fish for the winter." Quoted in Bartroli, "The Malaspina Expedition at Nootka," 95.

221 Marshall, "Political history of the Nuu-chah-nulth," 249-52.

222 This population data is discussed by Folan, "Community, settlement and subsistence patterns of the Nootka Sound area," 70-80.

223 Marshall, "Political history of the Nuu-chah-nulth," 166-68.

224 Leland Donald has synthesized references to slavery in the historical and ethnographic record, and he suggests that some Natives villages in the Northwest Coast may have had a slave population of up to 30 percent. It is impossible to arrive at a specific figure or percentage for Nootka Sound, however. See Leland Donald, "The slave trade on the northwest coast of North America," *Research in Economic Anthropology* 6 (1984): 121-58.

225 Colnett, "Journal," I, 71; Howay, *Voyages of the "Columbia,"* 190-93, 335-37, 371, 400-401.

226 John Boit, "Remarks on the ship Columbia's voyage," in Howay, *Voyages of the "Columbia,"* 401.

227 Kendrick, *Voyage of the Sutil and Mexicana*, 87.

228 Hayes, *Log of the Union*, 63-65.

229 Kaplanoff, *Joseph Ingraham's journal*, 208-12. For a summary of the activities of the Hope, see F.W. Howay, "The voyage of the Hope, 1790-1792," *Washington Historical Quarterly* 11, 1 (January 1920): 3-28.

230 Drucker, *Northern and central Nootkan tribes*, 222-25.

231 Ibid., 228.

Chapter 8: The Spatial Politics of Exchange at Clayoquot Sound

1 The observation comes from Barkley's wife, who accompanied him on his voyage and was the first White woman to visit the Northwest Coast. See Frances Barkley, "Reminiscences," 47, BCARS A/A/20/B24A. Barkley's trading journal has been lost; W. Kaye Lamb summarized what is known of this voyage in "The mystery of Mrs. Barkley's diary," *BCHQ* 6, 1 (January 1942): 31-59. The notion that Clayoquot Sound "belonged" to Wickaninish was also stressed by John Meares when he was interviewed by Britain's Privy Council in 1791. See Privy Council, Register, 8 February 1791, PRO PC 2/135, 443. Spanish explorers judged that Wickaninish was between forty and fifty years old, and described him as a plump, robust, impressive man. See Wagner, *Spanish explorations*, 83, 164.

2 The former figure was given by Sayaachapis, one of Sapir's informants. See Edward Sapir, Field Notebooks, "Nootka Notes," notebook 11, 14ff, Boas Collection, W2a.18, American Philosophical Society Library, photocopy in the possession of Richard Inglis, Royal British Columbia Museum; the latter figure, from Drucker's field notes, is cited in Richard I. Inglis and James C. Haggarty, "Pacific Rim National Park: Ethnographic history," unpublished report to Parks Canada, Calgary, 1986, 169. Curtis enumerated sixteen groups in *North American Indian*, vol. 9, 181-82.

3 Arcas Associates, "Patterns of settlement of the Ahousaht (Kelsemaht) and Clayoquot bands," unpublished report, Vancouver and Kamloops, 1989; Inglis and Haggarty, "Pacific Rim National Park," 166-72

There are conflicting accounts about the history of Opitsat. Vincent Koppert, an ethnographer, claimed that the Clayoquot displaced a Kelsemaht group from the village around 1780 and built around twenty houses there. See Koppert, *Contributions to Clayoquot ethnography* (Washington, DC: University of America, 1930), 1. Drucker, on the other hand, claimed that the village was captured from the Hisau'istaht. See Drucker, *Northern and central Nootkan tribes*, 240. But Arcas Associates point out that there is no mention of this capture in Drucker's field notes and that before the Clayoquot-Hisau'istaht war the site may have been occupied by some other Clayoquot Sound groups, including the Hohpitshaht. See Arcas Associates, "Patterns of settlement," 161.

4   This information, from Drucker's field notes, is summarized by Arcas Associates, "Patterns of settlement," 161-63.

5   Meares, *Voyages*, 143, 203. Another "mixed and split" expression, as Bhabha would have. Many traders were impressed by Native architecture and thought that it reflected complex socio-political arrangements. But they still tied such impressions to dualistic categories – in this case, the distinction between rude and polite society.

6   "Extract from Eliza's voyage," in Wagner, *Spanish explorations*, 146.

7   Howay, *Voyages of the "Columbia,"* 56, 391.

8   Meares, *Voyages*, 125

9   Ibid., 136.

10 The points in this paragraph are derived from Arcas Associates, "Settlement patterns," 159.

11 See ibid., 164; they note that this annual round persisted through the nineteenth century. This annual cycle, and the gendered division of labour that went with it, can also be pieced together from the historical record. See, especially, Meares, *Voyages*, 136-38, 143-48, 202-204, and Howay, *Voyages of the "Columbia,"* 45, 70, 248, 254, 257, 278-79, 315 and 390. The Clayoquot had taken over Indian Island, which was probably Hisau'istaht territory before the war. Echachist, a prime whaling spot, was probably owned by Hohpitshaht groups, but the Clayoquot seemed to have some rights to it before the war and were certainly living there on an annual basis by the late 1780s.

12 Meares, *Voyages*, 203.

13 Ibid., 141.

14 "Hoskins' narrative of the second voyage of the 'Columbia,'" in Howay, *Voyages of the "Columbia,"* 184

15 Meares, *Voyages*, 142-49.

16 Manuel Quimper's journal, in Wagner, *Spanish explorations*, 85. Other observers gave roughly the same description.

17 Meares, *Voyages*, 139.

18 Roe, *Journal and letters of Captain Charles Bishop*, 108.

19 "Haswell's log of the first voyage of the 'Columbia,'" in Howay, *Voyages of the "Columbia,"* 44.

20 The *Columbia* did a far better business at Clayoquot Sound on its second voyage, when it was stocked with copper and guns.

21 Meares and the officers of the *Columbia* gave lengthy descriptions of what they witnessed.

22 Hoskins was given a Native guard when he visited Opitsat in January 1792, but he could not ascertain whether Wickaninish was fearful of "other tribes attacking ... or of the wild beasts." Hoskins was told the latter but suspected the former. See "Hoskins' narrative of the second voyage of the 'Columbia,'" in Howay, *Voyages of the "Columbia,"* 261.

23 Meares, *Voyages*, 144-45.

24 Howay, *Journal of Captain James Colnett*, 201.

25 "Haswell's log of the first voyage of the 'Columbia,'" in Howay, *Voyages of the "Columbia,"* 57.

26 John Bartlett, "A narrative of events ... in the years 1790-1793, during voyages to Canton, the northwest coast of North America, and elsewhere," in *The sea, the ship, and the sailor: Tales of adventure from logs books and original narratives*, ed. Captain Elliot Snow (Salem MA: Marine Research Society, 1925), 287-337, at 297.

27 Meares, *Voyages*, 140.
28 Ibid.
29 When the Spanish visited Clayoquot Sound, they presented Wickaninish with shells and sheets of copper and were treated well by the chief. See Wagner, *Spanish explorations*, 86, 186.
30 "Hoskins' narrative of the second voyage of the 'Columbia,'" in Howay, *Voyages of the "Columbia,"* 183.
31 Ibid., 265.
32 Ibid., 186.
33 "Boit's log of the second voyage of the 'Columbia,'" in Howay, *Voyages of the "Columbia,"* 384-86; and see Hoskins's account, ibid., 260-65.
34 "Hoskins' narrative of the second voyage of the 'Columbia,'" in Howay, *Voyages of the "Columbia,"* 250.
35 Ibid., 270. In 1920, Clayoquot people told C.F. Newcombe that Gray built the vessel "on the South East point of the entrance to Disappointment Sound in Meares' Island, just opposite the present village of Opitsat." See Newcombe to Howay, 24 September 1921, Howay Papers, box 5, folder 12, UBCL-SC.
36 "Haswell's log of the second voyage of the 'Columbia,'" in Howay, *Voyages of the "Columbia,"* 312.
37 "Hoskins' narrative of the second voyage of the 'Columbia,'" in Howay, *Voyages of the "Columbia,"* 272.
38 Ibid., 275.
39 "Boit's log of the second voyage of the 'Columbia,'" in Howay, *Voyages of the "Columbia,"* 391. Boit lamented: "This fine Village, the Work of Ages, was in a short time totally destroy'd."
40 Marshall, "Political history of the Nuu-chah-nulth,' 227-28.
41 "Log of the Jefferson," 28 September 1793; Roe, *Journal and letters of Captain Charles Bishop*, 107.
42 "Log of the Jefferson," 13-14 June 1793; Howay, *Journal of Captain James Colnett*, 202.
43 "Log of the Jefferson," 13 June 1793.
44 Drucker, *Northern and central Nootkan tribes*, 110-11. For the Pacific Islands, see Thomas, *Entangled objects*.
45 Drucker, *Northern and central Nootkan tribes*, 110
46 Kaplanoff, *Joseph Ingraham's journal*, 224.
47 Ibid., 225.
48 "Log of the Jefferson," 13 June 1793.
49 Ibid.
50 Meares, *Voyages*, 230.
51 Ibid., 203-204. Vancouver was at Nootka Sound when Wickaninish arrived to strike this marriage arrangement. See Lamb, *Voyage of George Vancouver*, III, 917.
52 Meares observed this. See ibid., 175.
53 Meares noted that there was a fine line between "that rigour which begets discontent" and that idleness born from leisure that "so often appropriates to mischief." See ibid., 190.
54 Ibid., 145.
55 Although traders visited the sound less frequently after 1795.
56 For a checklist of the available data see E.W. Giesecke, "Search for the Tonquin," *Cumtux: Clatsop County Historical Society Quarterly* 10, 3 (1990): 3-8; Ibid., 10, 4 (1990): 3-14; Ibid., 11, 1 (1991): 23-40.
57 See Gabriel Franchère's account, excerpted in F.W. Howay, "The loss of the Tonquin," *Washington Historical Quarterly* 13, 2 (1922): 83-92, at 86; Robert Stuart's account, in *Nouvelles annales des voyages ...* , vol. X (1821), 5-8; and Edmund Fanning, *Voyages to the South Seas, Indian and Pacific Oceans ...* (New York: William M. Vermilye, 1838), 138-42.
58 W.E. Banfield, "Vancouver Island. Its topography, characteristics, &c., no. VII: Clayoquot Sound – The Tonquin massacre," *Daily Victoria Gazette*, 9 September 1858.

59 Meares, *Voyages*, 146-47.
60 See Howay, *Voyages of the 'Columbia'*, 261, 386; Saavedra, "Report on Nootka Sound," 1793-1794, Daylton, "Official documents," 300. Wickaninish and Hannape were cousins; Wickaninish was married to Tatoosh's sister; Wickaninish and Maquinna were parents-in-law and brothers-in-law.
61 See Walker, *Account of a voyage*, 59-60.
62 "Haswell's log of the first voyage of the 'Columbia,'" in Howay, *Voyages of the "Columbia,"* 79; "Log of the Jefferson," 1 June 1793. Although Wickaninish took sea otter furs from Barkley Sound, Magee of the *Jefferson* improvised, trading clamons (elk hides used as war dresses), which were prized by Native groups on the northern coast, and Haiqua (dentalia) shells, which Chinook people around the Columbia River used as currency.
63 "Log of the Jefferson," 28 September 1793-2 April 1794.
64 Roe, *Journal and letters of Captain Charles Bishop*, 105-107.
65 "Log of the Jefferson," 25 October 1793.
66 Sapir, "Nootka Notes," notebook 1 (Johnny Yocum informant), 10-11, and notebook 12 (Sayaachapis informant), 27-27v.
67 "Ucluelets seize Effingham Inlet," Sapir and Swadesh, *Native accounts of Nootka ethnography*, 368-77 (quotation is from 374-75).
68 "Boit's log of the second voyage of the 'Columbia,'" in Howay, *Voyages of the "Columbia,"* 389.
69 "Hoskins' narrative of the second voyage of the 'Columbia,'" in Howay, *Voyages of the "Columbia,"* 269.
70 "Haswell's log of the second voyage of the 'Columbia,'" in Howay, *Voyages of the "Columbia,"* 313.
71 Jewitt, *Journal*, 11.
72 Meares, *Voyages*, 212.
73 There are two exceptions to this statement about Clayoquot relations with northern groups. There is some suggestion in the Spanish record that the Clayoquot killed 70 Hesquiaht in 1793 (see Daylton, "Official documents," 267); and the Clayoquot, allied with the Mowachaht, attacked the Kyuquot in the mid-1850s (see Sproat, *Scenes and studies of savage life*, chap. 22, for a lengthy description).
74 The details in the following few paragraphs are derived from Inglis and Haggarty, "Pacific Rim National Park," and Blenkinsop to Simpson, 24 October 1852, PAC-HBCA, D.5/35, fol. 87-88.
75 Evidence for this comes from Banfield to Prevost, 30 October 1859, Church Missionary Society, North Pacific Mission, CMS 2./0, UBCL-SC; and Sherlock Gooch, "Across Vancouver Island," *Colburn's United Service Magazine* (1856), 516-541; Ibid., (1887), 28-40.
76 See "Log of the Jefferson," especially February to April 1794.
77 "The long war" is chronicled by Kwishanishim in Sapir and Swadesh, *Native account of Nootka ethnography*, 386-440.
78 Blenkinsop to Simpson, 24 October 1852, PAM-HBCA D.5/35, fols. 87-88; Blenkinsop to Devereux, 25 May 1896, John Devereux – Correspondence, 1890-1896, BCARS J/G/T61D.
79 Brabant to Devereux, 15 May 1896, Augustus J. Brabant, Miscellaneous Papers, BCARS E/D/B72.4.
80 Samuel Hancock, "Thirteen years residence on the north-west coast ...," fols. 264-69 (quotation is from fol. 266), Bancroft Library, Berkeley, HHB P-B29.
81 Eliza remarked that Barkley Sound had a larger population than either Nootka Sound or Clayoquot Sound. See "Extract from Eliza's voyage," 1791, Wagner, *Spanish explorations*, 149. And see "Report to the commissioner of Indian Affairs," signed by George Blenkinsop, 23 September 1874, Department of Indian Affairs, Black Series, Public Archives of Canada RG10, vol. 3614, file 4105.
82 This census is undated and the census-taker is unidentified. It appears in James Douglas, Private Papers, BCARS B20 1853, which is a compilation of censuses taken by the company between the 1830s and early 1850s, and it is reproduced in "Indian population, Vancouvers Island,

1856," J.S. Helmcken Papers, Add. MSS. 505. Roderick Finlayson, a Hudson's Bay Company factor at Fort Victoria, collected census information during the 1840s and passed it on to British naval personnel, but his figures for the west coast of Vancouver Island are vague and composite ("Nootka 1600"; "Klay-quoit 1100"). This information is enclosed in Great Britain, Admiralty, HMS Pandora, Correspondence of Lt. Wood, 1848, BCARS 0/A/P19W.

83 William Banfield, "Census" 1859, in Fort Victoria, Land Office, Register of land purchases from Indians," vol. 4, BCARS Add. MSS.772. See Galois, *Kwakwaka'wakw settlements*, appendix 1, for a discussion of the Hudson's Bay Company censuses.

84 See Inglis and Haggarty, "Pacific Rim National Park," 87-93 and passim.

85 The Ahousaht elder Peter Webster also suggested that the Ahousaht used guns during the Long War in Barkley Sound. See Webster, *As far as I know*, 59-60.

86 See Howay, *Voyages of the 'Columbia,'* 197-98, 380, 393-94. In the summer of 1788 Robert Duffin, Meares's first officer, was attacked while trading in a longboat. See Meares, *Voyages*, 175-77.

87 See Wagner, *Spanish explorations*, 109-27, 149-53, 171-90; Daylton, "Official documents," 159-97.

88 Peter Puget, "A log of the proceedings of his majesty's sloop Discovery," 4 January 1791-14 January 1793, PRO ADM 55/27, fol. 134.

89 Kendrick, *Voyage of the Sutil and Mexicana*, 116.

90 Cole Harris, "Voices of smallpox around the Strait of Georgia in 1782," in his *The resettlement of British Columbia: Essays on colonialism and geographical change* (Vancouver; UBC Press, 1997), chap. 1.

91 Finlayson to McLoughlin, 18 January 1845, PAM-HBCA B.226/b/1, fol. 13.

92 Howay, *Voyages of the 'Columbia'*, 197; Meares, *Voyages*, 180-84.

Chapter 9: Regional Geographies of Accommodation and Appropriation

1 The first quotation is from Howay's contribution to F.W. Howay, W.N. Sage, and H.F. Angus, eds., *British Columbia and the United States: The north Pacific slope from the fur trade to aviation* (New York: Russell and Russell, 1942), 13; the second quotation is from Howay, "Outline sketch of the maritime fur trade," 14.

2 Philip Drucker, *Indians of the northwest coast*, (Garden City, NY: Natural History, 1967), 30.

3 Edward Sapir, "Cultures, genuine and spurious," orig. pub. 1924, in Mandelbaum, *Selected writings of Edward Sapir*, 308-31 (quotation is from 318).

4 This quoted phrase is from Barry M. Gough, *The northwest coast: British navigation, trade and discoveries to 1812* (Vancouver: UBC Press, 1992), 50.

5 Joyce A. Wike, "The effect of the maritime fur trade on northwest coast Indian society" (PhD diss., Department of Political Science, Columbia Unversity, 1947), 91. Wike got some of her inspiration for this argument from the ethnographer Marius Barbeau. See Barbeau, "Totem poles: A by product of the fur trade," *Scientific Monthly*, December 1942, 507-14.

6 Robin Fisher, *Vancouver's voyage: Charting the northwest coast, 1791-1795* (Vancouver/Toronto: Douglas and McIntyre, 1992), 110.

7 Fisher, *Contact and conflict*, 17.

8 Ibid., 23; Fisher, "Indian control of the maritime fur trade and the northwest coast," in *Approaches to native history in Canada*, ed. D.A. Muise (Ottawa: National Museums of Canada, 1977), 65-86.

9 Thomas, *Entangled objects*, 83-84.

10 Joyce Wike, "Problems in fur trade analysis," *American Anthropologist* 60 (1958): 1,096-101.

11 He had less data to work with than we do now, but he continues to play down the impact of these destructive forces. See his Preface to the second edition of *Contact and conflict* (1992).

12 See David Harvey, *The urban experience* (Oxford: Blackwell, 1989); Harvey, *The limits to capital* (Oxford: Blackwell, 1982).

13 For a broader overview see Harris, "Social power and cultural change in pre-colonial British Columbia," especially 71-76.

14 Inglis and Haggarty, "Pacific Rim National Park," 12-13.
15 Marshall, "Political history of the Nuu-chah-nulth," 175.
16 Galois, *Kwakwaka'wakw settlements*, 223-76.
17 Extracts of "Edward Sapir's Correspondence," National Museums of Canada Mercury Series, in the possession of Richard Inglis, Royal British Columbia Museum, Victoria, Canada.

Part 3: Introduction

1 Sir Edward Belcher, *Narrative of a voyage round the world, performed in her majesty's ship Sulphur, during the years 1836-1842* ... , 2 vols., (Folkstone, UK: Dawsons, 1970 [orig. pub. 1843]), I, 107.
2 This is pointed out in Orsmby, *British Columbia*, 26, and many other studies.
3 For a brilliant elaboration of such ideas, see Said, *Orientalism*; Said, *Culture and imperialism*.
4 My epigraph is in the J.R. Anderson Papers, box 9, BCARS Add. MSS. 1912.
5 Alexander C. Anderson, "Notes on the Indian tribes of British North America, and the northwest coast," *The Historical Magazine* 7, 3 (1863): 73-81.

Chapter 10: The Ledger, the Map, and British Imperial Vision

1 Merry to Leeds, 4 January 1790, PRO FO 72/16, fol. 3-4.
2 Two more vague despatches came from Merry on 7 and 15 January 1790 – PRO FO 72/16, fols. 9, 64. In his despatch of 15 January, Merry enclosed extracts of a letter from Mexico dated 28 August 1789. By the start of January 1790, Count Floridablanca, Spain's first mininster, had fairly detailed knowledge of what had happened at Nootka Sound. He had received two letters written by the viceroy of Mexico that summarized Martínez's actions. The letter Merry saw was probably unofficial, and it was thin on detail. For more details see William R. Manning, "The Nootka Sound controversy," *Annual Report of the American Historical Association For the Year 1904*, 279-478, especially 334-67.
3 Leeds to Merry, 2 February 1790, PRO FO 72/16, fol. 87-88.
4 This quotation is from a draft of Leeds's letter, which was evidently written in a rage, in PRO FO 72/16, fols. 130-31.
5 English translation of Campo to Leeds, 10 February 1790, PRO 30/8/341, fols. 65-67; the Spanish text of this letter is in "Documents relating to the Nootka Sound controversy," 3 vols. UBCL-SC, II, 371-74.
6 Pitt to Leeds, 23 February, Leeds to Pitt, 23 February 1790, PRO 30/8/102, fol. 170, 30/8/151, fols. 55-56. Pitt was also agitated because Leeds had not given copies of his letter to the Cabinet.
7 Copy of Leeds to Campo, 26 February 1790, PRO FO 72/16, fols. 136-37. Leeds wrote to Campo de Alange under Pitt's supervision.
8 This point is stressed by John Ehrman in *The younger Pitt*, vol. 1: *The years of acclaim* (London: Constable, 1969), 556.
9 Furthermore, in February 1790 Pitt was concerned foremost with the military threat that France and the Austrian Netherlands posed to the newly independent Belgian states, and British diplomats were trying to hold together the Triple Alliance that Pitt had forged with Prussia and the United Provinces in 1788. See Jeremy Black, *British foreign policy in an age of revolutions, 1783-1793* (Cambridge: Cambridge University Press, 1994), chap. 5, which is the most recent and detailed analysis of the European dimensions of the Nootka Crisis
10 See Ehrman, *Pitt*, I, 467-574; J.M. Norris, "The policy of the British Cabinet in the Nootka crisis," *English Historical Review* 70 (October 1955): 562-80.
11 Merry to Leeds, 5 April 1790, PRO FO 72/16, fols. 245-47.
12 Merry to Leeds, 8, 18, and 25 February, 29 March, 12 and 19 April 1790, PRO FO 72/16 fols. 97-99, 109, 118, 239, 257, 270; Merry to Leeds, 3 May 1790, PRO FO 72/17, fol. 3. See also Paul Webb, "The naval aspects of the Nootka Sound crisis," *Mariner's Mirror* 61 (1975): 133-54.
13 Merry also doubted whether Spain had good enough finances to quckly muster a large military force.

14 See Miranda to Pitt, 8 September 1791, in Documents II, "English policy toward America in 1790-1791," introduced by Frederick J. Turner, *American Historical Review* 7, 4 (July 1902): 706-35, at 711-15. On the rise of South American resistance movements in Spanish America during this period see Colin M. MacLachlan, *Spain's empire in the New World: The role of ideas in institutional and social change* (Berkeley: University of California Press, 1988).

15 British business promoters still hoped that a Northwest Passage would be found. In July 1789, the British fur trader George Dixon wrote to Evan Nepean (undersecretary of state at the Home Office), arguing that a naval expedition should be sent to the Northwest Coast to establish a British settlement in order to prevent the Russians, Americans, and Spanish from colonizing the commerce of the region and to protect the coast for British traders "from both Hudson's Bay and Canada" in the event that a water passage across North America was discovered. Dixon's remarks were reiterated by Alexander Dalrymple, who, in September 1789, impressed on the Home Secretary the need to prevent the Northwest Passage from falling into Spain's hands. See Dixon to Nepean, (July) 1789, PRO CO 42/72, fol. 243-44; Dalrymple to Sydney, (September) 1789, PRO CO 42/61, fols. 56-62. These documents and developments are discussed in more detail in Alan Frost, "Nootka Sound and the beginnings of Britain's imperialism of free trade," in *From maps to metaphors: The Pacific world of George Vancouver*, ed. Robin Fisher and Hugh Johnston (Vancouver: UBC Press, 1993), 104-26.

16 Evan Nepean, Instructions to Captain Roberts, March 1790, PRO HO 28/61, fol. 249; Grenville to Cornwallis (secret), 31 March 1790, PRO HO 28/61, fol. 253-54. Overland expeditions in search of the Northwest Passage were also planned through the offices of the Hudson's Bay Company. See Glyndwr Williams, *The British search for the north west passage in the eighteenth century* (London: Longmans, Green, 1962), 239-40.

17 The handwritten draft of Meares's memorial is in PRO HO 28/61, fols. 291-373; it includes fourteen documentary appendices detailing Martínez's actions. On Meares's dealings with Grenville, see Norris, "Policy," 569, notes 1 and 2.

18 The *Iphigenia Nubiana*, commanded by William Douglas, was detained on 13 May but released two weeks later. The *North West America*, commanded by Robert Funter, was seized on 9 June. The *Argonaut*, commanded by James Colnett, was seized on 3 July. And the *Princess Royal* (then on its third trading trip to the Northwest Coast), commanded by Thomas Hudson, was seized on 13 July. The latter two vessels were taken to San Blas in the third week of July. The Spanish stripped all of these vessels of their sea otter furs, trade goods, and provisions, and Martínez renamed the *North West America* the *Gertrudis* and sent it on a trading trip for Spain's benefit. See Manning, "Nootka Sound controversy," 286-361; and Cook, *Flood tide of empire*, 146-99.

19 *The memorial of John Mears, lieutenant in his majesty's navy, to the Right Honourable William Wyndham Grenville ... dated 30th April 1790* (quotation is from 1-2 [emphasis in original]).

20 The quotation is from Leeds to Fitzherbert, 17 August 1790, PRO FO 72/18, fol. 189. The same point is made in Leeds to Pitt, 2 June, Leeds to Fitzherbert, 5 July 1790, PRO 30/8/151, fol. 57, PRO FO 72/18, fol. 22. And see Verus [Bland Burges], *Letters lately published in the Diary, on the subject of the present dispute with Spain* (London: G. Kearsley, 1790), letter III, 7: "no right but that of *actual possession* or *prior occupancy*, can amount to an exclusion of other nations." Burges was undersecretary of state at the Foreign Office and advised Leeds on legal matters.

21 See Argonaut [John Cadman Etches], *An authentic statement of all the facts relative to Nootka Sound ...* (London: Debrett, 1790), published in June, which points up some of the inaccuracies in Meares's statement of losses and gives his account of the sea otter trade. Etches was one of Meares's associates.

22 Leeds's interpretation of Campo's letter of 20 February, in Leeds to Merry, 4 May 1790, PRO FO 72/17, fol. 19.

23 Cabinet Minute, 30 April, Historical Manuscript Commission (HMC), *Dropmore Papers*, vol. 1 (London: HMSO, 1892), 579.

24 Grenville to George the Third, 1 and 2 May, George the Third to Grenville, 1 and 2 May, Grenville to Westmorland, 3 May 1790, HMC, *Dropmore*, I, 579-80.

25 See Webb, "Naval aspects."
26 See Frost, "Nootka Sound."
27 See Turner in "English policy towards America," 706-10; S.F. Bemis, "Relations between the Vermont Separatists and Great Britain, 1789-1791," *American Historical Review* 21, 1 (1916): 547-53.
28 Earl Stanhope, *Life of the Right Honourable William Pitt*, 4 vols., 3rd ed. (London: John Murray, 1867), II, 51.
29 Printed in William Cobbett, ed., *The parliamentary history of England* ... , vol. XXVIII (London: Hansard, 1816), 764-69. This message was prepared by Pitt, and the king considered it a "fair and concise narrative" of the issue. George the Third to Pitt, 5 May 1790, quoted in Donald Grove Banes, *George III and William Pitt, 1783-1806* (New York: Octagon, 1965), 227. Printed copies of Meares *Memorial* can be found in PRO HO 42/16, PRO FO 72/17 and FO 95/7/4.
30 These proceedings are documented in Great Britain, *Official papers relative to the dispute between the courts of Great Britain and Spain, on the subject of the ships captured in Nootka Sound ...* (London: J. Debrett, 1790), 27-38. A summary of Meares's memorial was published in the *Gentleman's Magazine* for June 1790, and these developments in early May can be tracked in the the *St. James Chronicle* and the London *Times*.
31 Cobbett, *Parliamentary history*, XXVIII, 770.
32 Leeds to Merry, 3, 4, and 5 May 1790, PRO FO 72/17, fols. 7-9, 15-21, 23-24.
33 Leeds to Merry, 4 May 1790, PRO FO 72/17, fol. 20.
34 Leeds, Draft instructions for Alleyne Fitzherbert, 7 May 1790, Leeds to Fitzherbert 16 May 1790, PRO FO 72/17, fols. 35-52, 54-59, 84-87 (quotation is from fol. 54 [my emphasis]).
35 J. Holland Rose, *A short life of William Pitt* (London: G. Bell and Sons, 1925), 82. Britain borrowed ten ships of the line from the Dutch and employed Portuguese spies to report on Spanish naval activities. See Robin Reilly, *Pitt the younger, 1759-1806* (London: Cassell, 1978), 180-81.
36 Fitzherbert to Leeds, 4 June, 5 and 29 July 1790, in "Nootka Sound controversy. Correspondence, 1789-1798," vol. 1, 98, 150, 169, BCARS A/A/10.1/Sp12. Prussia reluctantly agreed to provide military support to Britain if Austria, France, or Russia became involved in the dispute and war broke out in Europe. See Black, *British foreign policy in an age of revolutions*, for a detailed analysis of these diplomatic maneouvres
37 This declaration and Britain's counter-declaration are printed in Cobbett, *Parliamentary history*, XXVIII, 914-16, and *The annual register ... for the year 1790* (London: J. Dodsley, 1793), 300-301. On French attitudes towards the dispute, see Bland Burges, *A narrative of the negotiations occasioned by the dispute between England and Spain in the year 1790* (London: 1790), 212-133; William Doyle, *The Oxford history of the French Revolution* (Oxford and New York: Oxford University Press, 1990), 162-66.
38 This Convention was signed on 28 October 1790 and was published on 7 November. Copies can be found in PRO FO 72/20 and *The annual register*, 1790, 303-305.
39 The most authoritative account of Spain's handling of the dispute is Warren Cook's *Flood tide of empire: Spain and the Pacific northwest, 1543-1819* (New Haven: Yale University Press, 1973), especially 234-49.
40 J. Holland Rose, *William Pitt and national revival* (London: G. Bell and Sons, 1911), 567.
41 Indeed, John Derry notes that some British politicians seemed more interested in the diplomatic role that the French National Assembly played in the dispute than in the nature of the grievance with Spain; the dispute "allowed pro-French sympathisers to point to the [eventual] denunciation of the old Family Compact between the French and Spanish Bourbons [by Luzerne and Mirabeau] as evidence that the French reformers were acting up to their protestations of peace and their renunciation of dynastic ambitions." See John W. Derry, *Politics in the age of Fox, Pitt and Liverpool: Continuity and transformation* (London: Methuen, 1990), 80.
42 See, especially, E.J. Hobsbawm, *The age of revolution, 1789-1848* (New York: Mentor, 1962), 22-43.

43 Jean Comaroff and John Comaroff, *Of revelation and revolution: Christianity, colonialism and consciousness in South Africa* (Chicago and London: University of Chicago Press, 1991), 86.

44 See James Der Derian, *On diplomacy: A genealogy of western estrangement* (Oxford: Blackwell, 1987), who argues that multistate diplomacy in eighteenth-century Europe presupposed "a system of reciprocal orientations" and aimed to mediate "mutual estrangements between states" – that is, to mediate culturally and politically specific notions of foreignness (105-106).

45 On the differences between British, French, Portuguese, and Spanish interpretations of the Law of Nations, see L.C. Green and Olive Dickason, *The law of nations and the New World* (Edmonton: University of Alberta Press, 1989).

46 Michael Mann, *The sources of social power*, vol. 2: *The rise of classes and nation-states, 1760-1914* (Cambridge: Cambridge University Press, 1993), 254.

47 Colley, *Britons*, 59.

48 Ibid., 60.

49 These revenue figures are from J.V. Beckett and Michael Turner, "Taxation and economic growth in eighteenth-century Britain," *Economic History Review* (2nd series) 42, 3 (August 1990): 377-403, figure 1 at 379. The import and export figures are from C.H. Lee, *The British economy since 1700* (Cambridge: Cambridge University Press, 1986), chap. 6.

50 Patrick O'Brien, "Inseperable connections: Trade, economy, fiscal state, and the expansion of empire," in Marshall, *Oxford history of the British Empire*, II, 71-72.

51 These views are well articulated in Charles D'avenant's "Discourse on the plantation trade" (1698), in *The political and commercial works of ... Charles D'avenant*, 5 vols., ed. Sir Charles Whitworth (London: R. Horsfield et al., 1771), II; Malachy Postlethwayt, *The universal dictionary of trade and commerce ...* 2 vols., 4th ed. (London: 1774). On Adam Smith, see Bernard Semmel, *The liberal idea and the demons of empire: From Adam Smith to Lenin* (Baltimore: Johns Hopkins University Press, 1993), chap. 2.

52 See, especially, Appaduarai, *Modernity at large*, 114-35; John Brewer, *The sinews of power: War, money, and the English state, 1688-1783* (London: Unwin Hyman, 1989); Sudipta Kaviraj, "On the construction of colonial power: structure, discourse, hegemony," in *Contesting colonial hegemony: States and Society in Africa and India*, ed. Dagmar Engels and Shula Marks (London: Tauris, 1994), 19-54.

53 Kathleen Wilson, "The good, the bad, and the impotent: Imperialism and the politics of identity in Georgian Britain," in *The consumption of culture, 1600-1800*, ed. Ann Bermingham and John Brewer (London: Routledge, 1995), 237-62 (quotations are from 239-40). See also Brantlinger, *Fictions of the state*.

54 Brewer, *Sinews of power*. For another vivid account of these connections, see Langford, *A polite and commercial people*.

55 A. Dalrymple, *The Spanish memorial of 4th June considered* (London: George Bigg, 1790), 6. See also Burges, *Dispute with Spain*, letter 1; Leeds to Merry, 4 May 1790, PRO FO 72/17, fol. 15. The crisis was also dramatized. James Bryn's pantomime-opera, "Nootka Sound; or Britain prepar'd," opened at Covent Garden in June 1790. A typescript of the text is held at UBCL-SC.

56 Quoted in Marlies K. Danziger and Frank Brady, eds., *Boswell: The great biographer, 1789-1795* (London: Heinemann, 1989), 113. Pitt attended the banquet and was a member of the Grocer's Company of London. John Boydell was the world's leading merchant-printseller. He developed a huge export trade in English prints. See Timothy Clayton, *The English Print, 1688-1802* (New Haven and London: Yale University Press, 1997), 209-11.

57 Pitt worked with the philosophy of his father, who told Parliament at the start of the Anglo-Spanish war of 1739: "When trade is at stake it is your last retrenchment. You must defend it or perish." See Pitt (the elder), 8 March 1739, quoted in Reilly, *Pitt*, 181.

58 These quotations are from Palmerston to Mee, 12 May 1790, quoted in A. Aspinall, ed., *The later correspondence of George III*, vol. 1: *December 1783-January 1793* (Cambridge: Cambridge University Press, 1962), no. 589, note 1; Anonymous, *The errors of the British minister, in the negotiations with the court of Spain* (London: J. Debrett, 1790), 18.

59 During May and June 1790, Cabinet ministers were questioned by the Opposition about the value of the sea otter trade and whether it was likely to remain profitable. The debates can be followed in *Official documents relative to the dispute*. Commentators also argued over the value of the whale fishery. Some merchants claimed that whales caught in the Pacific sold for £90 in England, whereas Greenland whales were worth £170. Other merchants noted that whale oil from the Pacific sold for £50 a ton in London, whereas that from the north Atlantic was worth only £19 a ton. See P.S. Wilson, *Pitt, the younger* (Garden City, NY: Doubleday, 1930), 204.

60 Burges to Leeds, 27 June 1790, BM Add. MS. 28,066, fols. 55-56.

61 Fitzherbert to Leeds, 16 June 1790, BM Add. MS. 28,066, fols. 27-28.

62 Cobbett, *Parliamentary history*, XXVII, 979.

63 Steven, *Trade, tactics and territory*, 67.

64 Argonaut [John Cadman Etches], *A continuation of an authentic statement ...* (London: T. Beckett, 1790), 23.

65 Wilson, "The good, the bad, and the impotent," 241

66 Ehrman, *Pitt*, I, 354.

67 Ibid.

68 On Pitt's appreciation of British trade, see ibid., 329-436. On the whale and seal fishery, see MacKay, *In the wake of Cook*.

69 "Examination of Mr. Meares (fur trade)," 27 May 1790, PRO BT 5/6, fols. 113-19.

70 On Dalrymple's career, see "Memoir of Alexander Dalrymple," *The European Magazine and London Review* 42 (1802): 323-27, 421-24.

71 Dalrymple to Nepean, 3 July and 20 August 1790, PRO FO 95/7/4, fols. 339-40, 438. The two pamphlets are *Spanish pretensions*, published on 7 May, and *Spanish memorial*, published in mid-June.

72 Dalrymple, *The Spanish pretensions fairly discussed*, (London: George Bigg, 1790), 8 (emphasis in original).

73 Fitzherbert's translation, enclosed in Fitzherbert to Leeds, 16 June 1790, PRO FO 72/17, fols. 308-10. A slightly different translation can be found in *Official documents relative to the dispute*, 51-52, and *The annual register*, 1790, 294-98.

74 Leeds to Fitzherbert (private), 16 August 1790, BM Add. MS. 28,066 (quotation is from fol. 27). The reference is to Postlethwayt's *Universal dictionary of trade and commerce*.

75 Leeds to Fitzherbert, 17 August 1790, PRO FO 72/18, fols. 192-93. This *Noticias*, written by A.M. Burriel, *was* approved by the Spanish government.

76 Ehrman, *Pitt*, I, 348.

77 Alfred Cobban and Robert A. Smith, eds., *The correspondence of Edmund Burke*, vol. 6: *July 1789-December 1791* (Cambridge: Cambridge University Press, 1967), 118.

78 Said writes: "Imperialism is after all an act of geographical violence through which virtually every space in the world is explored, charted, and finally brought under control," See Said, *Culture and imperialism*, 225.

79 On these currents of thought, see Pratt, *Imperial eyes*, part 1; David N. Livingstone, *The geographical tradition: Episodes in the history of a contested discipline* (Oxford: Blackwell, 1992), chap. 4. On British views of Africa at the end of the eighteenth century, see Comaroff and Comaroff, *Revelation and revolution*, chap. 3. On these currents of thought in Spain and Spanish America, see Arthur Whittaker, "Changing and unchanging interpretations of the Enlightenment in Spanish America," *Proceedings of the American Philosophical Society* 114, 4 (1970): 256-71.

80 I am referring to Brewer's *Sinews of power*.

81 These quotations are from T. Bankes, ed., *A new, royal, and authentic system of geography ... containing a genuine history of and description of the whole world* (London: C. Cooke, [1790]), preface, n.p.; and George Augustus Baldwyn, ed., *A new, royal, complete, and universal system of geography ...* (London: Alex Hogg, [1785]), iii.

82 Brewer, *Sinews of power*, part five.
83 Ibid., 222.
84 See also Philip Corrigan and Derek Sayer, *The great arch: English state formation as cultural revolution* (Oxford: Blackwell, 1985), especially 124 ff.
85 Brewer, *Sinews of power*, 228, 230. However, we should acknowledge that the impact of "useful knowledge" on government was uneven. Brewer notes that the Excise Commission developed a sophisticated system of data collection and management. On the other hand, Bland Burges complained that when he joined the Foreign Office in 1789, "immense number[s] of dispatches" were "piled up in large presses, but no note of them is taken, nor is there even an index to them; so that, if anything is wanted, the whole year's accumulation must be rummaged over." See James Hutton, ed., *Selections from the letters and correspondence of Sir James Bland Burges ...* (London: John Murray, 1885), 131.
86 Nicholas Dirks, Foreward to Bernard Cohn, *Colonialism and its forms of knowledge: The British in India* (Princeton: Princeton University Press, 1996),
87 Michel Foucault, "Governmentality," in *The Foucault effect: Studies in governmentality*, ed. Graham Burchell, Colin Gordon, and Peter Miller (Hemel Hempstead: Harvester Wheatsheaf, 1991), 87-104 (quotation is from 102).
88 Kaviraj, "On the construction of colonial power," 31.
89 I am indebted to Barbara Belyea, who encouraged me to think through these issues.
90 David Philip Miller, "Joseph Banks, empire, and 'centers of calculation' in late Hanoverian London," in *Visions of empire: Voyages, botany, and representations of nature*, ed., David Philip Miller and Peter Hanns Reill (Cambridge: Cambridge University Press, 1996), 21-37 (quotation is from 23). Miller works with Latour's book *Science in action*.
91 Floridablanca to Merry, enclosure in Merry to Leeds, 4 June 1790, PRO FO 72/17, fols. 239-61; Floridablanca to Fitzherbert, translations and enclosures in Fitzherbert to Leeds, 16 June 1790, Leeds Papers, Add. MSS. 28066, fols. 27-55. The Latin and English text of this papal bull is printed in F.G. Davenport, *European treaties bearing on the history of the United States and its dependencies*, 4 vols. (Washington: Carnegie Endowment for International Peace, 1917), I, 72-75. Floridablanca's memorial of 13 June 1790 echoes the wording of Article 8 of the Treaty of Utrecht.
92 Revillagigedo to Valdes, 27 May 1790, quoted in Manning, "Nootka Sound controversy," 357-58; "Report of Don Juan Vicente de Guemes Pacheco de Padilla, Count Revilla Gigedo, Viceroy of New Spain on California, 1768-1793," *Land of Sunshine*, vol. 11 (June-November 1899), 32-41, 105-13, 168-73, 224-33, 282-89, at 168-170. The Treaty of Madrid is discussed in Green and Dickason, *Law of nations*, 60-61.
93 Dalrymple, *Spanish memorial*, 10-11; Leeds to Fitzherbert, 2 October 1790, PRO FO 72/19, fols. 93-109.
94 For all of their criticisms of the Cabinet for pushing Britain into a costly war over an obscure place, Opposition MPs agreed with Leeds on the point about sovereignty. Charles Fox, for example, argued in the Commons in May 1790 that "occupancy and possession should be considered as the only right to title." Quoted in Stanley Ayling, *Fox: The life of Charles James Fox* (London: Murray, 1991), 147.
95 Leeds to Fitzherbert, 5 July 1790, PRO FO 72/18, fols. 22-23.
96 Spain's invocation of the papal bull of 1493 inspired this rhyme by a political satirist, published on 12 May 1790:

> Your right so to do which you claim from the Pope
> We Britons dont value the end of a rope!
> It's a farce you make your Subjects believe,
> But our right's equal to yours from Adam and Eve.

Quoted in Ehrman, *Pitt*, I, 558.

97 Patricia Seed, "Taking possession and reading texts: Establishing the authority of overseas empire," *William and Mary Quarterly* (3rd ser.) 49, 2 (1992): 183-209 (quotation is from 200).
98 Ibid.
99 Leeds to Fitzherbert, 17 August 1790, PRO FO 72/18, fol. 75.
100 Daines Barrington, "Journal of a Spanish voyage in 1775," in his *Miscellanies* (London: J. Nicols, 1781), 469-534 (this footnote is on 505).
101 Leeds to Fitzherbert, 16 May 1790, PRO FO 72/17, fol. 84.
102 Rabasa, *Inventing America: Spanish historiography and the formation of Eurocentrism* (Norman: University of Oklahoma Press, 1993), 5-16 and passim. Rabasa explores how Spain invented (rather than discovered) America as "a new region of space," and a domain of Spanish dominance, by configuring the New World as a garden of imperial opportunity, a zoo of natural and human differences, and a book that could be read.
103 Leeds to Merry, 4 May and 22 June 1790, PRO FO 72/17, fols. 20, 343.
104 Anthony Pagden, *Lords of all the world: Ideologies of empire in Spain, Britain and France, c.1500-c.1800* (New Haven: Yale University Press, 1995), 74-75.
105 Arthur S. Keller, Oliver J. Lissitzyn, and Frederick J. Mann, *Creation of rights of sovereignty through symbolic acts, 1400-1800* (New York: Columbia University Press, 1938), 9.
106 Green and Dickason, *Law of nations and the New World*, 125.
107 Ibid., 126.
108 Privy Council Register, 8 and 11 February 1791, PRO PC 2/135, 439-53. This emphasis on the situation of Meares's purchases and the legal aspects of his actions in relation to Spain are revealed in marginalia on the draft documents of this interview. Privy councillors made notes about the spots of land Meares had occupied and raised questions about whether there were any lands adjoining these purchases and whether Meares continued to take possession of such spots each time he returned. See PRO PC 1/63/B22.
109 Dening, *Performances*, 109; Dalrymple, *Spanish pretensions*, 6-8 (emphasis in original).
110 Patricia Seed, *Ceremonies of possession in Europe's conquest of the New World, 1492-1640* (Cambirdge: Cambridge University Press, 1995), 3.
111 Dalrymple collected manuscript copies of the journals of the first British maritime fur traders, and, in 1789 and 1790, he published a collection of their maps. For lists, see "Catalogue of the extensive and valuable library of books; part 1, late the property of Alex. Dalrymple" (sold by auction, London, 1809), British Library; A. Dalrymple, *Memoir of a map of the lands around the north-pole* (London: George Bigg, 1789), iv.
112 Dalrymple, *Spanish pretensions*, 16.

Chapter 11: Circumscribing Vancouver Island

1 Lamb, *Voyage of George Vancouver,* IV, 1,390 (emphasis in original).
2 Menzies to Banks, 1 October 1794, Dawson Turner copies of the correspondence of Sir Joseph Banks, vol. IX, p. 108.
3 John Scouler, "Observations on the indigenous tribes of the n.w. coast of America," *Journal of the Royal Geographical Society* 11 (1841): 215-40 (quotation is from 215).
4 Berthold Seeman, *Narrative of the voyage of H.M.S. Herald during the years 1845-1851...,* 2 vols. (London: Reeve and Co., 1853), I, 99.
5 The results of Richards's labours are represented on numerous Hydrographic charts, and in his *The Vancouver Island pilot* (London: Hydrographic Office, 1864).
6 Quoted in Lamb, *Voyage of George Vancouver,* I, 208. Lamb charts much of the late nineteenth- and twentieth-century historiographical appreciation of Vancouver. The principal biographies of Vancouver are: Bern Anderson, *The life and voyages of Captain George Vancouver, surveyor of the sea* (Seattle: University of Washington Press, 1960); and George Godwin, *Vancouver: A life, 1757-1798* (New York: D. Appleton and Co., 1931). Lamb's introduction to the Hakluyt Society

edition of Vancouver's voyage is the most exhaustive account of Vancouver's survey. On Vancouver's dealings with Native peoples, see Fisher, *Vancouver's voyage*.

7 Glyndwr Williams, "Myth and reality: The theoretical geography of northwest America from Cook to Vancouver," in Fisher and Johnston, *From maps to metaphors*, 35-50 (quotation is from 50).

8 Fisher and Johnston, *From maps to metaphors*, introduction, 14

9 Lamb, *Voyage of George Vancouver*, I, 275-76.

10 Ibid., 276.

11 Ibid., IV, 1,390; I, 275.

12 Ibid., I, 281.

13 J.B. Harley, "Maps, knowledge, and power," in *The iconography of landscape*, ed. D. Cosgrove and S. Daniels (Cambridge: Cambridge University Press, 1988), 277-312 (quotations are from 279 and 303).

14 I will focus on the imperial tenor of Vancouver's cartography. This chapter avoids discussion of deeper epistemological questions of truth and reality in cartography but want to make one brief point about them. Arguments about the accuracy of Vancouver's survey re-endorse what Graham Huggan calls the "mimetic fallacy" at the heart of the scientific culture of imperialism: the idea that "an approximate, subjectively reconstituted and historically contingent model of the 'real' world" can be faithfully "passed off as an accurate, objectively presented and universally applicable copy." Vancouver's movements and dealings with Native peoples have been tracked in great detail, but his assumptions about truth and reality have barely been discussed. His survey had its own contingencies, but Vancouver passed it off as a reliable reconstruction of a geography that was *indubitably there all along*. Huggan claims that mimesis endorses a particular view or kind of reality: that of the West. The "imitative operations of mimesis can be seen to have stabilized (or attempted to stabilize) a falsely essentialist view of the world which negates or suppresses alternative views which might endanger the privileged position of its Western perceiver." Principally, Vancouver's cartography was falsely essentialist (incomplete) in that it erased most signs of Native territorial arrangements (I will rehearse some of these points in Chapter 11). Scholars such as Fisher, Johnston, and Williams do not comment on such issues, but they adopt a particular position on them: they collapse the distinction between what Huggan calls the "approximate function" of the map as a form of representation and its "authoritative status" as a form of knowledge that can induce effects of power. Vancouver's aim, they imply, was also his achievement: it was the plausibility (or accuracy) of his cartography that made his survey authoritative, not the Western views of the Northwest Coast that it licensed. See Graham Huggan, "Decolonizing the map: Post-colonialism, post-structuralism and the cartographic connection," *Ariel* 20, 4 (October 1989): 115-31 (quotations are from 116-18).

15 Fisher and Johnston, *From maps to metaphors*, 13-14.

16 See also Stephen Haycox, James Barnett, and Caedmon Liburd, eds., *Enlightenment and exploration in the north Pacific, 1741-1805* (Seattle and London: University of Washington Press, 1997); and Fisher, *Vancouver's voyage*. The principal exception to this generalization is Barbara Belyea, who has dealt with questions of truth, power, and mimesis in the eighteenth- and nineteenth-century cartography of North America and the Northwest Coast. See, especially, her "Images of power: Derrid/Foucault/Harley," *Cartographica* 29, 2 (summer 1992): 1-9.

17 Fisher and Johnston, *From maps to metaphors*, 6 (my emphasis).

18 See Lamb, *Voyage of George Vancouver*, I, 672.

19 Meares, Memorial to Grenville, 20 July 1790, PRO FO 95/7/4, fol. 415. Meares depicted Gray's circumnavigation in the vessel *Washington* on his map of the Northwest Coast, which was published in his *Voyages* (November 1790).

20 C.F. Newcombe, *The first circumnavigation of Vancouver Island*, Archives of British Columbia, Memoir 1 (Victoria: William H. Cullin, 1914), 21.

21 F.W. Howay, *Captain George Vancouver* (1943), quoted in Barry M. Gough, *The northwest coast:*

British navigation, trade, and discoveries to 1812 (Vancouver: UBC Press, 1992), 161.

22 Sproat to Scholefield (1908), "History of British Columbia," Sproat Papers, files 6 and 7.
23 Scholefield to Roberston (1912?), Newcombe Family Papers.
24 Victoria, *Colonist*, 20 January 1910, in John Walbran, "Scrapbook, 1909-1912," BCARS S/S/W14.
25 These links between imperialism and cartographic precision, emphasizd in the early twentieth century, have not entirely disappeared from scholarship on Vancouver, however. See, for example, John Naish, "The achievements of Captain George Vancouver: A reassessment after 200 years," *Mariner's Mirror* 80, 4 (November 1994): 418-30.
26 "General instruction for surveying," in the hand of Sir Joseph Banks, 21 February 1791, PRO HO 42/18, fol. 170.
27 Ibid., fols. 171-72.
28 Ibid., fol. 177.
29 Lamb, *Voyage of George Vancouver*, I, 283.
30 This quotation is from "Instructions to Menzies from Jos. Banks," Soho Square, 22 February 1791, BM Add. MS. 33,979, fol. 75. Banks sponsored Menzies and many other late eighteenth-century travellers.
31 A full list of the instruments and nautical and surveying texts used on Vancouver's voyage, prepared by Andrew David of the Hydrograhic Office in Taunton, UK, is published in Fisher and Johnston, *From maps to metaphors*, 291-93.
32 Banks to Grenville, 20 February 1791, PRO HO 42/18[33], fol. 168.
33 Lamb, *Voyage of George Vancouver*, IV, 1,391 (Vancouver's emphasis).
34 William Boelhower, "Inventing America: A model of cartographic semiosis," *Word and Image* 4, 2 (April-June 1988): 475-97 (quotation is from 479).
35 Ibid.
36 For a more rigorous discussion, see Andrew David, "Vancouver's survey methods and surveys," in Fisher and Johnston, *From maps to metaphors*, 51-69.
37 Lamb, *Voyage of George Vancouver*, II, 558.
38 Ibid., II, 628.
39 Ibid., 589.
40 Elaboration of this idea is hampered by the fact that Vancouver's log survey books are lost. This being the case, I consider his instructions in relation to his maps and journal.
41 Boelhower, "Inventing America," 479.
42 Lamb, *Voyage of George Vancouver*, II, 533 and 535.
43 Ibid., 573.
44 Ibid., 616 and 609; III, 1,026.
45 Ibid., II, 617.
46 Vancouver to Stephens, 6 December 1793, in ibid., IV, 1,588.
47 Vancouver to a friend, 2 October 1794, quoted in Gough, *Northwest coast*, 168.
48 Lamb, *Voyage of George Vancouver*, II, 589-96 (quotation is from 591).
49 See also José Rabasa, "Allegories of the *Atlas*," in *Europe and its others*, 2 vols., ed. Francis Barker, Peter Hulme, Margaret Iverson, and Diana Loxley (Colchester: University of Essex, 1985), vol. 2, 1-16. Rabasa argues that "the allegorization of the four continents [in Mercator's *Atlas*, 1595-1636] suppresses the colonialist machinery and fabricates an omnipotent European who can dominate the world from the cabinet, but it also produces a blind spot that dissolves history as a privileged modality of European culture" (12).
50 As Vancouver's log survey books are lost, I am restricted here to a comparison of Vancouver's maps and journal. See George Vancouver, *A voyage of discovery to the north Pacific Ocean and round the world.... Performed in the tears 1790, 1791, 1792, 1793, 1794, and 1795, in the Discovery sloop of war, and the armed tender Chatham, under the command of Captain George Vancouver* (London: G.G. and J. Robinson and J. Edwards, 1798). This was a revised version of Vancouver's journal. Vancouver noted that he drew on the journals, logs, charts, and drawings of his officers. This 1798 text was translated into French, German, Danish, and Swedish. In 1801, Vancouver's

brother, John, published a revised English edition in six octavio volumes. See Lamb, *Voyage*, introduction, 226. Lamb's 1984 edition is a reprint of the revised 1801 text, with appendices added but without the full collection of engraved charts.

51 I have worked with facsimiles from the 1798 edition.

52 It does not appear that the Admiralty gave Vancouver any specific instructions about what to include or highlight on the engravings. Correspondence over the engravings mainly concerns financial matters. See PRO ADM.1/2630 (1798), photostats in the W. Kaye Lamb Collection, box 10-3, UBCL-SC.

53 See Lamb, *Voyage of George Vancouver*, II, 591-92, 663.

54 On Spanish cartography see Wagner, *Spanish explorations in the Straits of Juan de Fuca*; Kendrick, *Voyage of the Sutil and Mexicana*; and Krauss, *The American west coast and Alaska.*

55 Lamb, *Voyage of George Vancouver*, I, 274, 592. On Vancouver's use of George Dixon's and Charles Duncan's charts see ibid., II, 592; III, 1,069, 1,071; IV, 1,322-26. Some of these traders, of course, had come out of the navy and had been trained by Cook. The importance of Duncan's discoveries were related to the Home Office in 1790, probably by Alexander Dalrymple, who had a copy of his journal and published two of his charts. See PRO HO 42/18[57]; Dalrymple, *Memoir of a map*, iv. Vancouver was more disparaging about Meares. When Vancouver met Gray at the mouth of the Strait of Juan de Fuca in April 1792, the American denied having ventured more than fifty miles into the Strait of Georgia. Meares exaggerated the American's achievements for his own ends. See Newcombe, *Circumnavigation of Vancouver Island*, 29-38.

56 Andrew Cook, personal communication. See also his "Alexander Dalrymple (1737-1808), hydrographer to the East India Company and to the Admiralty, as publisher," 3 vols. (PhD diss., University of St Andrews, 1992), especially vol. 1, 219-25.

57 See Lamb, *Voyage of George Vancouver*, I, introduction, 241; David, "Vancouver's survey methods".

58 Boelhower, "Inventing America," 484.

59 Rabasa, "Allegories of the *Atlas*," 3.

60 David Turnbull, *Maps are territories* (Chicago: University of Chicago Press, 1989), 26.

61 See, especially, Harley, "Rereading the maps of the Columbian encounter."

Chapter 12: Delineating the Oregon Territory

1 My epigraph is quoted in Howard Jones and Donald A. Rakestraw, *Prologue to manifest destiny: Anglo-American relations in the 1840s* (Wilmington: Books, 1997), 160.

2 Ibid., 151.

3 The classic account of the Oregon boundary dispute is Frederick Merk's *The Oregon question: essays in Anglo-American diplomacy and politics* (Cambridge, MA: Harvard University Press, 1967). Jones and Rakestraw connect the Oregon question to the Webster-Ashburton negotions of the northeast boundary and place both disputes in a broader Anglo-American political context.

4 See Gallatin and Rush (United States), Robinson and Goulburn (Britain), "Protocol of the third conference ... to negotiate a convention respecting fisheries, boundary and the restoration of slaves," 17 Septmeber 1818, in *Diplomatic correspondence of the United States: Canadian relations*, 5 vols. ed. William R. Manning, (Washington: Carnegie Endowment for International Peace, 1945), I, doc.629, 864-866.

5 See Merk, *Oregon question*, 37-59.

6 See Goetzmann, *New lands, new men*, 71-73, 150-55.

7 See *British diplomatic instructions, 1689-1789*, vol. 2: *France 1689-1721* (London: Royal Historical Society Publications, Camden 3rd ser. 35, 1925), 197; Max Savelle, *The diplomatic history of the Canadian boundary, 1749-1763* (New Haven: Yale University Press, 1940), chap. 1.

8 "Protocol of the sixth conference," 9 October 1818; Gallatin and Rush to Adams, 20 October 1823, Manning, *Diplomatic correspondence*, II, docs. 634 and 639, 872, 878. More immediately, Gallatin's formulation stemmed from the 1807 Anglo-American negotiations over the bound-

294 Notes to pages 207-10

ary between Louisana and Rupert's Land. American plenipoteniaries proposed the 49th parallel as the border from the Lake of the Woods "as far as the respective territories of the two parties extend in that quarter." Quoted in Jones and Rakestraw, *Prologue to manifest destiny*, 154-55.

9 On the importance of Mitchell's map in the geopolitical history of North America, see Seymour I. Schwartz and Ralph E. Ehrenberg, *The mapping of America* (New York: Abraams, 1980), 158-60, and passim. Mitchell was commissioned by the earl of Halifax, the president of Britain's Board of Trade. His maps figured in Anglo-American disputes over the northeastern boundary.

10 In his 1844 study of the Oregon Territory, Robert Greenhow, a librarian at the U.S. State Department, cited three "esteemed" maps depicting the 49th parallel as the border west of Lake of the Woods – Postlethwayt (1751), Palairet (1765), and Brown and Gibson (1775) (and he might have added to this list maps by Sculp and the Society of Anti-Gallicans, both 1755); another four maps showing alternative boundaries – Mitchell (1755), Smollett (1760), Bennet (1770), and Faden (1777); and he cites a number of maps that do not depict any boundary line in the region – most notably Popple (1738). See Robert Greenhow, *The History of Oregon and California* ... (Boston: Little and Brown, 1844), 281-83, 436-9. William Sturgis also discussed cartographic issues in "Oregon: The claims of Great Britain," *Hunt's Merchants' Magazine*, 12, 6 (June 1845), 520-38. He stated that "whether the forty-ninth degree was established as the boundary between the English and French possessions, agreeably to the treaty of Utrecht, cannot be determined," but he noted that many eighteenth-century American cartographers, such as Ewan Bowen, thought that the negotiators at the 1719 commission adopted the 49th parallel as the appropriate boundary. "This opinion appears to have been general," Sturgis suggested, "and was entertained by the [American and British] parties to the treaty of 1783" (530).

11 Albert Gallatin, *The Oregon question* (New York: Bartlett and Welford, 1846), 23-24.

12 Greenhow's book had an important influence on American thinking during the last round of diplomatic negotiations in 1845-46. He correctly judged that the 1719 commission did not institute the 49th parallel west from Lake of the Woods as the border, but he was unaware of these British diplomatic instructions, and he did not consider the role that cartography played in the negotiations of 1818. The following statement alludes to my thesis and undoes his view of these negotiations: "These discrepancies [between these maps with different boundaries] should excite no surprise; for maps, and books of geography, which are most frequently consulted in relation to boundaries, are, or rather have been, the very worst authorities on such subjects; as they are ordinarily *made by persons wholly unacquainted with political affairs.*" See Ibid., 437 (my emphasis).

13 Thompson to Colonial Office, 30 April 1842, enclosure 7, Foreign Office 5 – America: transcripts, BCARS GR327, vol. 4. Thompson was referring to the neogiations of 1818 and 1826.

14 Gallatin and Rush to Adams, 20 October 1818, Manning, *Diplomatic negotiations*, II, doc.639, 876-82. Adams sent a special agent to the Columbia to report on the activities of the North West Company. See ibid., I, doc.643, 886-92.

15 This proposal did not make it into the official diplomatic record. It was discovered by Merk. See *Oregon question*, 53-57. The text in question is Simon McGillivray, *Notice respecting the boundary* ... (London: B. M'Millan, 1817). This fictitious river is also depicted on the 1818 edition of Arrowsmith's *Map ... of North America*. The North West Company was viewed as a cartographic "authority" on North America. Thompson's maps of the Columbia River region were more detailed than McGillivray's, and his 1816 *Map of North America* does not depict the Caledonia River. See David Thompson, *Columbia journals*, ed. Barbara Belyea (Montreal, Kingston, London, Buffalo: McGill-Queen's University Press, 1994), 296-97.

16 Gallatin's proposal is recorded in the Journal of Richard Rush, 19 October 1818, quoted in Merk, *Oregon question*, 55.

17 Anglo-American attempts to determine a boundary in northeast America also turned around the interpretation of maps. See David Demeritt, "Representing the 'true' St. Croix; Knowledge and power in the partition of the northeast," *William and Mary Quarterly* (3rd ser.) 54, 3 (July 1997): 515-48; Jones and Rakestraw, *Prologue to manifest destiny*, chaps. 5 and 6.

18 Benedict Anderson, *Imagined communities: Reflections on the origin and spread of nationalism*

rev. ed. (London: Verso, 1991), 174.

19 Richard Helgerson, *Forms of nationhood: The Elizabethan writing of England* (Chicago: University of Chicago Press, 1992).

20 Jones and Rakestraw, *Prologue to manifest destiny*, 159 and passim.

21 Adams quoted in ibid., 161. And see Merk, *Oregon question*, 128 and passim.

22 Jones and Rakestraw, *Prologue to manifest destiny*, 162.

23 On the context of the negotiations, see Merk, *Oregon question*, 107-63.

24 On these developments, see Richard Mackie, *Trading beyond the mountains: The Hudson's Bay Company on the Pacific, 1793-1843* (Vancouver: UBC Press, 1997).

25 Pelly to Canning, 9 December 1825, in Frederick Merk, ed., *Fur trade and empire: George Simpson's journal ...* (Cambridge, MA: Harvard University Press, 1968), 259. On the Hudson's Bay Company's involvement in the dispute, see Galbraith, *The Hudson's Bay Company as an imperial factor*.

26 There had been a previous round of negotiations, in 1823-24, but they did not inject any new emphases into the boundary debate. Britain closed the negotiations by proposing a boundary along the 49th parallel to the Columbia and then down the river to the Pacific. Gallatin returned to London in 1826 with a counter-proposal, insisting on the 49th parallel to the Pacific but allowing British subjects use of the Columbia if it proved navigable from its point of intersection with the parallel. Britain rejected the offer but came back with a compromise, proposing the Columbia River as the main boundary but granting the United States what is now the Olympic Peninsula and, therefore, some good deep-water harbours in Puget Sound. Gallatin considered the offer offensive – an attempt to create an American island in British territory. Thus, soon after the 1826 negotiations started, Britain and the United States were back at square one. This correspondence can be tracked in Manning, *Diplomatic correspondence*, II, 55-76 and passim.

27 Gallatin to Clay, 16 November 1826, Manning, *Diplomatic correspondence*, II, doc.920, 529; III, doc.922, 536.

28 See Cole Harris, ed., *Historical atlas of Canada*, vol. 1: *From the beginning to 1800* (Toronto: University of Toronto Press, 1987), plate 66, "The maritime and land fur trade" (Robert M. Galois, Sheila Robinson), and plate 67, "Exploration in the far northwest" (Richard Ruggles).

29 Merk, *Fur trade and empire*, 124.

30 These formulations can be tracked in Manning, *Diplomatic correspondence*, II, docs. 920-31.

31 Memorandum of H.U. Addington, 6 May 1826, in Edward Stapleton ed., *Some official correspondence of George Canning*, 2 vols. (London: Longman's, Green and Co., 1887), II, 110-15 (the quotation is from 112 [emphasis in original]).

32 Gallatin to Clay, 25 November 1826, Manning, *Diplomatic correspondence*, II, doc.922, 536.

33 Stapleton, *Official correspondence of George Canning*, II, 113, 115.

34 Gallatin to Clay, 16 November 1826, Manning, *Diplomatic correspondence*, II, doc.920, 529-30; Gallatin also highlighted this in his reflections on these 1826 negotiations, printed in *The Oregon question*, 5, 18, 31-32. In reports prepared for the Foreign Office between 1823 and 1825, Stratford Canning, Britain's minister in Washington, highlighted that Britain could advance claims based on discovery and occupation that were exclusively its own, whereas many of those advanced by the U.S. were derived from Spain and had been denied by Britain during the Nootka Crisis. See Great Britain, Foreign Office, Papers Relating to the Northwest Coast of America, October 1823-March 1825, transcripts from the Stratford Canning Papers, F.O.352, bundle 8, BCARS D/A/G79/5.

35 Gallatin to Clay, 25 November 1826, Manning, *Diplomatic correspondence*, II, doc.922, 533.

36 Ibid.

37 Simpson to Addington, 5 Jan 1826, Merk, *Fur trade and empire*, 261-68.

38 Douglas to Simpson (private), 23 October 1843, PAM-HBCA D.5/9 fol. 119.

39 Thom to Simpson (private), 8 August 1842, PAM-HBCA D.5/7 fol. 184.

40 Howells to Aberdeen, 8 May 1845, FO 5 – America: transcripts, BCARS GR327, vol. 4.

41 Gallatin to Clay, 25 November 1826, Manning, *Diplomatic correspondence*, II, Doc.922, 538.

42　See Jones and Rakestraw, *Prologue to manifest destiny*, who discuss these issues in great detail.

43　David M. Pletcher, *The diplomacy of annexation: Texas, Oregon, and the Mexican War* (Columbia, MI: University of Missouri Press, 1973).

44　James K. Polk, "Message of the President," 2 December 1845, *Appendix to the Congressional Globe ... containing speeches and important state papers* (n.s) 1845-46 (Washington: Blair and Rives, 1846), 4. Also see President John Tyler's annual message to Congress (5 December 1843), in which he claimed that the US could claim the territory from 42°N to 54°40' N.

45　Wellington to Peel (private), 8 April 1845, in Kenneth Bourne, ed., *The foreign policy of Victorian England, 1830-1902* (Oxford: Clarendon, 1970), doc.35, 264.

46　*Hansard's parliamentary debates*, 3rd ser., vol. LXXIX (1845), col.123.

47　In February 1840, the Governor of the Hudson's Bay Company, Sir John Pelly, wrote to Lord Palmerston (then foreign secretary): "Should the United States Government be permitted to carry the measures proposed in those [Linn's] resolutions into effect, they will prove ruinous to the interests of the Hudson's Bay Company in that quarter, likewise to those of the Pugets Sound Agricultural Company, and deprive Great Britain of the only position on the shores of the Pacific, that can be valuable to the country either for colonization or commercial pursuits, while ... giving to them the command of the North Pacific." Pelly, quoted in Galbraith, *The Hudson's Bay Company as an imperial factor*, p. 219.

   Britain's political and diplomatic reaction to Polk's pronouncements can be tracked in "Correspondence relative to the negotiation of the question of disputed right to the Oregon Territory," *British parliamentary papers: Canadian boundary*, vol. 2 (Shannon: Irish University Press, 1969). The Hudson's Bay Company warned the Foreign Office about the implications of Polk's Democratic Presidency a number of times in 1843 and 1844. See Pelly to Aberdeen, 23 January 1843, FO 5/399, and passim, BCARS GR 327, vol. 4. For the results of this British expedition, see Leslie Scott, ed., "Report of Lieutenant Peel on Oregon in 1845-6," *Oregon Historical Quarterly* 29 (March 1928): 51-76. The United States despatched its own expedition to the region in 1841. See Charles Wilkes, "Report on the Territory of Oregon," *Quarterly of the Oregon Historical Society* 12 (1911): 269-99.

48　Galbraith, *The Hudson's Bay Company as an imperial factor*, p. 221.

49　Upshur to Everett, 9 October 1843, Manning, *Diplomatic correspondence*, III, 210-13 (emphasis in original).

50　John Calhoun, "Statement of the American plenipotentiary," encl. in Pakenham to Aberdeen, 12 September 1844; Buchanan to Pakenham, 12 July 1845; Pakenham to Buchanan, 29 July 1845, in Great Britain, "Correspondence relative to the negotiation of the question of disputed right to the Oregon Territory," *British Parliamentary papers: Canadian boundary*, vol. 2 (Shannon: Irish University Press, 1969), 13-39.

51　Buchanan to Pakenham, 12 July 1845, "Correspondence relative to ... the Oregon Territory."

52　The Hudson's Bay Company was willing to give up Fort Vancouver, partly because of the dangers of navigating the bar at the mouth of the Columbia River. In 1841 Simpson sent Douglas north to look for a new trade base. Douglas decided upon Fort Victoria, at the south end of Vancouver Island, in 1843. See Simpson to Pelly, 10 March 1842, Pelly to Foreign Office, 29 March 1842, PRO FO 5/388, BCARS GR 327, vol. 4. And see Margaret Ormsby, "Introduction," in *Fort Victoria letters, 1846-1851*, ed. Hartwell Bowsfield (Winnipeg: Hudson's Bay Record Society, 1979), xi-xix.

53　See Muriel E. Chamberlain, *Lord Aberdeen: A political biography* (London and New York: Longman, 1983).

54　Pletcher, *Diplomacy of annexation*, 603.

55　Gallatin, *The Oregon question*, 27

56　On the formation and articulation of such views, see Pletcher, *Diplomacy of annexation*.

57　See ibid., 584-91, for a discussion of Calhoun.

58　Douglas to Simpson (private), 23 October 1843, PAM-HBCA, D.5/9, fol. 119.

59　These letters are collected in *The Oregon question*.

60 London, *Times*, 27 March and 5 April 1845. On the role of the British periodical press in the dispute see Richard S. Cramer, "British magazines and the Oregon question," *Pacific Historical Quarterly* 32 (1963): 369-82.

61 See Chamberlain, *Aberdeen*, 331-40.

62 London *Times*, 3 January 1846.

63 *Edinburgh Review* 82, 165 (1845): 265, 261; London, *Examiner*, 26 April 1845.

64 Pakenham to Buchanan, 29 July 1845, encl. 2, letter 28, "Correspondence relative to ... the Oregon Territory," 43. Aberdeen also insisted that Britain should retain the right to navigate the Columbia River. He treated this as a point of national honour because it was enshrined in previous Anglo-American conventions, though he realized that the sandbar at the mouth of the river hampered traffic.

65 Mackie, *Trading beyond the mountains*, 256-61.

66 Adams to Rush, 22 July 1823, Manning, *Diplomatic correspondence*, II, doc.681, 58.

67 *The Gentleman's Magazine* (n.s.), XXIII (March 1845), 284. This reviewer was discussing John Dunn's *History of the Oregon Territory* (1944).

68 Jody Berland, "Space at the margin: Colonial spatiality and critical theory after Innis," *Topia* 1 (1997): 60.

69 See Wallis, "Cook's journals."

Chapter 13: Mythical Localities

1 Grey, memo on Pelly to Grey, 7 September 1846, PRO C.O.305/1, fol. 11. Before the Oregon Treaty was signed, the Colonial Office alerted the Foreign Office to "the great danger ... of allowing an ambitious Nation to pursue its own peculiar method of immigration and settlement with the avowed determination to annex the whole [Oregon] territory." See Hawes to Aberdeen, 10 February 1846, PRO FO 5/459, fol. 134.

2 See Mackie, *Trading beyond the mountains*, for an in-depth discussion of Hudson's Bay Company activities west of the Rockies to 1843.

3 Most of these schemes are printed in "Papers relating to the colonization of Vancouver Island," in *Report of the Provincial Archives, department of the province of British Columbia ... for 1913* (Victoria: King's Printer, 1914), v.49-84; and "Correspondence relative to the colonization of Vancouver's Island 1847-48," *British parliamentary papers* XLII (London: House of Commons, 1848), 619. The colonial correspondence surrounding them can be tracked in full in PRO C.O.305/1.

4 Cordua to McTavish, 24 June 1852, PAM-HBCA A.10/33, fol. 275.

5 John Dunn, *History of the Oregon Territory and British North American fur trade* (London: Edwards and Hughes, 1844), 298.

6 Charles Forbes, *Vancouver Island: Its resources and capabilities as a colony* (Victoria: The Colonial Government, 1862), 1-2.

7 George Hills, "General statement of the Diocese of Columbia for 1860," *Columbia Mission occasional paper* (London: Rivington, 1860), 25. See also Lieutenant H.S. Palmer, "Remarks upon the geography and natural capabilities of British Columbia ... ," *Journal of the Royal Geographical Society* 34 (1864): 171-95. Palmer worked with Dunn's imagery of the coast, presenting "a hasty geographical sketch" of its "numberless archipelagoes of rocky islets ... its inlets and numerous outlaying islands," its "extraordinary network of sheltered water-communication," and he gasped at the "extensive solitudes" of the interior. But he also refuted statements circulating in Britain that the region "swarms with blood thirsty savages" (172, 186).

8 Reginald H. Pidcock, "Adventures in Vancouver Island" (1862-65), Pidcock Family Papers, vol. 4, 7, BCARS Add. MSS. 728; Matthew Macfie, *Vancouver Island and British Columbia: Their history, resources and prospects* (London: Longman, Green, 1865), 58.

9 Dorothy Blakey Smith, ed., *The reminiscences of Doctor John Sebastian Helmcken* (Vancouver: UBC Press, 1975), 75.

10 Yonge to Barclay, 20 September 1849, PAM-HBCA, A.10/27, fol. 203. Such advertisements ap-

peared in the London *Times* and *Morning Chronicle*.

11 Charles Alfred Bayley, "Early life on Vancouver Island," 8, BCARS E/B/B34.2. This narrative was recorded by H.H. Bancroft in 1878.

12 See Roderick Finlayson, "History of Vancouver Island and the northwest coast," *Saint Louis University Studies* (ser. B) 1, 1 (1945): 69-84; James Dean, "Settlement of Vancouver Island" (1878), 14, BCARS E/B/D342 (written for H.H. Bancroft); Douglas to Barclay, 3 September 1849, *Fort Victoria letters*, 35-48; Augustus F. Pemberton, "Diary, January 1856-August 1858," BCARS E/B/P37.

13 This latter point was made emphatically by William Tolmie, a fur trader, who claimed that "white men do not take the same trouble to study the Indians that they take to study us." This changed as collectors, missionaries, and ethnographers arrived over the next thirty years. See W.F. Tolmie, "History of Puget Sound and the northwest coast" (1878), 32, William Fraser Tolmie Papers, vol. 1, file 11, BCARS Add. MSS. 557 (written for H.H. Bancroft).

14 The phrase is from Douglas to Smith, 4 August 1856, Fort Victoria, Correspondence on the affairs of Vancouver Island colony, BCARS A/C/20/Vi3. On colonists' fears, see, for example, Benjamin Pearse, "Early settlement of Vancouver Island" (1900), BCARS E/B/P31, and Blanshard to Grey, 18 August 1850, no. 5, in Richard Blanshard, *Despatches: Governor Blanshard to the secretary of state, 26th December 1849, to 30th August, 1851* (New Westminster: Government Printing Office, [1863]), 4. I discuss the response of the colonial government below.

15 J.W. Mckay, "Letterbook," 230, Joseph William Mckay Papers, BCARS Add. MSS. 2735.

16 Hills, *Columbia mission occasional paper*, 25.

17 This observation is in Richard Charles Mayne, "Journal kept in H.M.S. Plumper, February 1857-December 1860," 79, BCARS E/B/M45.

18 This phrase is from Frederick Dally, "Memorandum of trip around Vancouver Island ... 1866," Frederick Dally Papers, file 9, Add. MSS. 2443.

19 The quotation is from Bell to Thomson, James Bell, Correspondence Outward, 1859, BCARS E/B/B412.

20 Robert Brown, "Memoir on the geography of the interior of Vancouver Island," 4-5, Robert Brown Collection, box 1, file 10, BCARS Add. MSS.

21 J.R. Anderson, "Notes and comments on early days and events in British Columbia, Washington, and Oregon." See Anderson Papers, box 9, BCARS Add. MSS. 1912.

22 Robert Brown, "The first journey of exploration across Vancouver Island," in *Illustrated travels: A record of discovery, geography, and adventure*, vol. 1, ed., H.W. Bates (London: Cassell, Petter, and Galpin, [1969]), part 1, 254-55; part 2, 274-76; Part 3, 302-303; Part 4, 349-51 (quotation is from 254).

23 Robert Brown, "Diary," 23 March 1865, Robert Brown Collection, box 1, file 17. Brown saw himself in the mould of the explorer-hero, which was a general feature of Victorian exploration. In "The first journey of exploration" I, 254, he noted: "In the little frontier town where we start from, there are no philosophical instrument-makers to supply us with the tools for our work, no Geographical Society to advise us ...Apparatus has to be extemporised, and men found at short notice."

24 Robert Brown, "The present state of science on the north-western slopes of the Rocky Mountains," *Journal of Travel and Natural History* 1, 3 (1868): 173-80 (quotation is from 180).

25 Ibid.

26 John Emmerson, *British Columbia and Vancouver Island: Voyages, travels, and adventures* (London: Printed for the author, 1965), 92.

27 See, for example, Anderson and Co. to Colonial Secretary, 22 January 1864, British Columbia, Colonial Correspondence B-1300, microfilm held in the Department of Geography, UBC.

28 In fact, their views about the potential of the colony oscillated and their range of views reflects the fact that they were writing to different audiences. Hudson's Bay Company officials and the colonial office had different ideas about the purpose of colonialism on the island. When Douglas established Fort Victoria in 1843, he enthused to James Hargrave that the southern end of Vancouver Island appeared to be "a perfect 'Eden,' in the midst of the dreary wilderness of the

North west coast." See Douglas to Hargrave (private), 5 February 1843, Hargrave Collection, National Archives of Canada, MG 19, A21. Ten years later, Douglas was "not sanguine about the progress of the Colony" and informed Simpson that "I sincerely wish as you do, that the Hudson's Bay Compy. had never meddled in the colonization of Vancouver's Island, as it must involve a heavy expense." See Douglas to Simpson, 20 March 1854, and (private) 16 November 1854 PAM-HBCA B.226/b/11, fol. 38 and 86d. And see Barclay to Simpson (private), 13 October 1848, PAM-HBCA D.5/23, fol. 73d: Vancouver Island "is in my view worthless as [a] seat for a colony." But Douglas changed his opinion in 1856, when he visited the Cowichan Valley. He described the region as "extensive and valuable as an agricultural country" and had "bright hopes" about the future of the colony. Douglas to Tolmie, 5 and 6 September 1856, PAM-HBCA B.226/b/12, fols.108-109d.

29 See, especially, Edward Gibbon Wakefield, *A view of the art of colonization, with present reference to the British Empire; in letters between a statesman and a colonist* (London: John Parker, 1849).

30 Barclay to Douglas, 17 December 1849, BCARS A/C/20/Vi7.

31 See Tina Loo, *Making law, order and authority in British Columbia, 1821-1871* (Toronto: University of Toronto Press, 1994), chap. 2.

32 These quotations are from Pemberton to the Governor and Committee, 4 December 1851, Hudson's Bay Company, Land Office, Victoria, Correspondence Outward, signed by J.D. Pemberton, BCARS A/C/15/HB6P.

33 See Richard Mackie, "The colonization of Vancouver Island, 1849-1858," *BC Studies* 96 (Winter 1992-93): 3-40,

34 Joseph Despard Pemberton, *Facts and figures relating to Vancouver Island and British Columbia showing what to expect and how to get there* (London: Longman, Green, and Roberts, 1860), 58, 6-7.

35 Packington to Douglas, 22 August 1852, no. 7, Great Britain, Despatches to Vancouver Island, BCARS C/A/A/10.2/1A-4A.

36 Barclay to Douglas, 17 December 1849, Fort Victoria, Correspondence Inward, BCARS A/C/20/Vi7.

37 Richard Blanshard, the first colonial governor of Vancouver Island, was responsible for legal and constitutional matters. His colonial instructions, dated 16 July 1849, do not mention Native peoples. Douglas succeeded him as a governor in 1851. See Richard Blanshard Papers, file 8, BCARS Add. MSS. 611. The Charter of Grant is reprinted in a number of places. See "Despatches and other papers relating to Vancouver's Island and the Hudson's Bay Company," *British parliamentary papers* XXXV, 103 (London: House of Commons, 1849), 13-16.

38 Douglas to Barclay, 3 September 1849, *Fort Victoria letters*, 35-48. In fact, Barclay had written to him before about Native rights. See Barclay to Douglas and Ogden, 1 December 1848, PAM-HBCA A.6/27, fol. 335. On metropolitan reaction to Douglas's dealings with Native peoples, see, for example, Newcastle to Douglas, 12 April 1853, no.4 and 15 October 1853, no. 10; Labouchere to Douglas, 26 January 1856, no. 3 and 13 November 1856, no. 20, for the response of the Colonial Office to Douglas's military expeditions into the Cowichan Valley in 1853 and 1856. These documents are in Despatches to Vancouver Island. It was sometimes the permanent undersecretary at the Colonial Office, rather than the colonial secretary himself, who recommended that messages of "approbation" should be extended to governors over their handling of Native issues. See, for example, Merivale, memo on Douglas to Pakington, 21 January 1853, PRO C.O. 305/4, fol. 5d. Colonial secretaries sometimes added that Native-settler relations should be handled with "prudence" and "caution."

39 Barclay to Douglas, 17 December 1849, Fort Victoria, Correspondence Inward.

40 Hudson's Bay Company, "Return of treaties made by the Hudson's Bay Company with Indian tribes 1850-1854," BCARS F/53/H86; Hudson's Bay Company, Vancouver Island, colony account, 1848-1860, PAM-HBCA E.22/2, fols. 10-23. The quotation is from Douglas to Barclay, 16 May 1850, *Fort Victoria letters*, 95. Three other "treaties" were signed with Native groups of Fort Rupert and Nanaimo between 1851 and 1854. And see, especially, Wilson Duff, "The Fort Victoria treaties" *BC Studies* (1969), 3-57. Cole Harris's *The Indian land question in British Columbia*

(Vancouver: UBC Press, forthcoming) will revise and augment our understanding of Douglas's Native policy.

41 There is an enormous secondary literature on British imperial policy during this period, but one often gets a more vivid sense of what was at stake from primary sources. For a famous synthesis of British imperial thinking around 1850 see Lord John Russell's speech to the House of Commons on 8 February 1850, *Harsard's parliamentary debates*, 3rd ser., CVIII (1850), cols. 535-67.

42 Herman Merivale, *Lectures on colonization and colonies: Delivered before the University of Oxford in 1839, 1840, & 1841*, 2nd ed. (London: Longman, 1861), 492. And see David McNab, "Herman Merivale and the Native Question, 1837-1861," *Albion* 9, 4 (1977): 359-84.

43 Colonial secretaries expressed different degrees of interest in Native issues. Edward Bulwer Lytton and Lord Carnarvon were among the most attentive. On the establishment of the colony of British Columbia in 1858, Lytton told Douglas to "pay every regard to the interests of the Natives which an enlightened humanity can suggest," for "proofs are unhappily still too frequent of the neglect which Indians experience when the White man obtains possession of their Country and their claims to consideration are forgotten at the moment when equity most demands that the hand of the protector should be extended to help them." See Lytton to Douglas, 31 July 1858, no.6; Carnarvon to Douglas, 11 April 1859, no.49, Despatches to Vancouver Island.

44 On Hudson's Bay Company strategies of power, see Tina Loo, *Making law and authority in British Columbia*, chap .1; and Harris, *The resettlement of British Columbia*, chap. 2.

45 Duncan George Forbes Macdonald, *British Columbia and Vancouver Island ...* (London: Longman et al., 1862), 7.

46 Alexander Caulfield Anderson, *The dominion at the west: A brief history of the province of British Columbia, its climate and resources* (Victoria: Richard Wolfenden, 1872), 91.

47 "Journal of Sir James Douglas's trip to Europe, May 14 1864-May 16 1965," BCARS B/20/1864.

48 These quotations are from Douglas to Blenkinsop (private), 27 October and 13 November 1850, PAM-HBCA B.226/b/3, fol. 14d and 30; Douglas to Barclay, 21 March and 27 April 1852, Douglas to Smith, 6 September 1856, Fort Victoria, Correspondence on the affairs of Vancouver Island colony; Douglas to Pakington 21 January 1853, PRO C.O.305/4, fol. 1.

49 George Hastings Inskip, "Journal," 2 vols., I, 293 and passim, BCARS Add. MSS 805. And see Richards to Baynes, 17 August 1860, PRO ADM.1/5736, part II, Y168.

50 This phrase is from Douglas to Pakington, 21 January 1853, PRO C.O.305/4, fol. 1.

51 Douglas to Yale, 15 January 1853, PAM-HBCA B.226/b/7, fol. 58.

52 The quotation is from Douglas to Kingcombe, 6 July 1863, and see Douglas to Harding, (January) 1863, Vancouver Island, Governor, Naval Letters, BCARS GR 1308; and see Connolly to Bruce, 31 August 1856, PRO ADM.1/5672, on the deployment of gunboats "to give confidence to the settlers and to intimidate the Indians."

53 Douglas to Bruce, 27 July 1857, James Douglas, Private Papers, BCARS B/40/1.

54 Simon Ryan, *The cartographic eye: How explorers saw Australia* (Cambridge: Cambridge University Press, 1996), 4-5.

Chapter 14: Conclusion: The Loss of Locality

1 Louise Miranda and Philip Joe, "How the Squamish remember George Vancouver," in Fisher and Johnston, *From maps to metaphors*, 3-5.

2 Harley, "Rereading the maps of the Columbian encounter," *Annals of the Association of American Geographers* 83, 2 (1992): 522-42.

3 Said, *Culture and imperialism*, 225.

4 See, especially, Said, *Orientalism*; and Gayatri Chakravorty Spivak, *In other worlds* (New York: Methuen, 1987).

5 Timothy Mitchell, *Colonising Egypt* (Cambridge: Cambridge University Press, 1988).

6 See Bhabha, *The location of culture*; Gyan Prakash, "Who's afraid of postcoloniality?" *Social Text* 14, 4 (1996): 187-203.

Bibliography

Abbreviations

Add. MS.	Additonal Manuscript, BM
Add. MSS.	Additional Manuscripts, BCARS
ADM.	Admiralty Records, PRO
BCARS	British Columbia Archives and Records Service, Victoria, Canada
BCHQ	British Columbia Historical Quarterly
BM	British Museum, London, UK
BT	Board of Trade Records, PRO
FO	Foreign Office Records, PRO
HO	Home Office Records, PRO
n.d.	no date
n.p.	no pagination
PAM-HBCA	Provincial Archives of Manitoba – Hudson's Bay Company Archives, Winnipeg, Canada
PRO	Public Records Office, London, UK
UBCL-SC	University of British Columbia Library – University Archives and Special Collections Division, Vancouver, Canada

Primary

Manuscript Sources

Anderson, J.R. Papers. BCARS Add. MSS. 1912.

Anonymous of BCARS. "Directions for entering the principal harbours on the north west coast of America by different commanders." BCARS A/B/20.5/C76.

Anonymous of PRO. "A log of the proceedings of the Discovery, 29 November-28 December 1778." PRO ADM 51/4530.

Atahualpa of Boston. Log, 16 July-13 August 1812. Bancroft Library, Berkeley, P-K 211.

Bancroft, Hubert Howe. Miscellaneous Papers. BCARS E/C/B22.3.

Banks, Joseph. Dawson Turner copies of the correspondence of Sir Joseph Banks. British Museum (Natural History).

—. Papers, 1791. BM Add. MS. 33,979.

Barkley, Frances. "Reminiscences." BCARS A/A/20/B24A.

Bayley, Charles Alfred. "Early life on Vancouver Island." BCARS E/B/B34.2.

Bayly, William. "A log and journal kept on board his majesty's sloop Discovery." PRO ADM 55/20.
—. "Journals and a log kept on Capt. Cook's second and third voyages around the world." Alexander Turnbull Library, National Library of New Zealand.
Bell, James. Correspondence Outward, 1859. BCARS E/B/B412.
Blanshard, Richard. Papers. BCARS Add. MSS. 611.
Brabant, Augustin J. Miscellaneous Papers. BCARS E/D/B72.4.
Brown, Robert. Collection. BCARS Add. MSS. 794.
Burney, James. "Journal of a voyage in the Discovery." PRO ADM 51/4528/45.
Canada. Department of Indian Affairs, Black Series. Public Archives of Canada RG10, vol. 3614.
Church Missionary Society. North Pacific Mission. 2./0.-Original letters, journals and papers, incoming, 1859. UBCL-SC.
Clerke, Charles. "Log and proceedings, 10 February 1776-12 February 1779." PRO ADM 55/22.
Colnett, James. "The journal of James Colnett aboard the Prince of Wales and sloop Princess Royal from 16. Oct. 1786 to 7. Nov. 1788." 2 vols. Typescript of the original in the British Museum, London, UBCL-SC.
Dally, Frederick. Papers. BCARS Add. MSS. 2443.
Davidson, Alexander. "Invoice of sundry artices of merchandise on board his majesty's ship Discovery." PRO ADM 1/4156.
Daylton, Mary Elizabeth, trans. "Official documents relating to Spanish and Mexican voyages of navigation, exploration, and discovery, made in North America in the 18th century." BCARS A/A/10/M57t.
Dean, James. "Settlement of Vancouver Island" [1878]. BCARS E/B/D342.
Devereux, John. Correspondence, 1890-1896. BCARS J/G/T61D.
"Documents relating to the Nootka Sound controversy." 3 vols. UBCL-SC.
Dorr, Ebenezer. Papers. BCARS Add. MSS. 828.
Dorr, Ebenezer and Sons. Ship Hancock, Log Book [1798-1800]. UBCL-SC.
Douglas, James. Private Papers, 1835-1877. BCARS B/20-40.
Duff, Wilson. Papers. Microfilm from the Royal British Columbia Museum held in the Department of Geography, UBC.
Edgar, Thomas. "A journal of a voyage undertaken to the south seas by his majesty's ships Resolution and Discovery." BM Add. MS. 37,528.
—. "A log of the proceedings of his majesty's sloop Discovery, Charles Clerke, commander." PRO ADM 55/21.
—. "Incomplete journal." BCARS A/A/20/D63E.
Great Britain:
Admiralty. HMS Pandora-Correspondence of Lt. Wood, 1848. BCARS 0/A/P19W.
—. Records, 1778-1794, 1856-1860. PRO ADM.1, 51, 55.
Board of Trade. "Examination of Mr. Meares (fur trade)," 27 May 1790. PRO BT 5/6.
—. Records, 1789-1791. PRO BT 2/- and 5/-.
Colonial Office. Despatches to Vancouver Island, 1849-1859. BCARS C/AA/10.2/1A-4A.
—. Original Correspondence. Vancouver Island, 1846-1853. PRO C.O. 305/1-4.
Foreign Office. America-Correspondence, 1842-1846. BCARS GR 327.
—. Letters, 1846. PRO FO 5/459.
—. Miscellaneous, 1789-1791. PRO FO 95/7/-.
—. Papers Relating to the Northwest Coast of America, October 1823-March 1825. Transcripts from the Stratford Canning Papers, F.O.352, bundle 8, BCARS D/A/G79/5.
—. Spain-Letters, 1790-1791. PRO FO 72/16-20.
Home Office. Correspondence, Domestic (George III). PRO HO 28/- and 42/-.
India Office. Factory Records (China), vols. 86-94. BCARS GR 333.
Privy Council. Register, February 1791; and draft bundles. PRO PC 1/63/B22, 2/135.
Hancock, Samuel. "Thirteen years residence on the north-west coast ... " Bancroft Library, Berkeley, HHB P-B29.

[Hanna, James]. "Brig *Sea Otter* from Macao towards America through the Pacific Ocean." BCARS A/A/20.5/Se1H.

Hargrave, James. Hargrave Collection. National Archives of Canada, MG 19, A21.

Helmcken, John Sebastian. Papers. BCARS Add. MSS. 505.

Hewett, George Goodman. "Notes in Vancouver's voyages." BCARS A/A/20/V28H.

Hill, Samuel. "Autobiography." Photostat from New York Public Library, UBCL-SC.

Howay, F.W. Papers. UBCL-SC.

Hudson's Bay Company:

Fort Victoria. Correspondence Books, 1844-1856. PAM-HBCA B.226/b.1-12.

—. Correspondence on the affairs of Vancouver Island colony, 1850-1859. BCARS A/C/20/Vi2-3.

—. Correspondence Inward, 1849-1859, to James Douglas. BCARS A/C/20/Vi7.

Governor George Simpson. Correspondence Inward, 1842-1852. PAM-HBCA. D.5/7-35.

Land Office. Victoria. Correspondence Outward, 1851-1858, Signed by J.D. Pemberton. BCARS A/C/15/HB6P.

—. Register of land purchases from the Indians, 1850-1859. BCARS Add. MSS. 772.

—. Return of treaties made by the Hudson's Bay Company with Indian tribes 1850-1854. BCARS F/53/H86.

London. Correspondence Book Outward (official), 1848. PAM-HBCA A.6/27.

—. Correspondence Inward, 1849-1852. PAM-HBCA, A.10/27-33.

Vancouver Island. Colony account, 1848-1860. PAM-HBCA E.22/2.

Inskip, George Hastings. Journal. 2 vols. BCARS Add. MSS 805.

Lamb, Horatio Appleton. "Notes on trade with the northwest coast, 1790-1810." Photostat from the Houghton Library, Harvard University, UBCL-SC.

Lamb, W. Kaye. Collection. UBCL-SC.

Leeds, Duke [Carmarthen]. Papers, 1790. BM Add. MS. 28,066.

Mckay, Joseph William. Papers. BCARS Add. MSS. 2735.

Magee, Bernard. "Log of the Jefferson." Photostat from the Massachusetts Historical Society, UBCL-SC.

Malaspina, Alejandro. "Politico-scientific voyage round the world ... from 1789-1794." 3 books, Carl Robinson trans. UBCL-SC.

Manby, Thomas. "Log of the proceedings of his majesty's armed tender Chatham, 27 September 1792-8 October 1794." PRO ADM 51/2251.

—. "Manuscript journal of the voyage of H.M.S. *Discovery* and *Chatham,* Dec 10 1790-June 22 1793." Photostat from the Roberston Coe Collection, Yale University, W. Kaye Lamb Papers, 1-3, UBCL-SC.

Martin, Archer. "The inland tribes of Vancouver Island." BCARS F/1/M36.

Martínez, Don Estevan José. "Diary of the voyage ... in the present year 1789." William L Schurtz trans. UBCL-SC.

Mayne, Richard Charles. "Journal kept in H.M.S. *Plumper,* February 1857-December 1860." BCARS E/B/M45.

Moser, Charles. "Thirty years a missionary on the west coast of Vancouver Island." BCARS Add. MSS. 2172.

Navarrete, Martin F. "Viajes en las costa al norte de las Californias, 1774-1790." 1802 (1874 copy, George Davidson trans. Bancroft Library, Berkeley, P-B 26.)

Newcombe Family. Papers. BCARS Add. MSS. 1077.

"Nootka Sound controversy. Correspondence, 1789-1798." BCARS A/A/10.1/Sp12.

Pearse, Benjamin. "Early settlement of Vancouver Island" [1900]. BCARS E/B/P31.

Pemberton, Augustus F. Diary, January 1856-August 1858. BCARS E/B/P37.

Phelps, William D. "Solid men of Boston." Typescript from the Bancroft Library, Berkeley, BCARS A/A/30/So4.

Pidcock, Reginald H. Family Papers. BCARS Add. MSS. 728.

Pitt, William [Lord Chatham]. Chatham Papers. PRO 30/8/-.

Portlock, Nathaniel. "Log, November 1 1777-May 21 1778." PRO ADM 51/4531[68].

Quadra, Juan Francisco de la Bodega. "Voyage to the n.w. coast of North America by Don Juan Francisco de la Bodega y Quadra ... 1792." V.D. Webb trans., typescript of photostat in the Huntingdon Library, UBCL-SC.

Rickman, John. "Log." PRO ADM 51/4529[46].

Riou, Edward. "A log of the proceedings of his majesty's ship *Discovery*." PRO ADM 1/4529[42].

Roman Catholic Church. Diocese of Victoria. Papers, 1842-1912. BCARS Add. MSS. 2742.

Sage, Walter Noble. Papers. UBCL-SC.

Sapir, Edward. Extracts from his correspondence. Typescripts in the possession of Richard Inglis, Royal British Columbia Museum.

—. Field Notebooks, "Nootka Notes." From the Boas Collection, W2a.18, American Philosophical Society Library, Philadelphia. Photocopies in the possession of Richard Inglis, Royal British Columbia Museum.

Smithsonian Institution. National Anthropological Archives, Manuscript Collection, No. 4516, Philip Drucker, "II: The northwest coast: Nootka tribes," Part 23, "Nootka field notebooks, nos. 11-15." Photocopy, BCARS Add. MSS. 870.

Spain. Colonial Office. "Letters of Pedro Alberni, Commander Quadra, Gigedo and other Spanish officials concerning the Spanish occupation of the northwest coast of America." José Rodriguez trans. BCARS A/A/10.1/Sp1A.

Sproat, Gilbert Malcolm. Papers. BCARS Add. MSS. 257.

Sturgis, William. "Ms. of 3 lectures by Wm. Sturgis dealing with his voyages." Massachusetts Historical Society, Boston.

Tate Family. Papers. BCARS Add. MSS. 303.

Tolmie, William Fraser. Papers. BCARS Add. MSS. 557.

Tovell, Freeman. Collection. BCARS Add. MSS. 2826.

Trevenan, James. "Notes regarding the death of Captain Cook." BCARS A/A/40/C77T/A2.

Vancouver, George. "Papers relating to the voyage of the Discovery and Chatham, 1790-1795." BM Add. MS. 17,552.

Vancouver Island. Governor. Naval Letters. 1863-64. BCARS GR 1308.

Walbran, John. "Scrapbook, 1909-1912." BCARS S/S/W14.

Williamson, John. "Log of the proceedings of the Resolution." PRO ADM 55/117.

Published Sources

Anderson, Alexander Caulfield. *The dominion at the west: A brief history of the province of British Columbia, its climate and resources.* Victoria: Richard Wolfenden, 1872.

—. "Notes on the Indian tribes of British North America, and the northwest coast." *Historical Magazine* 7, 3 (1863): 73-81.

Anderson, Bern, ed. "The Vancouver expedition: Peter Puget's journal of the examination of Puget Sound May 7-June 11, 1792." *Pacific Northwest Quarterly* 30, 2 (1939): 177-217.

Anonymous. *Colonization of Vancouver's Island.* London: Burrup and Son, 1849.

Anonymous. *The errors of the British minister, in the negotiations with the court of Spain.* London: J. Debrett, 1790.

Argonaut [Etches, John Cadman]. *An authentic statement of the facts relative to Nootka Sound ... in an address to the King.* London: Debrett, 1790.

—. *A continuation of an authentic statement of the facts relative to Nootka Sound ...* London: T. Beckett, 1790.

Aspinall, A., ed. *The later correspondence of George III,* vol. 1: *December 1783-January 1793.* Cambridge: Cambridge University Press, 1962.

Baldwyn, George Augustus, ed. *A new, royal, authentic, complete, and universal system of geography ...* London: Alex Hogg, 1794.

Banfield, W.E. "Vancouver Island. Its topography, characteristics, and etc., no. VII: Clayoquot Sound-The Tonquin massacre." *Daily Victoria Gazette,* 9 September 1858.

Barrett, Charlotte, ed. *Diary and letters of Madame D'Arblay, vol. 1 (1778-June 1781)*. London: Macmillan, 1904.

Barrington, Daines. *Miscellanies*. London: J. Nicols, 1781.

Bartlett, John. "A narrative of events ... in the years 1790-1793, during voyages to Canton, the northwest coast of North America, and elsewhere," in *The sea, the ship, and the sailor: Tales of adventure from logs books and original narratives*, ed. Captain Elliot Snow. Salem MA: Marine Research Society, 1925.

Beaglehole, J.C., ed. *The journals of Captain James Cook on his voyages of discovery, vol. 1: The voyage of the Endeavour, 1768-1771*. Cambridge: Hakluyt Society, extra series xxxiv, 1955.

—. *The journals of Captain Cook on his voyages of discovery, vol. 3: The voyage of the Resolution and Discovery, 1776-1780*. 2 parts. Cambridge: Hakluyt Society, extra series xxxvi, 1967.

Beals, Herbert K., ed. *For Honor and country: The diary of Bruno de Hezeta*. Portland: Oregon Historical Society Press, 1985.

—. *Juan Perez on the northwest coast: Six documents of his expedition in 1774*. Portland: Oregon Historical Society Press, 1989.

Belcher, Sir Edward. *Narrative of a voyage round the world, performed in her majesty's ship* Sulphur, *during the years 1836-1842 ...* 2 vols. Folkstone and London: Dawsons, 1970.

Beresford, William. *A voyage round the world ... performed in 1785, 1786, 1787, and 1788, in the King George and Queen Charlotte, Captains Portlock and Dixon*. London: Geo. Goulding, 1789.

Blanshard, Richard. *Despatches: Governor Blanshard to the secretary of state, 26th December 1849, to 30th August, 1851*. New Westminster: Government Printing Office, 1863.

Bligh, William. *A voyage to the South Seas ... in his majesty's ship the Bounty*. London: G. Nicol, 1792.

Bond, Phineas. "Letters of Phineas Bond, British Consul at Philadelphia, to the Foreign Office of Great Britain, 1787, 1788, 1789." *Annual Report of the American Historical Association for the Year 1896*, 513-659.

Bowsfield, Hartwell, ed. *Fort Victoria letters, 1846-1851*. Winnipeg: Hudson's Bay Records Society, 1979.

Boswell, James. *The journals of James Boswell, 1760-1795*. Selected by John Wain. London: Heinemann, 1991.

Bougainville, Lewis de. *A voyage round the world. Performed by order of his most Catholic majesty, in the years 1766, 1767, 1768, and 1769*. London: J. Nourse and T. Davies, 1772.

British Columbia, Provincial Archives. *Report of the Provincial Archives ... for 1913*. Victoria: King's Printer, 1914.

British diplomatic instructions, 1689-1789, vol. 2: France 1689-1721. London: Royal Historical Society Publications, Camden Third Series XXXV, 1925.

Brosses, Charles de. *Histoire des navigations aux terres australes*. Paris: Durand, 1756.

Broughton, William Robert. *A voyage of discovery to the north Pacific Ocean ... performed in his majesty's sloop Providence, and her tender, in the years 1795, 1796, 1797, 1798*. London: T. Caddell and W. Davies, 1804.

Brown, Robert. "The first journey of exploration across Vancouver Island." In *Illustrated travels: A record of discovery, geography, and adventure*, vol. 1, ed. H.W. Bates. London: Cassell, Petter, and Galpin, 1869.

—. "The present state of science on the north-western slopes of the Rocky Mountains." *Journal of Travel and Natural History* 1, 3 (1868): 173-80.

Burges, Bland. *A narrative of the negotiations occasioned by the dispute between England and Spain in the year 1790*. London: Printed for the author, 1790.

Callender, John. *Terra australis cognita: Or, voyages to the terra australis, or southern hemisphere.* 3 vols. London and Edinburgh: A. Donaldson, 1766-68.

Cleveland, H.W.S. *Voyages of a northwest navigator ... compiled from the journals and letters of the late Richard J. Cleveland*. New York: Harper and Brothers, 1886.

Cleveland, Richard J. *A narrative of voyages and commercial enterprises ...* 2 vols. Cambridge, MA: John Owen, 1842.

Cobban, Alfred, and Robin A. Smith, eds. *The correspondence of Edmund Burke,* vol. 6: *July 1789-December 1791.* Cambridge: Cambridge University Press, 1967.

Cobbett, William, ed. *The parliamentary history of England* ... , vol. XXVIII. London: Hansard, 1816.

Cook, James. "The method taken for preserving the health of the Crew of his majesty's ship the *Resolution* during her late voyage round the world ... Addressed to Sir John Pringle March 5, 1776." Royal Society, *Philosophical Transactions* 66 (1776): 402-406.

Cook, James, and King, James. *A voyage to the Pacific Ocean ... performed under the direction of captains Cook, Clerke, and Gore, in his majesty's ships the* Resolution *and the* Discovery. *In the years 1776, 1777, 1778, 1779, and 1780.* 3 vols. and atlas. London: G. Nichol and T. Cadell, 1784.

Corning, Howard, ed. "Letters of Sullivan Dorr." *Proceedings of the Massachusetts Historical Society* 66 (October 1941-May 1944): 178-364.

Cutter, Donald, ed. *The California coast: A bilingual edition of documents from the Sutro Collection.* Norman: University of Oaklahoma Press, 1969.

D'Wolf, John. *A voyage to the north Pacific Ocean ...* Cambridge: Welch, Bigelow, 1806.

Dalrymple, Alexander. *An historical collection of the several voyages to the south Pacific Ocean.* 2 vols. London: J. Nourse, 1770-71.

—. *Memoir of a map of the lands around the north-pole.* London: George Bigg, 1789.

—. *Plan for promoting the fur-trade ...* London: George Bigg, 1789.

—. *The Spanish memorial of 4th June considered.* London: George Bigg, 1790.

—. *The Spanish pretensions fairly discussed.* London: George Bigg, 1790.

D'avenant, Charles. *Political and commercial works.* 5 vols., ed. Sir Charles Whitworth. London: R. Horsfield et al.., 1771.

Davenport, F.G. *European treaties bearing on the history of the United States and its dependencies.* 4 vols. Washington: Carnegie Endowment for International Peace, 1917.

Delano, Amasa. *A narrative of voyages and travels ... comprising three voyages round the world ...* Boston: E.G. House, 1817.

Dunn, John. *History of the Oregon Territory and British North America.* London: Edwards and Hughes, 1844.

Efrat, Barbara S., and W.J. Langlois, eds. "nu.tka.: Captain Cook and the Spanish explorers on the coast." *Sound Heritage* 7, 1 (1978).

Ellis, W. *An authentic account of a voyage performed by Captain Cook and Captain Clerke ...* 2 vols. London: Robinson, Sewell, and Debrett, 1782.

Emmerson, John. *British Columbia and Vancouver Island: Voyages, travels, and adventures.* London: Printed for the author, 1865.

Fanning, Edmund. *Voyages to the South Seas, Indian and Pacific Oceans ...* New York: William M. Vermilye, 1838.

Finlayson, Roderick. "History of Vancouver Island and the northwest coast." *Saint Louis University Studies* (ser. B) 1, 1 (1945): 69-84.

Fisher, Robin, and J.M. Bumstead, eds. *An account of a voyage to the northwest coast of America in 1785 and 1786 by Alexander Walker.* Vancouver/Seattle: Douglas and McIntyre/University of Washington Press, 1982.

Fleurieu, C.P. Claret. *A voyage round the world performed during the years 1790, 1791, and 1792, by Étienne Marchand.* 2 vols. London: Longman and Rees, Cadell and Davies, 1801.

Forbes, Charles. *Vancouver Island: Its resources and capabilities as a colony.* Victoria: The Colonial Government, 1862.

Gallatin, Albert. *The Oregon question.* New York: Bartlett and Welford, 1846.

Galois, Bob. "The voyage of James Hanna to the northwest coast: Two documents." *BC Studies* 103 (1994): 83-88.

[Gigedo, Count Revilla de]. "Report of Don Juan Vicente de Guemes Pacheco de Padilla, Count Revilla Gigedo, Viceroy of New Spain on California, 1768-1793." *Land of Sunshine* 11 (1899): 32-41, 105-13, 168-73, 224-33, 282-89.

Gooch, Sherlock. "Across Vancouver Island." *Colburn's United Service Magazine* (1856): 516-41; (1887): 28-40.

Great Britain. "Correspondence relative to the colonization of Vancouver's Island, 1847-48." In *British parliamentary papers*, vol. XLII (619). London: House of Commons, 1848.

—. "Correspondence relative to the negotiation of the question of disputed right to the Oregon Territory." In *British parliamentary papers. Colonies: Canadian boundary, 2*. Shannon: Irish University Press, 1969.

—. *Official papers relative to the dispute between the courts of Great Britain and Spain, on the subject of the ships captured in Nootka Sound ...* London: J. Debrett, 1790.

Hayes, Edmund, ed. *Log of the Union: John Boit's remarkable voyage to the northwest coast and around the world, 1794-1796*. Portland: Oregon Historical Society and Massachusetts Historical Society, 1981.

Hill, George Birkbeck, and L.F. Powell, eds. *Boswell's life of Johnson*, vol. 3: *1776-1780*. Oxford: Clarendon, 1971.

Hills, George. "General statement of the Diocese of Columbia for 1860." In *Columbia Mission occasional paper*. London: Rivington, 1860.

Historical Manuscript Commission. *Dropmore Papers*, vol. 1. London: H.M.S.O, 1892.

Holbrook, Silas P. *Sketches, by a traveller*. Boston: Carter and Hendee, 1830.

Holmes, Christine, ed. *Captain Cook's final voyage: The journal of midshipman George Gilbert*. Horsham: Caliban, 1982.

Howay, F.W. "A ballad of the northwest fur trade." *New England Quarterly* 1 (1928): 71-79.

—. "An early account of the loss of the Boston in 1803." *Washington Historical Quarterly* 17, 4 (October 1926): 280-88.

–, ed. "Four letters from Richard Cadman Etches to Sir Joseph Banks, 1788-92." *BCHQ* 3 (1942): 125-39.

–, ed. *Voyages of the "Columbia" to the northwest coast, 1787-1790 and 1790-1793*. Portland: Oregon Historical Society and the Massachusetts Historical Society, 1990.

–, ed. *The Dixon-Meares controversy*. Toronto: Ryerson, 1929.

–, ed. *The journal of Captain James Colnett aboard the "Argonaut" ...* Toronto: Champlain Society, 1940.

–, ed. *Zimmermann's Captain Cook: An Account of the third voyage of Captain Cook around the world, 1776-1780*. Toronto: Ryerson, 1930.

Hunt, George. "Nootka tales." In *Tsimshian Mythology*. Thirty-First Annual Report of the Bureau of American Ethnology, 1909-1910. Washington, DC: Government Printing Office, 1916.

Hutton, James, ed. *Selections from the letters and correspondence of Sir James Bland Burges ...* London: John Murray, 1885.

Jackman, S.W., ed. *The journal of William Sturgis*. Victoria: Sono Nis, 1978.

Jewitt, John R. *A journal kept at Nootka Sound*. Boston: Printed for the author, 1807.

—. *The adventures and sufferings of John R. Jewitt, captive among the Nootka, 1803-1805* [1824 edition, ed. Derek G. Smith]. Toronto: McCelland and Stewart, 1974.

Johnson, Ebenezer. *A short account of a northwest voyage, performed in the years 1796, 1797 and 1798*. Massachusetts: Printed for the author, 1798.

Kaplanoff, Mark D., ed. *Joseph Ingraham's journal of the brigantine HOPE on a voyage to the northwest coast of America, 1790-1792*. Barre, MA: Imprint Society, 1971.

Kendrick, John, trans. *The voyage of the Sutil and Mexicana, 1792: The last Spanish exploration of the northwest coast of America*. Spokane, WA: Clark, 1991.

Krauss, H.P., and Co. *The American west coast and Alaska: Original drawings and maps from the expedition to Nootka Sound of Juan Francisco de la Bodega y Quadra, 1792*. New York: Krauss, catalogue no. 144, 1976.

Lamb, W. Kaye, ed. *The voyage of George Vancouver 1791-1795*. 4 vols. London: The Hakluyt Society, 1984.

Ledyard, John. *A journal of Captain Cook's last voyage to the Pacific Ocean ... in the years 1776, 1777, 1778, and 1779*. Chicago: Quadrangle, 1963.

Lewis, W.S., ed. *The Yale edition of Horace Walpole's correspondence,* vol. 33. New Haven: Yale University Press, 1965.

Lloyd, Christopher, and R.C. Anderson, eds. *A memoir of James Trevenan.* London: Navy Records Society, 1959.

Macdonald, Duncan George Forbes. *British Columbia and Vancouver Island ...* London: Longman, 1862.

Macfie, Matthew. *Vancouver Island and British Columbia: Their history, resources and prospects.* London: Longman, Green, 1865.

Manning, William R., ed. *Diplomatic correspondence of the United States: Canadian relations.* 5 vols. Washington: Carnegie Endowment for International Peace, 1945.

Marshall, P.J., and John A. Woods, eds. *The correspondence of Edmund Burke,* vol. 7: *January 1792- August 1794.* Cambridge: Cambridge University Press, 1968.

Matthews. J.S., ed. *Early Vancouver: Narratives of pioneers of Vancouver B.C.* 2 vols. Vancouver: J.S. Matthews, 1933.

[McGillivray, Simon]. *Notice respecting the boundary ...* London: B. M'Millan, 1817.

Meany, Edmond S., ed. *A new Vancouver journal on the discovery of Puget Sound.* Seattle WA: n.p., 1915.

Meares, John. *The memorial of John Mears, lieutenant in his majesty's navy, to the Right Honourable William Wyndham Grenville ... dated 30th April 1790.* Published at the request of the British Government, 1790.

—. *Voyages made in the years 1788 and 1789, from China to the north west coast of America ...* London: Logographic Press, 1790.

"Memoir of Alexander Dalrymple." *The European Magazine and London Review* 42 (November/ December 1802): 323-27, 421-24.

Merivale, Herman. *Lectures on colonization and colonies. Delivered before the University of Oxford in 1839, 1840, and 1841.* London: Longman, 2nd ed., 1861.

Merk, Frederick, ed. *Fur trade and empire: George Simpson's journal ... 1824-25.* Cambridge, MA: Harvard University Press, 1968.

Milet-Mureau, L.A., ed. *A voyage round the world, performed in the years 1785, 1786, 1787, and 1788, by the Boussole and Astrolabe, under the command of J.F.G. De La Pérouse.* 2 vols. London: G.G. Robinson and J. Robinson, 1799.

Moziño, José Mariano. *Noticias de Nutka: An account of Nootka Sound in 1792.* Iris H. Wilson Engstrand, trans. and ed. Seattle/London: University of Washington Press; Vancouver/Toronto: Douglas and McIntyre, 1991.

Myers, John. *The life, voyages and travels of Capt. John Myers, detailing his adventures during four voyages round the world ...* London: Longman, Hurst, Rees, 1817.

Newcombe, C.F., ed. *Menzies' journal of Vancouver's voyage April to October, 1792.* Victoria: Archives of British Columbia Memoir no. 4, 1923.

Nicol, John. *The life and adventures of John Nicol, mariner.* London: T. Caddell, 1822.

Palmer, H.S. "Remarks upon the geography and natural capabilities of British Columbia." *Journal of the Royal Geographical Society* 34 (1864): 171-95.

Patterson, Samuel. *Narrative of the adventures and sufferings of Samuel Patterson ...* 1825 edition. Fairfield, WA: Ye Galleon, 1967.

Pemberton, Joseph Despard. *Facts and figures relating to Vancouver Island and British Columbia showing what to expect and how to get there.* London: Longman, Green, and Roberts, 1860.

Péron, François. *Mémoires du capitaine Péron, sur ses voyages.* 2 vols. Paris: Bissot-Thrivars, 1824.

Polk, James K. "Message of the President," 2 December 1845, in *Appendix to the Congressional Globe ... containing speeches and important state papers.* New Series 1845-6. Washington: Blair and Rives, 1846.

Portlock, Nathaniel. *A voyage round the world; but more particularly to the north-west coast of America: Performed in 1785, 1786, 1787, and 1788 ...* London: John Stockdale and George Goulding, 1789.

Postlethwayt, Malachy. *The universal dictionary of trade and commerce.* 5 vols. London: 1771.

Roe, Michael, ed. *The journal and letters of Captain Charles Bishop on the north-west coast of America, in the Pacific and in New South Wales, 1794-1799.* Cambridge: The Hakluyt Society, 1967.

Roquefeuil, M. Camille de. *A voyage round the world, between the years 1816-1819.* London: Sir Richard Phillips, 1823.

Sapir, Edward, and Swadesh, Morris. *Native accounts of Nootka ethnography.* New York: AMS Press, 1978.

Scouler, John. "Observations on the indigenous tribes of the n.w. coast of America." *Journal of the Royal Geographical Society* 11 (1841): 215-40.

Seeman, Berthold. *Narrative of the voyage of H.M.S. Herald during the years 1845-1851 ...* 2 vols. London: Reeve, 1851.

Shaler, William. "Journal of a voyage between China and the north-western coast of America, made in 1804." *American Register* 3, 1 (1808): 137-75.

Smith, Adam. *The Wealth of Nations.* Harmondsworth: Penguin, 1970.

Smith, Dorothy Blakey, ed. *The reminiscences of Doctor John Sebastian Helmcken.* Vancouver: UBC Press, 1975.

Sproat, Gilbert Malcolm. *The Nootka: Scenes and studies of savage life.* Charles Lillard, ed. Victoria: Sono Nis, 1987.

Stapleton, Edward, ed. *Some official correspondence of George Canning.* 2 vols. London: Longman's, Green, 1887.

Strange, James. *James Strange's journal and narrative of the commercial expedition from Bombay to the north-west coast of America.* Madras: Government Press, 1929.

Sturgis, William. "The northwest fur trade." Ed. Elliot C. Cowdin. *Hunt's Merchant's Magazine* 14, 6 (1846): 532-39.

—. "The northwest fur trade, and the Indians of the Oregon Country 1788-1830." Ed. S.E. Morrison. *Old Southern Leaflets,* no. 219, n.d.

Thompson, David. *Columbia journals.* Ed. Barbara Belyea. Montreal: McGill-Queen's University Press, 1994.

Vancouver, George. *A voyage of discovery to the North Pacific Ocean and round the world ... peformed in the years 1790, 1791, 1792, 1793, 1794, and 1795 ...* 3 vols. and atlas. London: G.G. and J. Robinson, 1798.

—. *A voyage of discovery to the North Pacific Ocean and round the world ...* New edition, with corrections. 6 vols. London: J. Stockdale, 1801.

Verus [Burges, Bland]. *Letters lately published in the* Diary, *on the subject of the present dispute with Spain.* London: G. Kearsley, 1790.

Wagner, Henry R., trans. and ed. "Journal of Tomás de Suria of his voyage with Malaspina to the northwest coast of America in 1791." *Pacific Historical Review* 5 (1936): 234-76.

—. *Spanish explorations in the Straits of Juan de Fuca.* Santa Ana, CA: Fine Arts Press, 1933.

Wagner, Henry R., Newcombe, W.A., eds. "The journal of Don Jacinto Caamaño." *BCHQ* 2 (1938): 189-222, 265-301.

Wakefield, Edward Gibbon. *A view of the art of colonization, with present reference to the British Empire; in letters between a statesman and a colonist.* London: John Parker, 1849.

Webster, Peter S. *As far as I know: Reminiscences of an Ahousaht elder.* Campbell River: Campbell River Museum and Archives, 1983.

White knight chapbooks: Pacific northwest series, no.4. San Francisco: White Knight, 1941.

Newspapers and Periodicals

B.C. Orphans' Friend, 1913
Daily Victoria Gazette, 1858
The Annual Register, 1784, 1790
The Daily Colonist, 1924, 1978
The Gentleman's Magazine, 1784, 1790

The Monthly Review, 1784
The Vancouver Sun, 1993
The Victoria Times, 1978
The Times, 1845-1846, 1864
Edinburgh Review, 1845
London Examiner, 1845

Secondary

Published

Anderson, Benedict. *Imagined communities: Reflections on the origin and spread of nationalism*. Rev. ed. London: Verso, 1991.

Anderson, Bern. *The life and voyages of Captain George Vancouver, surveyor of the sea*. Seattle: University of Washington Press, 1960.

Appadurai, Arjun, ed. *The social life of things: Commodities in cultural perspective*. Cambridge: Cambridge University Press, 1986.

—. *Modernity at large: Cultural dimensions of globalization*. Minneapolis: University of Minnesota Press, 1996.

Arima, E.Y. *The west coast people: The Nootka of Vancouver Island and Cape Flattery*. Victoria: British Columbia Provincial Museum, Special Publications, no. 6, 1983.

Arima, Eugene, and John Dewhirst. "Nootkans of Vancouver Island." In *Handbook of North American Indians*, vol. 7: *Northwest coast*, vol. ed. Wayne Suttles, general ed. William C. Sturevant. Washington: Smithsonian Institution, 1990, 391-411.

Ayling, Stanley. *Fox: The life of Charles James Fox*. London: Murray, 1991.

Bancroft, Hubert Howe. *History of the northwest coast*, vol. 1: *1543-1800*. San Francisco: A.L. Bancroft, 1884.

—. *The works of Hubert Howe Bancroft*, vol. XXXII: *History of British Columbia 1792-1887*. San Francisco: History Company, 1887.

Barbeau, Marius. "Totem poles: A by-product of the fur trade." *Scientific Monthly*, December 1942, 507-14.

Barnes, Donald Grove. *George III and William Pitt, 1783-1806*. New York: Octagon, 1965.

Barnes, Trevor, and Duncan James, eds. *Writing worlds: Discourse, text and metaphor in the representation of landscape*. London and New York: Routledge, 1992.

Barnett, James, Stephen Haycox, and Caedmon Liburd, eds. *Enlightenment and exploration in the north Pacific, 1741-1805*. Seattle: University of Washington Press, 1997.

Barrell, John. *English literature in history, 1730-80: An equal, wide view*. New York: St. Martin's, 1983.

Batten, Charles L. Jr. *Pleasurable instruction: Form and convention in eighteenth-century travel literature*. Berkeley: Univeristy of California Press, 1978.

Baudet, Henri. *Paradise on Earth: Some thoughts on European images of non-European man*. New Haven: Yale University Press, 1965.

Baugh, Daniel A. "Seapower and science: The motives for Pacific exploration." In *Background to discovery: Pacific exploration from Dampier to Cook*, ed., Derek Howse, 1-55. Berkeley, Los Angeles, Oxford: University of California Press, 1990.

Bayly, C.A. *Imperial meridian: The British Empire and the world, 1780-1830*. London and New York: Longman, 1989.

—. "The first age of global imperialism." *Journal of Imperial and Commonwealth History* 26, 3 (1998): 28-47.

BC Studies. 95 (Autumn 1992). Special issue: "Antropology and history in the courts."

Blackburn, Robin. *The making of New World slavery: From the baroque to the modern, 1492-1800*. London: Verso, 1997.

Beaglehole, J.C. "On the character of Captain James Cook." *Geographical Journal* 122, 4 (1956): 417-29.

—. *Cook the writer*. Sydney: Sydney University Press, 1970.

—. *The exploration of the Pacific*. London: Black, 1934.

—. *The life of Captain James Cook*. Stanford: Stanford University Press, 1974.

Beckett, J.V., and Michael Turner. "Taxation and economic growth in eighteenth-century Britain." *Economic History Review* (2nd ser.) 42, 3 (1990): 377-403.

Begg, Alexander. *History of British Columbia: From its earliest discovery to the present time*. Toronto: William Briggs, 1894.

Belyea, Barbara. "Images of power:Derrida/Foucault/Harley." *Cartographica* 29, 2 (1992): 1-9.

Bemis, S.F. "Relations between the Vermont Separatists and Great Britain, 1789-1791." *American Historical Review* 21, 1 (1916): 547-53.

Benjamin, Walter. *Illuminations*. New York: Schocken, 1969.

Berland, Jody. "Space at the margin: Colonial spatiality and critical theory after Innis." *Topia* 1 (1997): 60-78.

Bewell, Alan. "Constructed places, constructed peoples: Charting the improvement of the female body in the Pacific." *Eighteenth-Century Life* (n.s.) 18, 3 (1994): 37-54.

Bhabha, Homi K. *The location of culture*. London: Routledge, 1994.

Bitterli, Urs. *Cultures in conflict: Encounters between European and non-European cultures, 1492-1800*. Trans. Ritchie Roberston. Cambridge: Polity, 1989.

Black, Jeremy. *British foreign policy in an age of revolutions, 1783-1793*. Cambridge: Cambridge University Press, 1994.

Boas, Franz. *Kwakiutl ethnography*. Ed. Helen Codere. Chicago: University of Chicago Press, 1966.

Bodmer, Beatriz Pastor. *The armature of conquest: Spanish accounts of the discovery of America, 1492-1589*. Trans. Lydia Longstreth Hunt. Stanford: Stanford University Press, 1992.

Boelhower, William. "Inventing America: A model of cartographic semiosis." *Word and Image* 4, 2 (1988): 475-97.

Bourne, Kenneth, ed. *The foreign policy of Victorian England, 1830-1902*. Oxford: Clarendon, 1970.

Bowen, H.V. "British conceptions of global empire, 1756-83." *Journal of Imperial and Commonwealth History* 26, 3 (1998): 1-27.

Brantlinger, Patrick. *Fictions of the state: Culture and credit in Britain, 1694-1994*. Ithaca: Cornell University Press, 1996.

Braudel, Fernand. *Civilization and capitalism 15th-18th century*, vol. 3: *The perspective of the world*. Trans. Sian Reynolds. New York: Perennial Library Edition, 1986.

Brewer, John. *The sinews of power: War, money, and the English state, 1688-1783*. London: Unwin Hyman, 1989.

Buck-Morss, Susan. "Envisioning capital: Political economy on display." *Critical Inquiry* 21, 2 (1995): 434-65.

Carter, Paul. *The road to Botany Bay: An essay in spatial history*. London: Faber and Faber, 1987.

—. "Violent passages: Pacific histories." *Journal of Historical Geography* 20, 1 (1994): 81-86.

Chakrabarty, Dipesh. "Postcoloniality and the artifice of history: Who speaks for 'Indian' past?" *Representations* 37 (1992): 1-27.

Chamberlain, Muriel E. *Lord Aberdeen: A political biography*. London and New York: Longman, 1983.

Chapin, Chester. "Samuel Johnson, anthropologist." *Eighteenth-Century Life* 19 (1995): 22-37.

Clifford, James, and George Marcus, eds. *Writing culture: The poetics and politics of ethnography*. Berkeley: University of California Press, 1986.

Codere, Helen. *Fighting with property: A study of the Kwakiutl potlatching and warfare, 1792-1930*. Washington: American Ethnological Society, Monograph 18, 1950.

Cohn, Bernard. *Colonialism and its forms of knowledge: The British in India*. Princeton, NJ: Princeton University Press, 1996.

Colley, Linda. *Britons: Forging the nation, 1707-1837*. New Haven and London: Yale University Press, 1992.

Comaroff, Jean, and John Comaroff. *Of revelation and revolution: Christianity, colonialism and consciousness in South Africa*. Chicago and London: University of Chicago Press, 1991.

Conrad, Joseph. *Last essays*. New York: Doubleday, Page, 1926.

Cook, Warren L. *Flood tide of empire: Spain and the Pacific northwest, 1543-1819.* New Haven: Yale University Press, 1973.

Cooper, Frederick, and Laura Stoler, eds. *Tensions of empire: Colonial cultures in a bourgeois world.* Berkeley: University of California Press, 1997.

Corrigan, Philip, and Derek Sayer. *The great arch: English state formation as cultural revolution.* Oxford: Blackwell, 1985.

Cramer, Richard S. "British magazines and the Oregon question." *Pacific Historical Quarterly* 32 (1963): 369-82.

Crary, Jonathan. *Techniques of the observer: On vision and modernity in the nineteenth century.* Cambridge, MA: MIT Press, 1990.

Curtis, Edward. *The North American Indian,* vol. 11: *The Nootka; the Haida.* Ed. Frederick Webb Hodge. Norwood, MA: Plimpton, 1916.

Cutter, Donald C. *Malaspina and Galiano: Spanish voyages to the northwest coast, 1791 and 1792.* Seattle/Vancouver: University of Washington Press/Douglas and McIntyre, 1991.

Danziger, Marlies K., and Frank Brady, eds. *Boswell: The great biographer, 1789-1795.* London: Heinemann, 1989.

Daston, Lorraine. "Curiosity in the early modern period." *World and Image* 11, 4 (1995): 391-404.

David, Andrew. "Vancouver's survey methods and surveys." In Fisher and Johnston, *From maps to metaphors,* 51-69.

Dean, Mitchell. *The constitution of poverty: Towards a genealogy of liberal governance.* London and New York: Routledge, 1991.

Delgamuukw et al. v. the Queen. "Reasons for judgement of The Honourable Chief Justice Allan McEachern," 8 March 1991. B.C.S.C., Smithers Registry No. 0843.

Demeritt, David. "Representing the 'true' St. Croix; Knowledge and power in the partition of the northeast," *William and Mary Quarterly* (3rd ser.) 54, 3 (1997): 515-48.

Dening, Greg. *Islands and beaches. Discourse on a silent land: Marquesas 1774-1880.* Chicago: Dorsey, 1980.

—. *Mr Bligh's bad language: Passion, power and theatre on the Bounty.* Cambridge: Cambridge University Press (Canto ed.), 1994.

—. *Performances.* Chicago: University of Chicago Press, 1996.

Derian, James Der. *On diplomacy: A genealogy of western estrangement.* Oxford: Blackwell, 1987.

Derry, John W. *Politics in the age of Fox, Pitt and Liverpool: Continuity and transformation.* London: Methuen, 1990.

Dewhirst, John. "Nootka Sound: A 4,000 year perspective." In *Sound Heritage* 7, 2 (1978), ed. Barbara Efrat and W.J. Langlois, 1-29.

Dewhirst, John. "The Yuquot project 1: The indigenous archaeology of Yuquot, a Nootkan outside village." *History and Archaeology* 39 (1980), special issue.

Dillon, Richard H. "Archibald Menzies' trophies." *BCHQ* 15,3-4 (1951): 151-59.

Dirks, Nicholas B., ed. *Colonialism and culture.* Ann Arbor: University of Michigan Press, 1992.

Donald, Leland. "The slave trade on the northwest coast of North America." *Research in Economic Anthropology* 6 (1984): 121-58.

Doyle, William. *The Oxford history of the French Revolution.* Oxford and New York: Oxford University Press, 1990.

Driver, Felix. *Power and pauperism: The workhouse system, 1834-1884.* Cambridge: Cambridge University Press, 1993.

Drucker, Philip. "Ecology and political organization on the northwest coast of America." In *The development of political organization in native North America,* ed. Elizabeth Tooker, 4-15. Washington, DC: American Ethnological Society, 1983.

—. "Rank, wealth, and kinship in northwest coast society." In *Indians of the northwest coast,* ed. Tom McFeat, 134-46. Seattle and London: University of Washington Press, 1967.

—. *The northern and central Nootkan tribes.* Smithsonian Institution Bureau of American Ethnology, Bulletin 144. Washington, DC: US Government Printing Office, 1951.

Duff, Wilson. "The Fort Victoria treaties." *BC Studies* 3 (1969): 3-57.

Dunmore, John. *French explorers in the Pacific,* vol. 1: *The eighteenth century.* Oxford: Clarendon, 1965.

Dutton, Tom. "'Successful intercourse was had with the natives': Aspects of European contact methods in the Pacific." In *A world of language: Papers presented to Professor S.A. Wurm on his 65th birthday,* ed. Donald C. Laycock and Werner Winter, 153-71. Pacific Linguistics, C-100, 1987.

Eagleton, Terry. *The ideology of the aesthetic.* Oxford: Blackwell, 1990.

Eastwood, Terry. "R.E. Gosnell, E.O.S. Scholefield and the founding of the provincial archives of British Columbia, 1894-1919." *BC Studies* 54 (1982): 38-62.

Ehrman, John. *The younger Pitt,* vol. 1: *The years of acclaim.* London: Constable, 1969.

Ernst, Alice H. *The wolf ritual of the northwest coast.* Eugene: University of Oregon Press, 1952.

Ferguson, Brian R., and Neil L. Whitehead. *War in the tribal zone: Expanding states and indigenous warfare.* Santa Fe, NM: School of American Research Press, 1992.

Ferguson, Brian, ed. *Warfare, culture, and environment* London: Academic, 1984.

Fisher, Robin. "Arms and men on the northwest coast, 1774-1825." *BC Studies* 29 (1976): 3-18.

—. *Contact and conflict: Indian-European relations in British Columbia, 1774-1890.* Vancouver: UBC Press, 1977 (1992).

—. "Contact and trade, 1774-1849." In *The Pacific province: A history of British Columbia,* ed. Hugh J.M. Johnston. Vancouver/Toronto: Douglas and McIntyre, 1996.

—. "Indian control of the maritime fur trade and the northwest coast." In *Approaches to native history in Canada,* ed. D.A. Muise, 65-86. Ottawa: National Museums of Canada, 1977.

—. "Judging history: Reflections on the reasons for judgment in Delgamuukw v. B.C." *BC Studies* 95 (1992): 43-54.

—. *Vancouver's voyage: Charting the northwest coast, 1791-1795.* Vancouver/Toronto: Douglas and McIntyre, 1992.

Fisher, Robin, and Hugh Johnston, eds. *Captain James Cook and his times.* Seattle: University of Washington Press, 1979.

—. *From maps to metaphors: The Pacific world of George Vancouver.* Vancouver: UBC Press, 1993.

Folan, William J., and John T. Dewhirst. "Yuquot: Where the wind blows from all directions." *Archaeology* 23, 4 (1970): 276-86.

Foucault, Michel. *Discipline and punish: The birth of the prison.* Trans. Alan Sheridan. Harmondsworth, UK: Penguin, 1978.

—. "Governmentality." In *The Foucault effect: Studies in governmentality,* ed. Graham Burchell, Colin Gordon, and Peter Miller, 87-104. Hemel Hempstead: Harvester Wheatsheaf, 1991.

—. *Language, counter-memory, practice: Selected essays and interviews.* Ed. D. Bouchard. Ithaca, NY: Cornell University Press, 1977.

—. *Power/knowledge: Selected interviews and orher writings, 1972-1977.* Ed. Colin Gordon. New York: Pantheon, 1980.

—. *The birth of the clinic: An archaeology of medical perception.* London: Tavistock, 1973.

—. *The Foucault reader.* Ed. Paul Rabinow. New York: Pantheon, 1984.

Franco, Jean. "The noble savage." In *Literature and western civilization,* vol. 1: *The modern world,* ed. David Daiches and Anthony Thorlby, 565-93. London: Aldus, 1975.

Frost, Alan. "Nootka Sound and the beginnings of Britain's imperialism of free trade." In Fisher and Johnston, *From maps to metaphors,* 104-26.

Fry, Howard T. "Alexander Dalrymple and Captain Cook: The creative interplay of two careers." In Fisher and Johnston, *Captain James Cook and his times,* 41-57.

Galbraith, John S. *The Hudson's Bay Company as an imperial factor, 1821-1869.* Toronto: University of Toronto Press, 1957.

Galois, Robert M. *Kwakwaka'wakw settlements, 1775-1920: A geographical analysis and gazetteer.* Vancouver/Seattle: UBC Press/University of Washington Press, 1994.

—. "The Indian Rights Association, native protest activity and the 'land question' in British Columbia, 1903-1916." *Native Studies Review* 8, 2 (1992): 1-34.

Gandhi, Leela. *Postcolonial theory: A critical introduction*. Edinburgh: Edinburgh University Press, 1998.

Gerbi, Antonello. *The dispute of the New World: The history of a polemic, 1750-1900*. Trans. Jeremy Moyle. Pittsburgh: University of Pittsburgh Press, 1973.

Gibson, James R. *Otter skins, Boston ships, and China goods: The maritime fur trade of the northwest coast, 1785-1841*. Montreal, Kingston, London: McGill-Queen's University Press, 1992.

Giesecke, E.W. "Search for the Tonquin." *Cumtux: Clatsop County Historical Society Quarterly* 10 (1990): no. 3, 3-8, no. 4, 3-14; vol. 11 (1991): no. 1, 23-40.

Godwin, George. *Vancouver: A life, 1757-1798*. New York: Appleton, 1931.

Goetzmann, William H. *New lands, new men: America and the second great age of discovery*. New York: Viking, 1986.

Goldie, Terry. *Fear and temptation: The image of the indigene in Canadian, Australian, and New Zealand literatures*. Montreal: McGill-Queen's University Press, 1989.

Gosnell, R.E. *The year book of British Columbia and manual of provincial information*. Victoria: Government Printers, 1903.

Gough, Barry M. "India-based expeditions of trade and discovery in the north Pacific in the late eighteenth century." *Geographical Journal* 155, 2 (1989): 215-23.

—. *The northwest coast: British navigation, trade and discoveries to 1812*. Vancouver: UBC Press, 1992.

Green, L.C., and Olive P. Dickason. *The law of nations and the New World*. Edmonton: University of Alberta Press, 1989.

Greenblatt, Stephen. *Marvellous possessions: The wonder of the New World*. Chicago: University of Chicago Press, 1991.

Greenhow, Robert. *The History of Oregon and California ...* Boston: Little and Brown, 1844.

Gregory, Derek. *Geographical imaginations*. Oxford: Blackwell, 1994.

Guest, Harriet. "Curiously masked: Tattooing, masculinity, and nationality in eighteenth-century perceptions of the South Pacific." In *Painting and the politics of culture: New essays on British art, 1700-1850*, ed. John Barrell, 101-34. Oxford: Oxford University Press, 1992.

Harley, J. Brian. "Maps, knowledge, and power." In *The iconography of landscape*, ed. D. Cosgrove and S. Daniels, 277-312. Cambridge: Cambridge University Press, 1988.

—. "Rereading the maps of the Columbian encounter." *Annals of the Association of American Geographers* 83, 2 (1992): 522-42.

—. "Deconstructing the map." In Barnes and Duncan, *Writing worlds*, 231-47.

Harlow, Vincent T. *The founding of the second British Empire, 1763-1793*. 2 vols. London: Longmans, Green, 1953-64.

Harris, Cole, ed. *Historical atlas of Canada*, vol. 1: *From the beginning to 1800*. Toronto: University of Toronto Press, 1987.

—. *The resettlement of British Columbia: Essays on colonialism and geographical change*. Vancouver: UBC Press, 1996.

—. "Social power and cultural change in pre-colonial British Columbia." *BC Studies* 115-16 (1997-98): 45-82.

—. *The Indian land question in British Columbia*. Vancouver: UBC Press, forthcoming.

Harvey, David. *The urban experience*. Oxford: Blackwell, 1989.

—. *The limits to capital*. Oxford: Blackwell, 1982.

Helgerson, Richard. *Forms of nationhood: The Elizabethan writing of England*. Chicago: University of Chicago Press, 1992.

Helms, Mary W. *Ulysses' sail: An ethnographic odyssey of power, knowledge, and geographical distance*. Princeton: Princeton University Press, 1988.

Hoare, Michael E. "Two centuries of perception: George Forster to Beaglehole." In Fisher and Johnston, *Captain James Cook and his times*, 211-28.

Hobsbawm, E.J. *The age of revolution, 1789-1848*. New York: Mentor, 1962.

Howay, F.W. *British Columbia: The making of a province*. Toronto: Ryerson, 1928.

—. "Indian attacks upon maritime traders of the north-west coast, 1785-1805." *Canadian Historical Review* 6, 4 (1925): 287-309.

—. "Outline sketch of the maritime fur trade." *Canadian Historical Association, Annual Report*, 1932, 5-14.

—. "The earliest pages of the history of British Columbia." *First Annual Report of the British Columbia Historical Association*, 1923, 12-22.

—. "The fur trade in northwestern development." In *The Pacific Ocean in history*, ed. H. Morse Stevens and Herbert E. Bolton, 276-86. New York: Macmillan, 1917.

—. "The loss of the Tonquin." *Washington Historical Quarterly* 13, 2 (1922): 83-92.

—. "The voyage of the Hope: 1790-1792." *Washington Historical Quarterly* 11, 1 (1920): 3-28.

—. "Two memorable landmarks of British Columbia." *The Historic Landmarks of Canada, Annual Report*, 1921, 28-30.

Howay, F.W., W.N. Sage, and H.F. Angus. *British Columbia and the United States: The north Pacific slope from the fur trade to aviation*. New York: Russell and Russell, 1942.

Howay, F.W., and E.O.S. Scholefield. *British Columbia: From the earliest times to the present*. 4 vols. Vancouver: Clarke, 1914.

Howse, Derek. "The principal scientific instruments taken on Captain Cook's voyages." *Mariner's Mirror* 65, 2 (1979): 119-35.

Huggan, Graham. "Decolonizing the map: Post-colonialism, post-structuralism and the cartographic connection." *Ariel* 20, 4 (1989): 115-31.

Hulme, Peter. *Colonial encounters: Europe and the native Carribean, 1492-1797*. London: Metheun, 1986.

—. "Including America." *Ariel* 26, 1 (1995): 117-23.

Hunt, Margaret. "Racism, imperialism, and the traveller's gaze in eighteenth-century England." *Journal of British Studies* 32 (1993): 333-57.

Hyam, Ronald, and Martin Ged, eds. *Reappraisals in British imperial history*. London: Macmillan, 1975.

Inglis, Richard. "Foreword." In Alice W. Shurcliff and Sarah Shurcliff Ingelfinger, *Captive of the Nootka Indians: The northwest coast adventure of John R. Jewitt, 1802-1806*. Boston: Back Bay, 1993.

Inglis, Richard I., and James C. Haggarty. "Cook to Jewitt: Three decades of change in Nootka Sound." In *Le castor fait tout: Selected papers of the fifth North American fur trade conference, 1985*, ed. B. Trigger, T. Morantz, and L. Dechène, 193-222. Lake St. Louis Historical Society, 1987.

Inglis, Robin, ed. *Spain and the north Pacific coast: Essays in recognition of the bicentennial of the Malaspina expedition, 1791-1792*. Vancouver: Vancouver Maritime Museum Society, 1992.

Jones, Howard, and Donald A. Rakestraw. *Prologue to manifest destiny: Anglo-American relations in the 1840s*. Wilmington: SR Books, 1997.

Jopling, Carol F. "The coppers of the northwest coast Indians: Their origin, development, and possible antecendents." *Transactions of the American Philosophical Society* 79, 1 (1989): 1-164.

Joppien, Rudiger, and Bernard Smith. *The art of Captain Cook's voyages*, vol. 3: *The voyage of the Resolution and Discovery, 1776-1780*. 2 parts. Melbourne: Oxford University Press, 1987.

Joppien, Rudiger. "The artistic bequest of Captain Cook's voyages-popular imagery in European costume books of the late eighteenth and early nineteenth centuries." In Fisher and Johnston, *Captain James Cook and his times*, 187-210.

Kaeppler, Adrienne L., ed. *Cook voyage artifacts in Leningrad, Berne, and Florence museums*. Honolulu: Bishop Museum Press, 1978.

Kaviraj, Sudipta. "On the construction of colonial power: structure, discourse, hegemony." In *Contesting colonial hegemony: States and Society in Africa and India*, ed. Dagmar Engels and Shula Marks, 19-54. London and New York: Tauris, 1994.

Kant, Immanuel. *The critique of pure reason*. Trans. Norman Kemp Smith. London: Macmillan, 1929.

Keller, Arthur S., Oliver J. Lissitzyn, and Frederick J. Mann. *Creation of rights of sovereignty through symbolic acts, 1400-1800*. New York: Columbia University Press, 1938.

Kemp, Sandra. *Kipling's hidden narratives*. Oxford: Blackwell, 1988.

Kiernan, Victor. *Imperialism and its contradictions*. Ed. Harvey J. Kaye. New York: Routledge, 1995.

Kipling, Rudyard. *Rudyard Kipling's verse: Definitive edition*. London: Hodder and Stoughton, 1940.

Koppert, Vincent A. *Contributions to Clayoquot ethnography*. Washington, DC: University of America, 1930.

Kornfeld, Eve. "Encountering 'the Other': American intellectuals and Indians in the 1790s." *William and Mary Quarterly* (3rd ser) 52, 2 (1995): 287-314.

Kroeber, A.L. "American culture and the northwest coast." *American Anthropologist* (n.s.) 25 (1923): 1-20.

Kross, Herman E., and Charles Gilbert. *American business history*. Englewood Cliffs, NJ: Prentice-Hall, 1972.

Kumar, Krishan. *Utopia and anti-utopia in modern times*. Oxford: Blackwell, 1991.

Lamb, Jonathan. "Minute particulars and the representation of South Pacific discovery." *Eighteenth-Century Studies* 28, 3 (1995): 281-94.

Lamb, W. Kaye. "The mystery of Mrs. Barkley's diary." *BCHQ* 1 (1942): 31-59.

Lamb, W. Kaye, and Tomas Bartroli. "James Hanna and John Henry Cox: The first maritime fur trader and his sponsor." *BC Studies* 84 (1989-90): 3-36.

Langford, Paul. *A polite and commercial people: England 1727-1783*. Oxford: Oxford University Press, 1992.

Law, John. "On methods of long-distance control: Vessels, navigation and the Portuguese route to India." In *Power, action and belief: A new sociology of knowledge?* Ed. John Law, 234-63. London: Routledge and Kegan Paul, 1986.

Lawrence, Christopher. "Disciplining disease: Scurvy, the navy, and imperial expansion, 1750-1825." In Miller and Reill, *Visions of empire*, 80-106.

Lee, C.H. *The British economy since 1700*. Cambridge: Cambridge University Press, 1986.

Livingstone, David N. *The geographical tradition: Episodes in the history of a contested discipline*. Oxford: Blackwell, 1992.

Lloyd, T.O. *The British Empire, 1558-1983*. Oxford: Oxford University Press, 1984.

Loo, Tina. *Making law, order and authority in British Columbia, 1821-1871*. Toronto: University of Toronto Press, 1994.

Loomba, Ania. *Colonialism/postcolonialism*. London: Routledge, 1998.

Lowe, Lisa. *Critical terrains: French and British orientalisms*. Ithaca: Cornell University Press, 1992.

McNab, David. "Herman Merivale and the Native Question, 1837-1861." *Albion* 9, 4 (1977): 359-84.

Mackay, D.L. "Direction and purpose in British imperial policy, 1783-1801." *Historical Journal* 17, 3 (1974): 487-501.

Mackay, David. *In the wake of Cook: Exploration, science and empire, 1780-1801*. London: Croom Helm, 1985.

Mackie, Richard. "The colonization of Vancouver Island, 1849-1858." *BC Studies* 96 (1992-93): 3-40.

—. *Trading beyond the mountains: The British fur trade on the Pacific, 1793-1843*. Vancouver: UBC Press, 1997.

MacLachlan, Colin M. *Spain's empire in the New World: The role of ideas in institutional and social change*. Berkeley, Los Angeles: University of California Press, 1988.

MacLaren, I.S. "Exploration/travel literature and the evolution of the author." *International Journal of Canadian Studies* 5 (1992): 39-68.

Mann, Michael. *The sources of social power*, vol. 2: *The rise of classes and nation-states, 1760-1914*. Cambridge: Cambridge University Press, 1993.

Manning, William R. "The Nootka Sound controversy." *Annual Report of the American Historical Association For the Year 1904*, 279-478.

Manuel, Frank, and Fritzie Manuel. *Utopian thought in the western world.* Cambridge MA: Harvard University Press, 1979.

Marsden, Susan, and Robert Galois. "The Tsimshian, the Hudson's Bay Company, and the geopolitics of the northwest coast fur trade, 1787-1840." *Canadian Geographer* 39, 2 (1995): 169-83.

Marshall, P.J. *East India fortunes: The British in Bengal in the eighteenth century.* Oxford: Clarendon, 1976.

—. "The first and second British Empires: A question of demarcation." *History* 49 (1964): 13-23.

Marshall, P.J., ed. *The Oxford History of the British Empire,* vol. 2: *The eighteenth century.* Oxford: Oxford University Press, 1998.

Marshall, Yvonne. "Dangerous liaisons. Maquinna, Quadra, and Vancouver in Nootka Sound, 1790-5." In Fisher and Johnston, *From maps to metaphors,* 160-75.

Marx, Karl. *Capital,* vol. 1: *A critique of political economy.* Trans. Ben Fowkes. Harmondsworth, UK: Penguin, 1976.

Meek, Ronald L. *Social science and the ignoble savage.* Cambridge: Cambridge University Press, 1976.

Merk, Frederick. *The Oregon question: Essays in Anglo-American diplomacy and politics.* Cambridge, MA: Harvard University Press, 1967.

Miller, David Philip. "Joseph Banks, empire, and 'centers of calculation' in late Hanoverian London." In Miller and Reill, *Visions of empire,* 21-37.

Miller, David Philip, and Petter Hanns Reill, eds. *Visions of empire: Voyages, botany, and representations of nature.* Cambridge: Cambridge University Press, 1996

Mitchell, Timothy. *Colonising Egypt.* Cambridge: Cambridge University Press, 1988.

Moore-Gilbert, Bart. *Postcolonial theory: Contexts, practices, politics.* London: Verso, 1997.

Moorehead, Alan. *The fatal impact: An account of the invasion of the South Pacific, 1767-1840.* New York: Harper and Row, 1966.

Morrison, Samuel Eliot. *The maritime history of Massachusetts, 1783-1869.* Boston: Houghton Mifflin, 1921.

Naish, John. "The achievements of Captain George Vancouver: A reassessment after 200 years." *Mariner's Mirror* 60, 4 (1994): 418-30.

Newcombe, C.F. *The first circumnavigation of Vancouver Island.* Archives of British Columbia, Memoir 1. Victoria: William H. Cullin, 1914.

Niranjana, Tejaswini. *Siting translation: History, post-structuralism, and the colonial context.* Berkeley: University of California Press, 1992.

Norris, J.M. "The policy of the British Cabinet in the Nootka crisis." *English Historical Review* 70 (1955): 562-80.

Obeyesekere, Gananath. "'British Cannibals': Contemplation of an event in the death and resurrection of James Cook, explorer." *Critical Inquiry* 18, 4 (1992): 630-54.

—. *The apotheosis of Captain Cook: European mythmaking in the Pacific.* Princeton, NJ: Princeton University Press, 1992.

O'Brien, Patrick. "Inseperable connections: Trade, economy, fiscal state, and the expansion of empire." In Marshall, *Oxford history of the British Empire,* vol. 2.

Ormsby, Margaret A. *British Columbia: A history.* Toronto: Macmillan, 1971.

Orr, Bridget. "'Southern passions mix with northern art': Miscegenation and the *Endeavour* voyage." *Eighteenth-Century Life* (n.s.) 18, 3 (1994): 212-31.

Outram, Dorinda. *The Enlightenment.* Cambridge: Cambridge University Press, 1995.

Pagden, Anthony. *European encounters with the New World: From Renaissance to romanticism.* New Haven: Yale University Press, 1993.

Pagden, Anthony. *Lords of all the world: Ideologies of empire in Spain, Britain and France, c. 1500-c. 1800.* New Haven: Yale University Press, 1995.

Parry, Benita. "Signs of our times: Discussion of Homi Bhabha's *The location of culture*." *Third Text* 28-29 (1994): 5-24.

Pletcher, David M. *The diplomacy of annexation: Texas, Oregon, and the Mexican War.* Columbia, MO: University of Missouri Press, 1973.

Poole, Deborah. *Vision, race and modernity: A visual economy of the Andean image world.* Princeton: Princeton University Press, 1997.

Prakash, Gyan. "Who's afraid of postcoloniality?" *Social Text* 14, 4 (1996): 187-203.

Pratt, Mary Louise. *Imperial eyes: Travel writing and transculturation.* London: Routledge, 1993.

Rabasa, José. "Allegories of the *Atlas.*" In *Europe and its others,* vol. 2, ed. Francis Barker, Peter Hulme, Margaret Iverson, and Diana Loxley, 1-16. Colchester: University of Essex, 1985.

—. *Inventing America: Spanish historiography and the formation of Eurocentrism.* Norman, OK: University of Oklahoma Press, 1993.

Rediker, Marcus. *Between the devil and the deep blue sea.* Cambridge: Cambridge University Press, 1989.

Reilly, Robin. *Pitt the younger, 1759-1806.* London: Cassell, 1978.

Richards, Thomas. "Archive and utopia." *Representations* 37 (1992): 104-35.

Rogers, Pat. "The noblest savage of them all: Johnson, Omai, and other primitives." In *The age of Johnson: A scholarly annual,* vol. 5, ed. Paul J. Korshin, 281-302. New York: AMS Press, 1992.

Rose, Deborah Bird. *Dingo makes us human: Life and land in an Aboriginal Australian culture.* Cambridge: Cambridge Univeristy Press, 1992.

—. "Worshipping Captain Cook." *Social Analysis* 34 (1993): 43-49.

Rose, J. Holland. *A short life of William Pitt.* London: Bell and Sons, 1925.

—. *William Pitt and national revival.* London: Bell and Sons, 1911.

Rushdie, Salman. *Imaginary homelands: Essays and criticism, 1981-1991.* London: Penguin, 1991.

Ryan, Simon. *The cartographic eye: How explorers saw Australia.* Cambridge: Cambridge University Press, 1996.

Sage, W.N. "Some early historians of British Columbia." *BCHQ* 21, 1-4 (1958): 1-14.

—. "Towards new horizons in Canadian history." *Pacific Historical Review* 7, 1 (1939): 47-57.

—. "Unveiling of memorial tablet at Nootka Sound." *Second Annual Report and Proceedings of the British Columbia Historical Association,* 1924, 17-22.

Sahlins, Marshall. "Captain Cook at Hawaii." *Journal of Polynesian History* 98 (1989): 371-425.

—. "Goodbye to *tristes tropes*: Ethnography in the context of modern world history." *Journal of Modern History,* 65 (1993): 1-25.

—. "The apotheosis of Captain Cook." In *Between belief and transgression: Structuralist essays in religion, history and myth,* ed. Michael Izard and Pierre Smith, 73-102. Chicago: University of Chicago Press, 1982.

—. *What 'natives' think: About Captain Cook, for example.* Chicago and London: University of Chicago Press, 1995.

Said, Edward W. *Culture and imperialism.* New York: Knopf, 1993.

—. *Orientalism.* New York: Vintage, 1979.

Sanchez, Joseph P. "Pedro de Alberni and the Spanish claim to Nootka: The Catalonian Volunteers on the northwest coast." *Pacific Northwest Quarterly* (April 1980): 72-77.

Sapir, Edward. "Cultures, genuine and spurious." In *Selected writings of Edward Sapir in language, culture and personality,* ed. David G. Mandelbaum, 308-31. Berkeley: University of California Press, 1985.

—. "Sayach'apis, a Nootkan trader." In *American Indian life: By several of its students,* ed. Elise Clews Parsons, 297-323. New York: Huebsch, 1922.

—. "The social organisation of the west coast tribes." In *Selected writings of Edward Sapir in language, culture and personality,* ed. David G. Mandelbaum, 468-87. Berkeley: University of California Press, 1985.

Savelle, Max. *The diplomatic history of the Canadian boundary, 1749-1763.* New Haven: Yale University Press, 1940.

Schwartz, Seymour I, and Ralph E. Ehrenberg. *The mapping of America.* New York: Abraams, 1980.

Schwartz, Stuart B., ed. *Implicit understandings: Observing, reporting, and reflecting on the encounters between Europeans and other peoples in the early modern era.* Cambridge: Cambridge University Press, 1994.

Scott, David. "Colonial governmentality." *Social Text* 43 (1995): 191-220.

Seed, Patricia. *Ceremonies of possession in Europe's conquest of the New World, 1492-1640.* Cambirdge: Cambridge University Press, 1995.

—. "Taking possession and reading texts: Establishing the authority of overseas empire." *William and Mary Quarterly* (3rd ser.) 49, 2 (1992): 183-209.

Semmel, Bernard. *The liberal idea and the demons of empire: From Adam Smith to Lenin.* Baltimore: Johns Hopkins University Press, 1993.

Skelton, R.A. "Captain James Cook as a hydrographer." *Mariner's Mirror* 40 (1954): 92-119.

—. *Captain James Cook: After two hundred years.* London: The Hakluyt Society, 1969.

Smith, Allan. "The writing of British Columbia history." *BC Studies* 45 (1980): 73-102.

Smith, Bernard. "A comment." *Social Analysis* 34 (1993): 61-65.

—. "Cook's posthumous reputation." In *Captain James Cook and his times,* ed. Robin Fisher and Hugh Johnston, 159-86. Seattle: University of Washington Press, 1979.

—. *European vision and the South Pacific, 1768-1850: A study in the history of art and ideas.* Oxford: Clarendon, 1960.

—. *Imagining the Pacific: In the wake of the Cook voyages.* New Haven: Yale University Press, 1992.

—. *Style, information and image in the art of Cook's voyages.* Christchurch: School of Fine Arts, University of Canterbury, 1988.

Souvenir of the bi-centenary celebrations arranged in the Cleveland district. Middlesborough: Sanbride, 1928.

Spivak, Gayatri Chakravorty, *In other worlds.* New York: Methuen, 1987.

Stafford, Barbara Maria. *Voyage into substance: Art, science, and the illustrated travel account, 1760-1840.* London, UK: MIT Press, 1984.

Stanhope, Earl. *Life of the Right Honourable William Pitt.* 4 vols., 3rd ed. London: John Murray, 1867.

Steven, Margaret. *Trade, tactics and territory: Britain in the Pacific, 1783-1823.* Victoria: Melbourne University Press, 1983.

Stoddart, David. *On geography and its history.* Oxford: Blackwell, 1986.

Suleri, Sara. *The rhetoric of English India.* Chicago: University of Chicago Press, 1992.

Suttles, Wayne. *Coast Salish essays.* Seattle: University of Washington Press; Vancouver: Talon, 1987.

Swadesh, Morris. "Motivations in Nootkan warfare." *Southwestern Journal of Anthropology* 4, 1 (1948): 76-93.

Taussig, Michael. *Shamanism, colonialism, and the wild man: A study in terror and healing.* Chicago: University of Chicago Press, 1987.

Thomas, Nicholas. *Colonialism's culture: Anthropology, travel and government.* Princeton, NJ: Princeton University Press, 1994.

—. *Entangled objects: Exchange, material culture, and colonialism in the Pacific.* Cambridge, MA: Harvard University Press, 1991.

Thompson, E.P. *Customs in common: Studies in traditional popular culture.* New York: New Press, 1993.

Turnbull, David. *Maps are territories.* Chicago: University of Chicago Press, 1989.

Turner, Frederick J. "Documents II: English policy toward America in 1790-1791." *American Historical Review* 7, 4 (1902): 706-35.

Wallis, Helen. "Publication of Cook's journals: Some new sources and assessments." *Pacific Studies* 1, 2 (1978): 163-94.

Watt, Sir James. "Medical aspects and consequences of Cook's voyages." In Fisher and Johnston, *Captain James Cook and his times,* 129-57.

Webb, Paul. "The naval aspects of the Nootka Sound crisis." *Mariner's Mirror* 61 (1975): 133-54.

White, Richard. *The middle ground: Indians, empires, and republics in the Great Lakes region, 1650-1815.* Cambridge: Cambridge University Press, 1991.

Whittaker, Arthur P. "Changing and unchanging interpretations of the Enlightenment in Spanish America." *Proceedings of the American Philosophical Society* 114, 4 (1970): 256-71.

Wike, Joyce A. "A reevaluation of northwest coast cannibalism." In *The Tsimshian and their neighbors of the north Pacific coast*, ed. Jay Miller and Carol M. Eastman, 239-54. Seattle: University of Washington Press, 1984.

—. Wike, Joyce A. "Problems in fur trade analysis." *American Anthropologist* 60 (1958): 1,096-101.

Williams, Glyndwr. "The Pacific: Exploration and exploitation." In *Oxford History of the British Empire*, vol. 2: *The eighteenth century*, ed. P.J. Marshall, 552-75. Oxford and New York: Oxford University Press, 1998.

Williams, Glyndwr. "Buccaneers, castaways, and satirists: The south seas in the English consciousness before 1750." *Eighteenth-Century Life* 18 (n.s.) 3 (1994): 114-28.

—. "Myth and reality: The theoretical geography of northwest America from Cook to Vancouver." In Fisher and Johnston, *From maps to metaphors*, 35-50.

—. "Seamen and philosophers in the south seas in the age of Captain Cook." *Mariner's Mirror* 65, 1 (1979): 3-22.

—. *The British search for the north west passage in the eighteenth century*. London: Longmans, Green, 1962.

Wilson, Kathleen. "The good, the bad, and the impotent: Imperialism and the politics of identity in Georgian England." In *The consumption of culture, 1600-1800*, ed. Ann Bermingham and John Brewer, 237-62. London and New York: Routledge, 1995.

Wilson, P.W. *Pitt, the younger*. Garden City, NY: Doubleday, 1930.

Windsor, Justin, ed. *The memorial history of Boston ... 1630-1880*. 4 vols. Boston: James R. Osgood, 1881.

Withey, Lynne. *Voyages of discovery: Captain Cook and the exploration of the Pacific*. New York: Morrow, 1987.

Young, Robert J.C. *Colonial Desire: Hybridity, theory culture and race*. London: Routledge, 1995.

—. "Foucault on race and colonialism." *New Formations* 25 (1995): 57-65.

—. *White mythologies: Writing history and the West*. London: Routledge, 1992.

Unpublished

Arcas Associates. "Patterns of settlement of the Ahousaht (Kelsemaht) and Clayoquot bands." Vancouver and Kamloops, 1989.

Boyd, Robert Thomas. "The introduction of infectious diseases among the Indians of the Pacific northwest, 1774-1784." PhD diss., Department of Anthropology, University of Washington, 1985.

Braithwaite, Jean. "Genealogical and selected biographical data on the Mowachaht." Parks Canada, Calgary.

Cook, Andrew. "Alexander Dalrymple (1737-1808): hydrographer to the East India Company and to the Admiralty, as publisher." PhD diss., Department of History, University of St. Andrews, 1992.

Currie, Noel Elizabeth. "Captain Cook at Nootka Sound and some questions of colonial discourse." PhD diss., Department of English, University of British Columbia, 1994.

Dewhirst, John. "Mowachaht ownership and use of the salmon resources of the Leiner River and upper Tahsis Inlet, Nootka Sound, British Columbia." Archeo Tech Associates, Victoria, 1990.

Folan, William Joseph. "The community, settlement and subsistence patterns of the Nootka Sound area: A diachronic model." PhD diss., Department of Anthropology, Southern Illinois University, Carbondale, 1972.

Golla, Susan. "He has a name: History and social structure among the Indians of western Vancouver Island." PhD diss., Department of Anthropology, Columbia University, 1987.

Inglis, Richard I., and James C. Haggarty. "Pacific Rim National Park: Ethnographic history." Parks Canada, Calgary, 1986.

Malloy, Mary. "'Boston men' on the northwest coast: Commerce, collecting, and cultural perceptions in the American maritime fur trade, 1788-1844." PhD diss., Department of American Civilization, Brown University, 1994.

—. "The northwest coast voyage in American literature." UBCL-SC.

Marsden, Susan. "Controlling the flow of furs: Northcoast nations and the maritime fur trade." Paper presented at the BC Studies Conference, 1990.

Marshall, Yvonne. "A political history of the Nuu-chah-nulth: A case study of the Mowachaht and Muchalaht tribes." PhD diss., Department of Archaeology, Simon Fraser University, 1993.

Newman, Philip L. "An intergroup collectivity among the Nootka." MA thesis, Department of Anthropology, University of Washington, 1957.

Veit, Walter. "On the European imagining of the non-European world." In *Australia and the European imagination*. Papers from a conference held at the Humanities Research Centre, Australian National University, May 1981, 123-56.

Wike, Joyce A. "The effect of the maritime fur trade on northwest coast Indian society." PhD diss., Department of Political Science, Columbia Unversity, 1947.

Index

marriage alliances: chiefs, 114-15, 139, 143, 144, 280n60; Maquinna, Chief, 114, 115, 119, 124, 126

Martínez, Estevan José, 106, 112; seizure of British vessels, 168, 170. *See also* Nootka Sound Crisis

Mayne, Richard, 227

McCarthy, Grace, 59

McEachern, Allan, xx, 61-2

McGillivray, Simon, 208, 210

Meares, John, 84, 262n10, 293n55; accounts of fur trade, 98, 193-4; accounts of Wickaninish, 144; Columbia River and, 213; distortion of facts, 83, 86, 171; interview with Committee of Trade and Plantations, 178-9; land purchase, 170-1, 179, 186; Nootka Sound Crisis and, 112, 170-1; understanding of Native prestation system, 139-40, 141-2; views on Native peoples, 87, 108, 132, 142, 273n62; views on Native trading methods, 110, 124, 136

Menzies, Archibald, 86, 119, 196

mercantilism, 175

Merivale, Herman, 230

Merry, Anthony, 168, 172, 284n2

Miranda, Francisco de, 170

miscommunication: in Native-White relations, 79-80

Mississippi River, 207

Moffatt, Hamilton, 145

Morrison, Samuel Eliot, 84

Morton, earl of: instructions to Cook, 8-9

Moser, Charles, 4

Mowachaht confederacy, 126

Moziño, José Mariano, 22, 121, 245n3; view of Nuu-chah-nulth society, 102, 125, 126

Myers, John, 93

Nanaimis, Chief, 23

Naneguiyus, Chief, 115

Nasparti, 128-9

Native agency: control of fur trade by chiefs, xviii, 119, 151, 153; Native assumptions of cultural superiority, 153; practices of dominance, 241-2; role as partners in fur trade, 78-9

Native peoples: architecture, 280n5; attacks on traders, 96, 106, 127, 142, 143; attitudes to European goods, 75, 76, 87, 124-5, 199, 278n198; attitudes to trade and traders, 76, 78-9, 87, 92; competition between groups, 112-14, 116-19, 143-8, 154; effect of fur trade on settlement patterns, 127-8, 154, 157, 279n220; impact of fur trade, 126-8,

145-6, 154-7, 279n220; marginalization during commemoration of Cook's arrival, 51-5; marginalization of Native history, 52-3, 61-2, 65, 237; marginalization by Western accounts, 51-5, 58, 238, 239-40; as partners in trade, 78-9; presence among colonists, 226; representation by traders, 75-7, 78, 79, 86, 87, 90-1, 106, 108, 268n118; representations in 20th c. BC, 51-5; role of prestation in prestige system, 136, 138, 139-41, 142, 158; spiritual dimensions of contact, 158-9; strategies of power, 152, 154-5, 158; trade networks, 94, 100, 119-20, 148-9; villages as islands of cultural difference, 153; violence involving traders, 83-4, 91, 158; warfare between groups, xviii, 121-4, 132, 143-7, 148-9, 158, 159, 282n73. *See also* Native agency; Native populations; Native women; Nuu-chah-nulth peoples; names of specific peoples

Native populations, xix, xviii, 282n81; effects of disease, xviii, 146, 148, 157; effects of warfare, 146-7, 157; warfare, 145-6, 157

Native Rights Association, 52

Native women, 42; attitudes of Cook's crew towards, 45-6; prostitution, 111, 274n92

natural history: Foucault's views, 256n54

natural man concept, 37

Natzape, Chief, 114, 115, 123, 129, 278n207

Newcheasses people. *See* Nimpkish peoples

Newcombe, C.F., 56

Nichol, W.C., 4

Nimpkish peoples: conflict with Nuu-chah-nulth peoples, 123; conflicts with other Native peoples, 123; role in fur trade, 125, 126; trading partners, 125, 278n208

Nimpkish-Tahsis Trail, 125, 148

N-La' people, 122

noble savage concept, 8, 9, 12

Nootka peoples. *See* Nuu-chah-nulth peoples

Nootka Sound, 16, 96; abandonment by fur traders, 126, 130; base anchorage, 30-1; bicentenary celebrations of Cook's arrival, 59; as a centre of Native power, 154-5; commemoration of Cook's arrival, 3-4, 50-1; Cook's arrival, 16, 17-19, 23-7; Cook's departure from, 69, 70; map of contact impact, 155; map of settlement patterns, 107; map of sociopolitical arrangements, 107; name derivation, 245n3; as Native trading centre, 124-5; Spanish vessels, 22-3, 251n19, 252n20; trading vessels, 276n163; Webber panorama, 31, 255n7. *See also* Maquinna, Chief; Yuquot